SELECTED LETTERS
OF HANS HEYSEN
AND NORA HEYSEN

Edited and introduced by
Catherine Speck

Wakefield
Press

This book was produced with the support of the Nora Heysen Trust

Wakefield Press
16 Rose Street
Mile End
South Australia 5031
www.wakefieldpress.com.au

First published by the National Library of Australia 2011
This Wakefield Press edition published 2019

Original commissioning publisher: Susan Hall, National Library of Australia
Edited by Tina Mattei
Designed by Andrew Rankine, atypica
Printed and bound in Korea by Artin Printing Co., Ltd

ISBN 978 1 74305 641 7

A catalogue record for this
book is available from the
National Library of Australia

Cover images
top
Nora Heysen (1911–2003)
Self Portrait (detail) 1936

oil on canvas; 63.0 x 51.0 cm
Fred & Elinor Wrobel Collection
John Passmore Museum of Art

bottom
Ivor Hele (1912–1993)
Sir Hans Heysen, OBE (detail) 1959

oil on masonite; 106.6 x 81.3 cm
Gift of Mr and Mrs E.W. Hayward and
Ivor Hele 1959
Art Gallery of South Australia

Contents

ACKNOWLEDGEMENTS   vii

INTRODUCTION

    ON WRITING LETTERS   1

    ON HANS HEYSEN   5

    ON SALLIE HEYSEN   12

    ON NORA HEYSEN   13

    EDITOR'S NOTE   20

COSMOPOLITAN LONDON, 1934–1937   23

SYDNEY AND THE ARCHIBALD PRIZE, 1938–1943   87

LIFE AS AN OFFICIAL WAR ARTIST, 1943–1946   133

TO LIVERPOOL, LONDON AND BACK AGAIN, 1946–1953   173

TOURING THE PACIFIC AND SETTLING IN SYDNEY, 1953–1959   217

SUCCESS, ANXIETY AND CHANGE, 1960–1968   267

EPILOGUE   325

CHRONOLOGY   328

LIST OF ILLUSTRATIONS   337

INDEX   339

Acknowledgements

This book brings together letters from two separate collections, the Papers of Nora Heysen and the Papers of Hans Heysen, each held by the National Library of Australia. The aim has been to reveal a unique father–daughter relationship between two eminent Australian artists and to throw a spotlight on an aspect of the Australian art world often bypassed by more popular narratives. I wish to thank all who have made this possible. I would especially like to thank Lou Klepac and Peter Heysen, who granted me permission to access the respective sets of letters, Christopher Heysen, for permission to reproduce Hans' work, and the other members of the Heysen family, who placed their trust in me to produce this volume.

There are several people at the National Library of Australia to thank. The staff of the Manuscripts Section was very helpful in providing access to the complete holdings of correspondence, which I read during my six months of Sabbatical Leave in 2008 and during later visits. Margy Burn (Assistant Director-General, Australian Collections and Reader Services), Nat Williams (Director, Exhibitions) and Susan Hall (Manager, Publishing and Production) shared and encouraged my vision for this publication. Tina Mattei (Assistant Editor) and Felicity Harmey (Picture Researcher) ably assisted the production and Andrew Rankine (atypica) created an inspired design.

A frequent port of call in the process of assembling this book has been the Heysen family home and studio, 'The Cedars', in Hahndorf, South Australia. Curator Allan Campbell assisted in countless ways in illuminating the letters, often over morning tea in the kitchen at 'The Cedars'. Jill Swann's detective work at 'The Cedars' uncovered a set of letters to and from Liverpool in 1948 that was crucial in completing the correspondence from those years.

My colleague Professor Ian North, who was the Coordinating Curator of the all-important 1978 Hans Heysen exhibition at the Art Gallery of South Australia, provided wise counsel on the interpretation of events. Consultant curators Jane Hylton and Lou Klepac were very generous in answering queries about Nora Heysen, as was Hendrik Kolenberg (Art Gallery of New South Wales), and Craig Duberry and Andrew Flatau, both of whom knew Nora in her later years. Meredith Stokes shared memories of her mother Evie, Nora's lifelong friend, and Rosie Heysen lent me her copies of Nora's Pacific letters. Wende Dahl was an essential aid in transcribing many of the letters, while Peter Quigley's technical prowess turned digital images into print format.

Between 2009 and 2010, working on this volume mostly from Adelaide had many advantages. Hans Heysen was the longest-serving member of the Board of the Art Gallery of South Australia, and the resources of the Art Gallery of South Australia's Research Library and the skills of Jin Whittington (Information Manager) were invaluable in tracking down clues to comments made in the letters. Margaret Hosking (Barr Smith Library, University of Adelaide) also assisted greatly. Richard Heathcote (Director, Carrick Hill) answered many enquiries about Ursula and Bill Hayward, while the mystery of Carrick Hill's interior decorator was solved once a comment in Nora's letter was interpreted by design historian Professor Peter McNeil.

Joanna Mendelssohn (Associate Professor of Art History, University of New South Wales) answered queries about all things Sydney, while Glenn Cooke (former Research Curator of Queensland Heritage, Queensland Art Gallery) covered Brisbane. My thanks goes also to Kay Truelove (Art Gallery of New South Wales Library), Rebecca Capes-Baldwin (formerly Art Gallery of South Australia), Catherine Angove (Research Library, Australian Broadcasting Corporation), Lola Wilkins and Cherie Prosser (Australian War Memorial), Barbara Cotter (John Curtin Gallery, Curtin University), Edithe Piggott and Sue Grunstein (Archives of the Australian Red Cross, NSW Branch), and Hannah Kothe (University Art Gallery and Art Collection, Sydney University Museums). Two of my past postgraduate students, Tony King and Dr James Cooper, assisted with esoteric information about Hunters Hill cartoonists and architects of the Louvre.

The letters brought to light some little-known paintings by Hans and Nora, and I would to thank Michael Heysen, Susan Sideris (Kensington Gallery, Adelaide), Jock Duncan, Linda English, Fred and Elinor Wrobel and other private collectors. I also wish to acknowledge Lilian Mellink (Embassy of the Netherlands, Canberra), who facilitated my enquiry about the 'missing' Madame Elink Schuurman Archibald Prize portrait, and importantly Henri Elink Schuurman and Marcele van Berchem, who provided information about their mother, who is the painting's subject, and an accurate image of the painting.

The volume is rich in images and I would like to thank Tracey Dall, Georgia Hale and Laura Masters (Art Gallery of South Australia), Nick Nicholson (National Gallery of Australia), Tim Langford (National Portrait Gallery), Michelle Andringa and Tracey Keough (Art Gallery of New South Wales), David Whittaker (Australian War Memorial), Edward Bettella (Public Catalogue Foundation, London, and Liverpool Blue Coat School, Liverpool, UK), Richard Perram and Sarah Gurich (Bathurst Regional Art Gallery), Chris Read and Judy Lewis (State Library of South Australia), Julie Collett (Art Gallery of Ballarat), Rachael Rose (University Fine Art Collection, University of Tasmania) and photographers Michael Kluvanek (Adelaide), Peter Angus Robinson (Hobart) and Sue Blackburn (Sydney).

Thanks too to my Canberra family—Lorna Keany, Jane Keany and Tony Hill, and David Keany, who generously provided me with a second home when carrying out research at the National Library. Finally, my thanks go to my partner Chris Mortensen for his support and encouragement while this was being researched and written.

Introduction

On writing letters

The writing of letters is a dying art, yet not so long ago it was the main form of communication between family members, friends, colleagues and acquaintances. People made time to write letters, which were written on good quality paper or lighter airmail paper.[1] Most were written for private readers, although the notion of 'private' is elastic because letters were frequently read out to family members and shared with friends and relatives. People kept track of their correspondence and would apologise if a reply was tardy. Letters were kept and re-read at a later date. This culture of handwritten letters is disappearing quickly.

The letters between Nora Heysen, her father Hans Heysen and mother Sallie Heysen, which commenced in 1934 when Nora was in London, are an extended conversation about art, their lives and their work.

Hans Heysen (1877–1968) was a prominent landscape and still-life artist whose work is held in all major Australian galleries and in many private collections. He won the Wynne Prize for landscape painting nine times, was knighted for his services to the arts in 1959, and was the longest standing Board Member of the

---

1   An Australian airmail service to England commenced in the early 1930s. See 'Australia–England Air Mail', *Brisbane Courier*, 1 May 1931.

National Gallery of South Australia, as it was called until 1967, serving continuously from 1940 to 1968.

Daughter Nora Heysen (1911–2003) possessed prodigious talent. She was only 22 years of age when she held her first solo exhibition in 1933. By then she already had two paintings (*Petunias* and *Self Portrait*) acquired by the National Art Gallery of New South Wales, as it was known until 1958, as well as one by each of the Queensland Art Gallery (*A Mixed Bunch*), the National Gallery of South Australia (*Scabious*) and Armidale Teachers' College (*Still Life*). By the time she left Adelaide for London in 1934 she had won the South Australian Society of Arts Melrose Prize for *A Portrait Study*[2] and had painted her highly modernist portrait *Phyllis Paech* (1933). Nora's success continued when she returned from London. In 1939 she became the first woman artist to win the Archibald Prize and, in 1943, she was the first Australian woman to take up an appointment as an official war artist.[3] Later in life she received two notable honours: an Australia Council award for Achievement in the Arts in 1993 and an Order of Australia in 1998.

Letters were an integral part of the Heysen household. Hans corresponded regularly with many leading artists of the day, including Norman and Lionel Lindsay, Elioth Gruner, Harold Cazneaux, Lloyd Rees and Blamire Young. Hans and Sallie also wrote to their other children, once they had married and established homes and properties around South Australia. Nora moved around more than her siblings. From the 1930s to the 1960s, letters regularly went back and forth between the Heysen's family home, 'The Cedars', in Ambleside (later called Hahndorf), to London, where Nora was studying; to Sydney, where Nora moved permanently after her time overseas; to numerous locations in 'the Pacific' and northern Queensland, while Nora was an official war artist; and to Liverpool, in England, and the Trobriand and Solomon islands, where Nora accompanied Robert Black, whom she married in 1953.

When Nora was a young art student in London, her father frequently reminded her how much the family valued her letters, writing to her on 9 January 1935: 'it is a treat to have your letters, to look forward to each week and you don't know what joy they bring us'. Saturday morning was letter day at 'The Cedars' which Hans describes in detail on 21 June 1936:

---

2   In 1921 Alexander Melrose donated an annual prize for best portrait and figure painting, the Melrose Prize, to the Royal South Australian Society of Arts. One of the conditions of the non-acquisitive prize was that it not be won be the same artist more than twice in succession, and not more than four times in all. Administration of the prize was taken over by the National Gallery of South Australia in 1946. See 'Portrait and Figure Painting', *The Advertiser*, 19 May 1921.

3   Stella Bowen's appointment was announced at the same time as Nora Heysen's but Bowen did not take up hers until February 1944.

there was the usual scramble and general family gathering around a
Saturday morning cup of tea to hear all the news from Nora! And all
her doings, and no one is ever disappointed, for your letters are so
full of enthusiasm and so well expressed that they are a pleasure and
a joy to us all. They have become a weekly institution, and I do not
know what we would do without them.

Nora, likewise, valued what she called 'home news'. On 28 May 1935, she
comments that 'mail days are the bright spot of the week', and bemoans the days
when the mail failed to turn up or was late in arriving. Sallie would sometimes pop
a gum leaf or a perfumed flower in with a letter, as she did for one of the London
letters, Nora writing: 'in Mother's was a pale blue pansy and a poppy petal. It gave me
a little quick thrill of pleasure to find them there and the lovely soft colours looked
so charming on the grey blue paper'. As an art student in London, Nora read and re-
read her father's letters, which she called 'working letters', because they were mostly
about art.

Hans was a very practised writer of letters. Often he wrote drafts before
sending off his final version and, on 9 January 1935, he gently inducted his daughter
into the craft, praising her with: 'I think you write a really splendid descriptive letter,
so that we can share all your experiences—good and not so good'. Nora felt less
confident about her ability with words, commenting more than once that she could
not write as well as her father.

The letters between father and daughter are much more than a diary of
events. They are a discussion about how each was approaching their daily work and
the challenges they faced as artists. This extended to what could be called robust
criticism. For instance, in 1936 Hans saw his daughter's painting *Petunias* on display
in the National Art Gallery of New South Wales and comments to her: 'it lacked unity
and atmosphere, by unity I mean tone, due to each flower being seen somewhat
separately and not sufficiently as part of a whole. Still as I said, this is a youthful
fault and I liked the work'. Even when Nora was an established artist, her father still
reviewed her work. On 21 February 1951, he writes of Nora's Archibald entry, *Portrait
of Robert Black*:

it is the best thing you have so far done, in the portrait line. If I may
make a comment, the hills against the sky nearest the head seemed
too positive and detracted, and the folds in the right sleeve are not
sufficiently considered *in pattern* in relation to the whole. Still you
have done a jolly good job.

Hans for his part would speak of the difficulty of getting enough time to paint and, once having the time, knowing where to begin. For instance, on 5 December 1934, having recently returned from the extended trip to Germany and Britain, he writes:

> I have been cleaning up the studio and now all is more spick and span ready for work, all that is failing is how and where to start. For I am still quite at sea in regard to my work. When next I write I am hoping to tell you that I have once more begun and on what.

On 19 July 1936 Hans writes of his disappointment at seeing installed his painting *White Gums*, which had been commissioned by the Adelaide Steamship Company: 'in my picture I had kept the sky as a very fresh note of blue, but I was astounded how this was toned down almost to a grey in the suffused light in which it is hung, and also when lit by artificial light, in this respect it was an object lesson to me'.

Frequently a letter from either Nora or her father would be six handwritten pages, each describing his or her current work, exhibitions seen, art world events and gossip, art books read and family news. That number of pages was covered by a regular postage stamp and, thus, often a comment is made, such as 'I must stop, this will be overweight'. Also, in posting a letter overseas Hans, Nora and Sallie knew the news would be six weeks in reaching its destination, since letters went via surface mail. Should the news be urgent, an airmail letter was sent.

Letter writing takes time and the young student Nora occasionally complained about this. But the advice always came back that writing down one's ideas is a valuable exercise. On 21 June 1935 Hans says: 'Yes letter writing does take time, but you would not begrudge that when you realise what your letters mean to us, and I do also feel that letter writing does help one to express one's ideas and thoughts, and their benefit is not all single sided'.

The language of their letters differs from that of today. Farewells from Hans to his daughter were frequently long and very endearing, a quality more obvious when Nora was in her student days in London and Hans felt protective of her. In contrast to this openly sentimental quality, Hans, Sallie and Nora were not shy in making comments about people or events that would be incautious in today's world of email correspondence.

Many of the people discussed in the letters were influential friends of the Heysen family. Sydney Ure Smith was a publisher and president of the Society of Arts, in Sydney, and wool merchant James McGregor was a prominent art collector and friend of Robert Gordon Menzies—both were Trustees of the National Art Gallery of

New South Wales. Ursula and Bill Hayward were art collectors, and their home, Carrick Hill, and their art collection were bequeathed to South Australia. Ursula Hayward was also the first woman trustee on the on the board of the National Art Gallery of South Australia. Louis McCubbin was Director of that gallery from 1946 to 1950 and was on the Art Committee of the Australian War Memorial when Nora was appointed an official war artist. These people, who determined acquisitions in major galleries, headed up artist societies and lobbied major politicians, were integral to the course of Australian art from the 1920s to the early 1960s. The letters give glimpses into that era. However, by the 1950s and especially in the 1960s, they point to a changing art world, with the rise of commercial galleries, the decline of the Society of Artists, the development of abstraction and a new professionalism entering the museum world.

On Hans Heysen

Hans Heysen was an influential and well-connected figure in the Australian art world and his work was rapidly acquired. Apart from a period during the First World War, when he was forced to resign from every Australian art society because he was German-born and had refused to reaffirm his Australian citizenship on the grounds that his paintings of Australian sunlight spoke for him, he enjoyed much commercial success. His Sydney retrospective exhibition at the National Art Gallery of New South Wales in 1935, discussed in the letters, attracted crowds of up to 3000 per day. In 1952, buyers queued outside his David Jones exhibition and, once the doors opened, bought 11 pictures in 30 minutes. When his work was shown in 1960, crowds again flocked to see his paintings. *The Advertiser* reported on 14 March: 'a record crowd—unofficial estimate of 1200—filled the Hahndorf Gallery to hear Sir Richard Boyer open the Hans Heysen exhibition yesterday'. He was a popular painter and also highly esteemed by the art establishment.

His 1951 painting, *In the Flinders—Far North*, commissioned for the Australian Jubilee, was purchased by the Commonwealth Government and hung in the Australian Embassy in Paris for many years. When Queen Elizabeth II visited Australia in 1963, he was one of small number of Australian artists whose work was given to the Royal collection. A photograph in this volume shows him presenting the Queen and Duke of Edinburgh with his specially commissioned watercolour *White Gums, Summer Afternoon*. When Hans was knighted in 1959, Nora wrote home conveying the good wishes she had received from their mutual circle of Sydney friends, adding that the family's fame had spread to a story in *The Australian Women's Weekly*. She writes: 'the most popular knighthood ever bestowed I should think'.

Even as an elderly man in his eighties, Hans was still a celebrity appearing in the 1960s on two ABC television programs, *Shirley Abicair in Australia* and *The Lively Arts*. *Vogue Australia* ran a story in March 1968 of Adelaide arts identities. Hans appeared, along with fashionable bookseller and publisher Max Harris and debonair labour politician Don Dunstan. In Adelaide, Hans was regarded with great fondness. In 1967 when he tripped and cut his head at the art gallery following a Board meeting, the event was reported in the daily newspaper. Stewart Cockburn commented that after the wound had been treated, 'Sir Hans Heysen cheerfully continued with an unofficial inspection of some of his favourite paintings'.[4]

Despite being a popular painter and having the support of powerful politicians like Menzies, Hans' place in Australian art history has vacillated. Ure Smith publications, including *Art in Australia*, facilitated his reputation, with Lionel Lindsay the author of a special 'Hans Heysen' issue in 1920. Hans' foray into supporting the conservative but ill-conceived drive for an Australian Academy dented his reputation temporarily.[5] One reason for Hans' lack of location within a narrative of Australian art is that many accounts move rapidly from Heidelberg artists, who conveyed an intimate settled bush, to postwar modernism, and only lightly touch on landscape artists of the Edwardian and postwar eras, such as Hans Heysen, Elioth Gruner and Lloyd Rees.

In 1977, the Art Gallery of South Australia's *Hans Heysen Centenary Retrospective* went some way towards correcting this tendency. The Coordinating Curator of the exhibition, Ian North, observed: 'Heysen has succeeded in giving the Arcadian tradition in Australian painting a dimension at once humble and heroic. At the heart of his triumph was a wedding of humble subject matter, patiently observed, with grand European stylistic sources'.[6] Ten years later, Margaret Plant created an intellectual space in which to situate Hans' work, arguing that the historic moment of Federation provoked a sense of the history of grandeur and heroism for humans and nature alike, but noted Australian artists, like Hans, invoked British models, such as John Constable, to do so.[7]

Following soon after, Ian Burn credited Hans Heysen with presenting a new concept of the bush, that of inland Australia. Burn pointed to Hans' modernity

4   See Stewart Cockburn, 'Doyen of Painters Undeterred by Fall', *The Advertiser*, 12 September 1967.

5   There was strong opposition to an Academy from artists in many quarters and, as a result, in 1937 they formed the Contemporary Art Society in Melbourne, then in Sydney and Adelaide. By the end of the Second World War, the Academy's influence had waned.

6   See 'The Originality of Hans Heysen', in Ian North (ed.), *Hans Heysen*, Melbourne and Adelaide, Macmillan and Art Gallery of South Australia, 1979: 12.

7   See Margaret Plant, 'The Lost Art of Federation: Australia's Quest for Modernism', *Art Bulletin of Victoria*, no.28, 1987: 118–125.

in 'freeing the bush from its pastoral vision' and in painting the anatomy of the landscape of the Flinders Ranges in a neo-impressionist style. In identifying Hans' modern style in watercolours, like *The Land of the Oratunga* (1932), with their 'fierce colours, clear edges and the flat light creating crisp definitions of the landscape', Burn had done something the artist himself could never have done.[8] He had separated out the strands of modernism and differentiated mainstream modern art from what Nora called 'rank modernism', which is avant-gardism.[9] Hans also adopted a modern style in collapsing space in his Flinders Ranges work, which he described as having 'no appreciable atmospheric difference between the foreground and the middle distance; indeed hills, at least four miles away, appear to unite'.[10] Once again, in not differentiating between the different branches of modernism, Hans was unable to see how his approach to space, as portrayed in *Aroona* (1939), was modern.

There is yet another side to the artist's modernity. His Art Nouveau–inspired, hyper-real and exaggerated gum trees have a modern lineage too. They create, said Ian Burn, a 'mystique, even elements of fantasy [with] the giant trunk formation taking on a life force'.[11] Ian North had earlier pointed to this anthropomorphising of gum trees as 'humanoid in their heroic posturing'.[12] The artist himself had often enough provided the clue that his gums are his models but for Burn this hyper-real approach to composition does not present a sustained modernism, because they impose a 'classical order and moral stability'.[13] Already it is clear there is no easy fit for Heysen.

In his 2001 exhibition *Our Country: Australian Federation Landscapes, 1900–1914*, Ron Radford supplied the next piece in the jigsaw by situating Hans within a trajectory of Federation artists. Radford identified the importance of the political moment of Federation as signalling a change in how the late Heidelberg air of melancholy was traded for one of sober reflection. This shows up very early in paintings around early morning or late afternoon light, such as *Mystic Morn* (1904).

By the beginning of the second decade of the twentieth century, landscapes replete with sunshine were back. Hans described his new approach:

8   See Ian Burn, *National Life and Landscapes: Australian Painting, 1900–1940*, Sydney, Bay Books, 1991: 194.

9   Modernism is now increasingly being written about as encompassing more than its avant-garde arm, as was once popularly believed and peddled by Alfred Barr of the Museum of Modern Art in the 1930s. Christopher Green has said of French artists: 'most artists living in Montparnasse did not aspire to highly avant garde practices' but, nevertheless, worked as modernists. The same could be said of many British and Australian artists. See Christopher Green, *Art in France, 1900–1940*, New Haven and London, Yale University Press, 2000: 35.

10   Hans Heysen, quoted in Lionel Lindsay, 'Heysen's Recent Watercolours', *Art in Australia*, 24 June 1928: np.

11   See Ian Burn, *National Life and Landscapes: Australian Painting, 1900–1940*, Sydney, Bay Books, 1991: 48.

12   See Ian North, 'Gum-tree Imperial', in Daniel Thomas (ed.), *Creating Australia: 200 Years of Art, 1788–1988*, Sydney, International Cultural Corporation of Australia and Art Gallery Board of South Australia, 1988: 141.

13   See Ian Burn, *National Life and Landscapes: Australian Painting, 1900–1940*, Sydney, Bay Books, 1991: 48.

To give expression to that intangible stuff, light and atmosphere, is indeed a problem. Yet I feel these to be the essence of Australian landscape, they are what makes nature so various and fascinating. Sunshine, above all, is the essence of life, then atmosphere.[14]

Since then he has been equated with the Australian landscape, and even when drawing on European sources and living out a Barbizon ideal of working in harmony with nature, his art has been seen as wholly Australian.

But is that the whole story? Early in his career Hans spent four years in Europe and returned to Adelaide in 1903. These four years were much more important than many commentators have grasped, although Rebecca Andrews, in her 2009 touring exhibition *Hans Heysen*, drew attention to his European work produced in France, Holland, Italy, England and Scotland.[15] The letters provide an important clue: Hans returned home with a broad knowledge of international art and armed with a repertoire informed by international style. He was a keen student of impressionism and its later variant neo-impressionism, yet he has been overly constructed as a one-dimensional Australian artist.[16] Possibly he was complicit in this, given his traumatic experience of being identified as German in the First World War. But his first love is light; the subject, be it a gum tree or a rocky hillside, is secondary. Ian North identified this by suggesting that the gum tree was the prolonged subject of 'an artistic embrace'.[17] Hans, too, pointed to his broadly international, or what could be called his non-Australian, approach: 'While as an artist I love Australia, though art has no country, but is in essence cosmopolitan'.[18]

When in Belle Époque Paris, a beacon for art students from around the world, Hans had been immersed in a cosmopolitan art scene. He lived in fashionable Montparnasse, an area studded with artists' studios and ateliers set up for the foreign market. He took classes at the well-known Parisian art schools, Académie Julian and Académie Colarossi, both frequented by the large population of expatriate artists, and

---

14 Hans Heysen, quoted in Lionel Lindsay, 'The Art of Hans Heysen', in Sydney Ure Smith, Bertram Stevens and Charles Lloyd Jones (eds), *The Art of Hans Heysen*, an *Art in Australia* book, Sydney, Angus & Robertson, 1920: 8.

15 See Rebecca Andrews, *Hans Heysen*, Adelaide, Art Gallery of South Australia, 2009.

16 Even Ann Elias' analysis of Heysen's flower paintings, 'more Fantin than Fantin', situates him within the then fashionably British–Australian ethos. See Ann Elias, 'Fantin Latour in Australia', *Nineteenth-Century Art Worldwide*, vol.8, no.2, 2009: 9–19.

17 See Ian North, 'Gum-tree Imperial', in Daniel Thomas (ed.), *Creating Australia: 200 Years of Art, 1788–1988*, Sydney, International Cultural Corporation of Australia and Art Gallery Board of South Australia, 1988: 140.

18 Hans Heysen, quoted in 'A Difference Between Artists: Mr Heysen insulted', *The Herald*, Melbourne, 3 December 1921. The term 'non-Australian' is different from 'un-Australian', used by art historian Rex Butler to refer to work produced by Australian expatriates. See Rex Butler, 'A Short History of UnAustralian Art', in Ian North (ed.), *Visual Animals: Crossovers, Evolution and New Aesthetics*, Adelaide, Contemporary Art Centre of South Australia, 2007: 107–121.

above
Nora Heysen (1911–2003)
Self Portrait c.1932

oil on canvas; 64.0 x 50.0 cm
Pictures Collection, nla.pic-vn4179750
National Library of Australia

right
Unknown photographer
Hans and Sallie Heysen c.1920s

photograph
Manuscripts Collection, MS 5073
National Library of Australia

Nora Heysen (1911–2003)
Phyllis Paech 1933

oil on canvas; 48.6 x 39.0 cm
Nora Heysen Foundation Collection
The Cedars, Hahndorf
Photograph by Michael Kluvanek

Harold Cazneaux (1878–1953)
The Cedars 1926

photograph
The Cedars, Hahndorf

F.A. Joyner (1863–1945)
Heysen in the Flinders 1927

bromide photograph; 22.2 x 32.2 cm
(image), 31.6 x 39.2 cm (sheet)
Gift of Mrs Max Joyner 1981
Art Gallery of South Australia

right top
Hans Heysen (1877–1968)
The Land of the Oratunga 1932

watercolour on paper; 47.3 x 62.6 cm
South Australian Government Grant 1937
Art Gallery of South Australia

right
Hans Heysen (1877–1968)
Aroona 1939

watercolour on paper; 42.2 x 62.0 cm
Private collection

Nora Heysen (1911–2003)
Spring Light c.1938

oil on canvas; 51.0 x 41.0 cm
Nora Heysen Foundation Collection
The Cedars, Hahndorf
Photograph by Michael Kluvanek

Hans Heysen (1877–1968)
Flowers and Fruit (Zinnias) 1921

oil on canvas; 70.0 x 82.7 cm
Purchased 1921
Art Gallery of New South Wales
© C. Heysen, licensed by Viscopy

he was admitted to the École des Beaux-Arts.[19] Despite being hardworking and quiet by nature, he networked with fellow cosmopolitans of various national backgrounds, nationhood being transcended in this arena. His paintings and watercolours from those years show receptiveness to the modern ethos and, more importantly, a cosmopolitan outlook of cultural openness.[20]

Naturally he studied the work of the impressionists and the neo-impressionists. This becomes apparent in the letters when Hans discusses the possible purchase of a Camille Pissarro. He writes to Nora on 4 April 1937:

> I can well remember an exhibition at the Durand Ruel Galleries in
> Paris, of his late work in 1902. It was less coloured than his earlier
> work, and relied on subtle uses of pure white and grey whites more
> than on the spectrum, as Sisley or Monet did for obtaining light, and
> I still think he succeeded better than they in conveying the feeling of
> true light.

This close familiarity with impressionism continues in the London letters which, prompted by a large exhibition at Arthur Tooth and Sons, move onto a conversation about Monet and his creation of light, or lack thereof. Nora writes excitedly: 'One thing has a miracle of a sky that I never tire of looking at. It is a broken white cloudy sky with some trees against it on the right, a strip of still water and a piece of foreground'. Hans replies on 26 April 1936 that he looked up the *Illustrated London News* and found the Monets with the exhilarating sky: 'It was evidently painted before he "chopped" his technique into fragments, and not yet with sufficient impressionism to get "vibration"; with air and light. I know the Monets of that period and loved them'. Hans also had a keen appreciation of light in British work, having spent time during his summer holidays studying Turner and others in the London galleries.

On completing his tuition at ateliers in Paris, he spent close on a year studying art in the museums and galleries in Italy and painting in situ. It is as if he was seeing Italy through the eyes of J.M.W. Turner and of the French impressionists. Light infuses his watercolours especially those of Venice, of which he said: 'sometimes it looks as if the whole city hovers between water and air'.[21]

19   See John Milner, *The Studios of Paris*, New Haven, Yale University Press, 1988.

20   See Sarah Wilson, *Paris: Capital of the Arts, 1900–1968*, London, Royal Academy of the Arts, 2002: 51; Craig
        Calhoun, 'Cosmopolitanism and Nationalism', *Nations and Nationalism*, vol.14, no.3, 2008: 442.

21   Hans Heysen, quoted in Colin Thiele, *Heysen of Hahndorf*, Adelaide, Hyde Park Press, 2001: 68.

The letters provide clues as to how painterly approaches learned in Europe infused Hans' later working method. On 5 June 1936, he describes to Nora that in his commission for the ship *Manunda*, he had exaggerated the tree trunks and shown them as giants forging upwards to the sky and immersed in a strong blue light. His cropped style and zooming in on subject matter could be that of a modern photographer. He writes:

> The picture now awaits the approval of the Adelaide Steamship
> directors who are still quite in the dark as to the type of subject—
> so perhaps, it being only 'Gum trees' they want may not think it
> sufficiently exciting. It looks sunny and bright in the studio with a
> somewhat exaggerated blue in the sky.

This is one of many paintings in which light impelled Hans. His working with gum trees was almost a contingent factor, governed by his location. By reading his work with an 'internationalist' lens, the gum tree for Hans became what the haystack was to Monet—something that the French artist painted repeatedly as a subject of light and form. As Hans writes to Nora on 10 November 1935:

> The Gums down by the river are as fascinating as ever in their
> green setting—a green which has now become silvery in tone with
> flowering grasses, the lighting on the old stager was simply ripping
> with lovely modelling, and I could not resist having still another shot
> at him. One never seems to grow tired of these old Gums. Their old
> secrets are always as fresh as ever and awaken a thrill as if seen again
> for the first time.

The other element operating in Hans' work is form and, once again, his knowledge of British and Italian art is crucial. In 1936, when Nora and her friend Evie spent four months in Dorset immersed in nature as their subject, Hans writes on 5 June: 'You will be in Earnest Proctor's country and I am wondering if you will see *Eggardun*: the scene of his painting in our Gallery'. The bare bony hill structure in *Eggerdun*, a rocky hillside that was once a Roman fort, has a distinct similarity to the way Hans was portraying the Flinders Ranges, although Dorset's hills are much greener. Hans' time in Paris had opened up new ways of seeing and working, which is why, when faced with entirely new subject matter in the structure and form of the

Flinders Ranges, he was able to be so innovative in realising that 'the bare bones of the landscape' required a new approach.[22]

Hans spent the greater part of his working life in Australia but his time overseas from 1899 to 1903, and again for nine months in 1934, meant he was more international than is often realised. His remarks, 'I have often wondered how far I would have got in art if I hadn't been able to travel … [those years away] have done me untold good, given me quite a different grasp of art', lie at the heart of his work.[23]

The urge to travel and work overseas stayed with him, although Sallie comments in a letter to Nora on 3 June 1936 that Hans felt duty-bound to stay at home: 'Daddy is loving your letters and would give anything to be with you, but his non-conformist conscience is too strong for him, and the daily bread for all us looms large upon the horizon'. This sentiment is echoed in a letter to Nora on 19 July 1936, in which Hans says how much he wishes to join her wandering around Dorset: 'The very name of Corfe Castle conjures up all sorts of romantic visions and I ache to join you in wandering all over that rolling landscape'.

The letters show another side to Hans and how travel formed his art. He says that his daughter's letters from Paris brought back 'slumbering memories', and how the art to be seen in European museums reminds him of 'a dearth of mental food' back in Australia. His letters also show him throughout as having his finger on the pulse and reporting on significant gallery purchases and important gallery appointments across Australia. There also is the occasional bit of gossip, such as Max Meldrum narrowly missing out on the Director's position at the National Gallery of South Australia in 1936. Hans comments on 10 November 1934 about the difference that W.B. McInnes, even as a middling Acting Director, had made to the National Gallery of Victoria:

> He is I feel perfectly honest and cannot be bought over, but I cannot imagine him with the necessary qualifications for that important position. Already since his installment a number of pictures by Australian artists have been bought, and things that would never have been passed by Hall.

Much of this information is gleaned from Hans' extensive connections in the art world and also his close reading of magazines and newspapers. Hans' level of knowledge of the international art market, especially British, and current exhibitions is impressive, and makes for good conversation in the letters.

---

22   Hans Heysen, quoted in Colin Thiele, *Heysen of Hahndorf*, Adelaide, Hyde Park Press, 2001: 196.
23   Hans Heysen, quoted in Colin Thiele, *Heysen of Hahndorf*, Adelaide, Hyde Park Press, 2001: 74.

On Sallie Heysen

Sallie (born Selma Bartels), always 'Mother' in the letters, was the daughter of Adelaide's first German-born Mayor. She met Hans while attending his painting classes, which he conducted in the rooms of the Adelaide Steamship Company after returning home from four years overseas. They married in December 1904, Hans by then having sufficient income. His painting *Mystic Morn* (1904), which Sallie had named, had been recently purchased by the National Gallery of South Australia for 150 guineas.

Nora, the fourth of their eight children, was born in 1911, as Hans was being touted by *The Bulletin* as 'a great watercolour painter'. His second Melbourne exhibition brought in £1500, exactly enough to purchase the family's large and comfortable house, 'The Cedars', set in 36 acres in the picturesque South Australian district of Hahndorf.

Accounts of life at 'The Cedars' and of Sallie's organisational skills and social expertise thread their way through the letters. As Hans commented many years later: 'she knew how to send out invitations, how to address people, what to do and not to do'.[24] The list of famous visitors to 'The Cedars' is long and Sallie was an exceptional hostess and cook. After Nora met up with Colin Colahan at a London party, she writes home on 12 December 1948:

> who should be there but Colin Colahan, do you remember him?
> His memories of his visit to Hahndorf are still very fresh. When
> introduced to me he said—Oh yes, of course I remember, your Mother
> is the best cake maker in the world! And he went on to tell me in
> detail what he'd eaten on his last visit to the Cedars.

Sallie in her letters talks mostly about family and friends, much of which falls outside the scope of this book. The letters in which she focuses on art and which are included in the book, tend to be short. She names many of Hans' paintings and some of Nora's too, including her motherhood piece, *Dedication* (1941), which Nora initially called 'the Murray Madonna'. On occasion, Sallie lets loose and talks art but then stops herself, knowing that Hans and Nora have a special bond built around the subject. On 16 May 1954 she writes of work they had seen on display at the National Gallery of South Australia:

---

24   Hans Heysen, quoted in Colin Thiele, *Heysen of Hahndorf*, Adelaide, Hyde Park Press, 2001: 84.

Frances Hodgkins' work gave Daddy much pleasure. He admires her unerring colour sense—also the work of Barbara Hepworth, her *Trio: Surgeons and Theatre Sister* is most intriguing and made me think how you would enjoy it—she is a sculptress in the Henry Moore tradition Campbell said, this delicate study was a sheer joy—but you don't want to hear me talk art.

All the way through the letters Sallie sends special food parcels to Nora: jam to London and honey biscuits, fresh apples and metwurst to Sydney. Even when Nora was an official war artist working in remote parts of New Guinea, dried fruit would miraculously appear, sometimes weeks later than intended, but it found its way nevertheless. When Nora was painting portraits of the heads of the women's services in the war artist studios in the old Melbourne Morgue, the honey biscuits were handy and Nora writes home in January 1944: 'The biscuits too were very timely and for lunch and morning tea come in well. They are especially good biscuits and my present sitter Colonel Best and I are engaging in them to the full'.

Sallie, in her letters, had a different kind of relationship with her daughter to that of Hans. She was a caring mother but her remarks about art and life, unlike those of Hans, are generally brief and to the point.

On Nora Heysen

The chapters in this book are arranged around distinct phases in Nora's life, often marked by travel. They span the years 1934, just after she arrived in London to study art, to 1968, when her father Hans died. Nora's early success, followed by semi-obscurity, and then her 1980s revival amid a wider flurry of 'recovering' women artists, has puzzled writers. In 1989 Lou Klepac commented: 'she made her own way in the world, but her reserved nature ensured a rather restricted success. In her own words, she relished "comfortable obscurity"'.[25] He found it surprising that she had never had a solo exhibition in Sydney, her home for almost 60 years. By 2000 Klepac positions her as a 'recovered' artist, whose lacunae of reputation could be put down to the rise of abstraction which bypassed an entire group of realist painters, including Adrian Feint, Roland Wakelin and Douglas Dundas.[26] Certainly the advent of abstraction is part of the explanation. More recently, Jane Hylton noted that despite Nora dropping out of fashion she was 'irresistibly inspired by all that surrounded

---

25   See Lou Klepac, *Nora Heysen*, Roseville, New South Wales, Beagle Press, 1989: 15.
26   See Lou Klepac, *Nora Heysen*, Canberra, National Library of Australia, 2000: 5.

her—the colours of the flowers in her garden, the elegant curves of a sleeping cat or a reclining nude'. She found a determined 'pursuit of and love for light and life in her subjects'.[27]

The earlier letters show how crucial Nora's time was in cosmopolitan London, just as her father's time working in Belle Époque Paris had been for his later development. Like her father, Nora studied the work of the impressionists and neo-impressionists. After seeing an exhibition of French art at Burlington Gallery, she writes to her father on 3 November 1936 how greatly excited she is by the work of Vincent Van Gogh, Paul Cezanne, the Pissarros and Édouard Manet. She singles out Van Gogh's portrait of a sailor as the most vital and encloses a newspaper cutting for her father to see the work, to which he replies: 'It is quite uncanny with what simplicity of means Van Gogh produces a most convincing subject. I put it to his unnerving sense of design and extraordinarily original colour sense. I think his colour very beautiful'.

Light is a continual thread in the letters. On 30 January 1936, Nora writes about the light infusing her subject of flowers in a pot: 'the flowers bursting out of the leaves were so pure and beautiful flooded with light. I had a job painting them against a white muslin curtain. The leaves were the only dark note in the picture'. On 27 July 1937, writing home about her travels to Italy, Nora again focuses on light: 'The lovely Umbrian countryside was a revelation ... The luminous skies, the silvery blue distances ... I am longing to know which parts of Italy Daddy saw?'

Meeting Orovida Pissarro (1893–1968), who comments on her work, was one of a confluence of forces that led to a change in Nora's portraits, including her *Self Portrait* (1936), painted to mark her birthday. In the painting, Nora's palette is tipped forward, showing the new range of colours Orovida had suggested she use. It also reflects the neo-impressionist style Nora was now working in. Moreover, in the lively to-and-fro with her father, the letters show Nora emerging transformed and self-assured in her views on art. When she returned to 'The Cedars' in early October 1937 her work had loosened up, light was infusing it and the cosmopolitan experience had indeed rendered her work modern, as is evident in *Spring Light* (c.1938). The ensuing discussion is not recorded in the letters but Nora's paintings, such as *Corn Cobs* (1938) and her confident and modern *Self Portrait* (1938), filled with broken colour, were too modern for her father.[28]

Nora decided to move to Sydney to create her own professional identity and space. Once there, she began exhibiting with the Society of Artists and soon became a member. Her father, a fellow member, was a touchstone for conversation and she

---

27   See Jane Hylton, *Nora Heysen: Light and Life*, Adelaide, Wakefield Press, 2009: 11.
28   See Lou Klepac, *Nora Heysen*, Roseville, New South Wales, Beagle Press, 1989: 13–14.

was frequently asked to convey the good wishes of other artists, apologies that they didn't have time to visit 'The Cedars' when in Adelaide, or that they would soon be in Adelaide and would visit.

The Sydney years prior to the war were crucial for Nora in terms of establishing herself as portrait painter. Before long she was receiving commissions aplenty and entered two paintings in the Archibald Prize, winning the 1938 prize for her portrait *Madame Elink Schuurman*. A mere four years later, Nora was appointed an official war artist along with Stella Bowen. The letters from this period chart army life, complete with tales of living and working in remote parts of New Guinea, and the new subject matter Nora faces. Occasionally she met other artists, such as fellow official war artist Will Dargie, and writes home on 9 June 1945 of the relief to be able to talk art again: 'it is a God-send to talk to someone who understands the same language, and it was a tonic to talk art and laugh over our experiences as war artists'.

During the war years Nora met Doctor Robert Black and from the postwar years he features in the letters. She joined him in Liverpool, in the United Kingdom, in 1948. Her letters describe the hardships faced by a country recovering from a prolonged war. She also tells how a recently arrived Jeffrey Smart was astonished to find her in such surroundings painting flowers. Nora returned to Sydney in 1949, re-established herself in the Sydney art scene and the Society of Artists, and painted several portraits, including one of Robert. She entered that painting along with commissioned portraits of Camille Gheysens and of Norman Gratton, in the 1950 and 1951 Archibald Prizes respectively. Letters home describe the changing art scene, emerging stars like Sidney Nolan and the rise of abstraction.

Nora and Robert married in January 1953 and, soon after, set out on the first of three trips to the Pacific Islands, where Robert worked in tropical medicine. The letters from the Pacific describe how the couple had entered another world and, on occasion, revisited areas they had seen during the war. Nora used her time seeking out new subjects, as were other modern artists around this time. On returning to Australia, she examines her Pacific work and is shocked to see how 'the exotic colour and brown bare bodies seem strange in this grey atmosphere'.

Increasingly, the letters of the mid-1950s and early 1960s touch on the challenges of balancing a career with the demands of married life, such as entertaining Robert's colleagues. On 3 September 1962, she writes: 'we entertained a beautiful Indian woman doctor the other night. I'd rather had been painting her in her glorious rose silk sari than preparing a meal for her'. Art world figures also weave in and out of the letters, such as Thea Proctor, of whom Nora writes on 6 April 1960: 'she was there at the opening in all purple looking like a grand duchess'.

The letters also provide an insight into Nora's exhibitions. In 1939, she writes about arranging a solo show in Sydney at Grosvenor Galleries, which she delays when Australia enters the Second World War; the exhibition was never held. Throughout her letters from the 1950s and 1960s, Nora refers to several solo shows held outside of Sydney: in 1951 and 1956 at Heysen Gallery, Hahndorf, South Australia; in 1953 at Moreton Galleries, Brisbane; in 1957 at John Martin's Art Gallery, Adelaide; in March 1963 at the Masonic Centre, Millicent, South Australia; and in 1967 at North Adelaide Galleries, Adelaide. In April 1963, Nora also refers to a joint exhibition with her father held at Hamilton Art Gallery, Hamilton, Victoria. The majority of Nora's solo exhibitions were arranged either by her brother Stefan, when he ran the Heysen Gallery, or by another brother David, who managed the exhibitions in Hamilton and Millicent. Given that the family firm 'brand' was dominated by her father's work, by then popularised by David, who was printing editions of his father's paintings and watercolours, it is unsurprising that Nora felt a marginal visual identity.

Throughout her later career, Nora consistently had work on show in the Society of Artists exhibitions and entered the Archibald Prize, the Portia Geach Memorial Award, the Melrose Prize, *The Australian Women's Weekly* Prize and the Queensland Centenary Prize. She continued entering prizes and competitions into the 1970s. In all, this was a taxing schedule but she was less than strategic in not basing more solo exhibitions in Sydney. What the letters do not mention is that after the war, in late 1946, Nora was one of a number of Australians who had work exhibited in an important UNESCO exhibition *Exposition Internationale d'Art Moderne* at the Musée de Art Moderne in Paris, prior to her travelling back to Britain in 1948.[29]

Beyond Nora's well-known London, Archibald Prize and wartime portraits, as her letters reveal, is an artist who took on a steady stream of portrait commissions, far more than is widely realised. However, a good number, like those of Freda Nesbitt and Persia Porter, the latter entered in the Portia Geach Memorial Award in 1965, still remain in a private collections. One significant side to Nora losing control mid-career was that she worked in a genre—portraiture—which fell somewhat out of favour during the 1960s. Some artists, like Judy Cassab, incorporated abstract gestures into their work but others, like Nora, did not and it was difficult to continue working in that genre during this era.

Another factor in Nora's uneven modern profile was her practice of painting flowers, so much so that she said by the 1950s and the 1960s her work looked out of date. Her proclivity to paint flowers was something she felt she had little control over. On 13 November 1963 she writes: 'I've been painting all day and all night trying to

29   See 'Papers of Nora Heysen, 1913–2003', National Library of Australia, MS 10041.

get something of their illusive quality. This obsession to paint those roses. If I could just be content to look at them'. Flowers were a challenging subject, underpinned by that inevitable urgency to capture them when fresh. Her father, doubtless her first teacher and the one who encouraged her in this pursuit, understood this all too well. He was an exceptional flower painter, apparent in works like *Flowers and Fruit (Zinnias)* (1921). Writing for *Art in Australia*, Lionel Lindsay described how Hans 'works arduously while the light lasts, his eye on every form, every colour relation, painting with the assurance and ease of a ripe draughtsman'.[30]

The French nineteenth-century painter of flowers, Henri Fantin-Latour (1836–1904), who enjoyed great popularity in Britain, was their joint model.[31] Nora, whose London letters are filled with talk about light infusing her flower paintings, was apt to become discouraged that she could not achieve the perfection of Fantin. She was particularly discouraged when writing home on 18 August 1935: 'Yesterday I went into the National and had a good look at the Fantin flowers and when I came back I had a great desire to put my foot through all mine'. She was seeking a level of perfection that was no longer the currency of modern flower painters, like Jacob Epstein and Vanessa Bell, whose work she rejected. Her talk of painting flowers was close to becoming a private language with her father. He replies encouragingly on 6 October 1935: 'my advice would be don't bother too much about atmosphere just now, it will come naturally in time'. Hans adds on 26 November 1935: 'You need never regret having to paint flowers for a living, Fantin did it and it made him a fine painter to bring joy and pleasure into many a home.' Nora accepted his advice and her flower pieces sold well, so on one level she achieved what her father had suggested; but fashion passed her by. By 1967, critical reception of her work favoured her portraiture over her flowers, with Adelaide critic Ivor Francis commenting that her flower pieces 'did not afford the artist much opportunity to extend herself'.[32]

The letters hardly touch on Nora's extraordinary comment, made as a mid-career artist, in a 1962 interview with John Hetherington: 'because my father is Hans Heysen, I don't know if I exist in my own right or not. I suppose I never will know now'.[33] The only reference she made to it in the letters, once the Hetherington story had appeared in *The Age*, was to convey home two messages enquiring from readers of that story about her father! Doubtless there were other comments which she didn't relay home in letters.

---

30   Lionel Lindsay, 'Heysen's Flower Pieces', *Art in Australia*, June 1925: np.

31   The National Gallery of South Australia, under Honorary Curator Harry P. Gill, acquired two Henri Fantin-Latour paintings, *Zinnias* (c.1897–1889) in 1899 and *Poppies* (1891) in 1906.

32   See Ivor Francis, 'Two Stand Out', *Sunday Mail*, 2 September 1967.

33   See Nora Heysen, 'I don't Know if I Exist in my own Right', *The Age*, 6 October 1962.

Other women artists have not survived the famous-father syndrome. Orovida Pissarro dropped her family name and worked as 'Orovida' for many years in order to create her own identity, and adopted an orientalist style and medium quite different from that of her famous father Lucien, or grandfather Camille. She reverted to oil painting in the family's signature style of neo-impressionism in the mid-1940s, and after her father died.[34]

Nora did solve the father–daughter dilemma late in life, beyond the time span of these letters (1934–1968), but it plagued her for many years. In 1980, she observed: 'I've never tried to fight again to see if I was seen as a painter without my father's name. I really don't care anymore'.[35] It was only in 1989, following her important S.H. Ervin retrospective exhibition, that she commented: 'recognition has come a bit late but it's still very nice'.[36] Two months later, when the exhibition travelled to Adelaide, she added: 'I believe I am a painter in my own right and not just the talented daughter of the famous artist, Hans Heysen'.[37] Although she was still defining her career in terms of relationship with her father, it was now a relationship she had control over. In contrast, during the middle years of her working life, Nora's observations are starkly devoid of what Joy Hooton calls 'verbs of control, power and agency' and a 'power over circumstances'[38].

The letters go some way in explaining how Nora came to doubt herself mid-career and how she moved from being a successful artist to one on the sidelines. Even though she was living in Sydney, she was a perpetual conduit to her father. Sydney galleries would contact her to request a watercolour or painting by Hans for their forthcoming exhibition. Often enough she would arrange it and, in doing so, kept her father's reputation alive before the Sydney public. Private collectors, too, would contact her to see if she could facilitate their obtaining a Hans Heysen for their collection. Should one of her father's works go to auction, she would attend the auction and report home in the letters on the prices achieved, thus monitoring from Sydney the strength of the Hans Heysen market.

The mid-career years were difficult for Nora. She understandably felt she was the marginal Heysen to her father, still a giant in the art world. Another factor that stands outside the father–daughter relationship, and one hinted at in the letters to

---

34   See Kristen Erickson, 'The Art of Orovida', *Women's Art Journal*, vol.15, no.2, 1994–1995: 14–20.

35   Nora Heysen, quoted in Deborah Edwards, 'Nora Heysen', Honours Thesis, University of Sydney, 1980: 57.

36   Nora Heysen, interviewed by the author, 15 September 1989.

37   See 'When the Name is Heysen, you're in Demand', *The Advertiser*, 15 November 1989: 3.

38   See Joy Hooton, 'Autobiography and Gender', in Susan Magarey, Caroline Guerin and Paula Hamilton (eds), *Writing Lives: Feminist Autobiography and Gender*, Adelaide, Australian Feminist Studies, 1992: 29.

Hans, is the constant travelling of Nora's husband, Robert. She found his comings and goings difficult, as she comments on 13 October 1965:

> Robert returned from New Guinea on Sunday somewhat tired after his heavy schedule of meetings. He caught me in the middle of trying to clean up after an orgy of painting ... Now I'm frantically busy trying to restore order and get back to some sort of routine before Robert takes off again next Monday for Ceylon—before then all the clothes have to be washed and ironed, also I'm trying to finish the portrait of Charles Rowley and have a couple of sittings to cope with this week. Twenty four hours in a day are not near enough.

After her marriage failed in 1972, Nora's new status manifested itself in two magisterial portraits: the larger-than-life rendition of author and poet *Merv Lilley* (1977), held by the National Library of Australia, and the lively portrayal of the poet *Dorothy Hewitt* (1975), held by Curtin University, which shows a woman whose wild and uncontrollable hair signals her free spirit. This painting was entered in the 1975 Archibald Prize, as was *Merv Lilley* in 1983. Nora also entered her own less than flattering *Self Portrait*, of an ageing artist replete in her painting smock, in the Doug Moran Portrait Prize in 1988. This rush of portraits points to an artist who has regained her sense of control over her life.

For the last decades of her life, Nora knew that the letters her father received from her were housed in the National Library of Australia and, not long before she died, she agreed that her own letters would also be placed there. So within her own lifetime, she was aware their letters about their own working lives, and art, artists and exhibitions would be read by a wider audience than her family and friends. Hans and Nora read, talked about and exchanged books of letters from other artists, such as between the Pissarros and between Vincent van Gogh and his brother Theo. Little did they realise then that their letters would join the same pantheon.

Editor's note

The letters selected for this volume come from a much larger number sent between Nora Heysen, her father Hans and, to a lesser extent, her mother Sallie. In the main, the focus of this selection is on letters dealing with art and, for the most part, discussions between Nora and Hans outside of this broad topic have not been included. Due to consideration of space, some letters have been abridged.

The letters have been edited according to the National Library of Australia's style, while also retaining the individual voice, writing style and expression of the authors. In editing the letters for readability, punctuation has been added and modified, and grammar and spelling has sometimes been corrected. Correct names have been given for newspapers, for example the *London Illustrated* has been changed to *The Illustrated London News*, and a similar approach has been applied to titles of works of art. Dates and addresses have also been presented uniformly.

The Letters

Cosmopolitan London
1934–1937

The weekly letters from Nora Heysen to her parents, and theirs in reply, chronicle a period of remarkable change for Nora. Like numerous other Australian artists she headed to London, one of the two cosmopolitan centres (Paris being the other) to 'finish her education'. She funded her time there with the proceeds from her highly successful exhibition in Adelaide in 1933.

In 1934, Hans and Sallie and their four daughters travelled via Germany to London, where they spent several months 'installing' Nora in her new home. They enrolled her at London's Central School of Art, found her suitable and respectable studio accommodation in Church Street, Kensington, with the Reverend and Mrs Cornish, and introduced her to their circle of friends. The family then sailed back to Australia on *The Neptune* and the letters begin at that point, in October 1934, with Nora in London by herself. By late November her family were back home at 'The Cedars'.

Nora planned to spend one to two years away but extended the stay, returning in late 1937, when she was out of funds and felt ready to come home. As she wrote on 24 March 1937: 'it is now three years since I left my home country, it is a long time, quite long enough to be away from one's home country. I long for the bush and garden and the sun'.

The changes that Nora underwent were personal and professional. She has been frequently portrayed in her early years as shy and retiring but, by early December 1934, she reports: 'I'm very talkative when I go out, you would be surprised. I even astonish myself'. Her Adelaide friend Everton Stokes, who Nora calls 'Evie', joins her and this causes much family consternation and stern disapproval, resulting in Nora reminding her parents: 'we all have to branch out for ourselves at one time or another'.

Nora's work and her views on art change too, due to working in a cosmopolitan centre, where artists knowingly leave all that is safe and familiar behind and approach their work with an attitude of cultural openness. This can be seen in a series of self portraits that Nora paints. The first and most striking is *Self Portrait* (1934–1935), with its modern square modelling showing the influence of her modern teacher Bernard Meninsky (1891–1950). This is a presentation of self as alone and ready to face any challenges that may arise. Her manner of painting flowers also loosens up, as in *Spring Light* (c.1938), a work that was to become one of Hans' favourites.

Letters to her father focus on her work at the two art schools she attends, what she is painting in her studio and the art she sees in galleries and in exhibitions. She also establishes a practice of sending home 'snaps' of her sculpture and painting for comment, and a father-as-teacher element enters the conversation. His advice and feedback is sought and valued. Painterly and sculptural ideas of composition, tone, form and light are bandied back and forth. Nora, excited at each new discovery, writes letters that at times feel as if they are written at breakneck speed, while Hans replies with advice that draws on his already worked out ideas about light and form. He comments in January 1936: 'It's wonderful to read of your enthusiasm for your work, its ambitions, high hopes and disappointments. Lucky Beggar to feel like that, for I must confess that advancing years quietens that rush of blood along the veins'.

Hans engineers a meeting between his daughter and Orovida Pissarro, an artist whose work he has long admired, by writing to Pissarro and offering to buy a painting of hers. The two meet up to finalise the sale and, before long, Nora's way of painting and use of colour is challenged by her new friend. Her father welcomes this, commenting on 10 December 1935: 'Miss Pissarro comes from a long line of artists and her experience should have been a wide and wise one … Her palette sounds well worth experimenting with, in fact it is always wise from time to time to make a change'. In Orovida Nora finds another mentor and writes home on 4 February 1936: 'her opinion is frank and honest and is very helpful'.

Nora's travels to Paris and Florence take Hans back to his time as a student overseas from 1899 to 1903. His visual memory is remarkable and he recalls the time with clarity, such as seeing snow for the first time and how he 'can still clearly visualise [it], all so captivating and enchanting'. Similarly he writes with detail about paintings seen years earlier, such as one by Édouard Manet that he refers to in discussing the use of black and brown in painting:

> Did you see his Olympia in the Luxembourg Galleries? I think I like
> Manet quite as well, if not better, when he deals with blacks like in
> his Mexican soldier at the National Gallery [London] ... I can see it as
> distinctly as if I stood before it now and remains always a pleasure.

During his 1934 trip to London, Hans was a buyer for the National Gallery of South Australia and was always on the lookout for astute gallery purchases. This was the era of Australian galleries and private collectors, such as Heysen family friends James McGregor and Ursula and Bill Hayward, travelling to London to buy their paintings. At one stage, Nora mentions that she is going to look at an exhibition of Ernest Proctor's work and Hans asks her to send back a catalogue with marked-up prices, as he has recently purchased that artist's *Eggardun* for the Gallery. Hans had long wanted the Gallery to also have a Pissarro in its collection and Nora's friendship with Orovida leads eventually to filling this gap by facilitating the purchase of Lucien Pissarro's *Laurustinus* (now called *Campagne Orovida, the Laurustinus*).

While the letters ooze with talk about paintings and sculpture, the business side of working as an artist is never far from the surface. Nora was inducted into subjects, such as what price to charge, how often to hold exhibitions, what commissions to agree to and how to negotiate with dealers.

Against this background of art talk, Nora also refers to concerts and plays she has been to, and the names of performers, such as Gracie Fields, John Gielgud, Edith Evans and Elisabeth Schumann, pepper the conversation. She hears Walter de la Mare speak and reports home on 5 June 1936: 'little did I think when I was in Australia and used to read his poetry that I would ever see the man and hear him speak'. On another occasion, while immersed in a biography of George Bernard Shaw, Nora passes him on Piccadilly and writes home on 4 November 1935 that it was 'unmistakably Shaw, walking like a cat'.

World events weave in and out of the letters. The England-to-Melbourne Great Air Race was staged in 1934, as part of Melbourne's centenary celebrations. At a time when the trip by sea to Australia took six weeks, Nora writes it is almost 'more than one can grasp that the great distance was covered in less than three days'. The rise of Nazism also impinges on the German-Australian family and Sallie Heysen fears for family in Germany. Nora, too, observes that the world is heading towards another world war.

In late 1934 and early 1935 the young Nora had been dismissive of modern art and of Jacob Epstein's carved stone sculpture. By 1937, having looked at much modern British and French art and, in particular, neo-impressionist painting, a new understanding of the breadth of modernism infuses Nora's letters. She writes home how fellow Australian Roy de Maistre likes Pablo Picasso's work and, even though it challenges her, she adds: 'another man can come along with intelligence and knowledge and find expression and meaning there which he finds satisfying and interesting. What strangely conflicting views there are about'. She has become tolerant and mature in her views on art and returns home transformed. Her goals include winning the Archibald Prize, as she writes on 28 April 1936: 'Why can't someone paint a better portrait than Longstaff ... I'd like to win that prize away from him one day'.

5 Dukes Lane, London
21 October 1934

Dearest Mother and Daddy,

I am still alive and all goes fairly well so far. My thoughts are with you. I wonder where you are, what doing, how you find the boat and are the passengers interesting, and all the thousands of questions that cannot be answered.

Sundays seem very lonely days now and I cannot get used to no one coming, and sitting down to afternoon tea alone takes my appetite away completely. I can't help being reminded of the Sundays at home, a full table of coffee and brown cakes, and the smell of it and the clatter of many teacups.

My love to all,

Norrie

5 Dukes Lane, London
Monday 12 November 1934

Dear Mother and Daddy and everybody,

There is so much to tell you. I got a criticism on my drawing from Bernard Meninsky.[1] He was scathing and gave me the worst most damning criticism I've ever had. In fact he had not one good word to say—my drawing was lifeless, dull, formless and superficial and the technique was like sandpaper. He couldn't have said anything more disheartening and my conceit went a mighty crash. I don't know how far he is right, but it appears that he does not see my point of view at all and looks at the figure in a totally different way. He draws with a heavy line and square modelling, handling the pencil like a pen, whereas I draw with a single line and just use the shading to emphasise certain forms. It is very difficult to know how far to trust one's own judgement and how much to follow the masters. It isn't much good going to a school unless one is ready to knuckle under and learn from them, but on the other hand I don't want to give up my point of view for his, and we are both striving for something so completely different. He draws very well and I admire the solidity and movement he gets, but I don't want to draw like him.

Ever since I have felt very subdued and very discouraged, but I suppose there's nothing for it but to keep on.

It has been very cold … London appeals to me in this sort of atmosphere, it has charm. Lights are on now by three o'clock and it is already quite dark when I

---

1   Bernard Meninsky (1891–1950) exhibited with the progressive New English Art Club. His *Standing Female Nude in a Landscape* (c.1940–1943) is held by Tate Britain and *Nude* (1945) is held by the Art Gallery of South Australia.

get home from art school in the evenings. It is remarkable how quickly Winter has settled down in earnest. The whole of London has come out in fur coats and it is almost like being in a zoo, there are so many woolly bears about.

Now goodnight everybody,

Norrie

Ambleside, South Australia[2]
5 December 1934

My Dear Nora,

Our homecoming was really a very happy one—the roses were still all out in full bloom. The Grüss and Frau Karl are particularly beautiful and David had also filled the house with them.[3] Mother will have told you about the meeting at Port Adelaide and the wonderful Summer day to greet us at the Semaphore anchorage with an extraordinary glare of light which I had noticed for the first time again.

A week has now passed and already the whole trip is but a dream. It is actually very difficult to make oneself believe that I have been away at all.

With lots of love,

From Daddy

PS Adelaide seems very tiny, strangely small and provincial.

5 Dukes Lane, London
Wednesday 26 December 1934

Dearest Mother and Daddy,

At last the first news of the homecoming.

On Friday Evie was due to arrive but the boat was delayed at the last minute and didn't actually arrive until the Saturday. Jim, her brother, and I met her, then we came back here and lunched and great excitement and of course much talking and merriment.

On Monday we decorated the Christmas tree and it really did look quite nice, all silver standing against my dark curtain on the box in the window ... Tuesday the big day we cooked the turkey and the dinner and had a gay time. To begin with the clock stopped and we did not know the time, and by the time the dinner was cooked it was four in the afternoon and pitch dark. I don't think the

---

2   After the First World War, the South Australian Government revised German-sounding placenames. Hahndorf was called Ambleside until 1936.

3   'Grüss an Aachen' and 'Frau Karl Druschki' are roses.

dinner was much of a success. The turkey was overdone and the celery burnt and the water got into the pudding, but for all that we gloried in the fact that we were doing the thing properly, and eating a real Christmas dinner, and it was great fun cooking it.

I did not think the place was big enough to hold two, but we fit in very comfortably and take it in turns to do everything, and it is very nice to have someone to talk to and help do things.

I wish you could have seen my Christmas tree.

Goodbye and my love to all,

Norrie

Ambleside, South Australia
26 December 1934

My Dear Nora,

It was a delight to get your last letter with its more cheerful note and feeling that you are meeting some congenial company to give you the necessary change from your school and studio life.

The McGregors were here today and it was a delight to revive memories of pictures and painting with Jimmy, whose love of art is really a very genuine one.[4] We spent quite a time in your studio which I have arranged as a gallery of our possessions and it looks delightful. The Schoukhaeff, two Lamberts, Jacovleff, Clausen, Millet, two of your small flower studies, Connard, and the Batemans, also accompany my landscapes … and make quite an attractive show.[5]

Don't get too disheartened with Meninsky's criticism of your drawing—I think his main object is to insist on the pupil searching for movement and life.

Everything is looking particularly cheerful around your studio,

Daddy

---

4   James Robert McGregor (1889–1973) was a Sydney-based art collector, wool merchant and friend of the Heysen family.

5   Russian artist Basil Schoukhaeff's painting is *Cassis* (1928). The George Lamberts are *Head Study*, a pencil drawing, and *The Half Back*. Russian painter Alexandre Jacovleff's work is either *Fara Ali Afden, an Abyssinian* (1928) or *Abyssinian Landscape* (1928). George Clausen's work is one or all of *A Winter Morning, London*, *Thatched Cottages* and *The Farmyard*. The Philip Connard is *The Artist*. The Jean F. Millet is *Les lavandieres* (c.1875). The James Bateman is *The Farmyard* (1938). See Leonard Joel, *The Hans Heysen Collection*, Melbourne, Leonard Joel Pty Ltd, 1970: 3–45.

Ambleside, South Australia
23 January 1935

My Dear Nora,

My mind is still in the North, and all I have done since our homecoming is to overhaul the sketches of my last trip, and I find it rather surprising that I could put my finger on a number of passages awaiting to be developed and carried further, without much effort. Perhaps the 9 month spell is beginning to bear good fruit.

I was in the Gallery again yesterday morning to have another look at my purchases. The Reynolds portrait looks really good and I think you will like it. The Bateman, the Holmes, Lucien Simon—all carry splendidly on the walls.[6]

Time is up so I will stop so I will say goodnight dear Nora—take every care of yourself is the wish of us both,

From Daddy

Ambleside, South Australia
16 February 1935

My Dear Nora,

The routine now is to take them up to your studio to see the 'gallery'.

From Auntie Annie came pleading letters for help in supplying missing branches in their family tree! Hitler is on the Hebrew hunt and everyone must show a clear ancestry before they can hope for promotion. Auntie Dossie and I have been rushing around in search of records and touchstones but we can't find any legal information, and we wonder why on earth we never took any interest in our forefathers before this. Poor Auntie Annie is getting desperate, should we find anything I will send it airmail to you and ask you to forward it to her immediately. Things must be in a parlous state in Germany.

The jam looks ready so I'll be off.

Love from us all,

Mother

---

6   While overseas in 1934, Hans Heysen purchased 14 works for the National Gallery of South Australia, including Joshua Reynolds's *Dr John Armstrong* (1767) and James Bateman's *The Harvest*. See Edward Morgan, 'Gallery Buyers', *Art Gallery of South Australia Bulletin*, vol.33, no.3, 1972.

Ambleside, South Australia
18 February 1935

My Dear Nora,

Another fat letter, in fact two since last I wrote and a general family gathering to hear the latest from London making a most pleasant interlude in the Saturday morning's work. Of course everyone is immensely glad that you are feeling 'more at home', so to speak, in your London surroundings.

Mother lately she has not been as well as she should be ... I am afraid that Mother is worrying and feeling apprehensive about Effie's entrance into your studio. Not that this news came at all as a surprise, for Mother had long told me that that would happen. Unfortunately this apprehensive feeling has been aggravated by information that has come to her through others. You know exactly what we feel about the whole matter and there is enough evidence to show that our suspicions are justified. There is a very true saying 'that love is blind' and this may not only apply to when that state exists between man and woman but it is equally true and can happen between two persons of the same sex. Your letters sound perfectly happy—almost as if you were under such a spell.

I am writing quite openly dear Nora about my impressions, for I want you to be candid and open with us—it is the only way that our mutual love and an honest respect for your parents can be kept alive. Your Mother feels the position keenly and has taken it all very much to heart, and I am hoping a chain of circumstances may soon clear the air and free her from that anxiety, which I feel is partly responsible for her health, which should be better than it is, especially after our wonderful holiday.

We love your letters and I cannot repeat too often how great a pleasure and joy they are to us. Did I tell you in my last letter that the Sydney Art Gallery has asked me to hold a loan exhibition on my work in their Gallery? I had a letter from J.S. MacDonald, the Director, last week and already made out a list of those pictures by which I wish to be represented. This list comprises about 27 oils, 55 watercolours and 20 drawings drawn from Sydney, Melbourne and Adelaide. It has been quite a long and perplexing job to make out the list and brings back a memory over a period of 20 years and more.

We had news of Bernard Hall's sudden death in England! Now we are wondering who is to fill his place.[7]

My love goes with this,

From your Father

---

7   British artist Bernard Hall (1859–1935) was Director of the National Gallery of Victoria and Head of the National Gallery Art School from 1892. He was also a buyer for the Felton Bequest and died suddenly in London on a buying trip.

5 Dukes Lane, London
26 February 1935

Dearest Mother and Daddy and everyone,

The mail this week brought me Daddy's letter ... not forgetting the gum leaf which made me very homesick for the bush.

I have been hard at work over the weekend, yesterday and today painting, and the portrait is almost finished, it wants only a few touches to the head to complete it. I wonder if you would like it. I put the portrait of Ronda against it for comparison and it is infinitely better. Ronda looks hard and metallic and the flesh painting lifeless.[8] In the portrait I have painted the flesh very warm and feel that it has much more sense of flesh and blood. Today I painted in the sky, it is remarkable how quickly paint dries in this place. I am using pure oil as a medium, and yet it dries overnight. It must be the gas fire.

Goodnight with my love and best wishes to all,

Norrie

Ambleside, South Australia
5 March 1935

My Dear Nora,

The family excitement was very real over your last letter, we all enjoyed it thoroughly. The news of the first snow did certainly awaken the imagination and memories of my first snow seeing it softly falling towards evening from my sixth-storey window overlooking Boulevard Montparnasse.[9] It was all great fun, the hurrying down to Charenton on the next day and experiencing my first painting of snow. That wonderful transformation of the whole landscape I can still clearly visualise, all so captivating and enchanting.

It certainly is a great contrast to what we are experiencing here just now. No rain has fallen for a long time and the bush is as dry and brittle as no imagination can picture it. Yet with it all exists that peculiar fascination, and never have the trees and the bush been so beautiful for it is just that extra dryness that gives it the 'pastel quality'. We have now had more than a week of clear brilliant days and real Australian weather that we all love, it is an ideal Summer for the painter.

---

8   Ronda is the subject of Nora Heysen's *Ruth* (1933), purchased by the National Art Gallery of South Australia in 1933.

9   Between 1899 and 1903, Hans Heysen studied in Paris at the Académie Julian, under Jean Paul Laurens, at the Académie Colarossi and at the École de Beaux-Arts, under Léon Bonnat. He boarded at the Grand Hotel de la Haute-Loire on the corner of the Boulevard Raspail and Boulevard du Montparnasse. See Colin Thiele, *Heysen of Hahndorf*, Adelaide, Hyde Park Press, 2001: 50.

Goodnight and cheerio with love from everyone,

From Daddy

5 Dukes Lane, London
Tuesday 13 March 1935

Dearest Mother and Daddy,

I've just finished a long day's painting—been at it from early this morning
and now it is ten o'clock and I've just finished washing my brushes and cleaning
up. It is a self portrait I'm painting, just a head and shoulders full on.[10] I think it
is a better likeness than I usually aspire to and is a better painting, but I feel too
wearied out to care much.

Meninsky gave me a criticism on my drawing last week. He told me that
my work lacked feeling and any emotional quality, and that the technique was
uninteresting. I asked him for a remedy for such ills and he said that he could
not teach me any more, he advised studying the old masters, also he advised
experimenting more. He said I knew all that he could teach me about construction
and proportion, and the rest had to come from within myself. I feel that he is right,
so I am thinking of spending more time in the print room of the British Museum ...
So ends the term.

My love and thoughts to all,

Norrie

5 Dukes Lane, London
20 March 1935

Dear Mother and Daddy,

This week at last brought no home letters and I feel rather sad. I suppose I
know the reason well enough, no one will write while Evie is here.

I've been working on my Spring bunch and it is finished now. Yesterday
I put it alongside the little bunch I brought with me and was amazed to see the
difference. I feel it is a step forward and makes my cottage bunch look thick and
overcrowded and rather clumsy. I wish I could have your opinion.

My figure at the school is nearly finished I am sending a snap of the
torso ... will you tell me what you think?

Today I spent at the National ... I have been looking at the Dutch flower
pieces and the Fantin, and feel I want to paint flowers with the delicacy and
refinement and the beauty of detail the Dutchman achieves and yet with the feeling

---

10   This is *Self Portrait* (1934), held by the National Portrait Gallery.

and body of the Fantin flowers. For all the wonder of the Dutch flowers, I love the Fantin best and always pay it a visit.

My love and wishes to everyone,

Norrie

5 Dukes Lane, London
21 March 1935

Dearest Mother and Daddy,

Yesterday night brought me two letters and I felt much happier. I sat up late last night after the pictures reading them. It has made me happy to have Mother's letter for I have felt the silence more than I can say. I have never talked about this friendship, perhaps if I had it would have been better, feeling your intense dislike for Evie. I never wanted to, it was something I had apart and I suppose I resented not being able to have her at home, or to see her when I liked, or be able to talk about her or anything.

She was ill before she left, and I did not know till actually she had arrived at Port Said that she was coming. You say you could only see the cupidity of the move and how you had been hoodwinked, I cannot see that there was anything of that in it. I simply thought that if we were both here together studying we could be very happy living together. So I asked her to share with me. I knew you would not like it, but I did not think you could object to it so strongly and that it would cause so much upset. My love and loyalty I have for you will always be there.

My love to everyone,

Norrie

5 Dukes Lane, London
28 March 1935

Dearest Mother and Daddy,

I mentioned in my last letter that Evie was leaving me to stay with her Mother in a week or so. Your last letter sounded so worried about her staying here that I want to relieve further anxiety by sending this airmail. Evie leaves me in a day or two, on Monday, that will be good news for you. All this worry seems so useless, we have been very happy together. Is it not better to be happy, and have companionship, than to be lonely and miserable?

We all have to branch out for ourselves at one time or another. I have chosen Evie for a friend; whether it is just a spell, as you think it is, I don't know. It has lasted too long and stood too much to be just that.

Hope all is well, my love and all my thoughts go with this,

Norrie

Ambleside, South Australia
Tuesday 2 April 1935

My Dear Nora,

It was good to get your last letter with all its exciting news, and the family is becoming quite curious and interested over the new portrait. It sounds good and I certainly would love to see it and the progress you have made. You speak of too rapid drying of oils, quite probably the oil you are using contains too many dryers; an adulteration some colourmen use to accelerate its drying qualities purposely. There are slower drying oils made and it is worthwhile making enquiries at your colourman. Poppy oil should not dry as rapidly as you suggest even with a gas fire in the room. Had you thought of sending in to the Academy this year?

I was very interested to read of Ernest Proctor's exhibition, his work is I think very fine. The landscape I got for our Gallery carries beautifully on the wall and is a decided acquisition.[11]

I went down to the River amongst my Gums and enjoyed the gentle warmth of the sun and the warbling of the Magpies who were there in great numbers.

Again time is drawing near. I will close, goodnight dear Nora, and once more take care of yourself,

Dad

5 Dukes Lane, London
30 April 1935

Dearest Mother and Daddy,

This week I wanted to be able to tell you that I had two pictures accepted by the Academy. Instead there is no such joyful news, for I received a note at the very last minute saying my portrait had been accepted, but owing to lack of space

---

11   Hans Heysen purchased Ernest Proctor's *Eggardun, Dorset* for the National Gallery of South Australia in 1934.

not hung, and about the bunch of flowers I sent in I've received no news at all. Evidently had the same fate ... Bateman has been made an RA.[12]

I saw an exhibition of Dutch flower painting at Tooths', but there was nothing outstanding there.[13] They were not a patch on those in the National ... From that I went straight on to see a show of modern flower paintings by Vanessa Bell and Augustus John and various other moderns. The contrast was terrific. They made me feel sick, they were so crude and badly arranged, badly painted and messy in all ways. I have come to the conclusion that no one can paint flowers here.

All my love to Mother and Daddy,

Norrie

5 Dukes Lane, London

5 May 1935

Dearest Mother and Daddy,

I went in to see the Royal Academy and several exhibitions. There were no outstanding pictures and I didn't think the show was as interesting as last year ... The Spencers were the most original and novel, but even his did not come up to last year's. The Sickerts and Johns which the critics pick out as being the most important and best works in the show, I did not like. They were too dashed clever ... I was disappointed in the Batemans. The big one looked too wooden ... I'd rather have the little sketch you bought.

The picture that appealed to me most, and that made the most vivid impression, was a tempera painting by a woman called Orovida—the same artist who did the two decorative panels that you remarked on last year. The subject was a native mother and child with magnolia flowers. It was a most lovely and decorative thing, I could just picture it in my studio ... it was only £42.

My love to Mother and Daddy and all,

Norrie

---

12   British artist James Bateman (1893–1959) was a friend of Hans Heysen. RA stands for 'Royal Academician', a member of the Royal Academy of Arts, London. In 1935, Bateman was actually made an Associate Member of the Royal Academy (ARA). In 1942, he was promoted to RA. The Art Gallery of South Australia holds 29 works by Bateman.

13   Arthur Tooth & Sons was a London art dealer.

5 Dukes Lane, London
28 May 1935

Dearest Mother and Daddy,

Tomorrow is the opening of Daddy's exhibition.[14]

If I can possibly manage it I somehow want to go across to Paris next week. They are holding a marvellous exhibition of Italian art there and I am longing to see it. If I go, Evie is going with me as I wouldn't like to go alone, and we can have such fun together exploring a new town and the galleries and everything.

Later

Home from seeing Daddy's exhibition. It really looks splendid and made me feel very proud ... I just sat quietly in the room and felt at home again. It was wonderful, they looked so clean and fresh and full of vibrant sunshine.

The delicate watercolour of the white gums in the early morning, the silvery grey one, looked a dream. It recalled those misty mornings that I love so much and the great gum at Oakbank with cows resting under it looked so typically Australian and so full of its atmosphere.

I will go again and again. It would be wonderful if, after the exhibition is over, I could have one of the gums to hang in my studio until I go home. Or have you made arrangements to have them all packed?

My love to Mother and Daddy and everyone,

Norrie

Ambleside, South Australia
6 June 1936

My Dear Nora,

It is nearly 3 weeks since I last wrote and I have most certainly been conscious of my neglect, for my thoughts often migrate to London to be with you in your many activities.

How very fine of Bateman to get his ARA and to come when he most needed it too. But what bad luck the Academy returned your work ... it was also my fate when I sent to the Academy—'Rejected for lack of space'—but better luck next time.

---

14   When in London in 1934, Hans Heysen left some work to be shown at Colnaghi, one of Europe's oldest art
        galleries.

The pictures are all back once more from Sydney ... Taken all round, I think the Exhibition was a success.[15] Nearly 3,000 visited the Gallery on one Sunday.

Before leaving Sydney I spent a morning with Howard Hinton in his boarding house at Cremorne. He is a dear fellow and sends you his best wishes.

I will write more soon until then much love,

From Daddy

Hotel Liberia
Rue de la Grande Chaumière, Paris
10 June 1935

Dearest Mother and Daddy,

Paris comes up to all expectations, it is indeed a wonderful city full of art and artists.

This little place we are staying in is in a tiny street off the Boulevard Montparnasse next door to the Luxembourg Gardens. Daddy might know the whereabouts. It is in the Bohemian quarter of the city. Every shop almost in this little street sells artists' materials, and opposite is the atelier where Bourdelle the sculptor and Lucien Simon teach.[16] It is so fascinating to find these two big names in a funny little street like this. The art shops down the street are marvellous, crammed from floor to ceiling with canvases and sketchbooks, and great jars of brushes and so forth.

The first day Friday we spent at the Italian exhibition. We went early in the morning and spent seven hours there. It is a superb exhibition of masterpieces beautifully shown and in perfect taste. The whole thing just took my breath way. All the pictures I had admired in reproduction seemed to be there—there was too much. Oh dear, I wish Father had been there to see some of those pictures. The Raphaels were wonderful and the Leonardos and the Michelangelos and the Botticellis. I cannot begin to describe it all, and the impression it all gave me. The pictures were all hung in one row and the walls were draped in grey velvet, some rooms with wine red velvet, the grey was a beautiful setting for the pictures.

The next day Saturday we went to the Louvre. What a colossal place it is ... about ten times too big. The sculpture is amazing. The galleries have just

---

15   Hans Heysen's exhibition held between March and May 1935 at the National Art Gallery of New South Wales was his first solo exhibition.

16   This is the Académie de la Grande Chaumière, which opened in 1904.

been rebuilt by a genius of an architect and it is perfectly displayed.[17] It made a
great impression on me. Reminded me of the Pergamon in Berlin: the same idea of
bringing the atmosphere of open air and sunshine into the rooms. The great *Victory
of Samothrace* has a glorious position, a whole gallery like a wonderful interior
of a church built for her. I have spent hours there absolutely overwhelmed by the
beauty of that thing, it makes me cry it is so lovely. Standing at the head of some
thousand steps leading up in tiers, she seems to float in golden atmosphere, her
draperies flutter in the wind and she moves forward like some celestial heavenly
creature. The marble is a pale gold, age-worn in parts, and ... from every side and
every position she is superb.

The same architect who had done the sculpture rooms had arranged four
modern galleries with a single row of pictures round the room well placed.[18] It is a
great relief after the jumble and bad taste of other the galleries and the pictures
look well.

I've seen too much at the moment to write coherently at all,

Love Norrie

Ambleside, South Australia
13 June 1935

My Dear Nora,

Your last long letter with your description and your reactions to the Jubilee
Celebrations and quick survey of the Royal Academy were all extremely interesting.[19]

The Observer, *Times* and *Sketch* came to hand safely on Monday ... the
Academy illustrations and critics comments most entertaining. The John *Head*
illustration in *The Observer* I liked immensely, it suggested massiveness and yet
mobility. Certainly he makes his sitter live on canvas, so different from the ordinary
portrait. I too thought the Bateman disappointing, I agree with you.

I promised to tell you more of my show in Sydney, but I don't really think
there is very much to say ... Several pictures came as a pleasant surprise. *The
Farmyard Frosty Morning* looked crisp and cold and convincing. Its somewhat stiff
forms suited the time of the day and the cold air. Then came *The Brachina Gorge*
which carried well and looked 'big', and both *The Quarry Scenes*. Of the northern

---

17   Camille Lefèvre was chief architect at the Louvre when director Henri Verne carried out extensive
      reorganisation of the Louvre installations in the early 1930s. See L. Réau, 'Art Events of Interest in France',
      Parnassus, no.2, 1930: 11–13, 44; Christopher Green, *Art in France, 1900–1940*, New Haven, Connecticut, Yale
      University Press, 2000: 222.

18   This centre-line hang is much more modern than the dense salon-hang in other parts of the Louvre.

19   The Royal Jubilee, which was held on 6 May 1935, celebrated the 25-year reign of King George V (1865–
      1936).

oils *Sun-parched Hills* and *The Shadowed Hill* appealed most. I am glad we went to see it.

With lots of love from us all and from Daddy

5 Dukes Lane, London
25 June 1935

Dearest Mother and Daddy,

This week's mail was full of excitement. It brought your letters from Sydney and all about Daddy's show there.

I've been painting or at least repainting the sky of my portrait of Evie. After seeing the skies of the Italian painters I felt inspired to improve mine. It is a big improvement and the portrait is ever so much better, wonderful the difference a background can make to a picture.

I've decided to give up the Art School and work here spending the money on having a model occasionally. This week is my last week of the term and then I'll feel freer to get down to work. The figure I have been working in the modelling class has not got as far as I hoped … I felt bucked to hear your criticism on my two last efforts, I'm sure if I went on with it I could do something, if only cutting figures out of stone would satisfy me.

Sunday evening I spent with the Andersons. I had a long chat with Mr about art, he has no time for the Moderns, in that respect Bateman is far more open-minded.[20]

My thoughts are with you,
Norrie

5 Dukes Lane, London
27 July 1935

Dearest Mother and Daddy,

The picture had come, I carried it triumphantly up to my flat and opened it. Quite impossible to describe the great warm wave of feeling and happiness I had then, and read 'To Nora' on the bottom. It was a proud moment.

It is the first picture I have owned and what a picture! It gives out all the atmosphere of the gums and the dry grass, the rustle of the bank and it is the tree I always used to draw and that I loved so much.[21]

---

20   British artist Stanley Anderson (1884–1966) was a friend of Hans Heysen. Anderson was made an Associate of the Royal Academy of Arts in 1934 and a Royal Academician in 1941.

21   The watercolour is Hans Heysen's *Hillside by the River*, which is now in the Nora Heysen Foundation Collection, gifted by Nora in 2003.

How proudly I will show it to all who call. It looks well on the cream wall and the framing is excellent, some small yellow lines on the mount against the picture just sets it off, and the frame is excellent for a watercolour.

All my love,

Norrie

5 Dukes Lane, London
7 August 1935

Dearest Mother and Daddy,

A wonderful letter from Daddy this week, it warmed my heart ... It brought back all my experiences in Paris. I wish too that I could have been there with you and seen all the old haunts that you know so well.

I really didn't see much of Paris itself. There wasn't time, although staying out at Montparnasse as we did, I caught a real glimpse of the artist's life in Paris. In the mornings breakfasting at the counter of *the Dôme* we saw the most weird and wonderful types of artists and people.[22] We became quite familiar with some who used to come along every morning, and swallow down a glass of wine or cup of black coffee, and then walk off with their paints and canvases for the day's work. Some of them looked quite starved and yet quite happy. The cafés are fascinating.

London does grow on one, as people say. There are times when I loathe it every bit, but there are times when I like it. There is so much here. It is wonderful just to be able to hop on a bus and be at the National in a few minutes.

It almost looks as if the world is going to be shoved into another war. The papers here are full of it. I can't believe it possible, yet Mussolini means business evidently.

My gum looks wonderful this morning, dreaming in atmosphere.

My love to Mother and Daddy and everyone,

Norrie

5 Dukes Lane, London
10 August 1935

Dearest Mother,

This is a simply lovely present you have given me. I was so excited when it came, it is a beauty, the most gorgeous dressing gown I have seen, so soft and

---

22   The Dôme is the street-level café of the Grand Hotel de la Haute-Loire. Hans Heysen's apartment was in this building, from where he painted views of the street below in *From the Apartment Window, Paris* (1901). He frequented the Café du Dôme, a well-known place for artists and writers.

warm. It is the colour I love best. A lightish soft blue grey like my rug, with a buff coloured lining. Did you tell Mr McGregor exactly what I wanted?

I prepared a nice afternoon tea for Mr McGregor today and made everything look its best. This morning we baked cakes, homemade things look so nice on the table, a cake with nuts on it and a plate of scones and some brown bread and butter, and I made coffee which he appreciates. We talked art, he told me that you all looked well and he told me how well Daddy's exhibition in Sydney looked, and all about everything. Also he gave me a bit of a criticism on the work I had about. He thought my flower pieces were a big improvement, and had more atmosphere and more modelling. He liked the sky in my portrait of Evie, and the little landscape I did in Wales, all of which bucked me up.

My thoughts are with you all,

Norrie

5 Dukes Lane, London
18 August 1935

Dearest Mother and Daddy,

Yesterday I went into the National and had a good look at the Fantin flowers and when I came back I had a great desire to put my foot through all mine. He can envelope his flowers in atmosphere so beautifully, and although I try very hard to get atmosphere and unity into mine, I always seem to fail.

Yesterday I went into Colnaghi's to choose another watercolour. Really it is pure greed to have another one. When you wrote and said I was to keep one in my studio, I didn't know I was to have one of my own ... I chose the Quarry one. It looks beautiful on my wall ... Are you sure you can spare it until I get back?

On my way, I went into Tooths' to see the Spencer McGregor had bought.23 I think Spencer is the most original painter working here.

My love to all especially Mother and Daddy,

Norrie

23   Stanley Spencer's *Cookham Lock* (1935) was purchased by James McGregor, a Trustee of the National Art Gallery of New South Wales.

5 Dukes Lane, London
1 September 1935

Dearest Mother and Daddy,

On Thursday I had a wonderful treat. I heard Elisabeth Schumann singing at one of the Promenades. I'll never forget it. She was marvelous, and more lovely still than her records, and she was joy to watch.

Yesterday I took along two flower pieces to be framed today … I chose a very modern frame for the cornflowers of unpolished oak. It is an excellent frame for a modern work simple, and well made and excellent for a modern home … I'll wonder what you think of it. Probably think I'm going modern. I want things simple.

My love to all everyone,

Norrie

5 Dukes Lane, London
6 September 1935

Dearest Mother and Daddy,

I'm safely home again and feeling ever so much brighter after the three days of tramping under the sky. It was a grand change from this infernal city with its everlasting turmoil and noise…. Heavens it was too wonderful to smell the county again, all the old familiar smells of apples, of cows, of sweet hay and clover. It was intoxicating I just went mad with the joy of it … [We] arrived here at eleven last night. You have never seen two more weary individuals than we were then.

I feel myself expanding and growing and I think my work is improving I can tackle things with more freedom.

I've invested in a book on the modern Post-Impressionists—on Pissarro, Gauguin, Sisley, Degas, Manet, Monet, Bonnard and the others. It gives brief sketches of their lives and influences and numerous illustrations, all of which are very interesting and stimulating. There is something vigorous and fresh in this outlook which fascinates and stimulates me.

I'm going to dinner with Mrs Hayward with theatre to follow on Saturday.[24]

My love and thoughts,

Norrie

---

24   Ursula Hayward (1907–1970) was the daughter of the Barr Smiths, friends of the Heysen family. She and her husband, Edward 'Bill' Hayward (1903–1983), were in London on a year-long honeymoon, during which time they shopped for art.

Ambleside, South Australia
14 September 1935

My Dear Nora,

Spring is with us now in real earnest. The daffodils are scattered in profusion under the apple trees by the house, and in the top fruit garden. The plum trees have cast their white petals like a sheet of soft snow on the paths and grass, and covered themselves with tender green. There is warmth in the air and the double white violets by the lilacs are spreading their perfume right up to the top gate.

Was very interested to have your re-affirmation about Orovida's *Mother and Son* ... I have written to *Miss Pissarro* to purchase it.

I wish I could tell you more about the proposed new additions to our Art Gallery.[25] As far as I can make out they propose to build right down the west side 3 or 4 extra rooms for pictures, 2 or 3 for drawings and etchings with a series of ground rooms (underneath) to house their china and porcelain etc. There will be a new front entrance which comes in the centre of the new front, which will then lead into either of the galleries, and they will be joined again by cutting an opening through the end present gallery. What I am afraid of is that after all, it does not give us much extra space for pictures to allow of proper hanging.

Last week I had a cable from Colnaghi's—that they were returning 24 of my watercolours which means they sold 18 altogether, jolly good I think. It was awfully nice to feel your enthusiasm over the watercolours, that Gum was particularly fine last Summer, so cleansed and luminous.

All is well at this end and we all send our love,

From Daddy

Ambleside, South Australia
15 September 1935

My Dear Nora,

How very much we enjoyed your last letter—the oven was full of cakes, so the family gathered around in the kitchen while mother poured out the news.

Your idea to put school aside and devote more time to working in your studio and the Museum and National Gallery is very wise to me—for without interest and enthusiasm it is impossible to get real benefit from studies in a school.

---

25   Alex Melrose, a member of the Board of Governors of the Public Library, Museum and Art Gallery of South Australia, donated £10 000 toward extensions. He did so as part of the South Australian Centenary celebrations and in memory of his father, a pioneer. See William Moore, 'At Home and Abroad', *Art in Australia*, 15 February 1935: 63.

What a feast there is in store for you with the coming of the Chinese exhibition, I envy you Nora ... You will love the Chinese work, with its sense of serenity and expression of the infinite.

The Listener came to hand at last and in it there is quite a lot to interest one. Much as one may dislike Stanley Spencer's ideas, his pictures always interest. His uncommon outlook takes them away from the ordinary.

Was just reading through *The Artist*, an English art magazine, and came across, to my surprise, a short mention, quite complimentary too, on my exhibition at Colnaghi's in 'Shows of the Month'.

And now dear Nora it seems time is up. Mother sends her love to you, in which I must heartily join,

Your Dad

5 Dukes Lane, London
20 September 1935

Dear Daddy,

I have taken my studio for a further year. I think my money will hang out another year or so, with the help of a few sales over here I'll have plenty, if I am not too extravagant. Thank you for suggesting I could draw on yours if I did not have enough, I'll make mine last me out if it is possible.

This is a birthday letter with all my love and wishes,

Norrie

5 Dukes Lane, London
25 September 1935

Dearest Mother and Daddy,

I have been busy painting a gay little bunch of anemones on the striped cloth. I had a happy time painting it. The light streamed all through the flowers making them quite ethereal. The flowers were over a week old and on their last legs ... I wonder would you like the colour scheme and the way I have treated it. The flowers have more light and atmosphere in them than I have ever painted before. The background is all light, the cloth light with the few polish stripes, and the flowers are full of light.

Last night we had a grand celebration ... I was celebrating a sale. In the afternoon Anita brought Mrs Webster to buy a picture. She chose the little mixed bunch I brought with me from home. I thought as soon as I saw her that she would pick on that. She knew little of art, and had not much taste, and as long as the vase had as many flowers jammed into it as possible, and that they had plenty of light on them, she thought she was getting her money's worth. Compared with flower pieces I have painted here, it looks clumsy and overcrowded with a clever effect of light that doesn't really surround the flowers, but is just on the surface. So I have no qualms about parting with.

Evie is staying with me until December when she is marrying. It is wonderful to have her, and we do not get tired if each other. I think it a very good test if two people can share a flat, and be happy and work together. She helps my work. You will not believe *that*.

With every hope that all is well at home,

Norrie

Ambleside, South Australia
3 October 1935

Dearest Nora,

I have a commission from *Art in Australia* to select Adelaide's society beauties, gardens and interiors for Cazneaux to photograph. Cazneaux is being sent over next week and I am all hot and bothered about it. I don't know one house or garden let alone one beauty and wouldn't know how to approach them if I did—yet I'd like to do it. Cazneaux is such a delightful photographer.[26]

Did you ever have the negatives of your little figure enlarged—and would you let *Art in Australia* reproduce it or some flower studies—if you send one out would you like to see it reproduced? Syd is anxious to do something of yours, he writes me.

Goodnight my dear, take care of yourself,

Mother

Ambleside, South Australia
6 October 1935

My Dear Nora,

More exciting news for you! Had a cable from 'Orovida' (Miss Pissarro) this morning saying the *'picture is available'*, referring to the *Native Motherhood with Magnolia* ... Now I shall have to bother you so that we can get *possession* of the picture and *pay for it* on delivery to you. I am writing to her with this mail,

---

26   Harold Cazneaux (1878–1953), a friend of the Heysen family, called his house and garden in Dudley Avenue, Roseville, Sydney, 'Ambleside'. Cazneaux, like Heysen, was a keen gardener and had a studio in the garden. The photograph, *The Garden at 'Ambleside'*, is reproduced in Helen Ennis, *Cazneaux: The Quiet Observer*, Canberra, National Library of Australia, 1994: 4.

instructing her to communicate with you and then deliver the picture to No. 5 Dukes Lane, and that you will pay her by cheque on delivery.

It is splendid that you are getting so much pleasure out of *The Quarry*. I am glad to picture it in your studio and that it is bringing some sunshine into the London fog.

And now about a little remark in your recent letter—feeling rather despondent over your flower pictures after coming away from Fantin's picture in the National. I still think of this as the most perfect picture of flowers and even in the postcard reproduction it never fails to give pleasure. My advice would be—don't bother too much about atmosphere just now, it will come naturally in time—after the full meaning of form has been grasped with the pattern of your picture both in the distribution of darks and lights, and proportion of your colour masses. Although Fantin never makes you feel conscious of arrangement, he considers well the relative size of his flowers to his grey spaces, and size of canvas. Fantin creates his atmosphere—both by relative tonal values and undefined edges—which covers his later period when he gives more the *impression* of the flower without the definition of his early period.

Everyone sends their love and hearty cheerio,
From Dad

Ambleside, South Australia
21 October 1935

Dearest Nora,

Today brought your airmail letter written on the 4th of this month. The other snaps of your work were passed round; Daddy said 'full of painter's qualities' and 'what ripping modelling'. Stef said 'Nora's going modern' and between the head and foot of the family there is every degree of criticism passed over them—we are longing to see the colour. My imagination won't stretch far enough and I love the cornflower one best.

I'm so glad to report ... Daddy seems ever so much brighter and has been sketching over at Woodside, also painting a bunch of roses in your studio—the Stow jug.

Goodnight dear Nora,
Mother

5 Dukes Lane, London
Wednesday 30 October 1935

Dearest Mother and Daddy,

Thursday morning I had tea with Miss Pissarro and thereby hangs a long tale. I got a shock when she met me at the door, a great huge bulk of a woman in a brilliant red jumper and a mottled skirt and old slippers on her feet, a fat rosy face with short curled black hair, glasses, altogether the most unattractive presence imaginable ... However, once in her studio and talking art I forgot her appearance and saw only her alert intelligent eyes.

She was terribly excited about selling her *Mother and Son*, it was evidently quite an event ... I invited her back to see my studio and work and she expressed a wish to come. So on Saturday I entertained her and showed her my work to criticise. She came in like a bomb dropped out of the blue. She slatted me right and left, she said my paintings were muddy and 50 years behind time, and advised me to change my palette. She admitted that I could draw and had talent but that is all she allowed me. She thinks I use too much brown and black and yellow ochre and keep my colour too low in tone, I who pride myself on my fresh bright clean colour! You can imagine my surprise on hearing that. She hates yellow ochre and I love it and use it in everything almost, that is where we disagreed. She likes the interior I have just finished, and thought it the best bit of work, I agree there. She gave me a list of colours—an entirely new palette—mostly of cadmiums, excluding ochre, black and browns.

I'm going to try it and see what happens. I went immediately and got the colours from Blocks as they are the only safe makers for the cadmiums, and started on a bowl of fruit in a Chinese bowl. About my colour being muddy, I disagree with her, my flesh tones, yes; but not my flowers. I don't intend swallowing all she said, but it does no one harm to have a change of palette and experiment with new harmonies. You can certainly see a difference in the fruit I'm painting, it has more vibration and is more brilliant—it is painted with a palette consisting of white, cadmium red and pale-ultramarine—vert compose, cobalt and crimson and that is all. It is amazing the depth and richness of colour that can be got without using brown or black. It is a valuable hint to me—though I don't think I will ever desert the earth colour, to me just as beautiful harmonies can be achieved with them if used rightly.

Miss Pissarro is introducing me to her father Lucien Pissarro, that will be interesting. She was interested in the Sydney Gallery purchase.[27] She has, or her father has, several Camille Pissarros in his collection, very fine ones she says. I'm thinking of our Adelaide Gallery.

My love,
Norrie

27   The National Art Gallery of New South Wales purchased Camille Pissarro's *Peasants' Houses, Eragny* (1887).

5 Dukes Lane, London
Wednesday 19 November 1935

Dearest Mother and Daddy and all at home,

I have been working on a small interior, just a foot square, of Evie sitting reading in the blue dressing gown, the soft blue one. It was lovely to paint and I think I've made a good job of it. On the wall behind I have put in Daddy's watercolour of the gum which makes a perfect colour note in the picture, a bowl of fruit on the table completes the study. It is one of the simplest things I've painted and I have loved doing it, except for a few details, it is finished. Today I have put in the chair—these chairs of mine take some doing, but they are beautiful in an interior.[28]

Greetings and good wishes to you all,

Norrie

The Studio, South Australia
26 November 1935

My Dear Nora,

You need never regret having to paint flowers for a living. Fantin did it and it made him a fine painter to bring joy and pleasure into many a home—surely it was well worthwhile!

We send you much love,

From Daddy

5 Dukes Lane, London
Tuesday 3 December 1935

Dearest Mother and Daddy,

I have just come back from seeing the Chinese exhibition and feel stupefied with so much beauty.[29] Today I looked at the bronzes, three rooms of the most lovely shapes of vessels I have ever seen. Each one so exquisite in proportion and colour and showing so much originality and variety in shape. It was interesting to see that in most of them the artists had used the contrasts of plain surfaces with broken detailed surfaces. They seem never to make a mistake in their proportions and space, it is wonderful lesson. I want to study them as much as I can. I wish

---

28   This is Nora Heysen's *Interior* (1935).
29   The exhibition at Burlington House was reviewed by Alleyne Zander in 'International Exhibition of Chinese Art in London', *Art in Australia*, 15 February 1936: 51–55.

I could look at those books on Chinese art that you have. I didn't half appreciate them then.

I'm making an effort to hear Laurence Binyon speak on Chinese painting. All London is Chinese mad. People wear Chinese gowns, the shops are filled with Chinese materials and the antique dealers are filling their shops with Chinese articles of every description and the bookshops with books on Chinese art.

Goodnight to you all,

Norrie

5 Dukes Lane, London
Wednesday 10 December 1935

Dearest Mother and Daddy,

Did I tell you I went to a recital of Miriam Hyde's some time ago?[30] ... The recital was held in the hall of the Royal College of Music, a wretched cold tomb of a place all stark staring white, and dirty dingy portraits of all the famous musicians and those in connection with the Society hanging round the walls. There were about 50-odd people present huddled in the middle of the barn-like place, very little warmth or response for poor Miriam on her farewell recital. She played brilliantly though and her own compositions were clever, but somehow her playing lacks something, though technically she is excellent. I wonder what she will do when she gets back to Adelaide, teach I suppose. She'll find it uphill work. Adelaide is so small, especially where the arts are concerned.

It is very late, so goodnight all with love,

Norrie

Ambleside, South Australia
10 December 1935

My Dear Nora,

Your description of Miss Pissarro came like a douche of cold water ... but your meeting with Miss Pissarro has interested me immensely, and her remarks on your work.

Miss Pissarro comes from a long line of artists and her experience should have been a wide and wise one, so I was particularly anxious for you to meet her as I felt only good could come of it. Her palette sounds well worth experimenting

---

30   Miriam Hyde OBE AO (1913–2005), was an Adelaide-born Australian composer and pianist, educated at the Elder Conservatorium, University of Adelaide. She won the Elder Scholarship for Music to study at the Royal College of Music and in London from 1931 to 1933. She returned to Adelaide briefly in 1936 and then moved permanently to Sydney. Her papers are held by the National Library of Australia, MS 5260.

with—in fact, it is always wise from time to time to make a change—for by using always the same palette it is liable to lead to a formula in colouring, and this gives a crippling result ... Not that you need definitely to discard your black or brown, these also have their proper place.

> We send you our love,
> From Daddy

5 Dukes Lane, London
Thursday 19 December 1935

Dearest Mother and Daddy,

These days are awfully full and rushed. Evie is being married on Saturday morning at Shrewsbury. His people live there.

> All my love to Mother and Daddy,
> Norrie

5 Dukes Lane, London
7 January 1936

Dearest Mother and Daddy,

My birthday airmail letter has just come full of good wishes and exciting news ... I want to work out my life here. I want to work and justify myself and find myself, until I have done that I will not feel free to return. I want to absorb as much as possible to experiment to learn and later to exhibit a few things, some 15 of the best, at some gallery in London. I feel as if I am only just beginning to paint.

> My love to Mother and Daddy and cheerio to everyone,
> Norrie

5 Dukes Lane, London
12 January 1936

Dearest Mother and Daddy,

Well I'm now 25, a great age. I'm a young woman now and feel that I have left girlhood far behind. This last year of living here by myself in London and making my own decisions and having my own responsibilities has made me grow up three years in one. You probably celebrated the day more than I did. I spent it painting a self portrait.

I'm painting it all in a higher key using no black or brown on my palette and only a very little ochre ... In the self portrait I am doing myself in a blue smock against the wall and a part of my pink roses, the colour scheme is beautiful and I hope to make something good out of it.[31]

Thank you ever so much for sending the *Art in Australia*. I'm very interested in it and have gone through it many times over. It was good to read Daddy's article. I like the Ernest Proctor landscapes and I think the Reynolds excellent.

Goodnight all my wishes and love go with this,

Norrie

5 Dukes Lane, London
20 January 1936

Dearest Mother and Daddy,

This morning I painted on my self portrait, it is almost complete and I think it is the best self portrait I have painted. It is all very high in key.

Miss Orovida wrote the other day asking me to dinner tomorrow, I'm receiving the *Mother and Son* tomorrow … I have now received the picture, it hangs on my wall and looks absolutely lovely.

I had a very interesting evening on Tuesday when I went to see her … She is very interesting to talk to, and knows a great deal about art and artists. We had a talk, then she took me over to her father's studio, practically next door. He is a dear old man with a long grey beard, very like his father Camille Pissarro judging by the self portrait by him in the Tate.

I liked some of his work immensely, but most of it I thought looked thin and was too much all-over the same tone, without any contrast. They were like tone poems, very delightful, but lacking vigour and punch—but in them, all of them, was a very nice feeling as of a simple and sincere mind behind them. This colour scheme scarcely varies. There is a greeny blue predominantly in them, nearly all, they are very high in key and he uses a very short broken technique like Camille Pissarro, only he has carried it further and uses it without variation.

My love to all especially Mother and Daddy,

Norrie

5 Dukes Lane, London
23 January 1936

Dearest Mother and Daddy,

I've never felt more excited and enthusiastic in my life about painting. It's as if I had found a new base of life after seeing the Chinese exhibition, and having a rest from work these last two weeks. Now there is no end to what I'm going to do.

---

31   This is Nora Heysen's *Self Portrait* (1936).

I feel as if I'd only just begun to paint. I painted on a quick study of Evie, trying for life and vibration of colour using a high keyed palette, the scheme was delicate and subtle and I had a task. It is almost finished and is more alive than anything I have even painted. I put it against my last head and it was laughable to compare the two. The earlier was a dirty brown and looked rotten, I couldn't believe that I had painted it, and there and then it went into the rubbish bin.

Yesterday I spent at the Chinese exhibition looking at the paintings. That Chinese work has taught me a very great deal already. Their work is so refined, their outlook so aesthetic and beautiful, and they are masters of design and have such perfect taste. It is an object lesson to see how they conventionalize nature and make a picture of the simplest things, a twig on blade of grass, and the thing is perfect.

Now goodnight to you all.

My love to Mother and Daddy,

Norrie

Ambleside, South Australia
29 January 1936

My Dear Nora,

It's wonderful to read of your enthusiasm for your work, its ambitions, high hopes and disappointments. Lucky beggar to feel like that, for I must confess that advancing years quietens that rush of blood along the veins with excitement.

There will be genuine sadness in the whole of England today—for England did love their King, a real father of a Mighty Nation.[32] It will be an impressive sight you will witness and feel today.

L. McCubbin the new Director takes up his duties in June—I had a letter from him, saying how enthusiastic he feels over getting the job.[33] Did I tell you that Max Meldrum was runner up!

And now a little about the garden ... the Zinnias, the seed of which we brought from Germany, are showing a fine variety of colours and of a real Fantin quality and the Dahlias ... are showing some magnificent blooms, 10 inches across. The roses are still blooming, especially the Franz Karl, which are showing their golden centres. And now dear Nora once again I must close and say Goodbye!

Mother sends her love to you as does everyone else,

And your Dad also

---

32   King George V died on 20 January 1936.

33   Louis Frederick McCubbin (1890–1952), the son of Frederick McCubbin (1855–1917), was the Director of the National Art Gallery of South Australia from 1936 to 1950. See Anne Gray, 'McCubbin, Louis Frederick (1880–1952), *Australian Dictionary of Biography*, vol.10, Melbourne University Press, 1986: 243–244.

5 Dukes Lane, London
30 January 1936

Dearest Mother and Daddy,

I'm still working on my self-portrait. After seeing the Pissarros, I repainted the wall behind the head in broken colour and gave it much more vibration and light.

London is looking particularly bleak and drab, everything is draped in black and purple. The effect is too depressing for words and everyone is dressed in black to lend a still more dismal air. The funeral must have been a deeply moving spectacle. I was too busy painting to make an attempt to see it, but I turned on the wireless and heard a description of the whole thing. London is black in mourning her King.[34]

My love to you all,
Norrie

Hahndorf, South Australia
10 February 1936

My Dear Nora,

As you can see from the above, Hahndorf has now been officially restored together with Lobethal (Tweedvale) and Klemzig (Gaza). Klemzig is near Payneham on the Torrens and was the first and original German settlement. From there they migrated further out. Some of the very first cottages I painted in my youth were painted at Klemzig and I still have the clearest recollection of those whitewashed, thatched, mud and plaster houses with their high pitched roofs.

I have got so far without a word about your lovely letter on Saturday morning, again bubbling out with enthusiasm, and the will to make good. The right spirit 'old girl' and if you can still feel like that at 60 (and it's not such a very long way to look ahead after all) you will make good.[35] What did Hokusai the great Japanese artist say on his departing from this wonderful world at 99? 'I feel that I have just gained the knowledge to begin' meaning his heart was still young and courageous—and that is the secret. A great love for Nature—who will ever unfold all her secrets in any one of our lives.

Goodnight and good luck Nora with a cheerio,
From Dad

---

34   King George V's funeral was held on 29 January 1936.
35   Hans Heysen, then 59 years of age, was doubtless aware that his sixtieth birthday was to take place later that year.

Train to Scotland
Wednesday 17 February 1936

Dearest Mother and Daddy,

Well here I am gliding through the country bound for Minehead to the 'Lorna Doone' part of the world.

I felt I must get away for a few days so I took out my map of England and chose a spot furthest from London. I have always wanted to see Dartmoor and Exeter and go through the Doone country. So here I am dressed from top to toe in woollies, over all a red mackintosh, a toothbrush on one pocket and a few pound notes in the other, feeling as free as a bird and ready for any old adventure. Evie is with me, we intend walking all day and putting up at the village hotels or some farmhouses along the way.

I went out to see the Andersons on Sunday evening and spent a quiet evening sitting around the fire in the studio listening to Mr Anderson condemning Modern Art. He was very scathing. I don't agree with his narrow outlook and conservative views … He wishes me to remember him to Father and to apologise for not writing.

Goodbye for now my love to all,
Norrie

5 Dukes Lane, London
9 April 1936

Dearest Mother and Daddy,

Now where to begin in the magic of telling and answering news … I'm off to Paris on Monday for a week's holiday … Evie and I decided on the spur of the moment to go. We'll be staying at the same little place at Montparnasse all being well.

My love to you all,
Norrie

5 Dukes Lane, London
Easter Sunday 1936

Dear Everyone,

We leave at seven tomorrow morning … Funny to think that tomorrow evening I will be strolling along the Boulevard at Montparnasse watching café life.

I agree that art must come from within, but I don't agree with shutting oneself away from one's contemporaries. I think it is stimulating and necessary when one is young and studying to mix with fellow artists, discuss things and one another's work. I feel I want to be alive to life and impressions round me and to express beauty in the things I see round me.

I want to paint people, homely interiors, skies and trees and water and all that is living and vibrating around me. I feel in sympathy with the impressionists who wanted to break away from all the old traditions, and find a new way to express beauty in nature. I feel I am getting nearer to that. I ultimately want losing a little of my hitherto rather photographic outlook, and getting more art and feeling into things. I feel freer and surer of myself, and know what I want.

Goodbye for this time love to everyone,

Norrie

Studio, London
22 April 1936

Dearest Mother and Daddy,

Safely home again and nearly bursting with enthusiasm for work, never felt more stimulated in my life or so fresh and excited about painting.

Paris was not so gay this trip probably owing to the political situation. Everything was dearer. The cafés were half empty.

It was marvelous to see the Louvre again. The 'Winged Victory', 'Venus' the 'Pearl Necklace', the Fra Angelicos ... and all the other masterpieces. But those are my favourites, anyone of which alone I'd rave over to see. The little Vermeer seemed more beautiful than ever. I was disappointed in the modern rooms this time, didn't come up to expectations. I felt that work lacked design and punch.

There was a little Van Gogh street scene—a joyous lively thing that fascinated me, also some Sisleys that I liked. The Corots had been removed for an exhibition of his work. They were holding a retrospective exhibition of 100 of Corot's works at a big gallery by the Place de la Concord. I was lucky to have seen that. Daddy would have loved it. The show was beautifully hung and arranged on grey velvet. It was a fine exhibition and gave me a very comprehensive idea of the whole of Corot's work. There is tenderness and beauty in his work that no other painter possesses.

But most of our time was spent in the Louvre and the Luxembourg. I found the paintings in the Luxembourg very stimulating. There were hundreds of ideas in the work but badly painted, but the French painters get something in their work that the English never get. They have ideas and imagination.

This trip we went out to Montmartre. It was lovely out there, quite a different atmosphere from Paris or Montparnasse, freer and more bohemian. Oh, there is so much to tell you about, but it will have to wait as my flowers will not *wait* for me.

It is a lovely study and I'm *mad* to be painting—I'm really going to enjoy myself.

My love to everyone,
Norrie

PS I've had my pictures thrown out of the Academy, all three on a white ticket. The news was waiting for me when I reached home. I'm too busy with new ideas and excitement to be disappointed.

5 Dukes Lane, London
19 May 1936

Dearest Mother and Daddy and All,

Monday brought me a long letter from Daddy which I loved having and have gone though again and again.

I think I mentioned that I was entertaining the Batemans to dinner and theatre … Bateman came out at six and had a look at my work first, before Mrs B. arrived for dinner. I got a gruelling criticism from Bateman. He doesn't like my work evidently, and hasn't a good word to say for it. He thinks it lacks tone, that my technique is mechanical and that I'm trying to get light and vibration in the wrong way. All of which is very disheartening. But then he is biased against women painters and likes work that I don't like at all, so I cannot take it all as gospel truth. However, frank and same criticism from a man like Bateman is worth careful consideration, and I have thought a lot about it. About my work lacking tonal values he is right. I have rather been too apt lately of trying for fresh paint and colours and vitality, rather than truthfully representing tonal values. I suppose they are very important.

We nearly came to blows discussing women artists and their merits. In wishing to condemn someone's work he said 'Oh just like a woman's work' and that made me furious, and I stood up for them and defended them with all I had. Evidently he is rather bitter about Laura Knight getting all the limelight in this year's Academy, he thinks they are all making a frightful fuss over all and her work.

Personally he hates it. So do I, as a general rule, but her *Spring* landscape in this year's Academy I like very much indeed, and think it was by far the best picture in the exhibition … We were all too busy arguing to know what we ate, and before we'd finished we had to leave Bateman and rush off to the theatre.

Probably his criticism will do me a lot of good. At the moment I feel sore about it and a little resentful, as one usually does, after having had one's work pulled utterly to pieces. His views didn't tally at all with what Miss Pissarro thought, so where is one? I think that when all is said and done, one is very reliant upon oneself though. I think that occasional criticisms do pull one up and make one think.

It is funny in Australia I had a surfeit of praise, here I get nothing but adverse criticisms and jolts in all directions. Pity they couldn't be mixed a little more to even things out.

All my love goes with this,

Norrie

5 Dukes Lane, London
Sunday 1936

Dearest Mother and Daddy,

It seems as if the Australian Royal Academy will only be a weak replica of the English.[36] It will cause more wrangling and jealousy than it is worth. I can't see the sense of it, or really what good it is going to do.

How is our Gallery progressing? I'm longing to see what they'll make of it. I do hope foresight is used and they'll make a really good gallery of it while they are about it.

My love and good wishes to everyone,

Norrie

Train to Dorset
3 June 1936

Dearest Mother and Daddy,

Off at last—it is a pleasant feeling to be steaming further and further way from London. I'm bound for Wimborne in Dorset ... I'm hoping to get some fine weather for painting. I'm loaded up with sketching materials, in fact all my luggage consists of with a few blouses and underclothes.

On Thursday I saw the Chekov play *The Sea Gull*. It was tremendously interesting as a play and for the acting and producing. It was an all-star cast with Gielgud, Edith Evans and Peggy Ashcroft. Edith Evans was superb. You'll probably see a criticism of it in *The Illustrated London News*.

My love to you all,

Norrie

---

36   The push for an Australian Academy of Art was being backed by the Commonwealth Attorney-General, Robert Gordon Menzies.

Hahndorf, South Australia
3 June 1936

My Dear Nora,

Daddy is loving your letters and would give anything to be with you, but his non-conformist conscience is too strong for him, and the daily bread for us all looms large upon the horizon. When you come back you must try and persuade him to go with you, for I am sure you will never settle down for good here in Australia.

Cheerio for tonight,

Mother

Hahndorf, South Australia
5 June 1936

My Dear Nora,

Well here we are again, with another two weeks behind us and mighty little to show for it. The family rolled home on Friday evening in their brand new motorcar, a Ford V8, 1936 model. They didn't know themselves in this luxury—travelling without draughts and bumps, and from that you will gather it is a sedan. Well, it does really look a jolly nice car, dark blue with a really satisfying streamline. She is 8 cylinders and moves up the hills without any changing of gears.

I feel much happier now that the picture for the Manunda is complete, the last touch went on a few days ago.[37] The picture now awaits the approval of the Adelaide Steamship directors who are still quite in the dark as to the type of subject so perhaps, it being only 'Gum trees', they want may not think it sufficiently exciting. It looks sunny and bright in the studio with a somewhat exaggerated blue in the sky. This I did intentionally as blue so quickly loses its brilliance when taken away from the direct light, and the painting is set at the far end of a rather long saloon, lit by the porthole lights from either side of the ship.

It was as usual a great pleasure to get your letters written in the train going to Dorset on Saturday morning … You will be in Ernest Proctor's country and I am wondering if you will see Eggardun: the scene of his painting in our Gallery. It evidently is a beautiful rolling countryside and very paintable, if I remember Proctor's description of his surroundings.[38]

---

37 The painting is *White Gums*, which was commissioned for a fee of £200. TSMV *Manunda* was a Scottish-built ship that arrived in Australia in June 1929 and became the Adelaide Steamship Company's largest passenger and cargo ship, travelling between Sydney, Freemantle, Melbourne and Cairns.

38 *Eggardun*, the title of Ernest Proctor's painting, is the alternative name for Eggardon Hill, a Bronze Age hill fort in Dorset. The bare, bony hill structure in *Eggerdun* is somewhat akin to how Hans Heysen portrayed the South Australian Flinders Ranges, although Dorset's hills are much greener.

It was certainly welcome news that you intend sending me the two flower paintings, and shall look forward to their coming, and I am sure Howard Hinton will too.

Goodnight once more and may God bless you Nora,

Your Dad

Bye Ways, Corfe Mullen
10 June 1936

Dearest Mother and Daddy and all at home,

The English countryside has a soft quiet beauty ... one day we took the train to Corfe Castle which is only 9 miles away, and it is glorious country there. You would have loved it.

After much careful thought and consideration I have decided to keep on my flat in London for another year. I had to give the agents notice as to what I was doing. The decision rested entirely with me and I had to make up my mind. It was difficult, I felt torn a thousand ways, and still do, but I feel that I am not ready to go home yet. I have not proven myself, I have not done what I set out to do, it would be like turning back halfway and I feel I would always regret it.

My love to you all,

Norrie

Hahndorf, South Australia
21 June 1936

My Dear Nora,

Another week has flown and there was the usual scramble and general family gathering around a Saturday morning cup of tea to hear all the news from Nora! And all her doings—and no one is ever disappointed, for your letters are so full of enthusiasm and so well expressed that they are a pleasure and a joy to us all—they have become a weekly institution and I do not know what we would do without them.

I had a delightful and welcome letter from Bateman last week (per airmail) telling me of his visit with Mrs Bateman to your Studio ... and this is what he says:

> Her painting has altered very much. Now it is very much lighter
> in key and broken in colour. Her quality is not so good as her
> earlier work ... Now it is mannered. My own opinion is that she
> is too concerned with handling and technique. That comes to
> everyone naturally if one searches for truth. I tried to define art

as being an emphasis on some aspect of truth. Truth has many
sides to it and many aspects. In some cases I felt that Nora's
main aim was just clean colour. I cannot but feel this to be one
of the superficial qualities and one that will come naturally and
unconsciously in the pursuit of truth ... so without presuming, I
hope, I may just put my feeling to her a little clearer. I may say
that when she is through the wood, at least the present wood, she
will have definitely gained something.

I was very interested in this criticism as I regard Bateman as a very sound
critic, and absolutely outspoken and sincere. Never with the *wish* to condemn, but
if possible to advise, after all those are his observations. I am not a bit '*alarmed*'
by what he says, because it deals with a phase that most earnest of students go
through, a natural reaction from what they regard as '*stuffy*' and a strong impulse
to experiment, so as to graft onto qualities that you already possess, something that
you felt lacking.

I would regard and acknowledge Bateman's criticism in all sincerity—it
may be biased, but you will probably find on reflection that there is more than
merely a grain of truth in what he says. I feel sure that he, as well as I, have
complete faith in your stability and sanity of outlook and that there is no fear of
your ability leading you to shallowness and away from the searching after truth.
I think you will always have your feet on this earth, with your head up, looking
towards infinity, for any interpretation of nature—be it ever so humble—must
embrace some form of idealism. Bateman's insistence on tone or tonal values is
I feel very sound particularly for a young painter, for 'tone' is the substance and
colour decorates it. And there is no lasting satisfaction with a decoration that
has no 'body' or significance. Corot's saying or advice still holds good 'with never
failing draughtsmanship—truth of tone is essential', and this saying becomes more
convincing with ripened experience.

It is time to knock off and so my dear Nora I will say goodnight.
Mother and we all send you our love,
Cheerio Dad

Rempstone Farm, Dorset
Tuesday 1936

Dearest Mother and Daddy,

Tuesday's mail day and with it a big bunch of letters, Daddy's fat letters full of the advice of experience. I'm glad Bateman wrote and put his criticism of my work into his own words, it is more satisfactory that way. He is very right in most respects but I think everyone must find their own way ... when I am back in London again I will see Bateman and have another chat about art. For the present I want to work, and not talk about it.

So the weeks fly past and all my time and thoughts are taken up with that one little word 'art'. It takes all one has got and more. I have almost finished the portrait.

To wash a few clothes here is a day's work. Every drop of water has to be carried from the farmhouse, then a fire made outside to heat the water, then washing begins in a small basin with minimum amount of water. This, by the way, is the manner in which we have a bath ... The primitive life has its little drawbacks, but for the most part it is grand to be under the sky again overlooking distant hills and fields of waving grass.

My love to everyone,
Norrie

Hahndorf, South Australia
19 July 1936

My Dear Nora,

The news contained in your last letter that you had signed on for another 12 months came as a rather rude shock. Of course, we had been wondering along what lines your plans were developing, and I can quite imagine that when a decision had to be made, what your feelings were, for it would be no easy matter to make up your mind on so important a period in a young painter's life.

We loved your letter (arriving yesterday) dealing with your delightful description of Dorset countryside ... The very name of Corfe Castle conjures up all sorts of romantic visions, and I ache to join you in wandering all over that rolling landscape. I seem to know it all from Wilson Steer's pictures ... Then I remember Streeton's, quite a number of them dealing with that most paintable and delightful country.[39] Yes, do try and get there and paint me a little parcel of that landscape. I should love it, I know, those great rolling hills with a big clouded sky above, with masses of whites and greys.

Later

Ursula told me about her Gauguin and how much they liked it, so on our way to town this morning, to attend to the hanging of the *Manunda* picture, we called in at Birksgate and inspected the *Gauguin*—it is an early work before his departure for Tahiti probably painted in Breton.[40]

Well the picture for the *Manunda* was got safely on board and after a little trouble got into position, with a simple moulding on its boundary. I suppose a wave of disappointment comes over every artist, when he sees his picture under different surroundings than in that in which the work was painted, and certainly I did not feel very elated when I saw it there. Yet everyone else seemed very satisfied. Still, I must confess it is an improvement on what was there before. In my picture I had kept the sky as a very fresh note of blue, but I was astounded how this was toned down almost to a grey in the suffused light in which it is hung, and also when lit by artificial light. In this respect it was an object lesson to me.

And so dear Nora I will leave you once more—and we sincerely hope this will find you hearty and fit,

Cheerio from Dad

Hahndorf, South Australia
12 September 1936

My Dear Nora,

Daffodils, daffodils everywhere, seldom have I seen so many and never have we had more. The weather has been perfect to mature the buds slowly so that they have reached perfection. We have picked armfuls, and yet armfuls remain.

Last Saturday was the first day I have been out sketching. The family dropped me at 'Windy Corner' and I spent a couple of entrancing hours watching

---

39 Arthur Streeton (1867–1943) was in England for 20 years and frequently painted the landscape replete with its historic markers, such as in his painting, *Corfe Castle* (1909), held by the National Gallery of Victoria. See Geoffrey Smith, *Arthur Streeton*, Melbourne, National Gallery of Victoria, 1995: 150.

40 Ursula and Bill Hayward were building up an art collection for their home, Carrick Hill. This painting has since been reattributed to the *École de Pont-Aven*. Other work purchased during their 1935 trip to London include Stanley Spencer's *Zermatt* (1934), James Bateman's *Sketch Design for a Westmoreland Farm* (1935), Matthew Smith's *Nude with Pearl Necklace* (c.1930) and Jacob Epstein's *Neander* (1933). See James Schoff (ed.), *The British Collection at Carrick Hill: The Hayward Bequest of British Paintings*, Springfield, South Australia, Carrick Hill Trust, 1991.

the light play over those big green rolling hills. They are magnificent I think and make fine subject matter for someone, and they have never really been painted.

Hardy Wilson has been chosen as the new Director for the Melbourne Gallery. The choice I feel is a surprise to many. McDonald of Sydney, Daryl Lindsay and Basil Burdett applied and must have been in the running.

I seem to run out of news, so will stop now dear Nora, I might be able to add a few more words before the mail closes, so cheerio and *keep well*,

Your Dad

Tuesday

Was in town yesterday to adjudicate the portrait and landscape prizes together with Louis McCubbin. Ivor Hele carried off the portraits with quite a good thing of Brewster Jones, quite in Orpenesque style with Orpen's double lighting, his highlights and metallic flesh. Still it was by far the best things there.[41]

McCubbin took me all over the new additions to the Art Gallery, and told me his ideas and suggestions put to the Board regarding colour of walls and so on. I think you will be agreeably surprised when you see it completed, it promises well and will transform the whole gallery as a unit.[42] McCubbin is most enthusiastic and keen on his job and I feel he will be responsible for much good work and help raise enthusiasm for art here.

Goodbye once more and good luck Nora

Your Dad

Hahndorf, South Australia
26 September 1936

My Dear Nora,

I was immensely pleased with the good news your letter brought about Bateman's picture *Commotion in the Bull Ring* being bought by the Tate Gallery. What a genuine relief it will be for him, and what a splendid advertisement as well as an honour. Unfortunately one always has to look on the commercial side of these matters, for without sales the artist cannot go on, and this particular *sale* will mean a tremendous lot for Bateman.

---

41   Ivor Hele (1912–1993) was awarded the 1936 Melrose Prize for his portrait of Brewster Jones. In the same year, he also won the South Australian Centenary Prize, worth £200, for his painting *Reading the Proclamation*, which hangs in the Centre Hall of the Parliament of South Australia.

42   The Foundation Stone for the Melrose Wing had been laid on 5 June 1936. The building was due to be finished by September 1936 but the project was delayed by the death of the contractor.

It now appears that the directorship for the Melbourne Gallery had *not* been settled when I last wrote. Since then its aspect has changed completely and James McDonald has the position. The Victorian Government took the matter out of the Trustees' hands, vetoed their decision, and appointed McDonald. Very hard luck for Hardy Wilson with whom I deeply sympathise, for he had definitely been recommended after a personal interview with Trustees. Of course, the Sydney artists are really glad to get rid of McDonald, and I yet cannot understand why the Victorian artists cling to him, but they do.

My love,
Your Dad

Hahndorf, South Australia
22 October 1936

My Dear Nora,

Another long letter, brimming over with the most interesting news … Saturday morning is eagerly looked forward to by not only myself and Mother but the whole 'blooming family'. They will form a most complete diary of your London doings, and I know that Mr and Mrs Stow are equally enthusiastic so, my dear Nora, your letters really are being appreciated and the time you give to the making of them is not spent in vain.[43] For I do know, it takes a lot of time and one is often apt to think—'I wonder if it is worthwhile'. I can sincerely say 'it is'!

Yesterday brought an air letter with snaps of your more recent work. Thank you ever so much for sending us these, for every snapshot is welcome. Making allowance for some false colour values, I like all the flower studies. My first choice goes to the painting you are sending to Liverpool, then the anemones and the cornflowers, with the added piece on the left, this makes a charming study. In the anemones I can feel a greater spontaneity and more robust feeling for colour, actual paint quality.

Mother is writing—cheers Nora, take care of yourself,
With love from your Daddy

---

43   Catherine 'Katie' Stow (1856–1940), whose pen name was K. Langloh Parker, wrote *Woggheeguy: Australian Aboriginal Legends* (1930), illustrated by Nora Heysen. The original illustrations are held by the National Library of Australia. See 'Catherine Eliza Summerville (Katie) Stow (nee Field)' in Wilfrid Prest, *The Wakefield Companion to South Australian History*, Kent Town, South Australia, Wakefield Press, 2001: 518.

Rempstone Farm, Dorset
27 October 1936

Dearest Mother and Daddy,

Well here I am on the eve of going up to London. Nearly four months have passed. I wish that we were just beginning the Summer over again with better weather. I feel the weight of lost opportunities and wish that I could have done more work. As luck would have it, I have found a wonderful subject at the last moment so am working at a breakneck pace. The subject is a figure seated in a window resting. I want it to be symbolical of all working women. The simple setting here is perfect for her and I feel if I can't make a dash for it, I will never recapture my opportunity. Today I blocked the whole thing in thin colour getting the weight and bigness of the masses. Tomorrow I will have to use every hour of light to try and get in the background of window, wall and garden, the rest I will have to leave until I get up to my studio and pray that I will be able to get the same lighting effect.

All my love,
Norrie

Hahndorf, South Australia
3 November 1936

My Dear Nora,

Well! Here we are back home, after a most delightful trip … 'Mae West' behaved like a real lady despite her curves, she was extremely active and did everything that was expected of her under all conditions. She does 50 miles per hour quite comfortably, and hardly moves ever over rough roads. She has now done 4000 miles and this should be a sufficient test to show what she is made of.

My show with Fern in Melbourne opened successfully with the sale of 8 pictures and since then 3 more have been sold, at an average price of about 35gs each.[44] So I cannot complain. The show has another week to run.

Under separate cover I am sending you cuttings re 'the Australian Academy', 'for' and 'against', so you can draw your own conclusions as to the advisability of having it or not. Personally I agree with having some central authority as an Academy would give, but if possible to do away with the 'Royal'!

---

44   Hans Heysen's exhibition was at the Victorian Artists' Gallery, Melbourne.

Still I suppose it is the only '*sign*' that will give it the authority that it must have to do any good at all.[45]

My love goes with this,

Dad

5 *Dukes Lane, London*
3 *November 1936*

Dearest Mother and Daddy,

Well here we are and glad to be back. It was bewildering being back in a city the rush and tear and noise and bustle, the screaming buses full of people, the streets thronged, the gaily lighted shop windows, the excitement and sordidness of it all, and the heavy foggy atmosphere of it all wrapping it in.

The exhibition of French art at Burlington Galleries closed on Friday and we were just able to see it and I am glad, for there were some fine things there, the best collection of Van Goghs I have seen and probably will ever see here—I should say some of his finest things. His portrait of a sailor was to me the most vital and vivid and most original canvas there ... it made a bigger impression on me than anything there. It was so naive and fresh I can see it now. The sailor smiling with his hands folded on his knees in a bright blue jacket vigorously painted, full of movement and colour. He had a heavy old scarf round his neck, and a pale face with those strange far-seeing blue eyes peculiar to seamen, and on his head the most delightful straw-coloured hat turned up all round, and there he sat against his background of various little gaily coloured pictures (Japanese prints) so arranged to make a perfect design and with all being symbolic of the sailor and his travels.

All my love to you,

Norrie

5 *Dukes Lane, London*
Monday 9 November 1936

Dearest Mother and Daddy,

To get down to money matters, I have just paid off an accumulation of bills and find it leaves me with precious little to go on with. The inevitable day has come and I am broke and want to appeal for a loan from Daddy, that is, if you have not

---

45 The much debated Australian Academy of Art did eventuate at a meeting, presided over by the Attorney General, Robert Gordon Menzies, held at the Hotel Canberra on 21 June 1937. Ten artists representing each Australian state attended. Hans Heysen was the South Australian representative. Louis McCubbin declined an invitation to attend on the grounds that his position as gallery director required independence. See 'Australian Academy of Art. Gallery Director Declines Invitation', *The Advertiser*, 23 March 1937; 'Australian Academy of Art Founded', *The Advertiser*, 21 June 1937.

received the money for the two pictures I sent over. If you have sold them and you could send me the money, it would tide me over until I can sell more, but if they haven't, I'd be very thankful if Daddy could lend me £30.

The other day I summoned up the courage and wrote to Holmes asking him if I could bring a couple of things along for a criticism.

My love and thoughts go with this,
Norrie

Hahndorf, South Australia
17 November 1936

My Dear Nora,

Daddy's exhibition in Melbourne ... was a marvellous success and so many have sold. You can't think what a difference it makes to him after drawing a blank in New Zealand and in Sydney, with the foolish criticisms added, made him feel as though his work must be failing. Now he has brightened up quite a lot and has gained heart. Why must one be so dependent upon sales to prove the value of one's work? I feel Daddy lacks self-confidence because there is not an atom of conceit in his make-up. I wonder was there ever an artist who thought so little of his own comfort and welfare, or of his own amazing talents that could bring him all he could possibly wish for?

All our love dearest Nora, be happy,
Mother

Hahndorf, South Australia
18 November 1936

My Dear Nora,

I just want to add my note of once again my heartiest Christmas greetings, and hope that it will be a happy day for you.

I have had some good news from Melbourne—25 watercolours being sold with prospects of more. A splendid, and I will admit, a quite unexpected success. Mr Fern certainly deserves some compensation for his efforts. He offered to run the exhibition at his own expense and the usual commission of 15%.

Did I tell you in my last letter that I have booked up with Fuller for an exhibition at the SA Society of Arts rooms for October next to November 1? As I have not shown in Adelaide since 1922, it is time I think to venture again, with some confidence of success. I have enough watercolours on hand, big and small, but am practically cleared out of saleable oils as I have done no flowers or new landscapes, beyond the *Manunda* picture, since our homecoming. I never seem to be getting any further than putting my design to canvas with charcoal.

Again my very, very hearty wishes and love,

From your Dad

5 Dukes Lane, London
Monday 22 November 1936

Dearest Mother and Daddy,

I have the Holmes criticism to tell you about. He wrote making a time for me to call yesterday, so I chose what I thought to be four of my best efforts, and went along with a beating heart feeling much as one does when one is going to sit for an important examination. Still I went in with more faith than I came out. He gave me an adverse criticism, to put it into a nutshell. He thought my drawing was weak and had not improved since he last saw my work, my technique was bad and laboured, and he advised that I went to the Byam Shore School of Art and learnt to draw and paint there.[46]

My love to everyone at home,

Norrie

5 Dukes Lane, London
Tuesday 30 November 1936

Dearest Mother and Daddy,

What an enormous relief it is to have Daddy's airmail letter with an enclosed cheque. I cried with joy to get it and marvelled at the intuition that prompted the sending. For Daddy to feel prompted to sit down and write out a cheque for £30 on almost the exactly same day that I was driven to write airmail asking for just that same amount to tide me over. It is too strange and baffles all reasoning. I was just sitting up here wondering how much longer I could keep the framers and the Gas Company etc. waiting for their money. The Gas Company sent a note yesterday giving me five days in which to pay, and as I had no money, they probably would have cut me off.

Today I interviewed Mr Jackson, the Principal of the Byam Shore School. I told him that I wanted to learn to draw and paint and had been recommended to his school. He said that, as a rule, he didn't take beginners for less than a year, but

---

46   The Byam Shaw School of Art was founded in 1910 by John Byam Shaw and Rex Vicat Cole. The school merged with the Central Saint Martins College of Art and Design in 2003.

he'd make a concession as I was returning to Australia in eight months. So then and there I signed on for 6 months of 5 days a week drawing and painting—£22.

Mr Jackson makes a special feature of design, giving it a very important place in art teaching, so I think I'll benefit, and the good hard hours of drawing from the model will also do me good. Also the students are taught the chemistry of painting, and how to prepare canvases and so on.

There were several items in Holmes's criticism that I still cannot fathom. He said that my paintings of flowers looked dead and had no life as if I'd taken no pleasure in painting them. I can't understand it, if there is anything I love doing and find the greatest joy in doing, it's in painting flowers. Especially the one I took him of *Spring Flowers*, which I painted at the highest pitch of excitement, and enjoyed every moment of. I can't help but feel that some of what I felt is in the work, and I can't agree with his criticism on that point.

Well it is 'back to school day'. Thank goodness the first day is over.

My love to all at home,

Norrie

5 Dukes Lane, London
6 December 1936

Dearest Mother and Daddy,

Last night I went along to a little party of Australian artists—Murch and his lady were there. Murch looking quite spruce and tidy, but otherwise the same Murch with his theories and his droll sense of humour … A Mr Passmore, also a Sydney scholarship winner, was there. He has been over for four or five years and is now working at a business job in the daytime and studying at an art school in the evening. J. Cook they say is doing the same—the same old story, no one seems to be making a living out of art. It is a wrong state of affairs.

Miss Appleton, also a Sydney artist, was there, so altogether we were a little group all with ideals and no money, and with much to talk about. Not one of them wanted to go back to Australia. I was the only one—strange how people get better over here and don't want to return. I can't understand it. We talked far into the night which accounts for a heavy head this morning.

Well I've finished my first week at the Byam Shaw School and have learnt something about a nude, so far I have only drawn but next week will go into the design class and paint and see how I get on.

My love and wishes,

Norrie

5 Dukes Lane, London
8 December 1936

Dearest Mother and Daddy,

Many thanks for the batch of paper cuttings ... I was interested in the *fors* and *againsts* for the Australian Royal Academy. I can see that it will have advantages and disadvantages.

You will be sorry to hear of the death of Sir Charles Holmes, probably the news has already reached you in Australia.[47] He looked a very sick man when I saw him, evidently he never rallied after his last illness. He has done a tremendous amount for art and I am glad I was still able to meet him—though I'm afraid he was only a ghost of the former man.

Today I got a lesson from Mr Jackson. He didn't look at my work, but sat down and did a drawing explaining what he wanted, leaving me with a remark that it would take me two years before I could draw with his confidence. Very encouraging to be sure.

Murch has asked me to his studio with a small contingent of Australian artists, the same I met last Friday. I'm looking forward to seeing his work.

My love to you all at home,

Norrie

Hahndorf, South Australia
8 December 1936

My Dear Nora,

It has been a warm and glorious Summer's day, a deep blue sky with isolated, lit up and sundressed clouds floating here and there as if they enjoyed being up, high in the heavens.

Today I took the opportunity of starting a rather tender arrangement of mixed flowers in your studio and stuck at it all day, it's only a little bunch of light flowers in light against your bright wall and pale tablecloth.

It was exceedingly interesting to read of your interest in the Van Goghs and Renoirs. You are quite right with your remarks about both. It is quite uncanny with what simplicity of means Van Gogh produces a most convincing subject. I put it to his unnerving sense of design and extraordinarily original colour sense. I think his colour very beautiful ... I would like to have seen that show with you.

It's time to close this letter so dear Nora, once again, my hearty congratulations and wishes for a very happy birthday,

From Dad with love

---

47   Sir Charles Holmes (1868–1936) was the Director of the National Gallery, London, between 1916 and 1928.

5 Dukes Lane, London
4 January 1937

Dearest Mother and Daddy,

I have just come home from art school ... This term I feel I have a much better grip on my drawing and in my opinion have improved a good deal, being less mechanical and having more impression in my line. Mr Jackson occasionally gives me a lesson and says keep on searching and never put down a line that does not mean something.

It's difficult to think I will be 26 on Monday, old enough to be married and have a few children.

My love to everyone at home,
Norrie

5 Dukes Lane, London
20 January 1937

Dearest Mother and Daddy,

Orovida came to tea on Saturday. The same huge bulk in her red flannel dress, she is a character. Her criticism of my work was more encouraging this time, she thinks it has improved immensely in all ways, that my colour is cleaner and better and that I have lost a certain slickness that she didn't like at all.

She was anxious to know whether my father still wanted to buy a Lucien Pissarro, that was, I presume, the object of her visit. I thought there was a motive behind her looking me up. I am to have tea with her at Lucien Pissarro's studio on Saturday. Is the Adelaide Gallery still thinking of acquiring one of his? I told her that nothing was definite, but she seems terribly anxious to get a sale.

Goodbye for the present my love goes with this,
Norrie

5 Dukes Lane, London
9 February 1937

Dearest Mother and Daddy,

I'll begin by talking about my visit to Lucien Pissarro's studio. I had an interesting afternoon on Sunday looking at his work and talking art.

I wish the Adelaide Gallery could afford a Camille Pissarro. They have a lovely little tempera painting of his, £400, I'm sending a photograph of it, *The Peasant Woman*. It has a simple big feeling, is delightful in colour and a splendid

Unknown photographer
*Nora Heysen with her Parents
in Wales* 1934

photograph
Manuscripts Collection, MS 10041
National Library of Australia

Hans Heysen (1877–1968)
Brachina Gorge 1944

watercolour; 33.2 x 40.8 cm
Pictures Collection, nla.pic-an5837001
National Library of Australia

Unknown photographer
*Sallie Heysen in front of
Nora Heysen's Studio* c.1920s

photograph
The Cedars, Hahndorf

Harold Cazneaux (1878–1953)
*Hans Heysen in his Studio, Hahndorf,
South Australia* 1935

gelatin-silver photograph;
25.9 x 19.0 cm
Gift of the Cazneaux Family 1978
Art Gallery of South Australia

below
Nora Heysen (1911–2003)
Self Portrait 1934

oil on canvas; 60.8 x 53.5 cm
Purchased 1999
National Portrait Gallery

Constance Everton Stokes
(nee Wallis) (1906–1986)
Student Bust, London 1935

photograph
Manuscripts Collection, MS 10041
National Library of Australia

right
Nora Heysen (1911–2003)
Self Portrait 1936

oil on canvas; 63.0 x 51.0 cm
Fred & Elinor Wrobel Collection
John Passmore Museum of Art

far right
Nora Heysen (1911–2003)
Portrait of Everton (Evie) 1936

oil on canvas on board; 40.6 x 30.0 cm
Private collection

Nora Heysen (1911–2003)
Ruth 1933

oil on canvas; 81.5 x 64.2 cm
South Australian Government Grant 1934
Art Gallery of South Australia

Hans Heysen (1877–1968)
White Gums 1936

oil on canvas; 142.0 x 112.0 cm
Commissioned for TSMV *Manunda*
by the Adelaide Steamship Company
Private collection
Photograph by Michael Kluvanek

Nora Heysen (1911–2003)
Down and Out in London 1937

oil on canvas; 55.0 x 40.0 cm
South Australian Government Grant 1994
Art Gallery of South Australia

example of his figure painting. I liked it very much indeed. It interested me far more than any of Lucien Pissarro's work. To me Camille is the artist, and I would like to see one of his in the Adelaide Gallery. It is a chance for them to get one of his, if they didn't baulk at the price.

Lucien Pissarro's prices are, of course, a great deal less. The one I liked best was 157 guineas, it has a nice feeling and good colours, but lacks design somewhat, but it seemed to have more depth and to be a mature work compared with the others.

All his work is in a very high key, and after looking at many, one simply longs for some definite contrast and definition. They are all too much the same all over. They seem very anxious to sell.

My love to all,
Norrie

5 Dukes Lane, London
19 February 1937

Dearest Mother and Daddy,

The Pissarros came on Sunday. The two old people drove themselves in an old car, he is too old to get about much. I think they enjoyed their visit. I made some hot scones and cake which they did full justice to over tea. I showed my work to them and asked Pissarro for a criticism. It will amuse you to hear what he said, 'I mixed my colours too much and did not get light or atmosphere'. He advised me to try the Seurat method, that is, painting with spots of pure colour laid on side-by-side. That amused me. In a modified degree he himself uses that technique, that is why I suppose he thinks it is the only one. I intensely disagree with him and think that by copying a technique it would merely be forced and mechanical. He thinks that atmosphere and light are the two essentials of a landscape. I said what about design, and he said well of course that goes as a matter of course, one wouldn't paint if one didn't have a sense of design. I had a smile and inwardly came to the conclusion that artists were blind to their own work, for I feel that is just where he falls short himself.

Miss Pissarro had a photograph of the one I'd like to send to you. It has taken splendidly and will give you an idea of the picture. The colour scheme is in all purples and blues and greens. I wonder will you like it?

Miss Orovida wants me to join the Women's International Society of Artists. She arranged that I should be invited to join, but I didn't have the ready work at the time, but I will probably join later and send over from Australia, that is of course if I like the exhibition. It opens on Saturday. The Pissarros have invited me to meet people afterwards at a tea party.

Yesterday afternoon I went in after work to see a few shows ... I cannot arouse any enthusiasm about Holmes' work and have no sympathy with his outlook. Now I understand why he disliked my work, his pictures are low in tone and gloomy. There seems to be no joy in nature for him, but perhaps that is bias, for I still smart when I think of his remarks about my work.

Now to bed, love to everyone my thoughts go with this,
Norrie

5 Dukes Lane, London
26 February 1937

Dearest Mother and Daddy,

Miss Pissarro just rang to say would I like a loan of the Camille Pissarro's *Peasant Woman* and the Lucien Pissarro's *Laurustinus* while they are away in France for 3 months. They are insured of course, I jumped at the project.

Now goodnight with my love to everyone,
Love Norrie

5 Dukes Lane, London
1 March 1937

Dearest Mother and Daddy,

It has been an eventful week, first the arrival of the pictures. It was a thrill to see them on the walls and they both look splendid. The Lucien Pissarro has the big wall to itself over my divan. The Camille Pissarro hangs over the mantelpiece, and the Orovida by the wireless. Grandfather, father and daughter all represented.

The Lucien Pissarro has a lovely atmosphere and feeling, and there is a beauty and vibrancy in the way the paint is handled, being clear and crisp and yet having quality. I'm sure it would be a very popular picture if our Adelaide gallery could afford the £157 or guineas, I don't remember which. I'd like to see it there and the Gallery really should have a few examples of the Post Impressionists.

My love to all,
Norrie

5 Dukes Lane, London
15 March 1937

Dearest Mother and Daddy,

Yesterday I had the Batemans to tea ... Mr Bateman gave me a good and constructive criticism on my latest canvases. He seemed to think my work was a lot better, and liked some of it and where he found fault he had a good reason to back it up. He liked the Lucien Pissarro very much.

I am getting my things ready to send into the Academy. Since Bateman's criticism I have decided to alter all three.

My love to all and everyone,

Norrie

Hahndorf, South Australia
4 April 1937

My Dear Nora,

Your letter on Saturday contained really exciting news. It's great to have those two Pissarros on your walls ... On Wednesday I am seeing Louis McCubbin about it and have every hope that it will find its way into our Gallery.

I must try to get him interested in the Camille Pissarro, but if I have no luck, I propose sending both photographs to McDonald in Melbourne; for there is a faint chance that the Felton Trustees might be interested. I say a chance only—for they have that excellent example of a Paris Boulevard dated about 1892 or so[48]... I can well remember an exhibition at the Durand Ruel Galleries in Paris of his late work in 1902. It was less coloured than his earlier work, and relied on subtle uses of pure white and grey whites more than on the spectrum, as Sisley or Monet did for obtaining light, and I still think he succeeded better than they in conveying the feeling of true light.

When you get back you will notice some changes in our surroundings— more and more clearing is taking place ... that lovely old white Gum I have painted so often at Woodside has also gone. It felt like losing an old friend, and so one by one they go back to earth from whence they came.

Kramm brought us half a case of glorious grapes, large bluish-brown hamburgers. I wish you could see them, filled with Australian sunlight and fruitfulness. Your fingers would itch with an overwhelming wish to paint them. I want to paint them but with these wonderful days it is hard to resist being outside.

---

48 Camille Pissarro's *Boulevard Montmartre, Morning, Cloudy Weather* (1897), oil on canvas, was purchased through the Felton Bequest in 1905.

Our loves goes with this dear Nora—so for the present I will say goodnight,
Your Dad

5 Dukes Lane, London
14 April 1937

Dearest Mother and Daddy,
On Monday I was asked to a sherry party by Lady Young, sister to
Mrs Reynolds, who has several of Daddy's pictures. As a draw on the invitation I
was asked to meet some interesting people, artists and writers. I was curious and
went along. On arriving, I was introduced all round in a loud voice as the daughter
of the famous Australian painter Hans Heysen—I felt like an exhibit.

Roy de Maistre was among the exhibitors, I found him quite interesting to
speak to. He is a rank modern, thinks that Picasso and Henry Moore are the two
great men of the age. Picasso is holding an exhibition at present. I went to see it
and came away feeling that he was a charlatan. I simply couldn't take the work
seriously … but there you are, another man can come along with intelligence and
knowledge, and find expression and meaning there which he finds satisfying and
interesting. What strangely conflicting views there are about.

Must go, my love to all,
Norrie

5 Dukes Lane, London
21 April 1937

Dearest Mother and Daddy,
There is a quantity of news this week, pleasant and unpleasant. Three
buff tickets from the Academy saying politely that all my pictures have been
turned out has rather squashed any Spring feeling. However after throwing a few
temperamental fits, I have got over it and have started on an idea for a new canvas.
Evidently I am not to have any luck with the Academy.

Of most importance to me there are some fine modern pictures on loan to
the National Gallery. I went in on Tuesday and came back wildly excited. There is
a gem of a little Cezanne still life of just a pot plant, a pear and an apple. I have
fallen for it completely; then there is a magnificent Gauguin of two dark figures
seated against a decorative background. One that is often reproduced. It is lovely to
see the original which has glorious colouring, exotic and rich … Also there was the
famous Cezanne portrait of the man with pipe, but more about that later as I am
pushed for time and am due up at the art school.

Well I must bolt or I'll be turned out of the life class, and that hurts my pride.
My love to everyone,
Norrie

Hahndorf, South Australia
3 May 1937

My Dear Nora,

I have just come in with a basket full of lovely fresh mushrooms from
Spicer's paddock. Two days ago we had a wonderful soft rain which has transformed
our surroundings.

Lottie Lehmann, the German soprano, was singing some Deutsche Lieder
with a magnificent voice, undoubtedly the finest we have had in Australia for a
very, very long time. She comes to Adelaide in June so there is a treat in store for
us.

I wonder if you remember a Mrs Webster? You visited her in London and
she bought a flower study from you—she asked me to paint her a small zinnia study
and send on, which is now complete and ready to send on.

Cheerio Nora—with love from your Dad

5 Dukes Lane, London
4 May 1937

Dearest Mother and Daddy,

The Tate opens tomorrow with the Centenary exhibition of the work of
Constable. It is evidently going to be a great show, there being four rooms devoted
to his work. I am looking forward to seeing it and wish that Daddy were here to
enjoy it with me.

The money I have is not going to see me through ... this month I want to
book my passage ... This being how I stand, I will be called upon to beg yet again
another loan from Daddy. My debts are mounting fast. The first thing I will do
when I get home is mount a show and pray that the people will buy.

One by one I lugged my pictures home from the Academy and cursed the
RAs for not accepting at least one to repay me for all my work, worry and expense.

All my love to everyone,
Norrie

Hahndorf, South Australia
17 May 1937

My Dear Nora,

The weeks fly round, much sooner than I wish, for little seems accomplished towards new work for my show, one only comfort is I have until October![49]

I have good news for you re the Lucien Pissarro, for the Gallery has decided on the purchase. McCubbin gave me the news on Saturday. Mr Finlayson brought the question up again at their last meeting and its purchase was passed with promptitude.[50] I gave McCubbin Miss Pissarro's address ... I am glad they decided to buy, for I feel it helps to fill a gap which was wanting.

And now for Mrs Webster's Zinnias. This I am sending by registered post addressed to you by this mail. I hope you get it safely. I wrote to Mrs Webster ... and said that you would communicate with her immediately after the painting arrived, and perhaps discuss the framing of it with her and for which she will pay.

The price I am charging her is 60gs (Aus. money) approximately £47-5-0 in English. This I have asked her to pay over to you, and which amount you can put to your account, for I feel sure you will be wanting money by then.

Goodnight dear Nora (there is frost in the air—which says a wonderful Autumn morning, all sparkling and dancing in light. Now all is hushed.)

5 Dukes Lane, London
16 June 1937

Dearest Mother and Daddy,

First for the news. I'm off to Italy at the end of the month, McGregor has arranged the trip. It all sounds marvellous, I'm to see him tomorrow and will then know the plans. He has a friend at Cooks, which has helped, as he knows Italy so well and where all the art treasures are. I have been very thankful to leave it to him—Evie will probably join me and I cannot imagine doing the trip alone, so I'm hoping she can get away. I'm very enthusiastic and excited as you can imagine.

Fern was here on Saturday. I have given him four of my pictures to send back to Australia to sell, all 1935 work which he has a market for. I'm glad to get it off as I feel a little nearer to paying back some of my money debts to Daddy, it worries me to owe money when I know there are other calls on it.

---

49   Hans Heysen's exhibition was held in October 1937 at the Royal South Australian Society of Arts.

50   This was the second time the issue of acquiring Lucien Pissarro's *Laurustinus* had come before the Fine Arts Committee. It was raised at the 13 April 1937 meeting and rejected. See *Minutes of the Fine Arts Committee, 13 April 1937 and 11 May 1937*, Art Gallery of South Australia Research Library.

I'm looking forward to the arrival of the zinnia picture.

Goodnight to you all, my love to everyone ... the jam is disappearing fast and is jolly good,

Norrie

> *5 Dukes Lane, London*
> *23 June 1937*

Dearest Mother and Daddy,

I'm getting more and more excited about the trip to Italy and wish it were tomorrow instead of next week that we were leaving.

It is great news to hear that the Adelaide Gallery has purchased or rather is purchasing the Lucien Pissarro. I have just rung Orovida about it and she sounds thrilled, and is seeing her father who is still in France about the good news. She says it will cheer him up tremendously, as he has been feeling very despondent lately.

You must know how gratified I am for the loan and this will see me through with some to spare I hope. As soon as I get back I'll set to work to pay off my debts.

I must off to school and post this on the way.

My love to everyone especially Mother and Daddy,

Norrie

> *Hahndorf, South Australia*
> *Sunday 27 June 1937*

My Dear Nora,

It was great a pleasure for all of us (what is left of us) to have *two* letters from you this week.[51]

This week *Eric Wilson*, this year's Traveling Scholarship man from NSW, rang me. We could not arrange a meeting because we had other visitors. He asked me your address which I gave him, for I liked his voice and the way he spoke over the phone. He said he would like to have your advice re schools etc., so I call on you. He was staying somewhere in Kensington.

Streeton's show finished up with £2300 in Sydney according to Wall Taylor who managed it[52] ... It looks as if things have definitely swung round the right way. In Adelaide things are still stagnant.

---

51   The number of family members living at home was becoming less: Nora's sister, Deirdre, had married in April that year and her brother, David, had become engaged.

52   Arthur Streeton's solo exhibition was held in Sydney at David Jones Gallery and then in Melbourne at the Athenaeum.

The Brisbane show which the Sydney Society of Artists sent over barely paid expenses ... only 2 pictures were purchased by the Gallery including one of my small watercolours, *At Sunrise, Aroona.*

You have not told me anything about the Constable Show at the Tate, but perhaps you have not yet been there,

With love from your Dad

Train to Dover
1937

Dearest Mother and Daddy,

In the rush to get away I had no time to collect my wits for letter writing. Two days ago I saw a delightful little painting subject in the kitchen, myself sitting on the table with the washing as background. I knew that if I didn't do it then and there, it wouldn't be done at all, so everything went to the four winds.[53]

Daddy's *Zinnias* arrived on Saturday. I couldn't get the wrappings off fast enough. The glow of the colour that first met my eyes astonished me. Surely it is the richest zinnia study Daddy has ever painted. It is a lovely colour harmony and I like the rough painting quality of the background. The picture is so rich it knocks everything out in the studio. My work looks a pale silvery grey in comparison, in spite of the pure colours I use. The Pissarros also wouldn't stand against it. I rang Mrs Webster as soon as it arrived, she was very excited. When I showed her the picture, and Daddy need have no doubt as to her liking it or not, for she is thrilled with it, she paid me straight away the amount stated in Daddy's letter to her—£47-5-0.

There is a long day and night travelling ahead of me, and I'm feeling very churned up. I hope for a smooth crossing.

My love to you all,

Norrie

Hahndorf, South Australia
11 July 1937

My Dear Nora,

Your letter yesterday morning brought exciting news—a contemplated trip *to Italy*! ... Your suggestion brings with it a mountain of memories, mainly of Florence where I spent nearly 5 months ... I would say without hesitation, *Go.*

It's awfully good of Mr McGregor to pay you that visit and give you such an encouraging criticism. I have my faith in his judgement, 'but don't throw over

---

53   This is *Down and Out in London* (1937), oil on canvas, Art Gallery of South Australia.

tone too early'. It is so very important, and which lovers of Modern Art ignore and entirely lose sight of its value. I feel McGregor will come up to scratch and buy something.

I love to hear of McGregor buying the Jacovleff *Nude* for the Sydney gallery, and also the John's drawing and that he likes the Lucien.[54]

We were at the Russian Ballet last night—Mr and Mrs Hayward asked us down and although we were almost in the front row (stalls) we enjoyed the performance immensely. They had improved all round since we last saw them. We go again tomorrow night at the invitation of Monsieur Philipoff and his wife, a very beautiful and attractive woman. On Tuesday afternoon they are coming up to us. Monsieur Philipoff knows Jacovleff and knew Bakst the great ballet costume designer well—so it should prove quite an interesting visit.[55]

Goodnight Nora, love from us all goes with this and a special parcel from Dad and Mother. We are all very well.

Hahndorf, South Australia
25 July 1937

My Dear Nora,

Your letter with the wonderful news that you are to see Rome, Perugia, Padua, Venice and Milan and you will pass Spoleto and Assisi on your way! ... The memories of these places are still the clearest and strongest of my life and so they will be with you. What you will see will but whet the appetite.

In the end every artist must solve his own problems in his or her own way. But I see by your letters that you have come to this conclusion yourself. Your letters have been most interesting to me throughout, to feel the gradual change and development in your outlook and your reactions to the different schools of painting. They are not dissimilar to my own reflections and thoughts at that period of my studying years, and have revived many old memories.

Don't let the money question worry you Nora ... Did I tell you in a previous letter Mr R. Sedon came to see me from Melbourne for some of my work, and also to make enquiries about yours, for which he says he has buyers? I gave him seven, so far he has sold 5 for £300, including 2 northern oils which you know. The other two are to come back next week if unsold, and now he wants me to send more smaller

---

54   Alexandre Jacovleff's *Nude*, oil on canvas, entered the collection of the National Art Gallery New South Wales in 1937, as a gift from James McGregor.

55   Alexander Philipoff was the Executive Manager of Colonel de Basil's Ballets Russes.

works. So you see the picture market in Australia has certainly revived, and the same story comes from Sydney also.

Mother and I and Mike went into the new Gallery last week, and Mother was quite impressed with the great improvement the new additions have made to the Gallery as a whole. It is to be opened to the public next week. When the Entrance Hall and Sculpture Hall is completed, the print room and watercolour and 2 oil rooms are finished and hung, it will look *really* nice. And then all the basement with its ceramics, china and prints, and *odd watercolours* which McCubbin happily finds room for here, are all complete and well arranged. McCubbin tells me that a start will shortly be made with recolouring of the old walls which look surprisingly dingy. It will be a relief when this is finished so as to correspond with the new part.

Again goodnight dear Nora, we all send our love and keep well,

Your Dad

5 Dukes Lane, London
27 July 1937

Dearest Mother and Daddy,

Home safe and sound … I feel terribly glad I didn't go back to Australia without seeing Italy and its art treasures.

We arrived back last night after a choppy channel crossing.

I am longing to know which parts of Italy Daddy saw? … Florence is so rich in art treasures we just went from one masterpiece to another. I felt it a huge strain trying to absorb so much. The trip out to Arezzo from Florence was delightful and the Piero della Francesca's were superb, he seemed to combine every quality, beauty of colour and form and composition, and were completely satisfying. Imagine my thrill in seeing these things in their own setting.

The Tintoretto exhibition was another revelation; he has gone up tremendously in my estimation. The show was beautifully arranged and being on velvet the effect was rich and glorious and there is still a lurking romance in the canals at night. The whole city has a lacy feminine quality and has great exterior charm, whereas Florence has a more reticent quieter beauty.

Milan didn't interest me as much as the other cities, the cathedral of course was magnificent and there were many gems in the Brera. Bellini's Pieta was there, its appeal was as strong as ever, it is the finest thing he ever painted.

Then Paris, we stayed at the same little place out at Montparnasse and spent the days seeing a few exhibitions and galleries, or else wandering in the

Luxembourg Gardens. One day we spent at the Great Paris Exhibition.[56] It is simply enormous, beyond conception. It stretches for miles on either side of the Seine from the Louvre way up past the Eiffel Tower.

The thing that interested me was an exhibition of the work of Van Gogh, a lovely show, so tastefully arranged, his sketches and drawings and letters also were very interesting. There were some fine paintings, beauties that I hadn't seen before and altogether it left one with a great admiration for the man. There was one glorious golden landscape with a blue cart that was so alive I could smell the grass. His work has a strange vitality and always leaves me excited and stimulated. I walked into that room feeling utterly weary after miles of walking in trying to find the place, but the moment I saw those canvases all so alive, so vital and intense, I forgot it all. Also saw an exhibition of very modern work—Braque, Picasso, Vlaminck, Modigliani, Maillol and others.

My love to all,

Norrie

Hahndorf, South Australia
27 July 1937

Dearest Nora,

Even the papers are beginning to mention your arrival in October and they ought to know.

Mother

Hahndorf, South Australia
3 August 1937

My Dear Nora,

Your last letter was again all excitement written on the train to Dover, and now we are wondering what news next Saturday will bring us.

Mr Battarbee, who is now holding a show at the Society Rooms, came yesterday afternoon and he had many interesting things to tell me about Hermannsburg Mission Station and the surrounding country, quite enough to really whet my appetite for another trip to the Far North, but this time into the real centre.[57] His exhibition deals

---

56   This was the all-important *Exposition Internationale des Arts et Technique dans La Vie Moderne*, which was held from May to September 1937 and included pavilions from many nations.

57   Rex Battarbee (1893–1973) was a Victorian watercolourist who first visited the Lutheran mission at Hermannsburg in 1932 and again in 1934, when he met Albert Namatjira (1902–1959). When Battarbee returned in 1936, Namatjira, already accomplished in pokerwork on wood, wanted to learn how to use watercolours. The two men worked collaboratively, each teaching the other. See Alison French, *Seeing the Centre: The Art of Albert Namatjira, 1902–1959*, Canberra, National Gallery of Australia, 2002: 9.

with Alice Springs and all around Hermannsburg, and in some respects is quite good, and here and there the work brings conviction.

He tells me of a brilliantly clever Black at Hermannsburg who has taken to watercolours and within two weeks of watching him (Battarbee) paint, he turned out some remarkable watercolours, with good colour and a fine feeling for light—in fact he said he knows of no one in Australia who could paint light better! He has brought 3 of his paintings down with him and are on show at the Rooms. We go down tomorrow when I shall be eager to see them. It sounds all too good to be true doesn't it, as I am quite prepared to be disappointed. Yet McCubbin seemed astounded when he saw the work so there must be something in it.[58]

Goodnight dear Nora and may God bless you. All serene at home and Mother sends her love along with mine,

From Dad

Hahndorf, South Australia
17 August 1937

My Dear Nora,

Your letter although a sketchy one was a joy to us … it speaks of your thrills and intense enthusiasm for Giotto and all those wonderful things to be seen and *felt* in Florence—the queen of cities. I knew you would be treading on thin air when once you got there and would go through all those exquisite feelings that I experienced in 1902! But enough of Italy and its art treasures until your letter comes along with your experiences, told in a calmer mood when back in London. We shall look forward to that letter.

The last evening we attended the opening of our new Art Gallery … there were some 500 people present and the new rooms looked delightful, a real credit to McCubbin who was also instrumental in having all the sculpture dragged out of

58 Pastor F.W. Albrecht, the mission supervisor, sent Namatjira's watercolours to Battarbee to include in the July 1937 exhibition. In the exhibition catalogue, the work is not listed by Namatjira's name but by his language group. McCubbin purchased Namatjira's *Illum-baura (Haasts Bluff), Central Australia* from *An Exhibition of Central Australian Watercolours by Rex Battarbee*, Royal South Australian Society of Arts Gallery, 19 May to 3 June 1939. Namatjira is listed as 'Albert Namatjira (Arunta artist)' in the 1939 catalogue but the title of his work is not given. Battarbee supplied the gallery with a handwritten 'certificate of authentication', stating that Namatjira 'painted these three watercolours absolutely on his own, he also picked his own subjects'. See Albert Namatjira's file, Art Gallery of South Australia. Hans Heysen owned two Namatjira watercolours: *Gum Tree* and *Mount Giles* (both c.1938–1939), the latter purchased in 1939.

the Old Gallery on that very morning—the difference! ... Once again our Gallery is spacious.[59]

Goodnight dear Nora—and good luck with lots of love,
Dad

5 Dukes Lane, London
6 o'clock, 19 August 1937

Dearest Mother and Daddy,

I'm leaving in half an hour so this is just to give you a few more particulars. The *Thermopylae* is due in Adelaide on the 6th of October so I'll be home for Daddy's birthday.[60]

McGregor has been a great friend to me over here and has been an invaluable help in fixing up my passage. I have letters of introduction from him to the Captain and he has done everything possible to make the journey comfortable. Tomorrow I spend in Antwerp and sail from there in the evening, so it is the Channel for me tonight and then all aboard for home.

The studio looks bare and desolate with a huddle of cases in one corner ... I'll soon be with you all.

Much love,
Norrie

These letters come from the National Library of Australia's 'Papers of Sir Hans Heysen, c.1880–1973', MS 5073, series 2, folders 143, 146, 147, 148, 149, 150, 151, 152, 153, 154, 156; and 'Papers of Nora Heysen, 1913–2003', MS 10041, series 1.3, folders 31, 32, 33, 36, 37, 38.

59   The Gallery extensions, consisting of the Melrose Wing and the new façade, were opened on 16 August. The Gallery had improved natural and artificial lighting, with McCubbin reporting that it was the most up to date and best lit of public galleries in the Commonwealth. See *Annual Report of the Public Library, Museum and Art Gallery of South Australia for the Year Ended 30 June 1938*.

60   This was on 8 October.

Sydney and the Archibald Prize
1938–1943

The years in Sydney from 1938 to when she was appointed a Second World War official war artist saw Nora Heysen quickly reaping the benefits of her overseas training. She established herself as a serious professional and, by the end of that year, had entered two paintings into the Archibald Prize. That same year, the National Art Gallery of New South Wales purchased one of her paintings from the annual Society of Arts show. The letters home, which now carry the more adult signature line of 'Nora' in place of London's 'Norrie', chart a string of portrait commissions and flower paintings. Success came quickly and not only did she win the Archibald Prize in 1939 for her portrait of *Madame Elink Schuurman* but in 1941 also won the South Australian Melrose Prize for her painting *Motherhood*. Unfortunately the Archibald Prize resulted in unfair accusations by a group of disgruntled artists of her father's undue influence.

Evie weaves in and out of these letters. She left England on the last ship out as war broke out and with her husband Henry posted to Singapore and Evie expecting their first child, she joined Nora in Sydney. Tragedy too struck the Heysen family in 1938 when their eldest daughter Josephine died suddenly as a result of complications from childbirth. In accord with their dying daughter's wish and with the agreement of their son in law, Hans and Sallie then took over looking after newborn Josephine (Jill).

The letters frequently report on who is doing what in the Sydney art scene, what is being shown and importantly, what is being purchased. The business side to working as an artist is to the fore, so the studio is not only a place of work but also a place to display one's paintings to purchasers. Nora recounts how a sale is often assisted by good coffee and cake. Finding suitable accommodation with room for a studio is difficult and Nora and her flatmate Evie move several times during this period.

The artists Nora meets and mixes with regularly are drawn very much from the Society of Artists with which she and her father both exhibit. Her father's influential friends Sydney Ure Smith and James McGregor rapidly become Nora's friends too. Through the Society of Artists she meets a host of artists more her age, including Adrian Feint, John Brackenreg and William Dobell, while artists she met in London, Eric Wilson, Arthur Murch and Jack Carrington Smith, are also a part of this wider group. She leads a busy life, professionally but also socially, taking in the theatre, concerts, ballet and films.

The letters home often convey messages from Hans' Sydney contacts, so much so that her father never seems far away, even though Nora is working in another city and in the portrait genre her father no longer practises. Flower painting they each share, even though Hans has little time for it now. While Nora refers in her letters to advice she receives from her father, only one letter from Hans to his daughter survives from this period. Like many of the London letters, he asks Nora to describe how she is approaching her portrait painting, which she duly does in the following letters.

Home in South Australia is frequently a reference point in Nora's letters and no letters from home signal some form of disapproval. It is the place of retreat at Christmas, the site of the bush that Nora replicates in Sydney with an escape to Kurrajong and from where produce is ever-present and emanates. There is a permeation of social borders between home and away, with guests moving between Sydney and 'The Cedars'.

The effects of Australia's entry into the war become more marked as the letters unfold. Artists enlist, art-related businesses collapse, sales are fewer and then Sydney itself is under threat, as Nora prepares to leave for the country in Canberra, where Evie lives with her husband Henry.

'St Ravenna'
37 Elizabeth Bay Road
Elizabeth Bay, Sydney
Wednesday 15th 1938

Dearest Mother and Daddy,

Well here I am established, or partly established, in a little flat in Elizabeth Bay. Somewhere at last to drop my belongings and set up my easel. It has been a weary trek hunting down a room that was liveable. On the point of desperation we chanced upon this place which, though very small and boxy, has two great compensations: a view overlooking Rushcutters Bay, and a flood of morning sunshine. It's airy too, being high up and has running hot water which is a God send, but gosh the woodwork and doors and windows are ugly.

We moved last night, so all is in chaos. I'm sitting writing on my stretcher bed—the only article of furniture I have purchased so far. From the kitchen issues forth the welcome smell of stew and all round come the subdued noises of other people living. Flat life again—I don't love it, and I sigh for the trees and the bush and the garden. I have no mind for writing. There is no peace and quiet in this city life.

No letter from home. I have called at the bank several times, and back at the hotel at Cremorne Point, but there was nothing. I received those Daddy re-addressed.

Flat hunting here is just as depressing as in London, rents are high. To begin with, there are no studios and well-lighted rooms are as rare as masterpieces, or rather I should say, for the price I want to pay. Then this turned up. Boxall has his quarters only two doors away, and Beaumont is within cooee. McLeay Street runs parallel, so Mr Ure Smith is almost a neighbour. Also Hera Roberts lives down the same street.

I am longing for news from home.

My love to all,

Nora

'St Ravenna'
37 Elizabeth Bay Road
Elizabeth Bay, Sydney
21 June 1938

Dearest Mother and Daddy,

Great excitement, the cases have arrived. Everything in perfect order thanks to Daddy's packing. It was a joy to open up and find all intact, and I am so glad to have the books coming into these four bare walls. I began to regret more and more that I had not stretched a point and brought some books. It was very good of Daddy to pack things for me. I know the time and experience that goes into such a job. Glad also to have the easel, and the table is a God send. We have been living in suitcases, using them as tables, chair and cupboards, everything. My patience and temper were at breaking point, and my spirits down to zero. Now things look a little brighter, and I am beginning to feel a little of my own atmosphere. Until now, the atmosphere has consisted of the smell of stale eucalyptus and gas.

To have carpet on the floor improves matters, and we have just begun to make the place a little more liveable with muslin curtains and few pictures on the walls. What a difference a few pictures make. The red and black striped curtains come in beautifully. I don't think I told you much about the flat, or of what it consisted. There are only two very small rooms, and a tiny kitchenette and very small bathroom.

The room I am going to use as my studio has a little alcove with a large window opening out with a view overlooking rooftops, with Rushcutters Bay beyond. The little glimpse of the peaceful bay with white yachts lying there gives me great joy. If it was not for that glimpse, I could never have reconciled myself to these boxy rooms. And the sunshine is good, it streams in through all the windows and gives a wonderful brightness and hope.

Daddy's letter on Saturday was doubly welcome, I was glad to have all the news of home.

Goodnight to all, my love to everyone,

Nora

'St Ravenna'
37 Elizabeth Bay Road
Elizabeth Bay, Sydney
Sunday 14 July 1938

Dearest Mother and Daddy,

I don't know where the last week has flown—when I'm painting I lose track of all time. All week I have been solidly at work on my still life and today saw it finished at last ... I'll probably send it to the Society of Arts show. The notice you sent on today made me realise that the sending-in day is alarmingly near. Before then I want to do a large portrait and some flower pieces, so it is straight onto the next.

On Monday evening I met Syd Ure Smith and had a chat with him.[1] Cousin Anita invited him and Evie and myself to a sherry and we had a pleasant time. Syd Ure Smith is entertaining with his wonderful stories. It is so good to have a laugh occasionally, and what a gift he has. I'm waiting until I get straight before inviting people here, but next week I hope to do a little entertaining. Fern sold my large flower piece, the news cheered me up immensely, and he asks for more so I'm sending him *The Blue Hyacinth*, as the buyer Wal Taylor found for me seems to have been a myth.[2]

Boxall has asked me in to supper on Sunday evening to meet Dundas and his lady friend and Beaumont and his lady friend. I'm looking forward to a chat.

The letterbox for the past fortnight has remained empty and I begin to feel anxious to know all is well at home.

My love to all,

Nora

'St Ravenna'
37 Elizabeth Bay Road
Elizabeth Bay, Sydney
Wednesday 5 1938

Dearest Mother and Daddy,

I have started on a still life study of the Ming bowl and some fruit and wine and tapestry, a rich study full of beautiful edges and subtle tones. It is just to get my eye in so I can start on some flowers.

---

1   Sydney Ure Smith (1887–1949) was editor of *Art in Australia* and *Home*, and President of the Society of Artists.

2   Wal Taylor ran Grosvenor Galleries, which was located at 219 George Street, Sydney.

It is a full life working and looking after a flat, even though it is so small, and the general muddle of not yet having a place to put things, and not being able to find them. Living has been rather a trial.

It is back to London days, with a line of inevitable wet washing hanging over one's head, with the smell of linseed and turps, and the study that can't be moved. Boxall and Beaumont dropped in to tea on Sunday. Boxall bought a huge pineapple, and was full of talk about people and shows, and what all the artists were doing.

All my love,
Nora

'St Ravenna'
37 Elizabeth Bay Road
Elizabeth Bay, Sydney
Sunday 10 August 1938

Dearest Mother and Daddy,

Lunch at McGregor's was a handsome affair and ah, the wine—some rare old vintage in whose presence one could but talk in whispers and sip in ecstasy. Mr Ure Smith was a guest and Hera Roberts, Mrs Rutherford and a Peter Whitehead. Mostly I enjoyed his collection of pictures and fell in love with a little Lambert flower piece (the one reproduced in the Lambert book). It is a little masterpiece, so reserved and subtle. What a versatile artist was Lambert, I only wish he were still alive to add his zest to paintings. I do envy McGregor that picture.

I have asked the whole party in to a sherry on Friday evening, I don't know where they'll sit, or stand for that matter, but it is the only way in which I can return any hospitality.

My love to all,
Nora

'St Ravenna'
37 Elizabeth Bay Road
Elizabeth Bay, Sydney
Thursday 1938

Dearest Mother and Daddy,

At the moment I am pretty busy getting my pictures ready, as the sending-in day is on next Friday. I have to have them all ready to be called for. I'm sending in seven or eight—the full quota—and am hoping to sell. Madame Schuurman has offered to sit for me this week but I have postponed it until I get back.[3]

The sherry party I held was quite a success and everyone seemed to enjoy themselves. Last night Sydney Ure Smith asked me in to a sherry to meet Adrian Feint and some German people. I didn't get back until nearly midnight so am feeling the effects today.

I am looking forward to seeing Daddy's show over here. I haven't been to see David Jones' Gallery yet.[4]

My love,
Nora

'St Ravenna'
37 Elizabeth Bay Road
Elizabeth Bay, Sydney
5 September 1938

Dearest Mother and Daddy,

Mother's letter has just arrived—I didn't know of the Gallery purchase until Friday afternoon when I went along to the private view and then I only by chance saw the ticket on my flower piece.[5] It was a welcome surprise, and right on top of that, Ure Smith came over and told me that I had been elected a member of the Society of Arts. News that I was a member was especially cheering. The flower piece is the large one I painted over here, mixed flowers, camellias, lupins, jonquils and ageratum and some other flowers, very strong in colour relieved by grey background. On Saturday I sold my little picture of pompom dahlias. So for the moment, I'm off the rocks and feel almost rich.

---

3   Madame Adine Michele Elink Schuurman (1913–1986) was in Sydney with her husband Tom, who was Consul General of the Netherlands. She had married in 1933 and was 25 years of age when she sat for the portrait.

4   Hans Heysen had a successful exhibition at Sydney's David Jones Gallery.

5   The National Art Gallery of New South Wales purchased Nora Heysen's *Spring Flowers* from the 1938 Society of Arts exhibition.

My first impression of the show was good, fewer pictures and well hung. Daddy's two big watercolours have an excellent position and show out from amongst the other work. The green hills is a beauty and looks splendid. There isn't an outstanding panel this year. Gruner has some nice things, beautiful in feeling and tone but lacking, I think, quality and substance. The two Johns are outstanding and R.J. McGregors' Stanley Spencer looks good, the Picasso and the Marie Laurencin leave me cold.

On Sunday McGregor invited me to lunch. S. Ure Smith and Hera and Mrs Nesbitt, and McGregor was a liberal host—he has offered me a large room to do portraits in and the loan of any of his vases. He is very kind.

Tomorrow Madame Schuurman is coming to sit for me, so I'm busy stretching down a big canvas in readiness.

My love to all at home,

Nora

'St Ravenna'
37 Elizabeth Bay Road
Elizabeth Bay, Sydney
11 September 1938

Dearest Mother and Daddy,

I was offered £50 for my still life study *The Ming Bowl* and although I had marked it 'not for sale' I couldn't afford to keep it at that price. I was also offered eight pounds less than the price I wanted for *The Chestnut Tree*, but that I cannot accept, as it is not fair to those that pay the full price, and I don't approve of bargaining with pictures.

My love to all,

Nora

Nora's sister Josephine dies suddenly

'St Ravenna'
37 Elizabeth Bay Road
Elizabeth Bay, Sydney
Monday 1938

Dear Mother and Daddy,

My thoughts are all with you, and I have tried again and again to write but that awful feeling of helplessness to say anything dogs me, and the terrible reality blots everything out. It all seems so wrong, so terribly wrong.

I cannot say anything, but my heart goes out to you and is leaden with thoughts of your suffering. I feel numb and desperate with the reality of it all.

My love and all my thoughts,

Nora

'St Ravenna'
37 Elizabeth Bay Road
Elizabeth Bay, Sydney
Tuesday 1938

Dearest Mother and Daddy,

In my free moments I have been looking for another flat, and today I found one that is more pleasant. It is only a little further down the street in a new block of flats that is still in the making, two fairly large rooms overlooking the harbour, a little balcony leading out from the one I'll use as a studio, for the rest there is a modern kitchen all new and clean with plenty of cupboard space and a refrigerator and a nice little bathroom. It is indeed quite a luxurious place after this little box of a doll's house. This cramped way of living amongst paints and half finished work was 'getting me down'.

We can't move in until some of the workmen move out but, as these places seem to consist of cardboard and bits of wire and go up overnight, I'll be moving by early next week. I have started on John Lane Mullins, and Madame is nearly complete.[6] Also there are few more commissions in the wind and I have enough to keep me busy now, more than enough.

On Sunday McGregor asked me to lunch and the usual people were there and we enjoyed a good lunch and excellent wine. Then one day McGregor came in

---

6   John Lane Mullins (1857–1939) was a prominent patron of the arts; Member of the New South Wales Legislative Assembly from 1917 to 1933; Trustee of the National Art Gallery of New South Wales from 1916 and President from 1938 to 1939; and Secretary and Treasurer of the Society of Artists from 1907 to 1939. His art collection included bookplates by Adrian Feint (1894–1971). See Mark Lyons, 'Mullins, John Lane (1857–1939)', *Australian Dictionary of Biography*, vol.10, Melbourne University Press, 1986: 608–609.

with Lionel Lindsay and Ure Smith to see the sketch of J. Lane Mullins and other work, with the idea of giving me another commission. I have been trying to paint Madame's coat from various models and have been having an exasperating time. My sitter has just arrived so I must get to my paints.

My thought is so often with you these days,

All my love,

Nora

'Westchester'
24/8 Onslow Avenue
Elizabeth Bay, Sydney
15 November 1938

Dearest Mother and Daddy,

Well I have moved at last and am more or less settled into my new home. It is a great relief being out of those cramped little rooms. I feel I can at last breathe again in this comparative luxury and housekeeping becomes almost a pleasure. Everything is brand new and clean. The kitchen is all tiled and the most modern bathroom. The rooms too are a fair size and the view of the harbour a joy forever. I have been very busy trotting to and fro with baskets of belongings, and as well, have been working every day on the portrait of John Lane Mullins. He is very good sitter and gives me every help and encouragement. I have tackled a very large canvas of him and have my work cut out.

My love to all,

Nora

Hahndorf, South Australia
20 November 1938

My Dear Nora,

It seems a very long while ago since last I wrote to you but that does not mean that my thoughts have not been with you very often, wondering how your health was and how you were solving the occasional problems in paint that you had set yourself. Anyway, Mother and I were sincerely relieved to hear you had shifted into your new rooms. And it sounds all very nice indeed. Good health is absolutely essential to a painter's job and you cannot retain it if you have to sleep and live with your canvases, in fact live on the smell of paint. Lead is extremely injurious to both the stomach and lungs, and I know of cases where painters have been permanently affected by its fumes, so it pays to be careful in this subject.

I would like to hear more in your letters of how you are getting on with the two portraits. I am always eager to hear from what angle you are approaching your subject matter. To me, the course of a portrait painter is full of irritations and pitfalls. The vexed question must always arise between painting a straight-out portrait or treating your subject as a colour problem. The painter who can combine the two successfully is rare, and this is where so many portraits come to grief. They fall between two stools. Even Orpen with all his technical abilities rarely put it over completely. It is unwise to mix the issue and I feel that all the great portraits, like those of Holbein, Durer and the Italians, depend on their searching for the character of the subject.

Do you know our Trustees turned the purchase of the Lambert *Lady with Fan* down? I was deeply annoyed at this decision as, after their first meeting, I asked them to reconsider their verdict, and again pointed out why they should buy it.[7] They said they had enough women portraits by him, then why the — did they ask me to report on it when they knew it was a female portrait.

In your letter you suggested coming over for Christmas if you could rake up the funds. Mother and I would love you to come and especially under the present circumstances, as it is difficult for us to reconcile ourselves to Josephine's death. It has been a ghastly strain on Mother … I have a suggestion to make. Come over and paint or draw a portrait of Steve for us—he would make a ripping subject.[8] I feel you would get something worthwhile but there is always something fascinating in a young male developing into manhood. He is just at that stage now. I enclose my £20 now which will cover your fare, as barter for the portrait. Then there is another suggestion in your letter regarding Nurse Bone, she would make a fine painting.[9] She is looking fine, although old. She is still very capable with that wonderfully calm expression. If you could paint her just as she was when we saw her last week, she should make a really fine painting in her working clothes. She loves little Josephine and will find it hard to give her up. It is only a matter of days and Mother will bring her home … I don't know how Mother will manage it, for it is not easy for an older person to adjust themselves to the constant demand.[10] Later on we have someone who can look after Baby for part of the day at least, for I can see she will be a restless infant.

---

7   George Lambert's *Lady with a Fan* was on offer for £244 and was not acquired because the Gallery held the artist's *Dorothea in Fancy Dress*. See Fine Arts Committee Report, 8 November 1938, Public Library, Museum and Art Gallery of South Australia.

8   Steve is Nora's brother, also called Stef and Stefan.

9   Nurse Bone was looking after baby Josephine. Sallie Heysen had a nurse to tend to all of her children and, in this case, grandchildren.

10   Hans and Sally adopted baby Josephine.

It was good to have Lionel Lindsay with us; he stayed only three days and left Adelaide rather sooner than he intended, as his wife was left alone at Wahroonga. The exhibition went off well, sales had reached £550 after the first 4 days, so Lionel was quite delighted.[11]

Now I must close. Mother is writing too. I do sincerely hope you will be with us for Christmas.

We all send you love and hope all is well,

Your Dad

'Westchester'
24/8 Onslow Avenue
Elizabeth Bay, Sydney
Wednesday 1938

Dearest Mother and Daddy,

It was good to have Daddy's letter this morning, the first to arrive at the new address in the brand new letterbox. Now I feel more or less established. Thank you for the cheque, it means home for Christmas and that is good to think about. I was wondering how I would manage it, for I have to make what I hold last until I can have an exhibition, as I do not want to sell work until then. That means a constant flowing out and nothing coming in.

I have spent myself on John Lane and feel more or less flat—the muggy heat of late adds to that condition. The portrait is nearing completion. Successful or not, I am much too wound up in it to know, but am glad that it is so far and that the worst is over. John Lane sits likes a brick and does not spare himself, so both artist and model are exhausted. I have practically been working every day and all day on it.

I had lunch at McGregor's on Sunday, the usual lunch gathering and very enjoyable, and from there went to the Gallery to study Lambert's portraits. *The Lady with the Fan* is hanging there next to his *Self Portrait*.

The portrait of Madame Schuurman still wants the finishing touches. I have been trying to pin the illusive little lady down for the final sittings, but so far with no success. The nursemaid is ill so she has to stay home and mind the children. If it isn't the children it's a social engagement, so I have let her be for the time being until she has run out of excuses. Such are the joys of a portrait.

---

11   Lionel Lindsay's exhibition of watercolours, etching and woodcuts opened on 9 November 1938. Hans had somewhat reluctantly volunteered to open his friend's exhibition but was so averse to public speaking that he had to turn his back to the audience and read his speech facing the wall. See Colin Thiele, *Heysen of Hahndorf*, Adelaide, Hyde Park Press, 2001: 247.

The portrait of Madame I'm treating purely as a decoration and a colour scheme, the portrait of John Lane I'm trying for character and tone with subdued colours and a background of books. Every portrait is a different problem.

My love to all,

Nora

'Westchester'
24/8 Onslow Avenue
Elizabeth Bay, Sydney
7 December 1938

Dearest Mother and Daddy,

The completion of the John Lane portrait has taken me much longer than I thought, in fact I am still on it. The treatment of the books in the background has been my difficulty. The actual portrait is finished and I am satisfied it is the best head I have painted. I could not have found a more sympathetic and patient sitter than in John Lane. Madame also remains unfinished. She has had various troubles at home. It is a long business this portrait painting and can't be hurried.

Last night a few people came in—a little house warming party to which I invited Shirley Jones to meet some people. John Lane and he clicked, and he seemed to enjoy meeting Howard Hinton and Will Ashton, in fact he was the colour note of the party in his canary yellow suit and red tie. Everyone wanted to be introduced to him and he thoroughly enjoyed his prominence. The kind old man arrived with a bunch of roses and a cerise jerkin he had bought in Paris and thought would come in useful in my colour schemes.

I am afraid it will be next door to Christmas before I can get away. I have first to see both portraits finished and framed and sent in for the Archibald competition, and I have also a small still life group mapped out to do, so have been up to my neck. John Lane and family all seemed very pleased with the portrait, and pronounce it a very good likeness.

Sydney is all-agog with ballet and everyone is talking about it and comparing ballerinas. With a small portion of Daddy's cheque I booked a seat one night and went and thoroughly enjoyed it. Shirley Jones invited me to dine

first at the Australia so I went well primed up.[12] The principal ballerina of this
company is Baronova. She is truly lovely, not a Pavlova but she has charm.[13]

My love to all,
Nora

'Westchester'
24/8 Onslow Avenue
Elizabeth Bay, Sydney
Thursday December 1938

Dearest Mother and Daddy,

Just say that I have booked for Monday, and will be with you on
Wednesday, 21st of December.

At the last moment, I decided to entirely repaint the background of books
to the John Lane portrait, as I thought it interfered with the head. A nasty job,
but it has been accomplished at last, and is I think a very great improvement.
McGregor loaned me the books and helped me out.

I had a last sitting on Madame this morning, and are now going in to see
Will Ashton about filling in forms and so on. Must post on the way for this to reach
you in time.

Love to all,
Nora

Nora wins the Archibald Prize

'Westchester'
24/8 Onslow Avenue
Elizabeth Bay, Sydney
Sunday January 1939

Dearest Mother and Daddy,

It was good to have your telegram yesterday morning, the first to arrive.
After two days of rather bewildering notoriety and excitement, today the reaction
has settled in and I'm glad to spend a quiet day in my studio.[14] I have been
beset with reporters and photographers, and their battery of cross-questioning.

---

12   The Hotel Australia extension was completed in a stylish Art Deco style by Emil Sodersteen, Robertson and
      Marks Architects and was featured in *Art in Australia* on 15 February 1936: 75–77.

13   Irina Baronova was in the second Australian tour of the Ballets Russes.

14   Nora Heysen had won the 1938 Archibald Prize. The exhibition ran from 21 January to 20 February 1939.

Now I have a vague idea of the life of a movie star. Thank goodness that it lasts for a brief day, and what is news one day is forgotten the next, and I can settle back and paint in comfortable obscurity. I did not know that the Archibald was to be judged on Friday, just as well, as I'd have been on tenterhooks. I was out swimming in Rushcutters Bay, and got back in the evening to frantic telephone calls and photographers waiting on the doorstep. I was dumb with amazement and excitement. McGregor came to the rescue with his car and chauffeur and rushed me off to the Gallery, and then I walked in to a veritable hornet's nest of reporters, and the whole board of trustees and judges waiting to congratulate me.

The biggest surprise of all was the portrait of Madame Schuurman winning it, and not John Lane. I hadn't in my wildest dreams entertained the thought of her doing it. Poor old John Lane was terribly disappointed. He is in bed with the after-effects of a heart attack. I went to see him yesterday, and it was quite sad to see him trying to cover up his disappointment. I feel that I have let him down.

Of course, Madame is elated. She came in radiant and all the trial of model and artist were forgotten. On the auspicious Friday night, cousin Paul and Alphonso came in and we celebrated with a few drinks all round. I can't yet grasp the fact that I've won the thing, and yesterday when I went in to see the collection I thought I was very lucky to carry it off.

My portrait of Mr McCormack is well on the way I have had two or three sittings and he is a good sitter, very vitally alive and fresh looking. He should make a good clean direct portrait.

You'll laugh at the attack of Meldrum's.[15] The reporters all want to urge me into battle defending women's rights, but I have no wish to be drawn into it especially as it becomes personal. Here is Meldrum's article.

Love to you all,

Nora

---

15   Max Meldrum (1875–1955), a fellow entrant, went so far as to declare: '[If] I were a woman I would prefer raising a healthy family to a career in art. They are more attached to the physical things in life'. See 'Domestic Ties Downfall of Women Art Careerists', *Brisbane Mail*, 23 January 1939.

'Westchester'
24/8 Onslow Avenue
Elizabeth Bay, Sydney
Monday 29 January 1939

Dearest Mother and Daddy,

All is once more normal and the feeling of momentary success has been thoroughly swamped by the difficulties and problems of another portrait. I don't know how a portrait painter can ever hope to buoy himself up with conceit. The very fact of being confronted with a person whom one has to portray on canvas, their character their atmosphere, with all the subtleties of flesh painting of God knows what else, is enough to humble one to the dust. My sitter is sun bathing at Palm Beach today so I'm having a holiday.

I have just come back from the Gallery, so while my mind is fresh with impressions will write a bit about the entries for the Archibald and Wynn prizes. There were record entries for the Archibald this year, and so far there have been record attendances to view the show. Today you could hardly move, there were so many people, I didn't realise that the show created so much interest. Will Ashton has done a lot towards awaking it, and everywhere there are notices posted up and instructions where to go.

My first impression was of surprise at the number of good portraits and sound work, but on a closer examination today, I was very disappointed. There seems a general lack of ideas and originality. For the most part, the portraits are dull. The same old drab colour skies and lifeless spouses and muddy flesh painting. Nothing outstanding. Meldrum, I think, had the best exhibit and I liked his *Self Portrait with a Model* and it nearly arrived at something, but lacked quality of paint and subtlety. The McInnes' were poor and not up to standard, and there was no Longstaff, a lucky year for me, and as well, it is a good lesson to see one's work amongst others. I have learnt a great deal. How a Lambert would have shone out amongst that group. There have been no more criticisms of the picture, only Wilkinson's cursory comments which I sent you in *The Herald*.

Goodness knows why the Wynne Prize was given to Syd Long. I can't see any merit in his landscape. It looks just like a clever poster and has no particular design or beauty of paint, just an effect. Daddy's watercolour of the gum in morning light looked fine and was well hung, it shone out from amongst the others. The Gruner had a very good landscape, very poetic and serene in feeling, a blue river winding out through gently undulating country.

Daddy's letter was very welcome and I appreciated his 'well done' with advice against getting a swollen head. Not much fear of that. Many thanks for posting on the telegrams. I have been inundated with them. Now comes the answering of them. Not so good.

My love to all and the baby,
Nora

> 'Westchester'
> 24/8 Onslow Avenue
> Elizabeth Bay, Sydney
> 26 February 1939

Dearest Mother and Daddy,

Many happy returns for Mother on the 1st. After a brief respite I have begun on another portrait, and am up to my neck in it again. This time my victim is Mrs Ernest Watt. I'm doing a full-length portrait of her in a white evening frock. She should make a very feminine and charming portrait if I can manage it, but at this stage, confronted by an enormous white canvas, I feel as if my idea of the finished creation is a very long way off. I want to have it finished for the Academy show in Melbourne, so you can imagine I'm working full out.

Lionel Lindsay and McGregor dropped in one day to see the portrait of McCormack, and both thought it a better head than when I sent into the Archibald, that is encouraging. Also there is another commission in the wind which means a trip to Brisbane, but so far nothing definite. I had thought to hold my show in June, but now might postpone it to the Spring, as I'm afraid that by taking commissions I will not leave myself enough time.

You will be sad to know that John Lane died on Friday. It gave me a shock to hear the news, as a short while ago when I was down to see him, there was every prospect he was well and would be up and about in a few days. I must on with work as my sitter has just arrived.

With birthday greetings and my love,
Nora

'Westchester'
24/8 Onslow Avenue
Elizabeth Bay, Sydney
Sunday 1939

Dearest Mother and Daddy,

Life for one this last week has been a hectic rush, what with painting against time, and people continually blowing in to see my sitter and the portrait in progress. I don't know which way to turn. The portrait progresses slowly. Constant interruptions are no good for work, and still to keep my sitter interested. I have to make concessions and learn to put up with it, though how I curse when I'm in the middle of a ticklish piece of modelling to be interrupted. Such are the troubles of a portrait painter. Every day they seem to mount up until I wonder why I chose this walk of life.

On Wednesday I was hauled into a luncheon given by the South Australian Women's Association at Farmers'.[16] Lillie Wallace over here is responsible. How I bless her, she has pestered me till I had to go. Last luncheon I conveniently forgot the date and didn't turn up, so this time to make up for my rudeness gave in and went. A most boring ceremony and the eats, a slice of cold meat and a lettuce leaf did nothing to atone for a wasted three hours. I was supposed to be guest of honour.

This Archibald Prize has brought not only blessings on my shoulders, but by some trick it seems to have made me a few enemies. There are still irate and seething letters in the papers against my portrait and the judges' decision, the papers rang to know what I think of it. I have nothing to say, so probably they will grow tired of it.[17]

This week the portrait has to be in, so until that is over, I will not be able to breathe.

My love to all,
Nora

---

16 Farmers (now Myers) was fashionable Sydney department store in Market Street. It housed Blaxland Gallery and also had a cafeteria and a restaurant.

17 Reports, such as 'Artist-father Helped. Archibald Prize Won by Woman', *The Sydney Morning Herald*, 21 January 1939, linked Nora's win to her father. Some artists were convinced that influential Heysen family friends had been involved in the judging and that it was decided on 'some other basis', and called for an enquiry. See 'Archibald Prize: Enquiry Urged', *The Argus*, 11 March 1939; 'Knockabout', *Daily News*, 13 March 1939 and 'Letter to the Editor', *The Sydney Morning Herald*, 14 March 1939.

Nora Heysen (1911–2003)
Poppies 1938

oil on canvas; 54.0 x 44.0 cm
Private collection
Photograph by Michael Kluvanek

Nora Heysen (1911–2003)
Madame Elink Schuurman 1938

oil on canvas; 87.0 x 68.0 cm
Private collection

right
Nora Heysen (1911–2003)
Motherhood 1941

oil on canvas; 76.3 x 64.5 cm
Martha K. Pinkerton Bequest Fund 1942
City of Ballarat Fine Art Gallery

Nora Heysen (1911–2003)
Adrian Feint 1940

oil on plywood; 88.0 x 66.0 cm
Pictures Collection, nla.pic-an7021886
National Library of Australia

Nora Heysen (1911–2003)
White Cacti c.1941

oil on panel; 39.7 x 29.2 cm
Elder Bequest Fund 1941
Art Gallery of South Australia

'Westchester'
24/8 Onslow Avenue
Elizabeth Bay, Sydney
4 April 1939

Dearest Mother and Daddy,

Mother's letter was very welcome bringing good tidings all round.
McGregor left on Friday, and while he is away he has loaned me his Lambert flower
piece and the John drawing of Lamb. It is a treat to have them to study.
The Lambert has always been a favourite of mine and the John is fine. These
should inspire me to do some good work. There's no end to McGregor's kindness.

Mary Edwards is enemy No. 1 over here and it is she who heads the
meetings.[18] I have nothing against her and was surprised the other day to get a
letter from her saying that she noticed that I avoided her in the street and that she
wished me to understand that her attack was not personal, but that she felt that
all the artists in Sydney had been wronged by my gaining the prize and although it
hurt her to distress me, she felt it her duty and so on. The woman's mad. She must
have had a guilty conscience, for I didn't even see her. I have only one wish to steer
clear of all these petty jealousies and bickering amongst the artists.

This must go if I am to get my good wishes for Easter there in time.

My love to all,

Nora

'Westchester'
24/8 Onslow Avenue
Elizabeth Bay, Sydney
20 April 1939

Dearest Mother and Daddy,

It's the first touch of winter today, terribly cold. This is going to be a cold
flat in the winter, too many windows and cracks, and no adequate heating.

Did I tell you Mr Johnson bought a small white rose study of mine just
recently and presented it to the Australian Club? Very handsome of him, as the
picture is to have pride of place in the new Annexe that has just been completed.[19]
Also Ernest Watt bought the white roses that I painted 10 years ago, and brought

18   Soon after the announcement of the winner of the Archibald Prize, Mary Edwards wrote to Nora Heysen
     suggesting she didn't deserve the award and should return the prize money. Nora Heysen, interviewed by the
     author, 15 September 1989.

19   See 'Hospitality for Women Guests. Australian Club Annexe', *The Sydney Morning Herald*, 12 April 1939.

over Mrs Watt; she fell for it and received it as a present from him because she was so good in sitting.

Sydney is to have a new movie theatre that is to show only Continental films. It opens on Friday.

I have a commission to paint Mrs McCormack, not an easy subject, as she is self-conscious and doesn't look a bit like herself when she sits. On Thursday she sat all day and I tried to draw her out without success.

My love to all and the baby,

Nora

'Westchester'
24/8 Onslow Avenue
Elizabeth Bay, Sydney
2 May 1939

Dearest Mother and Daddy,

Mother's letter breathes of a lovely Autumn. I can close my eyes and imagine it all, the misty mornings and beautiful Autumn days and all the fruits and flowers. Here in the city, one scarcely notices the changing of the seasons. Only now are there mists over the harbour, and the air is sharper in the evenings.

Gruner called in to see me on Monday. It was nice of him to come and I enjoyed a chat with him. Also he was very helpful with a criticism of my work and was altogether most charming. Also Brackenreg brought Dobell in to see me one evening. Dobell was a scholarship winner and has just returned after having been away for seven years, but I'm afraid not to stay, as he speaks of getting back as soon as he can to make some money. He's been very bitten with the French school and his work is very influenced by Renoir. No one in Australia is any good, not even Lambert. I nearly came to blows with the young man.[20]

Mr Johnston has been sending in the most magnificent roses to paint. It is embarrassing and bewildering, however I have painted three studies of them and on Tuesday night invited he and his wife to tea. He came with another armful so I'm painting again. No peace for the wicked. The Autumn roses are so lovely I can't resist them, yet I feel I should be drawing and painting portraits.

Sydney Ure Smith came in the other evening and gave me the good news that I have sold my flower piece in the Academy show.[21] As the sales for the entire show amounted to £150's worth, I think I was jolly lucky and on the strength of it

---

20   In fact, William Dobell was born in 1899 and was 12 years older than Nora.
21   This was the second Australian Academy of Art exhibition.

shouted myself to a Greek play, and have had some dark blinds put in my studio. They pull up from the bottom so block out low light, which helps tremendously.

I enclose a cheque for £112 which goes a little way towards paying off my debts. My love to all,

Nora

PS Have received my Archibald cheque £422, so feel almost wealthy.

'Westchester'
24/8 Onslow Avenue
Elizabeth Bay, Sydney
Tuesday 1939

Dearest Mother and Daddy,

Last night Sydney Ure Smith invited me in to meet Larry Adler and his wife.[22] Max Dupain was also there with a portfolio of his photographs under one arm. I was interested to see his work, some good things amongst them but most rather too abstract. Photography seems to me is out of its depth when it tackles the abstract. Larry Adler and his vivacious young wife were the life of the party. Both have travelled the world with a wide-awake intelligence, so are interesting to talk to.

All my spare time these days seems to be given over to answering letters, they keep flooding in. Invitations, congratulations and letters of kindly advice. Some are awfully funny, and as for the people who sat next to me at school, they are mounting up daily.

My love to all,

Nora

'Westchester'
24/8 Onslow Avenue
Elizabeth Bay, Sydney
18 May 1939

Dearest Mother and Daddy,

I've been busy still painting roses. Festivities have been few and the last two weeks have been quiet. One evening Mr Johnston invited me to dine at the Australian Club and see a show afterwards ... I was glad to see my *White Roses*

---

22   Larry Adler, the American harmonica player, performed in his first Australian concert with the Sydney Symphony Orchestra in 1939.

in the new Women's Annexe—it looked really well, as if the room had been made for it, and it is the only picture in the room. Johnston is tremendously proud of presenting it. He is terribly keen at the moment to patronise artists and I think it is a jolly good idea.

The mornings have been glorious, fresh and dewy—at nine every day I take my bathers and towel and walk down to Rushcutters Bay baths and swim. The water is cold and exhilarating and the exercise is splendid.

My own show is booked for October, and the Society of Arts is in July and I want good things for them both. Also Brackenreg is holding a show of drawings in November, he's very keen on arousing all the artists to draw, and is encouraging them for all he is worth. About time, I think.

Last Friday I was guest of honour at a Lyceum Club luncheon.

My love to all,

Nora

'Westchester'
24/8 Onslow Avenue
Elizabeth Bay, Sydney
Monday 13 June 1939

Dearest Mother and Daddy,

Sorry you didn't like my portrait of Madame Schuurman. I'm interested to know how the Academy show looked in the Adelaide Gallery and if the sales were any better.

The Society of Arts show gives promise of being a good one this year. Murch has sent out some good things, a nude and several landscapes, he is arriving in a few weeks time. Also Dobell is showing some very interesting work. Did I tell you that the Gallery had brought a little interior of his—a very beautiful little thing with all the qualities of a Vermeer, also I saw a nude of his the other day which I thought the best nude I've seen painted in Australia.[23] Dobell is coming to live in the Cross so we'll soon be a little class up here.

One evening I went along to the Julian Ashton School; I heard Norman Lindsay give a lecture to the students—my first introduction to Norman Lindsay and I hope not the last. He'd make a most interesting painting.

My love and hope that things are brighter,

Nora

---

23   The National Art Gallery of New South Wales purchased *Boy at the Basin* in 1939.

'Westchester'
24/8 Onslow Avenue
Elizabeth Bay, Sydney
24 July 1939

Dearest Mother and Daddy,

I have just straightened out my mind and my flat after a week's frantic painting ... I have just worked painting—painting morning, noon and night with no thoughts left for anything else. To begin with I painted a few camellias, the creamy white ones with few pink stripes. I summed up enough courage to go and demand them from the Botanical Gardens. I chose a very simple scheme, just four or five flowers surrounded by their decorative leaves against a pale grey background, and pale yellow foreground, all very silvery and austere. It is a success I think.

Sending in for the Society of Arts is this Friday, so I have a busy week ahead, finishing, varnishing and framing all these details seem to take time and as well I have a drawing to finish and my model has gone and got the flu so I don't know what I'm going to do. Draw her in bed I suppose.

I was very interested to hear all about Mrs Hayward's grand new home, it must be rather lovely—Mrs du Boulay was telling me a bit about it.[24] She is from King's Cross and runs a furnishing shop and helped Mrs Hayward with colour schemes. She has good taste and probably a number of the schemes are hers. But what a foolish mistake not to have a picture gallery—with all that money and all those rooms. I can't understand it.

What did you think of the new *Australia*.[25] I thought the reproduction of Daddy's gum excellent. Everyone is saying how much they like it and whenever I see the magazine advertised, it is open at that page. I do hope Daddy is able to get away on a sketching trip.

My love to all,

Nora

---

24 Merle du Boulay was an interior designer of the more 'fussy' style; she assisted with the interior design of Carrick Hill, in Springfield, South Australia. After the war, she had a shop in Sydney in Castlereagh Street. See Margaret Lord, *A Decorator's World: Living with Art and International Design*, Sydney, Ure Smith, 1969: 99.

25 *Australia, National Journal* was the new Sydney Ure Smith venture. It ran from 1939 to 1947 and had financial backing from James McGregor, Charles Lloyd Jones and Mrs James Burns. Hans Heysen was also approached. Fairfax Press had taken over the ailing Ure Smith publications, *Art in Australia* and *Home*, in 1934. Ure Smith stayed on and thought the two magazines would survive. Four years later, he was forced to resign. See Nancy Underhill, *Making Australian Art, 1916–49: Sydney Ure Smith Patron and Publisher*, South Melbourne, Oxford University Press, 1991: 164–167, 260–261.

'Westchester'
24/8 Onslow Avenue
Elizabeth Bay, Sydney
14 August 1939

Dearest Mother and Daddy,

The Society of Arts show opened on Friday I went along to hear the Governor's speech and see the doings. There was a tremendous crowd, the usual social gathering with a few stray artists looking incongruous amongst the furs and feathers ... No one is buying pictures. It's a rotten outlook for artists, so far 16 have been sold, all lowly priced things, bringing the total to only £500.

The Dobell nude is, in my opinion, the best thing in the show of the Australian work. It's a fine piece of painting with great feeling of weight and flesh, and the colour is rich and full, and the whole thing has a most interesting paint quality. Dobell's work stands out this year, and he deserves the praise he is getting from all sides. The paper criticisms have been particularly poor and not worth sending. Howard Ashton had his usual grouch and flayed the lot. His is a one-eyed narrow-eyed dyspeptic, and wouldn't even give Dobell his due.

Over the weekend I painted some roses, very old-fashioned pink ones, and tomorrow am starting on a Spring bunch. The time is passing at an alarming rate and when I think of my show only eight weeks ahead my knees tremble and I can't help worrying. What a curse exhibitions are. I loathe being tied down to a date.

Mrs Malcolm Reid rang the other day and asked if she could see my work, as she wanted to buy a flower piece. She bought along a sister and friend and I fed them on cream cakes and coffee and I believe sold a mixed bunch. She is to come and have another look tomorrow morning and finally decide.

My love to all,

Nora

'Westchester'
24/8 Onslow Avenue
Elizabeth Bay, Sydney
25 August 1939

Dearest Mother and Daddy,

Mother's letter yesterday relieved my anxiety over lack of news—knowing that Freya's time was drawing near[26] ... What is the use of bringing children into this world at the moment I can't think. The last news of Germany's pact with

---

26   Freya is one of Nora's sisters.

Russia came like a bombshell, and now it seems that only a miracle can save the world from another 1914. I find it all too disturbing—somehow even over here, with all this glorious sunshine, one can't remain impervious to the shifting of world powers and the terrific anxiety and strain that has gripped England and Europe. One thinks war an impossibility—and yet?

Everyone over here is depressed. Brackenreg came down on Monday looking very gloomy and despondent. It has just dawned on him that artists are in for some lean years and that prospects are desperate. On the last night of the Society of Arts show Syd Ure Smith had arranged for a beer and cheese party to be held up in the rooms, and members and exhibitors were going to invite their friends and everything promised to be rather jolly, and it all fell through. No money—the sales this year were so poor that the artists were even chary of parting up with 2/6 a piece.

My love to all,
Nora

'Westchester'
24/8 Onslow Avenue
Elizabeth Bay, Sydney
Monday 11 September 1939

Dearest Mother and Daddy,

I have put off writing ... I think it is useless holding a show, and have postponed it until later in the year, and even then it is doubtful. In the meantime I have undertaken two commissions. Mrs Nesbitt I'd agreed to paint as soon as she'd returned from abroad, and now she is back and wants to begin sittings, then there's the Johnston's young daughter, so I'm tied down to working here for a bit. On the other hand I feel too unsettled to do anything and painting seems impossible, it seems equally impossible not to work. A few days of idleness away from my painting and I feel I have lost my identity, and life for me becomes futile.

When I heard the declaration of war my first thought was for Mike, with every fresh assurance that men will not be sent from here I feel intensely relieved. Stef seems better fitted for the battles of this world.[27] One can only hope and pray that this terrible madness will stop before we are too far in to withdraw. Every morning I awake to realise it afresh.

McGregor arrived back on Monday last and I lunched with him on Sunday—the usual party was there, Mrs Nesbitt, Hera, Syd Ure Smith, Adrian

27 Australia entered the Second World War on 3 September 1939. Mike and Stef are Nora's brothers.

and the Churches, and McGregor, poor man, looks worn out and hasn't had a moment's rest. He's already been to Canberra and Melbourne twice, and was that same evening off again to Melbourne. His views on art and the situation abroad were of course intensely interesting, and he bought back some new pictures, some lovely books and a cellar of wine. How good that wine tasted. It was hard to realise that even as one drank, the valley where it came from was being smashed with war. You'll probably hear from McGregor. In the meantime, he wanted to be remembered and inquired after all and everyone.

Daddy's letter last week was truly welcome and I read the criticism of the Impressionists with interest and anticipation.[28] I'm impatient to see the Van Gogh and the Matisse. It still seems doubtful whether or not Sydney is to have the pleasure of seeing it. Negotiations have all been pushed to the background, and art these days is the last thing anyone thinks of. Thank you for the catalogue and the cuttings. I passed them onto Brackenreg and he's even more eager than I to see work that will be so new to him. He bought down *the* print to show me before he sent it and I thought it excellent, the best print of a watercolour I have ever seen. Brackenreg was so excited about it that he even thought of flying it over himself to be able to talk it over with you and get any suggestions.[29]

I want this to catch today's mail, so my love to all,

Nora

'Westchester'
24/8 Onslow Avenue
Elizabeth Bay, Sydney
1 October 1939

Dearest Mother and Daddy,

I find it difficult to realise that suddenly I have become an aunt four times over and in the same breath realise I'm almost 30.[30] The weeks fly by and I feel desperate when I think of holding a show and completing the work. As things stand I'll hold it sometime in November, the later the better, that is of course if the situation abroad allows it. From what I can see things are going to get a great deal worse before they can improve and Goodness only knows what is going to happen or what remains after this earthquake. What strange bewildering times we live in.

---

28   *The Herald's Exhibition of French and British Contemporary Art* was on show at the National Gallery of South Australia from 21 August to 17 September 1939.

29   John Brackenreg ran the fine art publishing company, Legend Press, and made prints of Hans Heysen's watercolours and paintings.

30   Nora's siblings by now have young children.

I have given up trying to follow events in the newspapers and have at last settled more or less down to work again. I have just finished some white azaleas in a pewter pot and some fruit, and tomorrow I start the portrait of Mrs Nesbitt. In the evenings Brackenreg and I have been sharing a model and are drawing again.

Brackenreg, Dobell and I called one night on Fleischmann, the Hungarian artist. He has a colossal studio down McLeay St—a private ballroom in one of the old homes. Around the entire length of the walls he has photographs of his work most artistically taken and his work is good. You saw some of his photographs of Balinese women in the last *Australia*. He has thousands of them and is completely under the spell of their charm and beauty.

I have just come back from a Sunday lunch at McGregor's and feel mellow with good wine and food. It was McGregor's birthday and the usual party was there and we all ate a lot, drank a lot and talked a lot and now I only feel fit to sleep. McGregor looked rather worn and tired, but is ever the grand host. He sent me home with an armful of tapestry, very lovely pieces which will come in handy for still lifes.

I'm to begin on Mrs Nesbitt on Wednesday. It's going to be a difficult job and I'm worried even before I begin, especially as McGregor wants a tapestry background (the material of the dining room curtains at home) which is going to be the very devil to put behind a head, however here goes. I suppose one problem is as difficult as another in painting, but I fear I'm courting trouble but McGregor is set on it.

Is there any hope of Daddy getting away to do some work? Really there's nothing like painting; the only thing worth living for I think.

Brackenreg has generously presented me with a print of Daddy's red gums, it looks fine on my cream walls. He's certainly done a good job, the best reproduction of a watercolour I've ever seen.

My love to all,
Nora

'Westchester'
24/8 Onslow Avenue
Elizabeth Bay, Sydney
28 October 1939

Dearest Mother and Daddy,

In the rush of the last few weeks no thoughts or thanks have reached paper, and now I realise suddenly it is a fortnight since I last wrote. Trying to make a successful portrait of Mrs Nesbitt has absorbed and worried me, it is a difficult job, well nigh an impossible one. I have made several pencil drawings, and have started on a large canvas, but can't feel very sanguine as to the finished result. I'm painting her in black against a tapestry background—the flesh is interesting, but there is so little to get hold of and I'm in a perpetual state of despair.

I lunched at McGregor's on Sunday and enjoyed his lavish hospitality. All the Sydney people seem tired and worried these days. Everyone has aged. Will Ashton whom I saw at the Gallery the other day looks five years older, I was quite shocked at the difference. He seems to have taken the worries of the artists on his shoulders and I believe is fretting too that he can't get on with his own work. He enquired after you and sends his regards. McGregor looks worn out and Syd Ure Smith's ill with overwork and worry. As he says, what will happen to the artists? It is indeed a poor outlook. I'm still waiting to see how things will go before definitely deciding to hold a show.

Mrs McCormack told me the other day her mother, Lady McCormack, is very anxious to have a watercolour of Daddy's and the price is immaterial.

My love to all,

Nora

'Westchester'
24/8 Onslow Avenue
Elizabeth Bay, Sydney
24 November 1939

Dearest Mother and Daddy,

I have definitely decided not to hold a show this year, instead I am sending in 6 to 8 flower pieces to Taylor and am hopeful about him being able to sell two or three. Adrian Feint opened his show at the Grosvenor Galleries yesterday, and I went along to pay my respects and help swell the little gathering. It was quite a good show and I liked some of his flower pieces for their decorative quality and nice sense of taste and colour. Adrian was feeling very bucked as he'd sold nine things which I thought was excellent. Old Howard Hinton bought two for the Teacher's College. I met him there and had a long chat. He particularly wants to be remembered to all at home. If only there were a few more Howard Hintons in this world, it would be a pleasanter place for the artists. Ure Smith opened the show and gave a very laudatory little speech.

I also saw the French Impressionists show which is being held at David Jones.[31] I missed Renoir and Monet and Degas, but on the whole there were better examples of Van Gogh, Gauguin and Utrillo and Matisse than I had expected. It will take another visit to sort things out, but on a first impression I liked the Van Gogh portrait, the Gauguin still life, and the grey street scene of Utrillo, also the little Christopher Wood, although I thought the English section disappointing, especially the Johns. The show has been getting a great deal of publicity over here with every day several columns in the paper and talks over the air. Syd Ure Smith gave an excellent talk last week which came over splendidly, and Margaret Preston speaks this week. The show will probably have a big influence on painters over here, and I can already visualise the next Society of Artists show.

Dobell and Brackenreg combined last week and threw a party which was rather fun—both their flats adjoin, and both have a rather fascinating balcony looking down onto the plane trees and Kings Cross. Dobell's an interesting character, I only hope society doesn't spoil him. At present people are falling over themselves to meet him, and I believe he doesn't find much time for his work. It's impossible to combine the two I think. If the people over here satisfied their insatiable curiosity, one wouldn't be allowed to work at all.

My love to all,

Nora

'Westchester'
24/8 Onslow Avenue
Elizabeth Bay, Sydney
1939

Dearest Mother and Daddy,

I'm trying to get the portrait of Mrs Nesbitt finished so as to be able to come home before Christmas, unfortunately there have been a lot of interruptions. McGregor saw it and didn't like the background and eyes and mouth and so on. One wants a great deal of patience besides the hundred and one other gifts to succeed at this game. At the moment I vow I'll never take another commission, or if I do I'll see that I make a few clauses before I begin.

It will be good to get home and quietly paint some flowers. I'm longing to try the pink roses again and hope our rose bush has some buds ready.

---

31   *The Herald's Exhibition of French and British Contemporary Art Show* had reached Sydney and was on show at David Jones Art Gallery from 20 November to 16 December 1939.

Last week I had dinner one night at the Buckles. They had quite a large gathering, Max Dupain and his wife, Wal Taylor, Brackenreg, and Mr Buckle's brother. I've had two or three visits to the big exhibition and have enjoyed a number of pictures, the Tonks and the Utrillo grey street scene with Wilson Steer landscapes, the little Christopher Wood are the ones that interest me most.

My love to all,

Nora

'Westchester'
24/8 Onslow Avenue
Elizabeth Bay, Sydney
14 March 1940

Dearest Mother and Daddy,

I have been hard at it and have finished two more still life studies, one by night light and one by day, both of vegetables—tomatoes and onions and egg fruit; also have done another pencil head of Adrian Feint which I think is the best up to date. Adrian has a fine head to draw. When I first met him he was just handsome, but now he has character and something to it, well worth trying to portray. I've enjoyed doing him and he's quiet and good company, a rare nature amongst the others.

McGregor has found me another commission to draw, a young woman over from Melbourne. I'm to meet the lady over at luncheon at McGregor's on Sunday and start work on her on Monday.

Sending-in day for the Academy is coming all too near. I'm sending in the portrait of Mrs Nesbitt and flower piece. I have only planned out another portrait and won't have it finished. The weather has been too hot and unpleasant to ask anyone to sit for any length of time. I don't like the sound of the selection committee: Margaret Preston, Thea Proctor, Douglas Dundas and Lloyd Rees. It seems ridiculous to have two women on the same committee. Is Daddy sending over?

My love to all,

Nora

'Westchester'
24/8 Onslow Avenue
Elizabeth Bay, Sydney
Wednesday 1940

Dearest Mother and Daddy,

Mother's airmail on Monday was very welcome … Today I started painting again just a small study of purple grapes and peaches to get my hand in for a portrait. The Mullins have commissioned me to do a nephew of theirs, and I also have a drawing to do of an old lady, also another of Adrian and after these I'll feel ready to tackle McGregor. I have only been drawing lately, the weather has been too unpleasant for consistent work.

The ballet is flourishing in spite of the heat and the prices are higher than ever … The Tatlock Miller collection of ballet drawings is showing at David Jones.[32] I heard today that the Australian artist amongst them, Sainthill, has sold almost his whole exhibit of over 60 works.[33] It is amazing I think in these times. Of course the prices were low, ranging from 10 to 15 guineas, but even then it's wonderful. The exhibition was very well arranged and interesting. Sainthill's work was outstanding, original in colour scheme and very decorative, he'd captured something of the spirit of ballet.

On Saturday night Madame Schuurman invited me to a dinner party. It was a huge affair with 50 to 60 guests. Mr and Mrs Menzies were there and the big wigs of society. McGregor and Mrs Nesbitt, Norman Lindsay, Dobell and the Medworths, Murch and the Lloyd Jones, others I didn't know. Madame has at length decided not to buy the portrait so that is that.

This must go tonight. My love to all,

Nora

PS If you could send along my smock, the one I left, I would be glad as I haven't one here.

---

32   This British Council exhibition opened in February 1940. The show of 500 works around the subject of the theatre and dance was assembled in response to the interest in the Ballets Russes. Exhibitors included Jacob Epstein, Laura Knight, Duncan Grant, Augustus John and Edgar Degas. See Steven Miller and Eileen Chanin, *Degenerates and Perverts: The 1939 Herald Exhibition of French and British Contemporary Art*, Melbourne, Miegunyah Press, 2005: 68.

33   Tasmanian-born artist Loudon Sainthill (1918–1969) was inspired by the Ballets Russes tours of 1936–1937 and 1938–1939. Sainthill's work was so successful that he returned to London with the ballet company in May 1939, along with his partner Harry Tatlock Miller. Then, with Rex Nan Kivell's help, Sainthill exhibited at London's Redfern Gallery the work he completed during the return voyage. See Sallie O'Neill, 'Sainthill Loudon (1918–69)', *Australian Dictionary of Biography*, vol.16, Melbourne University Press, 2002: 166.

'Westchester'
24/8 Onslow Avenue
Elizabeth Bay, Sydney
Tuesday 1940

Dearest Mother and Daddy,

Mother's letter was welcome on Monday. I went in on Saturday to hear Menzies open the Academy show.[34] He made a wonderful speech and crowds were there to appreciate it—the usual gathering of society and a sprinkling of artists. I had tea with the Buckles and met Margaret Preston, and also hosts of people I know. I couldn't see much of the pictures, but am going again tomorrow, so will report later. Criticisms here have been scathing in the paper. Howard Ashton, as usual, dispensed of it as mediocre and gave a vindictive and biased report which has roused the artists almost as a body against him. I saw in last night's paper Ure Smith replied to it in no uncertain terms. Except for these damning criticisms, the Academy has had no advertising whatsoever.

As far as I could see for people it didn't seem a bad show, up to standard, I thought, with a few good things, two Dobells, and an excellent still life by Joshua Smith, good Margaret Prestons, some interesting Eric Wilsons, two Murches, and a good head in sculpture of his. Of course, I always think that in these mixed exhibitions nothing really shows to advantage. I don't know why, but the good work suffers. Daddy's watercolours looked well and had a good central position. I'm only showing a rather lame exhibit of two flower pieces. McGregor did not want me to show Mrs Nesbitt, so at the last moment I was stranded with nothing framed.

My portrait of Adrian Feint is coming on slowly, as sittings have been spasmodic and the weather heavy. I hope to have it ready for the Society of Artists.

My love,
Nora

'Westchester'
24/8 Onslow Avenue
Elizabeth Bay, Sydney
Monday 1940

Dearest Mother and Daddy,

I meant to follow up my last brief letter long before this, but a week has flown goodness where. A week of portrait sittings has taken time and thought, and any spare moment I have has been devoted to flat hunting. I'm looking for a large

34   This was the third Australian Academy exhibition.

room where I can paint—such a thing is not being built these days, and in the older places one has cockroaches and no conveniences.

I suppose these early Autumn days are lovely at home—I often look back and remember them and then feel fed up with the city and flat life.

In the afternoons Adrian has been sitting and the portrait has gone a few paces ahead. I'm trying to put an outdoor background behind him, always a problem. I don't know how the old masters achieved it and attained such unity.

This afternoon, as the day was glorious, I walked along to the Gallery to see the Gruner Memorial Exhibition, and the scholarship entries.[35] I thought Gruner's work would fail in the mass but I was agreeably surprised—the show looks good and there are some lovely little landscapes full of poetry and feeling. He may lack strong design and draughtsmanship, but he gets a something into his work, a quality of his own which will assure his place amongst Australian landscape painters in spite of what his non-admirers think. I still like best his early period and find his later work rather thin, flat and formalised. His flower pieces I don't care for, but they lend variety to the show which was inclined to suffer from a sameness. I suppose with a large exhibition of one man's work that is unavoidable.

The Academy's reception here was very lukewarm, and it closed lamely with the total of sales under three hundred—not very encouraging to all concerned. I didn't get in to see it again, but heard today that someone had made an offer for a flower piece of mine, which I accepted. Prices are low and going lower and it is difficult to know what stand to take. However low one's prices, there will always be someone to beat one down.

My love to all,

Nora

'Westchester'
24/8 Onslow Avenue
Elizabeth Bay, Sydney
Wednesday 1940

Dearest Mother and Daddy,

Mother's letter came on Monday and home news was very welcome and also some happy snaps … a healthy baby and some security in these anxious times. It is good to think of them as so contented and happy, and occasionally I feel almost

---

35   Elioth Gruner (1882–1939) died in October 1939. *Art in Australia* in November 1939 carried a tribute to him
by William G. Buckle, who commented that Gruner's work 'stood alone for its lyrical quality, its poetry and its
tenderness'. His Memorial Exhibition was at the National Art Gallery of New South Wales from 17 April to 31
May 1940.

envious. In the life of an artist, there is no contentment and no security, a game of chance and gamble, and a game with odds well against me. Now, more than ever, the outlook for artists is pretty hopeless.

It becomes daily more difficult to concentrate on any work, and quite impossible to shut out that daily millions are being slaughtered, and millions suffering the loss of all they possess. Today is a glorious Autumn day with the harbour sparkling in the sun—no wonder we out here find it difficult to realise the horror in Europe.

My love to all,

Nora

7 Montague Place, Sydney
Saturday 1940

Dearest Mother and Daddy,

Mother's letter found me in the throes of moving. At last I have found a flat suitable—in the end the chance popped up quite unexpectedly, as is their want after months of solid hunting, and we moved in overnight as it were.

More space makes life happier and I have a large airy studio overlooking Rushcutters Bay. A delightful outlook very similar to the Lane Mullins view, as these flats face the same direction—the bay full of boats is an endless attraction and the headland beyond is very paintable, and I'm longing to get settled in, so I can begin on some studies. A fireplace also adds to comfort, and although it is only gas, it is cheery and warming on these cold evenings. The weather has been glorious, fine and sunny, and this flat, thank goodness, catches the morning sun which is ideal for the baby.[36] Altogether there are four rooms, two large and two medium, with a big sunny kitchen and a nice bathroom. The disadvantages are that hot water is not laid on and the floors squeak, however there's always something.

Over here everyone is gloomy, and the one topic is war news—it is hard to combat the depression, and work on, when the whole world seem to be toppling round our heads. Every time I see Brackenreg he tells of another collapse. Business after business is closing down—he says that Buckle is ill in bed with worry and strain. It is hard on people who have spent their lives building things up, only to see them crash round their ears, just when they are ready to sit back and reap some of the rewards. I was sorry to hear Ure Smith has had to give up.[37] This is no age for art of any description.

---

36   This is Evie's baby, whom Nora Heysen painted in *Merrie at Six Months* (1941), private collection.

37   Ure Smith's new publication *Australia* was in trouble, with the other directors wanting to cease publication. He continued with it on a monthly basis and in a new format. See Nancy Underhill, *Making Australian Art 1916–49: Sydney Ure Smith, Patron and Publisher*, Melbourne, Oxford University Press, 1991: 172.

I had a few people in the other evening for a chat. Murch amongst them, and his latest girl friend. The same old Murch. He hasn't changed a bit—he's got a job at the Sydney Technical which is keeping him going and he's come to settle in the Cross.

My love to all,
Nora

7 Montague Place, Sydney
Wednesday 1940

Dearest Mother and Daddy,

It seems an age since I've heard from home, but I'm expecting a letter any day … I'm gradually settling into my new quarters and have started work again. Adrian has been able to give me some more sittings, and the portrait nears completion, thank goodness, as both sitter and artist are exhausted. I hope to show the portrait in the Society of Artists show. Also I have started on a view from my window looking out over the park, with some buildings and in the background a table and painting gear. The double interest scheme is going to be difficult to pull off, but it is an interesting venture and something new for me.

This must go, my love to all,
Nora

7 Montague Place, Sydney
10 August 1940

Dearest Mother and Daddy,

Last week I made a last effort and finalised Adrian—a great relief to both sitter and artist for it has been a long ordeal. I think it is the best portrait I have painted up to date. But until I see it freshly in the exhibition feel I cannot judge it fairly. The style of painting is more akin to *Ruth* in the Adelaide Gallery, than anything I have done since. I have painted it on wood and have kept all technique very quiet and subdued. The colour scheme too is low in tone consisting mainly of plums and blues in varying shades.

My love to all,
Nora

7 Montague Place, Sydney
Sunday 1940

Dearest Mother and Daddy,

The sausages have arrived in first-rate condition and a great thrill it was to receive them. If anyone asked me what my greatest gustatory adventure was I would say the first mouthful of mettwurst every season. It is better than ever and never has it tasted so good. Adrian was thrilled with his. I'm so glad that you included one, as no one could appreciate it more, especially as he's hard up. I had been waiting before writing so to first deliver them to their respective owners, but so far only Adrian has his. McGregor is away for a few days in Melbourne, and I have rung Ure Smith several times but haven't been able to find him—probably he's rushed right now getting the Society of Arts exhibition arranged.

This week has been a battle against time to get my pictures into the exhibition and to paint a bunch of Spring flowers. I sent seven things into the Society show and am hoping they will give me a good hanging.

I know some people here, the Blundens, who have a country shack up at Kurrajong and they bought down a huge basket of blossoms and have camellias and daffodils, hence the rush of painting. Mrs Blunden has asked me up to stay for a week and I think I'll go and get a breath of country air.

My only outing since last writing was a farewell evening given in honour of Dadswell who has enlisted and is going away. The evening was held at the Ure Smiths and all the artists were there. I don't know why but a gathering of artists is always a lame affair. We all sat and looked at each other, the bright spot of the evening was Hetty's supper.

I've forgotten to say that I now have a pupil. I hesitated when Mrs Tansy rang and asked me would I take her Peter as a pupil, as I thought teaching would be the last thing I'd tackle, however with things in the state they are for artists, I felt I should consider it. Peter is only eight, but frightfully enthusiastic. Just how it will last remains to be seen. Yesterday afternoon was the first lesson.

My love to all,

Nora

7 Montague Place, Sydney
21 September 1940

Dearest Mother and Daddy,

I have been meaning to write for days to give you news of the exhibition.[38] I was speaking to Brackenreg and he said he posted Daddy all the news concerning the show—paper cuttings were practically non-existent and only *The Herald* had a brief survey and Howard Ashton had his usual splenetic paragraph, the latter rousing a bitter protest from Syd Ure Smith and Lloyd Jones. I think it is about time H. Ashton ceased to act as a critic, he does a lot of harm in his biased attack.

I am glad the Adelaide Gallery bought an Adrian Feint and a Dobell.[39] I'll be interested to hear your verdict on them. The Dobell is interesting but I don't think it is the best of his work. I like his portrait of Miss Crookston much better, in fact it is a little masterpiece and unfortunately it wasn't for sale. Adrian seems at last to have caught up with the success he deserves—all seven of the things he sent in were sold and two Gallery purchases! It's wonderful for him. His landscapes are not as strong as his flower pieces—he is still feeling his way in the Stanley Spencer approach, but in his flower pieces he has definitely arrived and in the piece the Sydney Gallery bought I think he's achieved his high-water mark.[40]

I sold the other drawing I had of the American woman, Mrs Edwards. Dr Constance Darcy bought it and I was very pleased, as it is an unexpected thrill to sell a picture these days, let alone a drawing. McGregor bought my small still life study. I'm to lunch with him on Sunday and am to deliver the sausage. Have been trying for three weeks to get it to him. The 'modern' tendency in the show this year has called forth a deal of criticism. It is true that it could have been a show held anywhere in Europe for all the Australian feeling there was about the work—a pity, but still with so many of our artists just arriving back from Europe with their heads and canvases crammed full of influences, how can one expect anything else. Dobell has had a big influence, one can see it everywhere, the joke of the show was Joshua Smith going all abstract to the signature of 'Josh'.

In a sea of European influences Daddy's gums and landscapes looked sane and original with their lovely Australian atmosphere. I liked the big one of the gums the best I think. More about the show when I have had a quiet look about. I must post this on the way up to the Cross to buy some dinner.

---

38   This is the 1940 Society of Arts exhibition.
39   The National Gallery of South Australia purchased Adrian Feint's *Morning in Onslow Street* (1940), oil on canvas, and William Dobell's *The Yellow Glove* (1940), oil on board.
40   The National Art Gallery of New South Wales purchased Feint's *Flowers in Sunlight* (1940), oil on canvas.

Sydney's going modern mad. All papers are giving undue attention to any artist with abstract views—here's a cutting to tell you about it.

My love to all,

Nora

7 Montague Place, Sydney

5 October 1940

Dearest Mother and Daddy,

Just a short note to wish Daddy many happy returns for this birthday on the eighth. The Contemporary Society exhibition at David Jones is causing a fine stir and everyone is having a ding-dong go at each other. Sydney Ure Smith and John Moore are having a few words, and I noticed that John Moore didn't turn up at the Society of Arts meeting on Tuesday, so I hope he's not going to resign or something.

I went along to the opening out of curiosity, and I found that the same impulse had drawn a couple of thousand others.[41] All society was there and a very arty crowd of the younger set. As for the show, it was very good imitation of the British and French contemporary art that was held in the same gallery last year. Most of the things were so derivative that one couldn't consider them. A few were interesting experiments, fresh and with good design. Of course drawings were non-existent, perhaps one would have more confidence in this abstract art if one felt that behind it there some knowledge and draughtsmanship, instead one couldn't help feeling all this so-called modern and new outlook was only a cloak. However, they have a big following, and this exhibition and its popularity is a sign that Sydney is going modern with a vengeance.

I'm enclosing a snap of the drawing of *Peter*. Fleischmann took it for me, but strange the background has come out dark, whereas really it is drawn on cream paper, but it may give you some idea. Peter is here this afternoon so I must get on with my lesson.

With love and the best of wishes for the 8th,

Nora

41   The Contemporary Art Society Annual Exhibition opened on 24 September 1940.

7 Montague Place, Sydney
Tuesday 1940

Dearest Mother and Daddy,

Here are some of the letters which will amuse you. Lionel Lindsay certainly stirred up the troubled waters afresh and things are humming. I read in today's paper that the exhibition of contemporary art had already had an attendance of 11 000 and they were extending the show for another week. The Society of Arts will have to wake up and take notice. I can feel dissatisfaction amongst the members, but we lack a leader and as long as the shows are held in the Department of Education rooms, they'll never get the attendance. I think it was a mixed blessing when the Society was donated the Gallery free.

I asked Eric Wilson to dine with me one night last week. It was interesting meeting him again and we had a long chat about London days.[42] He brought his collection of prints which he'd gathered on his trip and going through all one's favourites was a stimulating tonic.

Wilson has swung over to the teaching of Ozenfant and the abstract school—he's mad on Braque and Picasso and Segantini and, as far as I can judge, slavishly copying these men. He's frightfully enthusiastic to get on, but I think he's finding it difficult to settle down again. It is strange to find an artist with a keen religious faith these days. He's a Puritan and a Seventh Day Adventist rolled into one. A fact I believe which rather estranges him from his fellow artists. They can't understand him at all. I think he's lonely.

I'm glad you like *Peter*. I'll ask Fleischmann if he'll pull some more proofs. The garden sounds a joy. I wish I could see it.

My love to all,

Nora

7 Montague Place, Sydney
Wednesday 31 March 1941

Dearest Mother and Daddy,

Back safely and all went well on the trip. Sydney has greeted me with hot sultry weather, and all that glorious Autumn weather at home seems a wonderful dream. Coming back into the Cross was like entering a hothouse full of petrol fumes and the smells of the city—one is doubly more conscious of it after the freshness of the country. On my shopping excursion I ran into Dobell and a few of the clan all looking jaded and tired. I realised then how much fresher I felt in every

---

42   Eric Wilson was in London from 1937 to 1939, returning to Australia in December 1939.

way. It was a great change and a wonderful holiday just to be at home, to have the freedom of mind to quickly work in a lovely atmosphere. I can tell you I appreciated it especially after battling in a city.

Thanks to Daddy's care, the canvas unrolled intact in this atmosphere. My *Madonna of the Murray* looks quite startlingly fresh.

Love to you all,

Nora

7 Montague Place, Sydney
18 July 1941

Dearest Mother and Daddy,

Although I had half expected it, the news that Mike and Stef had joined up came as a shock[43] ... it is sickening to see the great liners storm out with their cargo of youth for the slaughter yard—it fills one with a bitter resentment against the futility and horror of the war. Day by day the casualty lists grow, the headlines become more bloody and things everywhere are tightening up and changing. Menzies' speech tonight enforcing dictatorship measures was depressing. It is all rather bewildering and terrifying.

McGregor blew in yesterday and bought a flower piece, awfully good of him and very cheering. He also gave me a commission for a portrait drawing, the subject to be Michael Whitehead. I think you may have met him at McGregor's. He's a very likeable young man of 26 with an alert keenly cut face that should be good for the pencil. It will be nice to do some drawing again. I'm looking forward to it. McGregor looked tired and strained and very pessimistic about the future.

I have sent instructions for my *Motherhood* to be returned to Adelaide. I'll show it there in the Spring Exhibition.

My love to all,

Nora

7 Montague Place, Sydney
7 August 1941

Dearest Mother and Daddy,

Daddy's letter over the weekend was extra welcome as the last news from home was rather worrying with illness and trouble the order of the day.

43   Nora's brothers both joined the Royal Australian Air Force.

Thanks for the information regarding the Society of Arts show. I would like to show both *Motherhood* and the *Scabious*, for cataloguing they can keep their titles, and, as for prices, I think 75 guineas for my Mother fair, and 30 guineas for the flowers. Could Bayly make me a frame for the *Scabious*? The flower piece I'm sending from here I think I'll send framed by mail. At present it is in at Taylor's Galleries. I'm calling for it tomorrow, so will then either take it out of its frame or roll it and post it as Daddy suggested, or get it sent as it is in its frame. The expense would work out much the same. I doubt if there would be time to have a frame made.

How quickly these sending-in dates descend on one. The Society of Arts is the next consideration. I'm sending in *My Murray Madonna*, which I'm calling *Dedication* after Mother's advice, also several flower pieces and a couple of drawings. What is Daddy sending over this year?

My love to you all,
Nora

7 Montague Place, Sydney
20 September 1941

Dearest Mother and Daddy,

Yes I did receive the wine and was it welcome! The first contribution my Mothers have brought me in. The Wire was worded 'Congratulations Melrose Prize'.[44] On the strength of it I bought myself a Spring hat and a book. I didn't expect the Gallery to buy, I knew they'd think it too much like *Ruth*. Perhaps had I swapped 'Mother' I would have had more luck. McGregor over here thought the Sydney Gallery might have bought Patricia, he liked it better than *Dedication*, however I'm lucky to have won the prize. It at least covers framing and model fees and that is all one can expect these days.

Over here I have been negotiating a few sales. The McEacherns whom I wrote that I had met came to tea last week and bought a flower piece, one that I had just finished off, Spring flowers against a blue background. Did I tell you they had commissioned me to paint a bunch of wild flowers? To gather the flowers they hired a car for the day and took me for a lovely day's outing out to Church Point and Palm Beach. It was a day after rain and the bush was heavenly and gay with flowers. We gathered armfuls, some of the most fascinating varieties amongst them, but not until we came to the flannel flowers could I see a beginning to my

44   This was the second time Nora Heysen won the National Gallery of South Australia's Melrose Prize for portraiture. She also won it in 1933 for *A Portrait Study* (1933).

arrangement. I have used them as a central note and found them beautiful and fascinating to paint. This texture and tone of grey-green is like no other flower. All the other little bits and pieces fell into place around them, and I think the bunch is successful. I have just put the finishing touches to it and feel satisfied that I have captured a bit of their charm. I hope they'll like it as I feel I want them to have the best, for they have the scheme of holding an exhibition of Australian works that they have collected in London immediately the war is over. He is a wealthy man and has the means as well as the enthusiasm to carry out his idea, that is, to advertise Australian art in London. It was good to be in the bush again and enjoy a picnic hamper with wine and chicken and coffee and homemade cakes. It made me think of home, only the apple pie was missing.

I am glad to hear that Daddy is feeling better.

My love to all there,

Nora

> 7 Montague Place, Sydney
> Friday 24 October 1941

Dearest Mother and Daddy,

It was good to get Daddy's letter yesterday it brought with it the scent of lilac and a vision of apple blossom and a haze of blue and primrose. I'm glad the Epstein is proving readable. I had time to read a passage or two and thought it entertaining, like his work, full of vitality and a quick lucid summing up of essentials.

I was glad to hear that the Adelaide Gallery was considering my *White Cacti*. Ure Smith rang me about it yesterday, the three things on consideration are being sent over on approval and I'm taking in my *Cacti* today. It's a very small thing and I haven't much hope that the other members of the Trustee Board will like it.[45]

Did I tell you that Madame Schuurman had at last bought her portrait? I thought that the 'lend for one night' had gone on long enough, and so I rang saying that I thought that someone else was interested, and after that her husband decided that rather than let his wife pass into someone else's hands, he'd part up.

I hope the new land turns up trumps.[46] I can see no end to this ghastly war mess—it is a depressing thought to wake up to each morning. Fleischmann took some snaps of my *Dedication* I'll post you a print next time. It has come out quite well. I'll show it in the Autumn in Adelaide and will probably bring it back with me

---

45   The National Art Gallery of South Australia purchased *White Cacti* in 1941 from Elder Bequest funds.

46   Hans and Sallie Heysen purchased two adjoining properties, taking the size of 'The Cedars' to 150 acres.

when I come home for Christmas. I'd like it to go into the Adelaide Gallery one day, I have always thought it better than the other.

I'll post this on my way in with the *Cacti*.

My love to all,

Nora

7 Ulverstone
Elizabeth Bay, Sydney
Saturday 1941

Dearest Mother and Daddy,

Just a word to confirm dates. I have booked for the 21st which gets me home on the 23rd, that is Tuesday week. Luckily I booked before the Japs decided to crash in so was able to get a sleeping berth at least for half the way. Should Sydney get a bomb before then things will be in the air, but so far so good. Blackouts are threatening, and restrictions are closing in. It seems fantastic to think that the same ghastly destruction can happen here, and one avoids thinking of how inadequate air protection is. Sydney still dreams on under a cloudless blue sky, and we all go blissfully on.

The portrait is finished. Sir Lionel seemed pleased, and everyone judges it a speaking likeness. McGregor blew in for a preview yesterday and was satisfied that it was a good portrait and a good likeness. He also pleasantly surprised me by saying that he had commissioned it, and was taking control of the framing. I feel myself that it is very like the man and has vitality and life, but how could I but help to get these qualities. As you say just to be in contact with him is an inspiration.

I have a hectic week ahead preparing the flat and generally fixing things here. Some people are taking over the flat, so it has to be brightened up. Also I have to finish the McEachern's flower piece, and what with one thing and another, do not know if I am coming or going.

This must go, goodbye till Tuesday,

Nora

7 Ulverstone
Elizabeth Bay, Sydney
1942

Dearest Mother and Daddy,

Sydney at last, but a very different Sydney. One's first impulse is to get out of it as quickly as possible—the streets are deserted and the park looks desolate and dusty. The journey seemed interminably long and hot, the only bright spots were bottles of lemonade and honey biscuits.

I'll be here for a week at least. It will take us that time to get things packed and finalised, and to find a place in the country. Canberra will probably be the next move if there is a home to be got there, anyway I'll let you know when and where.[47]

My love to all,

Nora

7 Ulverstone
Elizabeth Bay, Sydney
Monday 16 March 1942

Dearest Mother and Daddy,

As you can see I am still in Sydney, likely to remain for a week or so until I can decide where to turn and what to do next. It is very wearing living in state of indecision.[48] I'll be immensely glad to get settled somewhere. The problem of what to do with one's possessions is the curse. The last two or three days I have spent in packing frames and pictures, an endless job, the difficulty is to get hold of cases. Wood here seems as precious as diamonds. So far trying to find a place in the country has failed. Everyone seems to have had the same idea and the agents have taken advantage of the situation by charging exorbitant rents—rents seem to be higher in the country now than in the city.

I walked across to the Gallery on Sunday afternoon and was delighted to find several early Streetons and Roberts showing—a lovely little landscape of Roberts' of Coogee Beach attracted me a lot. It had a lovely quality, also a very early Streeton of Redfern Station with wet streets and grey buildings sensitively handled with beautiful passages of greys and delicately drawn figures and carriages influenced by Conder. Those men got something. Looking from those little canvases to some of the more modern work I couldn't help thinking how obvious and crude it

---

47   Evie and her husband Henry lived in Canberra.
48   Nora included a newspaper cutting from *The Daily Telegraph* that ran with the headline 'Harbour Lights Shock Heffron. Will Prosecute Owners of Unscreened Lights', showing lights from homes visible in the night sky.

looked, no tenderness, no true feeling, none of that precious quality that seems to me to make painting worthwhile.

The Gallery was being prepared for the exhibition of Dobell's and Margaret Preston's work which opens on Thursday.[49] I'm curious to see their work and will go along to the opening.

We have had four or five air raid scares here, but nothing happened and I didn't even hear the sirens.

My love to all,
Nora

These letters come from the National Library of Australia's 'Papers of Sir Hans Heysen, c.1880–1973', MS 5073, series 2, folders 152, 155, 156, 159, 160, 161 and 168; and 'Papers of Nora Heysen, 1913–2003', MS 10041, series 1.3, folder 32.

---

49   This was *Margaret Preston and William Dobell Loan Exhibition*, National Art Gallery of New South Wales, 1942.

Life as an official war artist
1943–1946

These letters also present a rather one-sided dialogue between Nora and her father and mother. This may be due to the fact that some letters Nora received did not survive her constant movement with the Australian Imperial Force (AIF). Also Sallie Heysen seems to have written more than Hans, who may have been very busy at this stage of his career. Letters and food parcels play a large part in military life, and in August 1944, midway through her time in New Guinea, Nora comments they 'mean more than anything else here'. Sallie's parcels, which contained home-baked biscuits, dried fruits and other necessities, were always very welcome. There is less commentary on art, and more on life as an official war artist. Art talk often gets down to basics, such as requests for materials like tubes of paint and red chalk.

Even though Hans himself is less evident, his presence is everywhere. Nora relates how she meets people who proudly own one of her father's paintings and how many of the artists she meets know her father or have visited 'The Cedars'. She writes in one letter in 1943, while still in Melbourne, how fellow artist Harold Herbert recalled over dinner his visit there, and how he thought 'I was the image of my Dad and got quite sentimental'; while Dobell sends his apologies, via Nora, to Hans because he didn't have time to call on him while in Adelaide. Her father's name comes in handy too. In New Guinea, she encounters the Quartermaster on a naval ship who had served on the *Manunda* and knew 'Daddy's picture', *White Gums*, well. She writes home: 'his enthusiasm spread to me bearing the name and he couldn't do enough, and suddenly good fresh food arrived and for a week we ate like Lords.

Despite her protestation once again that she can't write like her father, Nora's letters convey beautifully the terrain in which she works, the people she meets and especially those she portrays. Her descriptions are those of a portraitist who studies every aspect of the persona to capture the essence of personality on canvas, such as that of 'Bluey', the Queensland logger who cleared areas of New Guinea jungle with his bulldozer 'Dearest', so soldiers could advance, and of Major Josephine Mackerras, the entomologist at the Cairns Medical Research Centre, who worked on malaria.

The letters chart Nora Heysen's time in Melbourne, prior to going to New Guinea, her return to Adelaide due to dermatitis in later 1944, her reappearance in Melbourne in late 1944, her posting to the Red Cross Blood Bank in Sydney in 1945, followed in the same year by transfers to Townsville and Cairns, in North Queensland, and Morotai. Running throughout all these moves is reference to 'the Colonel', who is Colonel John Treloar. He ran the War Artists Scheme from the Military History Headquarters, in Melbourne. Nora clashed with Treloar because he was critical of her New Guinea work, and he intended to terminate her appointment at the end of 1944. What is not described in the letters is the pressure Treloar came under from Hans' influential friends to keep Nora, and how Louis McCubbin, a member of the War Artists Committee, drove up to 'The Cedars', looked over Nora's work while she was recuperating in late 1944 and recommended an extension of her appointment. What is described in the letters is how she rebuked Treloar's criticisms point by point. She refers to her family 'being blessed with a certain amount of persistence'.

A war was going on but art still sold. Hans relates to Nora, in New Guinea, art auction prices in a buoyant art market, recent works aquired by the National Gallery of South Australia and various purchases of Nora's work. And even while in the AIF, Nora enters three of her portraits in the Archibald Prize. Talk about art books also continues where possible. When back in Melbourne after time in the tropics, Hans writes to Nora that he is ordering a copy of Camille Pissarro's letters to his son, Lucien. Close to the end of her appointment as an official war artist, Nora in turn mentions that she has heard a new book on Australian art by one 'B. Smith' has appeared, as if to signal her reintegration into the art scene.

'Menzies', Melbourne
Thursday 1943

Dearest Mother and Daddy,

I'm still hovering on the brink, but any day now expect to get that final push into the world of officialdom. I saw Treloar today and hope then that he will announce the news that my appointment has gone through. Until then, I'm still supposed to be tongue-tied. Stewart is sworn to discretion.[1] I dined last night with Harold Herbert and his wife. McGregor had us all for a dinner party here, and it was full of reminiscences of his visit to 'The Cedars' and he remembered it all to the slightest detail and probably a lot that never happened. Thought I was the image of my Dad and got quite sentimental. He's good company.

I can't buy red chalk here or in Sydney and remember that I have a box somewhere in my studio at home, a small flat brown box full of sticks I bought in Paris. It is probably in the sideboard drawers. If you could locate it I should be very glad to have them as pencil seems too slight a medium for swift action. I am remaining here until my appointment goes through, and hope it won't be long for more than one reason.

Will write at length when I have more time in the army.

My love to all,

Nora

'Menzies', Melbourne
12 October 1943

Dearest Mother and Daddy,

They are trying to get war artists on an army status. Previously they were attached on the same basis as war correspondents. Now we've joined the army and thereby given a few privileges and loose a deal of freedom. Anyway I'm in for it now, and am just beginning to realise what I am signing away. They say getting in is as difficult as getting out, and I quite believe it.

My position is a curious one and seems to cause worry and confusion all round. I am looked upon as some queer specimen that doesn't quite belong anywhere. What seems to disturb them most is that I have no number. A number, it would seem, is one's identity. Without it, I am as dust. I am given the rank of Captain with the pay women receive, less of course than the men, but this they promise me will be rectified—several years hence I should imagine.

---

1   Stewart Cockburn was a journalist and family friend. See 'Woman as War Artist. Miss Nora Heysen',
     The Sydney Morning Herald, 12 August 1943.

Yesterday I had a chat to Daryl Lindsay at the Gallery and saw the exhibition of War Work held there.[2] Ivor Hele's work was outstanding.

My love to all, this is in haste between appointments,

Nora

'Menzies', Melbourne

Thursday 4 November 1943

Dearest Mother and Daddy,

Have just received the bad news of Daddy's accident and I cannot help but worry ... What a shock and nightmare it must have been. Seeing Daddy on the roof has always given me the shudders, and a fall just then on the cement must have been horrible.

I have just returned from 3 days down at Queenscliff. My first taste of camp life, straw mattresses and stews and cold water. Queenscliff is on the coast some 70 miles out of Melbourne on Port Phillip. There are large camps down there and women are helping protect our coast.

The War Museum are now paying my expenses, and I'm about to start work on the portraits of the head women in the various branches of the services.[3] My first victim is Second Officer McClemans of the WRANS.[4] I meet her tomorrow and begin work. I have been allotted a small room out at the Military History Headquarters out in St Kilda Rd.

My love and wishes,

Nora

'Menzies', Melbourne

Sunday 28 November 1943

Dearest Mother and Daddy,

At last for a breather and to collect my scattered wits. I have been immersed in my khaki scheme and, as if once having mixed the colours, I couldn't get enough of it. I was tackling the whole thing in that tone, with the only relief the red stripes on the lapels and ribbons on the chest. It will either hit or make a very bad miss, and at the moment it is half way between the two, and I feel irritated

---

2   *Exhibition of Paintings, Drawing and Sculpture* opened at the National Gallery of Victoria on 16 September 1943. Paintings in this exhibition, by male official war artists only, pre-date the appointment of women. Daryl Lindsay (1889–1976) was Director of the National Gallery of Victoria.

3   Nora Heysen took up the position on 18 October 1943. The War Museum is the Australian War Memorial; the name had changed from 'museum' to 'memorial' in 1923.

4   Women's Royal Australian Naval Service.

and on edge. My sitter is overworked and tired, and can spare me a bare hour a day which is not enough, and working in brief snatches like that is very unsatisfactory. One just gets started and time is up, however Colonel Irving has a fine and strong head, domineering and efficient, highly capable with penetrating blue eyes and a sense of humour.

My next is a WAAAF and I begin her on Wednesday—but haven't as yet seen her.[5] My appointment is still two days ahead.

The exhibition of British War Work is here at the Gallery and it's a stimulating show and there are some interesting things—two magnificent Muirhead Bone drawings, some good Kennington pastel portraits of airmen and some very interesting things by a John Piper of a ruined church.[6] In none of them is there any sentiment or human appeal, but there are well-designed canvases and good quality of paints. One feels that the artists have, one and all, approached the war as a means of creating works of art out of the subject matter offered.

My love to all,

Nora

'Menzies', Melbourne
Wednesday 8th 1943

Dearest Mother and Daddy,

My portrait of Sybil Irving is at last complete, but the next hangs fire as my sitter is ill and won't be out of hospital until next week. I'm going down to Pt Cook to have a look about for air force material.

I met Mainwaring for the first time the other day.[7] He's just down from New Guinea and has brought back piles of work and ideas. He's a nice fellow, full of enthusiasm and vitality, his work is capable and fresh, rather topographical but well drawn and he seems to be a prolific worker. I hear Will Ashton has resigned his directorship.[8] I wonder who will succeed him? Daryl Lindsay has asked me to sign one of Daddy's drawings. Evidently one was missed.

My last sitter, Sybil Irving, has asked me out to dine with her and I'm looking forward to meeting her unprofessionally and getting to know her—if only

---

5   Women's Auxiliary Australian Air Force.

6   *Exhibition of British War Pictures*, which included work by Ethel Gabain (1883–1950), toured all Australian state art galleries.

7   Geoffrey Mainwaring (1912–2000) was an Australian official war artist in New Guinea between 1942 and 1947.

8   Will Ashton resigned due to poor health in November 1943. He continued at the National Art Gallery of New South Wales until mid-1944, when he became Director of David Jones Art Gallery in 1944. See Silas Clifford Smith, 'Will Ashton', *Dictionary of Australian Artists Online*, http://www.daao.org.au, accessed 20 August 2010.

one could do so before painting them. The conditions one works under are not favourable. The light is bad and there is nothing to aid one, just four bare walls and a hard chair. Khaki is a foul colour to paint and doesn't suit women. My present sitter insists on wearing her air force cap because she is the only woman who wears gold braid on hers. What with the cap and the khaki uniform, I have a few square inches of face in between in which to get some human streak. In this case, those few inches are not prepossessing—a very hard mouth, and undistinguished features. Oh dear, where does the artist come in. These women are most capable and efficient, I have the greatest respect for them.

My love to all,

Nora

'Menzies', Melbourne
Sunday

Dearest Mother and Daddy,

Just a note to say there is a hope of my coming home for Christmas for a couple of days. I have the Colonel's consent, now it is just a matter of getting on the train.

I have yet to complete my air force portrait before leaving, but it is well on the way, and fortunately this time I have perfect cooperation with my sitter and all goes smoothly. On getting back I want to repaint Colonel Sybil Irving, and it still has to be in time for the Archibald as it will not be tactful to show the Heads of both WAAAF and WRANS without the army—my first portrait of the woman was not a success.[9] I battled with it for the best part of a month, and now have decided to paint her again. Meanwhile I have come to know her and having seen and studied her in her own home, and out of uniform, and I think I have a better chance as well as a better understanding.

My appointment is now finalised, has been so the Colonel informed me, since October. Now I have to wait for a Commission.

My love to all,

Nora

---

9   Nora Heysen entered all three portraits in the 1944 Archibald Prize: *Colonel Sybil H. Irving, Controller, AWAS* (1943), oil on canvas, Australian War Memorial (ART22220); *Group Officer Clare Stevenson* (1943), oil on canvas, Australian War Memorial (ART22215); *First Officer Sheila McClemans, WRANS* (1943), oil on canvas, Australian War Memorial (ART23416).

'Menzies', Melbourne
Monday January 1944

Dearest Mother and Daddy,

My commission is now through and I'm a Captain (still out of uniform). Now that I'm entitled to wear the thing, I'm loathe to put it on feeling apprehensive of all it entails. Instead of going through an Officer's School, it has at last been decided to give me private tuition in army etiquette until I can at least salute. I feel I cannot don my khaki, it's going to be most embarrassing (especially as everyone out at the Military History Section knows me just as a plain civilian). To roll up with pips all readymade, and a higher rank than the other artists, is going to be awkward to say the least. Then I in my turn, when my sitters roll up here, have got to salute them.

The second portrait of Colonel Irving is almost complete, and is much better thank goodness. Another sitting will see it finished and then I'm off to camp. My first port of call is Darby up at Bacchus Marsh and then onto Albury. On Sunday I went out to Colonel Irving's home in Toorak and helped plant zinnias and asters and lunched in the garden. It was a glorious day, and good to be out in it messing about with the good earth. Colonel Best sat for a drawing in the afternoon, and later we all went out to tea at the Hordern's, kindly old people with quite a collection of pictures and furniture and china.[10] They have a couple of Daddy's watercolours, and a flower piece of mine.

My love to all at home,
Nora

'Menzies', Melbourne
Wednesday 19 January 1944

Dearest Mother and Daddy,

I've expected long before this to add to my last scratchy letter, but have been caught up in a whirl of activity which has ended in my finally being cast into khaki—it took me two hours on Sunday to dress myself for my first rehearsal ... I was expected out to lunch at Sybil Irving's so was expected to be regimentally correct in every detail. Finally I walked stiffly out feeling very compressed and awkward, and rather damp from exertion. The high stiff collar is very hard to get used to, and my feet are blistered and sore in army shoes, but I dare say I'll get

---

10 Colonel Kathleen Best was Assistant Adjutant General (Women's Services) and coordinated AWAS (Australian Women's Army Service), AANS (Australian Army Nursing Service) and AAMWS (Australian Army Medical Women's Service).

used to it in due course. At the moment I feel rather as if I was minus my identity and playing a part on the stage. When someone saluted me in the street the other day, I looked around to see whom it was they were saluting, then suddenly realised it was myself. These days I dodge everything with red on its uniform, and I don't know which embarrasses me more, having to salute or being saluted. I had three hours drill in army etiquette on Sunday, but still feel a very raw recruit.

Today I bought Mother's Christmas present, a very nice pig-skin folio to hang from my shoulders. It is the most useful and the most comfortable part of my attire and I'm already attached to it, for it holds brushes and sketchbooks and all my oddments, and as well leaves my hands free. All the official business of getting into the army is upon me, and I spend half my days signing here, trying on clothes there, and being injected. The injections alone carry one over two months. Now at last I have a number 'VFX 94085 Captain Heysen. N. AIF' for future reference. I was interviewed and photographed yesterday—I'll send along a picture of myself in uniform so you can recognise me on the next occasion.[11]

My portrait of Colonel Best is almost complete and now it seems I'm still going on with portraits.[12] The war artists are being moved into the city to new rooms with better lighting (the building was lately the morgue). The entrance was shuddering, but up on the fourth floor one looks over the Gardens and Flinders Street Railway Station, and the light is good, which is the main thing. There is a creaky old lift going up made in the shape of a coffin and dismal dark alleyways—the place has an atmosphere all its own—would suit Daumier or El Greco.

The biscuits are proving a tremendous success, and are an added inducement to my sitters.

My love to all there,

Nora

'Menzies', Melbourne
Sunday 1944

Dearest Mother and Daddy,

At the moment I am working on Matron Sage and am painting her in a white cap and red cape. She has a fine head and the whole thing is like a Flemish Old Master—Van Eyck would have loved her. The white head-dress is such a

---

11 The photograph taken by Ronald Munro on 17 January 1944 is *VFX94085 Captain Nora Heysen, Official War Artist, Military History Section, Land Headquarters*, Australian War Memorial (062802).

12 This painting is *Lieutenant Colonel Kathleen Best* (1944), oil on canvas, Australian War Memorial (ART22216).

lovely setting for the face, and with the simple red cape makes a good design.[13] Unfortunately time is my enemy once again, and I have only six brief sittings, as my subject leaves for New Guinea this week.

We have settled into our new quarters and I'm enjoying having a decent light to work in and plenty of room to walk back. At the moment only myself and Mainwaring are working there, we have one floor each. It's very noisy on account of being over the electric trains, and one of the noisiest thoroughfares. One cannot talk to one's sitters, nor have the windows open, but the outlook is quite fascinating and I've started a canvas of the railway lines and trains.[14] The best way to combat a noise, I find, is to try and paint it.

The Archibald win seems to be creating a bigger stir than usual. I cannot myself hold with such obvious distortion as Dobell has seen fit to display, but all the artists seem to agree that it is a fine painting and more like Joshua Smith than he is himself. I'll send a few cuttings about it. McGregor was here during the week and he told me all about it—he's all for Dobell and has completely swung over. I dined tonight with him and Harold Herbert, plus a couple of wool brokers and Mrs Menzies and Mrs Herbert, and the arguments were fierce.

My love to all,
Nora

'Menzies', Melbourne
Friday 24th

Dearest Mother and Daddy,

The precious bundle of paint rags and the equally precious fixative spray arrived a couple of days ago, and both went straight into action. After having been brought so low as to use newspaper instead of paint rags, that fine quality singlet was pure aesthetic joy. Never again will I squander paint rags, and these will last me a long time. As I'm drawing mostly in chalks and carbon pencils, it is essential to have a sprayer and it has retrieved a lot of badly rubbed drawings.

Must back to business. This 9 to 6 working by the clock makes me squirm.

My love to all round,
Nora

---

13   This painting is *Matron Annie Sage, Matron in Chief, AANS, Melbourne* (1944), oil on canvas, Australian War Memorial (ART22218).

14   This is *Flinders Street Station*, private collection.

'Menzies', Melbourne
Wednesday 1944

Dearest Mother and Daddy,

I'm taking time off to munch on honey biscuits and to say many thanks for them.

My plans today have been once more altered. I have just been talking to Colonel Treloar, and have reached the decision that I move up to New Guinea as soon as arrangements can be made. I feel that to do the work they require of me that I must be right on the spot, and the further up north I can go, and the nearer the fighting areas, the better the atmosphere for war activities.

My activities will be with the nursing women, and now that they have pushed into Lae, there will be good pioneering work to be done. In the meantime I have two further portraits to complete—both matrons.

Ursula Hayward is here again, also James McGregor, so I do not lack for cheer. Have settled down at Menzies and since my Captaincy have had marked attention. Remarkable how a couple of pips can change peoples' attitude.

My love to all there,
Nora

In camp, Brisbane
Tuesday 4 April 1944

Dearest Mother and Daddy,

I had thought to be in New Guinea by now, but am still waiting to be flown over. My plane leaves tomorrow at dawn—a non-stop flight of 12 hours, a rather large mouthful for my first taste of air travel, and as I'll be the only woman on a service plane, I'm hoping I won't disgrace myself.

Two days notice in Melbourne only allowed me sufficient time to get equipped and packed, then I stayed up the best part of two nights so as to be ready in time. The train trip up from Sydney was long and hot and now I'm in camp on a hill overlooking the city. This space is overrun with Americans like a plague of locusts. They have stripped the shops bare. Once again I sleep on straw and cover myself with a dingy grey army rug, and gaze at the deal furniture and bare boards. I'm trying to juggle my luggage into 60lbs and what, with my painting gear and all my tropical equipment, I'm having a heart breaking time. It becomes a tube of paint or a jar of face cream.

McGregor saw me off in Melbourne armed with a cocktail of three large packets of calsellettes.[15] I drove off in an army truck, gasmask, steel helmet and

---

15   'Deal' refers to pine furniture. Nora might be referring to 'Calsallettes', a brand of laxative.

first aid and dixies and what-not strung on. All I lack is a rifle and swearing vocabulary to be completely war minded.

My love to all at home,

Nora

Port Moresby, Papua
8 April 1944

Dearest Mother and Daddy,

A word before I take off for Finschhafen ... Strangely enough, after dreading going up, I enjoyed the trip here. It was exhilarating and beautiful taking off into the early dawn at Brisbane. I was the only woman and Australian in an American Lockheed, an honour I'm told.

Flying these days seems as casual as catching a taxi. It amazed me taking off with so little fuss on such a long trip. Passengers and luggage were piled in haphazardly with rubber tyres, and jeeps and soldiers, all on top of each other. A young fellow with rolled-up shirt sleeves took his place at the engines, and off we went with a cheery call to hang on, as everything tipped down to the tail end. Here everyone travels by air, and so I'll be getting plenty of it.

I'm living with the sisters and have been allotted a tent to myself. One sleeps on a straw mattress and under a net, and everything creeps and crawls and smells of mildew.

Yesterday Roy Hodgkinson, a war artist at present here, took me for a trip up into the hills in an old truck—and what a ride! I'm still sore. The bumping and rattling and the hairpin bends over precipices, it was amazing that any locomotive could take it. We were on the beginning of the Kokoda Trail and the scenery was magnificent, volcanic mountains, ravines, waterfalls, all on a grand scale. Roy admitted when we got back that it was his first experience of that track.

My tent looks out onto the Owen Stanleys and just outside are growing paw paws and bananas. Five months at the Menzies was not the best training for this life.

Have an early date at the aerodrome, so must get some sleep. I'd love some home news, and feel strange and very isolated way up here.

My love to all at home,

Nora

VFX 94085 Capt. N. Heysen
CCS, AIF NGF[16]
17 April 1944

Dearest Mother and Daddy,

There is much to tell you and little time in which to say it ... I haven't quite recovered from the shock of suddenly finding myself here.

A hectic naval party helped to clear the air and was it a party. I joined in with half a dozen sisters and jeeped it to Finschhafen. Drinks flowed—a potent cocktail of whiskey, gin and rum was carried round in buckets, and one drank it out of large shaving mugs. A half a dozen of these on an empty tum, and I was set to enjoy myself. A cheery band, gay flags and 200-odd men to choose from, Australians and Americans from every service, and most of them hadn't seen a woman for 8 or 9 months. Two bearded Aussies off a Corvette took me in charge, we danced on a gravel patch on the water's edge and supped on Edgell asparagus and fresh tomatoes and every conceivable savoury. They do things well, the navy. The two beards have asked me to dine on their Corvette this week, and I'm to choose my own menu, fresh lobster salad and roast chicken and fruit salad and ice cream. I'm saving up for it. This life is a curious mixture of hardship and luxury.

I have started on several subjects—a view overlooking Scarlet Beach, and a strafed coconut grove with some curious volcanic hills in the background, also have painted some native berries and done some chalk drawings of the natives. The Papuan natives have fine heads and are most interesting to draw. There is subject matter in plenty, but how to tackle it? I feel like a raw beginner and quite at a loss.

When I go out painting for the day, they pack me up whitebait and asparagus and tinned orange juice, and I sit and lunch on a blasted coconut stump or on the edge of a bomb crater, and find myself wondering how many died on just that spot only 5 short months ago. Incredible to try and picture it.

I wear the men's jungle green uniform and the AIF hat and plod about in my heavy boots. Washing here is a problem with no hot water, and flat irons heated on a primus make it a long process. I just haven't the energy and go dirty.

There are 14 women here. They do not accept me as one of themselves, and I live isolated in my little tent apart from their quarters, and they have built-in sheds with electric light, wardrobes and soft mattresses. The conversation centres around illness and operations.

My love to all,

Nora

---

16   Casualty Clearing Station, Australian Imperial Force, New Guinea Force.

VFX 94085 Capt. N. Heysen
Att. 106 CCS, AIF
1 May 1944

Dearest Mother and Daddy,

News from home at last and two letters on the same day. It was very exciting and how I welcomed them. One feels so isolated up here in strange surroundings and company.

So far I've escaped dengue and malaria, but the mosquitoes eat me alive through all my thick clothes and all last night there was a wild excitement in the camp. Five American negroes dared to enter the sisters' area and there was pandemonium. One was caught and shot and the others escaped. I slept through it all ... Today the men have been busy putting barbed-wire entanglements round our enclosure, the sentries have been doubled and no one is allowed out without an armed escort.

Life has plenty of thrills up here. Yesterday I adventured up Satelberg escorted by four soldiers, a butterfly enthusiast, an amateur artist and a photographer with a driver just out of bed with malaria, an experience I'll never forget. The track was hair-raising. We were stuck half a dozen times and had to pull ourselves out of feet of mud, for the rest we were jolted and bumped till we were black and blue and seat sore. Eventually we got within a mile of the top and trudged the rest with my paint box and gear and our lunch. It was worth it though.

The views were magnificent and everything of interest. The old German mission up there of course is razed to the ground, and the place is a shambles. Everywhere live bombs were still lying around. One found a Chinese cabbage growing out of an old German bible, sewing machines and silver entrée dishes, bomb craters 20 feet deep and the place a warren of foxholes, trees stripped bare, gaunt and broken. Only the cross of the Church is still standing, and the pulpit carved and painted by the natives. I found a very nice piece of board amongst the wreckage and put up my paint box on a piece of old school desk and I sat in a foxhole and proceeded to paint the view looking over the scene where our men fought and struggled the bitter way. Everything was serene and blue with white cockatoos floating overhead. After working away quietly for some time I became more and more aware of a horrid smell, and looking down found I was quartered on the remains of a dead Jap.

Then the rain came and we started the slippery trek home. I was nursing a wet canvas and an exotic white lily I found up there, but on arriving back the painting was covered in mud and the beautiful white lily broken and bespattered, and we looked a sorry crew. Jeep travelling in these parts takes experiencing to be believed. They achieve the impossible.

This week I've spent a good deal of time in the operating theatre doing preliminary sketches for a painting of an operation in progress. Three appendix operations in succession made me feel green about the gills, and I did a hasty exit. The surgeon, who is an artist at his job, will always bring me over when he pulls out the culprit to show me the inflammation. After the patient has been carried out, we all sit round in the theatre and drink and eat, with the bucket of blood swabs sitting under the table. Before I'm allowed into the theatre, I have to don mask and gown. The poor patient, lying there waiting to be put under, views my entry as if to say what instrument of torture is this. It is quite fantastic to find myself in that atmosphere. This war does strange and unpredictable things to us.

My love to all at home,
Nora

Hahndorf, South Australia
8 May 1944

Dearest Nora,

Your letter dated 1st May arrived this morning—it brings you somewhat nearer to know that we can hear from you within a week. For with all those hair-raising incidents, we will be glad indeed to know that all is well with you, and the sooner news comes that you have left the jungle behind the happier we will be. It is all too disturbing to think of. One can only hope that your work will benefit, and that you will come through unscathed, mosquitoes, Negroes, flying foxes, operations and dead Japs. You will have to paint thrillers or write them out of your system!

I wish I could fulfill your request for pillowslips adequately, some fine coloured linen would be ideal, alas it is unprocurable. Washing must be a great problem. I have just packed a box for you—biscuits, dried figs etc and 2 white pillowslips, somewhat thin but soft and 1 pink hand towel. Please mention anything you can think of that might add to your comfort and convenience— surely they can provide mosquito scarers or sprays. For Heaven's sake, don't let a malaria one get you.

By the way, there is an offer from the Geelong Gallery per Daryl Lindsay for that flower piece of yours in the collection, the lovely grey-blue vase and the big white rose—should you agree to sell, will you write the price. The entrance to your studio is gaily festooned with pink passion flowers. I feel I must emulate the wattle bird warning, go careful, go careful.

All our love to you my dear,

Mother

VFX 94085 Capt. N. Heysen
Att. 106 CCS, AIF
Sunday 8 May 1944

Dearest Mother and Daddy,

Mother's letter has just come and home news is more than ever welcome. No sign of the prunes yet, but they'll be welcome when they do come. Today my trunk actually arrived after over a month on the journey. I'm thankful to see it, as it held the bulk of my painting equipment, clothes and the linen bag and shoe bag you made for my birthday. These I have sadly missed, as in my tent there is nowhere to put anything—a table, a chair, a bed and a few ropes strung across, as well all my painting gear to cope with. Bags are a blessing.

This last week it has rained or rather poured continuously, everywhere mud ankle deep and the smell of mildew and rotting. One's clothes get in a frightful state, damp and muddy. I've spent the days painting in my little tent, my feet on a box to keep them dry, my canvas perched on a chair and my bunk a litter of paints and papers. If law and order can come out of chaos, then it's going to be hard put to emerge out of this. My paintings mildew overnight, they'll be old masters before I get them back. My tin trunk has put in a timely appearance.

Every time a patient comes in for an operation, the surgeon rings me up and I go and get my impressions in the theatre. Yesterday had a native with a badly crushed foot. The surgeon did a delicate skin graft over the wound when he'd sewn the tendons and joined the splintered bones. The skin graft is wonderful and horrifying to watch. It is only by going out from time to time, and coming at it again, that I can watch and draw these things, and I wish someone else had been detailed off to do this job. There's no doubt it's interesting, but I can't get the things I see out of my mind. This composition progresses slowly. The surgeon is an artist at his job and one watches him sew up a vein with the delicate touch of a woman. He operated all through the London Blitz.

The CCS (Casualty Clearing Station) is moving up further north in a few weeks. If they do move, I think I'll go with them though, at the moment, it is doubtful if the sisters will go and, if not, a lone woman will not be viewed with favour. They are getting more or less used to me here now.

My love to all at home,

Nora

Hahndorf, South Australia
16 May 1944

Dearest Nora,

Your letter dated 8th May has just arrived and has given us our fill of thrills and chills of fear and anxieties. What a terrifying experience it all is, and can it all creep into your pictures along with mildew and what not! At any rate life can hold no nervous shocks for you once you are back in Australia again.

We will be glad when the New Guinea trip is fait accompli ... McGregor rang up just now, he is on a flying trip over, he tells of your great send off from Menzies! He was delighted to have news of you.

We all wish you luck and good health and much love,

Mother

VFX 94085 Capt. N. Heysen
Att. 106 CCS, AIF
30 May 1944

Dearest Mother and Daddy,

After a week of no mail, today they came in a big batch and I took the afternoon off to read and enjoy them.

I met a young Adelaide boy the other day, Capt. Mates. I went with him for a picnic up Satelberg—halfway the jeep got bogged and slipped over the side, and there we were with no hope of any passerby to extricate us. We pinned a message on the track in the hope, asking whoever it was to ring for a jeep to come up and get us. Meanwhile we walked down to the river and had a swim in the most picturesque and romantic spot, sparkling waterfalls and limpid pools overhung with jungle fern-like foliage, the sun splashing through in dazzling spots. On arriving back, we found the jeep gone and our tea with it. Nothing to do but to hike it. By then, it was dark and no light, a muddy jungle track through eerie blackness and 6 miles of it, with a very doubtful reception on arrival. After interminable hours of feeling our way through mud, we met an American truck and got a lift for a mile, then that also got bogged. By that time it was after 10 o'clock and off we squelched again, then were met by a rescue party. The men who extricated our jeep realised, on getting back, that the occupants must still be up there. They with kindly intentions had driven the thing back. Well we nearly got back when the lights on the jeep failed, then it began to pour, and eventually we walked in bedraggled and weary, far too tired to cope with the medicine that awaited us. I haven't lived it down yet and that incident has earned me a reputation of a rebel. It is true, I have managed to break every rule peculiar to this place.

This week I've been busy with bulldozers and have been introduced to the Mechanical Engineering Company, meeting thereby Bulldozer Bluey otherwise Sapper Bashful (believe it or not that is his name). Bluey is a character that one would meet only once in a lifetime. A lumber man from Queensland, a hulking great fellow 6 ft 4 and ginger, with pale blue eyes with that distant horizon look, red headed, red moustache and red hairs all over his brawny chest. It was Bluey who blazed the trail for the tanks to get up Satelberg, and who mowed down the jungle to make roads, all under Japanese fire. He and *Dearest*, as he calls his Bulldozer, were a law unto themselves. No one dared to give Bluey orders and he and *Dearest* went their own dangerous way. He's up for a Military Cross. He has an enormous red moustache and beard. What a man and yet, sitting for his portrait, he was blushing like a schoolgirl.[17]

Another I met and drew, 'Shorty', a handsome Scotchman with black beret at a rakish angle and merry blue eyes. Have spent every morning down at their camp on the banks of the Song River—Someone boils the billy at 10 and the cook pays me homage by turning out a batch of whopping great scones, and we all sit round on our haunches and the men yarn. Someone smears the scones with tropical spread, and we sip tea out of battered tin mugs. Shorty made me a stool, and another somehow produced a tin of turkey, an unheard of luxury, and there's nothing they wouldn't do for me—one advantage of being a woman up here. Shorty took me for an all-day picnic up the Massawang the other day, and we explored unknown fields. He taught me to shoot with an Owen gun, and I won a bet shooting the mark 6 times in succession.

My love to all at home,
Nora

17   This painting is *Bluey* (1944), oil on canvas, Australian War Memorial (ART23417).

VFX 94085 Capt. N. Heysen
Att. 106 CCS, AIF
29 June 1944

Dearest Mother and Daddy,

I have been trying to get to this letter for days, but life has been a turmoil and not knowing hourly if I was to be moved back or not. Had just begun on a large bunch of tropical flowers and was in the midst of it, when a movement order came through to return to Lae immediately and my plane seat was already booked. I dug my heels in and started battling, as the only reason for my return to Lae was for a rest prior to my move to Madang. Last night I was told I had to move this morning, but told them it was impossible as I hadn't finished my flowers, and now I'm waiting repercussions, probably a court martial or I'll be shot at dawn, or else. Being a woman they may allow for whims. This has gone on for three days and through them I've painted from dawn to dusk interrupted by the telephone. The flowers are lovely here—there was an old mission house on this hill with an old garden. Hibiscus, frangipani, lilies, cannas and coral flowers and a host of other little things new to me. Here I am at home and have enjoyed the escape from military subjects.

Here is a snap of me at last in captivity, not very good but it may give you an idea of what I look like in my jungle greens, also a reassurance that I am fit and well.

Mother's letter dated the 14th June came two or three days ago and it was good to hear all the news ... Everyone here is jubilant at the apparent success of the invasion, and in a way it is heartening as it seems to be the beginning of the end, but the price of it![18]

Have been called before the CO, went down quaking at the knees to be relieved by hearing that I was to be allowed a week's grace and that all was well. I can breathe again and return to my flowers. After the 8th I will be at Lae. It is indefinite how long I'll be there before moving on to Madang or further. Sorry to report that the fruits and pillowslip have not come—I'm still hoping.

My love to all,

Nora

---

18   Nora Heysen is referring to the landing at Normandy on 6 June 1944.

VFX 94085 Capt. N. Heysen
Att. 2/7 AGH, Lae
14 July 1944

Dearest Mother and Daddy,

Two home letters in as many days, and my word it is good to have them. Mine also seem to have been mislaid.

It would seem that I'll be here for another fortnight, as the women haven't moved up to Madang yet, and they do not encourage my going alone.

The sisters live in long native huts and are very comfortably off. The river is the only outlet to one's thoughts, the hills hem one in, beautiful they are, a hazy blue with little white clouds lying between in an absurd way that one wouldn't believe. Living amongst a crowd has the one advantage that one is left entirely alone, so I spend a great deal of time in my little tent—a concert, a movie the sole distraction!

Have started working on some chalk drawings, one of natives building a hut and the other of two little native girls sewing strips of coconut matting together for the sisters' mess. Here natives do all the work about the place, and they are fascinating to watch. The little girls who do the ironing are rather sweet with their graceful dignified little ways, their happy laughter at everything and their twitter, like a flock of young birdlings. One came running through my tent just now chasing a kitten, and catching sight of my flower piece I had hanging on the flap of my tent, she stopped dead and walking over gently touched the central white hibiscus with her long black fingers, then peered behind the canvas and looked back at me with a strange little smile of wonder.

Why not spend next winter in the tropics, parts of it really are very pleasant? I enjoyed Finschhafen and hated leaving for this.

My love to all and a hope that Daddy is well again,

Nora

VFX 94085 Capt. N. Heysen
Att. 111 CCS, AIF
29 July 1944

Dearest Mother and Daddy,

Just to say that I'm on the move again, and this will be my address. They promise to fly me up to Alexishafen tomorrow. Up to date there are only four women there. I want to be there so as to see the pioneering stages of setting up a CCS.

Things have just been so-so, this place sits like a weight on my spirits and it has rained ceaselessly. For all that, there's been no water owing to pipes being washed away. The only way of washing body and clothes is the Busu River which runs a muddy stony course just below. I go for a dip in it morning and night, but come out far greyer than in I went. This treatment has brought about a tinea infection and a prickly heat rash, not warranted to improve my temper. And lastly to dispatch the worst first—I had a letter from Col Treloar saying that he was disappointed and dissatisfied with my New Guinea work, and wished my immediate return to Melbourne.

I feel it is a rather unjustified and hasty attack, considering that he has only seen part of the work done here in the first 2 ½ months while I was trying to work my way in through new and trying conditions. Still, it is very depressing having done one's best, and to put it mildly, I'm fed up. I wrote back in an angry mood giving my comment on his every accusation and insinuation, and now I'm hastily getting out to escape repercussions. But just how long it will be before his authority catches up with me, is a matter for conjecture. I fear that my short career as a War Artist is fast drawing to a stormy close.

The gist of his criticism was that I had not immortalised the war work of the Florence Nightingales. In fact, had gone so far as to undermine their prestige by depicting them in social mood, dancing and holding a tea party, and crime of crimes, I drew them in the bath tub.

Also that I had drawn too many undistinguished people, and had done no active war scenes and that I hadn't touched upon the work done here by the AAMWS, the latter argument was in my favour, since there are no women of that service up here. So much for so little, and let's get onto brighter things. The dried fruit and chocks have been a tonic, the prunes delicious and the figs a treat indeed. Also I don't know myself sleeping on linen again, so life has a few compensations.

Jimmy Cook blew in the other day—he has the job of being the artist attached to the Comforts Fund and has just arrived in New Guinea. It was stimulating to talk to someone after my numb and dumb existence here, and we both enjoyed a good chat. He is in his element and very excited at the subject matter and keen as mustard. He should fit right into this position as he has experience and knowledge, and an illustrative turn of mind so necessary in this job. Treloar turned him down, also Dobell and Drysdale. Now I hear that since Dobell's success he is trying to get his services, but Bill isn't having any of it, and I don't blame him.

If one were allowed a free reign, there is plenty of subject matter here. I jeeped up to Nadzab the other day and marvelled at the beauty of the hills. Bare and volcanic in formation, very magnificent shapes, and in that setting, the enormous Flying Fortresses and Liberator bombers looked truly superb as they rested like enormous monster birds glistening silver in the sun.[19] Yet strange and terrible to think that their sole purpose is destruction, death and futility. It seems that these scientific marvels are only inspired by war and hatred—a sad misguided world, and no mistake. On my return here, I shall try and do a little work up there and blast the Colonel. I'm afraid that living exclusively with women and hospitals does not inspire one to paint them.

Have been working on red chalk drawings, and a few odd watercolours round the place. Yes, watercolours! I have taken it up hoping that the multiple difficulties will distract my thoughts, and I must admit that watercolour painting doesn't allow a wandering mind. My admiration for Daddy increases every day, if that were possible.

The mess bell has gone and so it is the sheep to the slaughter or to food, or rather to slaughtered food.

My love to all at home, with a hope that all is well,
Nora

VFX 94085 Capt. N. Heysen
Att. 111 CCS, AIF
9 August 1944

Dearest Mother and Daddy,

No mail has caught up with me yet, and I miss it sadly. Only a week I have been here, or a little over and it has seemed a long time. After having been so free of skin troubles, I have now developed every brand peculiar to these parts and one all my own. This latter unfortunately is all over my hands. The doctors say sitting out in the sun painting has caused it, and that I must wear gloves, keep them greased and not get heated or sit in the sun. All things which I'm unable to do, however they are so swollen and irritated that it is difficult to work and what with prickly heat over my entire body, and dermatitis and tinea to boot, my life is made a little miserable at times.

Worse than all this are the rats. They are here in millions, every night one gets into my bed. They eat their way through everything, crawl all over everything and smell. If there is one thing I hate it is rats in my bed, and one lies awake watching for them. What they don't eat goes mildewy and musty. Sometimes it just gets me down, and I wonder what the Hell—is anything worth it?

---

19   In 1910 a Lutheran mission was established at Nadzab, where an airfield was built during the Second World War for use by the American and Australian air forces in repelling the Japanese.

At the moment, I'm drinking warm gin and water preparing myself for my nightly companions the rats. About the only way one gets any sleep at all. Liquor has come to the island, and we all have our donation for the month dealt out to us. My wine cellar is quite spectacular. A bottle of whiskey, one of gin and three of beer, but all warm, hence not very alluring.

I'm working on half a dozen subjects at once. A portrait of the theatre sisters in cap and mask and gloves preparing the instruments of torture.[20] As the theatre is the coolest place here, that subject is welcome. Also am doing or rather painting a blood transfusion on a native, a scene of the wounded being unloaded on stretchers off a barge, and a composition of men working amid the ruins constructing a picture theatre—the seats coconut logs, the screen a fantastic structure of bamboo stems. The men here are a mahogany colour, they work just in jungle-green trousers and leggings, and make beautiful studies. One of these subjects alone could take months of study. I live and work in a daze of bewildered subject matter, and heat and mosquitoes and flies and smells.

I still have a few biscuits. They have been a boon—sitting on the Nadzab airstrip without food for 24 hours, I suddenly remembered them in my kit bag and they saved my life. I shared them with my driver in the cold light of the dawn.

This place has a character of its own—a lovely silvery quality of grey that is fascinating. All the coconut palms are decapitated and dead and a lovely cool grey. All the derelict wooden sun-bleached ruins are grey, and the skies are overcast and grey, a luminous grey.

Well to bed, my love and thoughts,

Nora

VFX 94085 Capt. N. Heysen
Att. 111 CCS, AIF
12 August 1944

Dearest Mother and Daddy,

At last my mail has caught up with me. Twelve letters all in one big bunch, I half went crazy with delight.

Life in a CCS is interesting—the MO's, pathologists, surgeons, dispensers, the adjutants, the quarter masters, all individuals, of course not forgetting the sisters who all seem avid for publicity. To protect myself from everlasting requests to paint them and their gardens and houses, I persuaded the war photographer to do his bit.

---

20   This is *Theatre Sister Margaret Sullivan* (1944), oil on canvas, Australian War Memorial (ART22234).

I have a lot of subjects on the way and occasionally I stick a woman in edgeways to appease the Colonel. Have started on a portrait of the theatre sister in white gown and cap and mask and gloved hands—in the light of the window against an old whitewashed wall. It makes a subtle and fascinating scheme. Am also painting the surgeon, the blood bank with sisters in attendance, the x-ray scene and a blood transfusion on a native. Enough to keep me busy. The days have been very hot and in the heat, my rashes drive me mad. Have had advice from all the MO's, endless prescriptions, the only cure to get out of New Guinea, and that of course I can't do. The diet I think really is the cause. Haven't seen fruit nor any vegetables for 2 months. Today, the great exception, as we had Adelaide celery for lunch. It tasted marvellous, though it was brown, and I ate it, strings and all. Most of the men look ill and we women all yellow and patchy. There's no doubt that this climate ages one quickly. My hair shows decided tendencies to greyness, and my skin is a horror to the touch. I look at my hands in revolt.

You will be welcoming the first signs of Spring. How remote all that sweet freshness seems from this. Here the air is permeated still with the smell of decayed Japanese food, and bodies and camp refuse. One can hear crocodiles in the river at the back.

My love to all at home,
Nora

VFX 94085 Capt. N. Heysen
Att. 111 CCS, AIF
19 August 1944

Dearest Mother and Daddy,

Mother's letter dated 4th has just found me ... letters mean more than anything here and if it comes in at midnight, the word goes round like lightning and everyone's astir 'Any for me?'

For a short while things have been much better. The navy came to the rescue, the quartermaster on a ship that came into port here knew the *Manunda* well and Daddy's picture and his enthusiasm spread to me as bearing the name, and he couldn't do enough.[21] Every morning there arrived a hamper of fresh fruit, eggs, meat and butter and many little accessories. For a week, one ate like Lords, even to cold chicken and Stilton cheese. The Navy entertained us on their ship in gallant style, the most beautiful fresh salads and icy cold beer, as much as

21   During the war, the *Manunda* was converted into a hospital ship serving in the Middle East and the Pacific. She was damaged during the air raid on Darwin in 1942 and, once repaired, was based at Milne Bay, New Guinea.

one could hold. Also they produced a board for me to pin my canvases to, and are making me an easel. That picture of Daddy's has had very happy repercussions. Sad to say we had a farewell party to them yesterday, and at dawn this morning I watched her sail out.

I have finished my painting of the theatre sisters. To paint again in a studio will be heavenly. Here I usually prop my doings up on a chair balanced on blocks and sit on a petrol drum in the blazing heat and glare. The operating theatre provided relief with its stone floor and white-washed walls. I was frowned on by the surgeon until I made a drawing of the theatre sister for him, and now he's co-operative and we take the use of the theatre turn and turn about. There I work in the sterile atmosphere of ether and whiteness. The surgeon is my next victim. At present I'm doing the blood and serum sisters and a transfusion scene. My model for this, a native boy, died unfortunately and next I found myself a spectator at his post mortem. This time, not to watch, but to draw but not first enquiring whose the body was, I got a nasty turn to find my favourite native boy stiff and cold.

The crowning insult last night, a rat brought a biscuit from outside into my bed and ate it under my pillow, quite unbeknown to me. Is that not intimate proof that I've been broken in? This morning I spent at the tub trying to get rat out of my clothing and mind. I'm just setting off to the pictures under a starry sky.

My love to all at home, hoping all is well all round,

Nora

VFX 94085 Capt. N. Heysen
Att. 111 CCS, AIF
31 August 1944

Dearest Mother and Daddy,

Expecting everyday to receive my marching orders, I'm working against time. It is a stupid way to work and I don't feel I can do my best, harried perpetually from headquarters. I feel I have no freedom. At the moment, I'm working on portraits of all the sisters, they are willing but not very interesting sitters. I alternate them with men and natives. The natives are marvellous models, unselfconscious, patient and understanding. They are so right in this setting and have such natural graceful movements that it is hard to look the other way towards subjects of military interest.

The hills, too, are beautiful even though the place is a shambles, dead trees and bomb craters. There is much beauty, the skies sunfilled with beautiful cloud effects, and the moonlit nights unbelievable. A party of us paddled across to one of the islands in a native lakatoie the other evening, taking our tea and some bottles of beer, and spent half the night on a moonlit beach hung over with coconut palms. The war seemed very remote. The sisters are a nice friendly crowd here, and often invite me to their outings.

There's a skin specialist up here at the moment, and I'm going to see what he can do for me.

My love to all at home,

Nora

> *VFX 94085 Capt. N. Heysen*
> *Att. 111 CCS, AIF*
> *3 September 1944*

Dearest Mother and Daddy,

Three home letters on three consecutive days, a happy surprise. Probably I will be returning at the end of this month. Any day the Colonel is likely to haul me in. If he does not, I'll finish the work I have in mind, and take steps towards home. Physically, as the men say, 'I've had it'. My skin complaints are getting me down and I feel that nothing but a cool climate will help. There was the skin specialist for New Guinea up here the other day, and I took myself along for advice and was informed that I had eczema on my hands and reek tinea under my arms, and prickly heat turning to dermatitis over the rest of my body. A complete example of New Guinea skin diseases, isn't that lovely? Remedy prescribed, no soap, one shower a day, no washing, a liquid chocolate mess to be applied throughout four times a day, ether soap for my head ... gentian violet for the tinea and a green paint for spots. I can see I'll have very little time for painting, outside the old body.

My love to all at home and a big thank you for the good things,

Nora

VFX 94085 Capt. N. Heysen
Att. 111 CCS, AIF
18 September 1944

Dearest Mother and Daddy,

My ultimatum has been signed just now by the skin specialist, and I'm making plans to fly direct to Australia as per flying boat as soon as can be managed. It will probably be a fortnight before my movement order is produced, but things are underway. It seems useless to hang on further, my skin condition becomes worse. When he gave me the once over today, he gave me the alternative of remaining here in bed or else returning as soon as possible. So that's that.

What my movements will be on returning, I don't quite know. I suppose I'll have to report at Headquarters, and will then apply for leave and go home to shed some of my New Guinea skin. I wish, like a snake, I could just crawl out of it and leave my troubles behind, twined round a bush to frighten the unwary.

My love to all at home,

Nora

Hahndorf, South Australia
22 September 1944

My Dear Nora,

It's been a boon right along to have your letters—Mother and I have enjoyed every one of them with their pen pictures of every scenery and personal happenings. What an experience! Sometimes I wish I could be with you to explore new fields, for your descriptions whet my appetite for fresh subject matter, but I draw the line at the conditions you have to work under.

The problems of art are bad enough in themselves, but when handicapped by all the 'evils' of that country, well I realise all that which yet remains to be done in this land of ours. Brimming over with subtle beauties quite untouched, no one as far as I know at the moment, is even attempting to explore even the simpler problems. They are all more or less concerned with 'isms' of art, swamping all their love for this country with its peculiar subtleties of form, colour and atmosphere.

At present there is a Memorial Exhibition of Streeton's work at the National Gallery in Melbourne which may prove a stimulus to some of our younger painters to get back to the Australian landscape.[22] McGregor writes me, 'It's

---

22   Arthur Streeton died on 1 September 1943. The Memorial Exhibition at the National Gallery of Victoria
      included 100 paintings and 30 watercolours drawn from all state galleries and private collections. High
      attendance resulted in the exhibition being extended for two weeks. See 'Streeton Exhibition Extended',
      The Argus, 28 September 1944.

extremely fine and surprisingly versatile', he wishes that I could come over to see it. It will be coming, or the greater part of it, to Adelaide. We could not manage the whole on account of the excessive insurance values, and our Gallery is 'hard up' as to funds that can be diverted to this purpose. It would have to come from the Government, and they give us nothing beyond staff and cleaning expenses.

The South Australian Society of Arts here has just closed, we bought two— one by Smart for 15gs and another for 10gs.[23] I was unable to attend the meeting, so have not seen the pictures.

We sent McCubbin over, with £200 to buy from the Society of Artists Sydney, and he bought back an Adrian Feint *The Happy Landing* for £100 and *At the Window* by Murch for 75gs. McGregor thinks it is the best thing Feint has painted, which applies also to Murch.

When I looked at the London 'price lists' at auction sales in the *Connoisseur* I realised a decided reaction towards the more popular type of picture—Stubbs is certainly coming into his own, his top price being 6,000gs. The Society of Artists Sydney closed with record sales, and the same state of affairs comes from Melbourne. Will Ashton's exhibition with Sedon realised over 3,000gs before opening day, and all old work too. His top value being 250gs each for two Paris scenes. Both John Rowell and Johnson topped the 2,000 mark and each had to pay over £900 income tax. I am not listening to any of the dealers personally as to holding an exhibition. I would sooner keep what I have than give them to the Government, but everything sells that I let go out! Quite evidently there is *great* deal of money about.

When in town I paid the Geelong cheque for your flower piece 35gs into your account. Mother will have told you that I had paid Sedon's cheque of £52 and something into your account for the large flower study—also Fern had paid into your Melbourne account a cheque for the *Scabious*. And I must not forget there is a cheque of £35 from Holman I paid into the bank for you.

Time is up so must stop. We all send our love in the hope that we will see you with us very soon. In the meanwhile 'see it through' and cheerio,

From your Dad

Nora returns to 'The Cedars' for four weeks[24]

---

23   The Jeffrey Smart was *Water Towers* (1944), oil on canvas.
24   To read an account of Louis McCubbin's report on Nora's official war art he saw at 'The Cedars', see 'Nora Heysen's View from the Pacific Region' in Catherine Speck, *Painting Ghosts: Australian Women Artists in Wartime*, Melbourne, Craftsman House and Thames and Hudson, 2004.

Wentworth Hotel, Sydney
Thursday 7th 1944

Dearest Mother and Daddy,

A word to say I'm home safe and sound. In Melbourne I met fresh obstacles … When I met Colonel Treloar on arriving he seemed surprised and knew nothing of my coming over, nor of my proposed trip to Sydney—the letter I had written to him a week previously had gone astray, 'wouldn't it'. Hence nothing had been arranged for me to travel on, nor to work here, and he said it was impossible to do anything on that day as it was too late for movement order tickets etc. Well, a little thing like that wasn't likely to stop me, so I went and saw him and eventually, though it took me all day to achieve it, I got on that train. The Wentworth couldn't take me in when I arrived, so I walked the streets for three hours with the Domain looming nearer and nearer with every step, so came back looking so pathetic that the manager here suddenly found a room for me. Thank God this family is blessed with a certain amount of persistence. I didn't notice the train journey, eight in the carriage all the way, servicemen and myself, the only female, and no sleep—the chocolate my only sustenance, as I refused to battle for my food en route. I was thankful for the chocolate, and nearly tackled the sausage bread.

Sybil Irving was thrilled with the 'bag' of country produce and was touched with the little bag of bread and butter so neatly tied. The roses were still wet and fresh, the gift a great success.

McGregor was at the Menzies, I had a drink with him as a send-off, most pleased to see each other. He sends his love. On the spot he rang though to his friend the skin specialist here, a Dr Grant Linderman (related to the wines) and made an appointment for me. Have just returned from seeing him with a fresh dose of prescriptions and advice. I'm to leave off taking Atabrin[25] as that, in his opinion, is responsible for my skin and half the New Guinea skins. He gave me X-ray treatment and a lot of other sundries to swallow and apply. We shall see what happens. So far I've done nothing much but rest. I begin working tomorrow.

Everyone thinks I look miles better than when I went through last, and so I should. There is no place like one's own home to set one on their feet again. I'm ready again for the next 'do'. It was good to have those four weeks.

My love to all at home,

Nora

---

25   A drug used to ward off malaria.

Wentworth Hotel, Sydney
14 December 1944

Dearest Mother and Daddy,

The parcel has just arrived with all I wanted, plus the biscuits—the delicious accompanying smell, a whiff of Christmas. The paints will see me through the Blood Bank.[26] There is nothing to be had here, not a tube of paint nor anything to paint on. I'm glad to have the shirts and to see the open necks—it has been very hot and sticky, and starched collars don't help one to keep cool. I've written asking the Colonel for a few days to go home for Christmas. So far I haven't had his reply, but I think he will be on my side.

The Blood Bank here wants me to hold an exhibition of the work I have done before I leave so that everyone represented or not can bring along their relatives to see. So I am faced with the dreadful idea of showing a lot of raw canvases and drawings unmounted, a prospect I hate. I'm scratching my head to try and think of something to help me, at least a boundary to help the canvases, but the shops squash every idea. The allowance is one sheet of poor cardboard.

I have done a fair amount of work, and will be glad to have a few days' spell. This nine-to-five racket is only endurable in short spasms.

I'm writing this in amongst the blood and serum and cannot concentrate, so will come to this again. My love to all at home with the thought of being there soon,

Nora

'Menzies', Melbourne
Wednesday 10 January 1945

Dearest Mother and Daddy,

Since last writing I have settled in somewhat with a little of my equilibrium regained. There is nothing like painting to restore balance to a confused mind. Back in the 'Morgue' with the trams and trains rattling past, telephones ringing and other roar of continual traffic, peace, perfect peace!

I'm hard at work on a large canvas of the New Guinea Blood Transfusion and having once goaded myself into tackling that white canvas, I feel slightly more resigned to working here. There are a handful of leftover artists working somewhere on another floor of the building. Occasionally I hear a bellow from their vicinity when the billy has been brewed for morning tea, otherwise I am quite detached, which is a blessing. Hele, Dargie, Mainwaring, Hodgkinson, Norton are all away *covering* the offensive.

---

26   The blood bank was an AIF unit based at Sydney Hospital.

Ivor Hele's New Guinea work was on view for a couple of days for General Blamey's inspection. I was lucky to just see it on the day of my arrival, before it was taken down. The drawings were first rate, the best I've seen come out of this war, but his paintings were a disappointment. They seemed confused and muddled.

On Sunday I worked in Colonel Irving's garden, the day was lovely and the work interspersed with beer and music on the lawn.

Not only is Daddy inundated with congratulations, even I am receiving them thick and fast on his behalf. Quite half a dozen people have said 'Congratulations on the OBE'.[27] I don't know what the answer to that is … it is rather nice.

I must resume my transfusion. My love to all at home,

Nora

'Menzies', Melbourne
Monday 29 January 1945

Dearest Mother and Daddy,

The days pass and I do not remember when last I wrote, it must be some time ago since the biscuit tin is almost empty.

As you no doubt know, McCubbin was over here for a week making a selection of work for a contemplated large mixed show of Australian War Artists' work—about 200 pictures in all. It is extraordinary I think that one man is entrusted with the selection. Probably there is a final judgement. McCubbin made no hesitation in his choice, and went through the work like a whirlwind … and said he'd have that, and that, and was out again in five minutes. I was left somewhat bewildered and dazed. However, on thinking over his choice, it is the one I should have made myself, so there you are. Ten paintings and ten drawings of mine to be included.

McCubbin tells me that Col Treloar is still under the impression that I hate him and he's frightened to come near me. Since he is far more considerate under that impression, it can stand and I can work in peace. My blood transfusion is now finished, for better or worse, and for relief I have turned to the dance subject.

As far as I can see, to complete my New Guinea work is going to take months. Two stray canvases found their way home from Bougainville the other day. They got lost in transport.

My love to all at home,

Nora

27   Hans Heysen was awarded an OBE for his services to art in the New Year's Honours List of January 1945.

PS Ivor Hele has just arrived back from New Guinea. He called in the other day on his way home. He's certainly 'had it' this time and looks a wreck. A bad jeep accident has smashed his nose in and a few teeth, and he was unconscious for 3 days and is still very nervous and shaky.

'Menzies', Melbourne
Wednesday 21 February 1945

Dearest Mother and Daddy,

Ure Smith was over for a week. I breakfasted with him for a couple of mornings, and he came down to see my work—was enthusiastic and wants to publish some in his next volume on Australian Art.—He says he wants to reproduce some of the war artists' work, but Treloar won't have it, as he thinks all proceeds or more should go to the Australian War Museum. It seems wrong that the work of the American War artists has been given so much publicity, while ours is neglected and the artists, by being in this job, are out of circulation and the public eye.[28]

Ure Smith looked well and enjoyed his stay—he wanted to know all the home news and said he was writing. He also had only just heard of Daddy's OBE, it evidently didn't reach Sydney … On several occasions I lunched with Jim McGregor. His company is always stimulating and I look forward to his flying visits.

Has Daddy the new Phaidon book on Augustus John's work? I bought it with a portion of my Christmas £5. I would like to give it to Daddy in exchange for the Wilson Steer which he already had.

My love to all at home,

Nora

Hahndorf, South Australia
Monday 12 March 1945

My Dear Nora,

'At last' you may say. Well it's about time I did write and tell you the happenings and arrival of the John book. And now for John. It's a fine selection of his portrait work and I like most of them immensely, so virile and so lifelike and

---

28   Artists were critical of the limited appointments to the official war art scheme and that the work was not being widely exhibited. See 'The Second World War: Women Artists Respond' in Catherine Speck, *Painting Ghosts: Australian Women Artists in Wartime*, Melbourne, Craftsman House and Thames and Hudson, 2004. The confrontational American war art received much publicity and Russell Drysdale described it as possessing 'a power and a force which is refreshing to see'. See 'Frankly Shocking Realism in Pacific War Art', *Sunday Sun*, 7 January 1945.

so fine in character. The selection of his 'compositions' not so good or representative. I know of several that should have been included, the same with the Wilson Steer book. Thank you ever so much for sending this home, it's well worth having. Would you like me to send the Wilson Steer on to you? Or perhaps you don't want to be bothered with it just now? Just give the word and I will pack and send on to the Menzies.

I have just read in *The Connoisseur* that McColl is writing a book on Wilson Steer but doesn't say when it is to be published and evidently Phaidon Press got in first. Another review mentioned was the letters of Camille Pissarro to his son Lucien covering a period of very many years. This sounds interesting, and I am writing to Preece to get a copy to send to you.[29] Evidently in many of these letters he stresses the importance of drawing, draw, draw, draw he says! Did you see in the *Bulletin* the prices realised at a public auction in Sydney lately? Norman Lindsay's soared up—a small watercolour 12 x 9 brought 90gs. And some higher, Gruner up to 180gs (small canvases) and one of my small things *A Pastoral* 90gs!

When last in town I just missed 2 tubes of Viridian—but she is keeping some for me out of the next lot—about 2 months, she thought. 5 small cobalts is all I got, these I will send on to you with a Studio Burnt Sienna. Don't forget to write, we always love having your letters, hope the skin trouble is clearing up, again thank you for the John book.

With love from your Dad

'Menzies', Melbourne
Friday 16 March 1945

Dearest Mother and Daddy,

A letter from Daddy, a rare pleasure. As my plans are so indecisive, I think it would be wisest to hold the Wilson Steer. I just can't cope with books travelling, much as I should like to have them with me. I think I must have procured the last John book to be bought in Melbourne. It is amazing how quickly new art books are snapped up. One day every bookshop seems to have dozens, and the next they are all gone.

Stanley Spencer is next on the Phaidon Press list and I want to add that to my Christmas present. The Camille Pissarro sounds interesting and I know I'd like his outlook. So if you could order me a copy I'd be very glad.

Bill and Ursula Hayward stayed at the Menzies a couple of days en route to Adelaide, and I enjoyed a couple of cheery dinners and shows with them. Bill

---

29   Preece was a well-known Adelaide bookshop that also held exhibitions.

Hayward was keen to see the work I'd done in New Guinea and was enthusiastic.[30] I am always glad when someone who has been there, and knows, likes the work and can appreciate in them some of their own experiences and impressions. You will no doubt be seeing them as they promise themselves a trip up and are looking forward to seeing you again.

I am still working on New Guinea stuff, but feel that I have almost finished what I can do with it. It is so difficult, I find, to retain spirit and life working only from notes and memory.

Seven new artists have been appointed. Donald Friend is already working here and has unfortunately the room next mine. He giggles incessantly and entertains. I don't mind the racket of trains and trams, but that giggling is an irritant. He wears heavy gold rings on his fingers, long hair and the work I've seen up to date repulses me. I'm convinced that he is a fake, no doubt a very amusing and witty one with pretty camouflage, but my back bristles.

There's another woman too, a Sybil Craig, elderly and a painter of flowers so they tell me.[31] Max Ragless and John Goodchild from Adelaide, Solomon Herman and James Flett from Sydney. These appointments are I think for six months only, and only 4 of them are to be official war artists.

Ivor Hele opens his show here next week. He is at present in hospital having his nose put straight, and then goes back home to work.

My love to all at home,

Nora

VFX 94085 Capt. N. Heysen
c/- Sec. Officer Barnes
RAAF Group 824 Cairns
2 June 1945

Dearest Mother and Daddy,

At last a little stability in which to write and let you know what I am doing, and where. You will have received my telegram, I hope, but as mails from here are censored strictly, it is difficult to know what goes through.

---

30   Bill Hayward (Sir Edward) served in the AIF in the Middle East and New Guinea, rising to the rank of Lieutenant Colonel.

31   On Sybil Craig's time as an official war artist, see 'Sybil Craig's View from the Home Front' in Catherine Speck, *Painting Ghosts: Australian Women Artists in Wartime*, Melbourne, Craftsman House and Thames and Hudson, 2004.

Just a week since I left Melbourne at 4 am, one bleak morning. I made Townsville late that same night, after a bumpy trip and a very long one in a transport plane. Once again the only woman.

On reaching Townsville, no one owned me. The army sent me to the air force, and the air force to the army, bandied back and forth and, very weary, I spent almost two hours on the airstrip trying to find a pillow for my head that night. Eventually I was taken to an air force mess into the midst of a heavy Saturday night session, and was brought round or rather finished off with a couple of whiskies. Everyone was very merry and it was midnight before I found a straw bed in the barracks. It was discovered in the morning that I had no authority to go on to Cairns, as I had no ticket, no priority, or movement order. Goodness knows how I got so far. Evidently I should have had a ticket which was never given me. However all was well. I promised a portrait here and there and got away on a very luxurious passenger plane. My first taste of travelling in comfort. An air hostess popping barley sugar into one's mouth every few minutes, lounge chairs, paper bags and curtains. One engine broke down, but no one knew till we were safely down.

Cairns is a lovely spot surrounded with high mountains and the climate good at this time of the year. I'm stationed about four miles out of town on a hill by the sea. It has rained ever since I arrived, heavy tropical rain and my paper was too sodden to work, like New Guinea again.

I feel a little lost. My room is a petitioned off part of an army hut and the mattress of straw seems very hard again. Once again life is boiled down to necessities.

One thing I forgot on leaving home, and that is my watercolour box. I cannot locate it so think I must have left it in my studio or in the lobby where I was packing. Could you possibly send it to me if it is there, as I had counted on making some watercolour sketches.

My love to all at home,
Nora

> VFX 94085 Capt. N. Heysen
> Att. 106 CCS, AIF
> 9 June 1945

Dearest Mother and Daddy,

I'm still here still waiting day by day for word to move up further north, very shortly we'll be the only Australians here, and I'm impatient to get on.

I have been doing a little gun practice, drawing a 6-pounder anti-tank gun and crew in action, and learning a little about the mechanisms of war. Can't get up much interest in drawing guns and machinery, but feel it a necessary part of my equipment for the job.

Dargie arrived here unexpectedly for a couple of days. On his way up North to Aitapi, he slipped and cut his hand and knees on coral, and was put off here for medical attention. I welcomed the coincidence, as it is a godsend to talk to someone who understands the same language, and it was a tonic to talk art and laugh over our experiences as war artists. For all the time I've been here and with all the people I've met from every walk of life, not one has any knowledge or real interest in art. One begins to feel strangely apart, almost an outcast.

I have been working on the subject of a native being attended by a sister. The dark body of the native on the white sheets in contrast to the white woman—Manet's *Olympia* in reverse and a painter's subject, and one I enjoy doing. The only trouble is I have to work in a crowded ward, and the spectators drive me mad.

It is still indefinite where I move. Wewak is contemplated and I'm hoping this is so, as I'll be nearer what I want.

Hope all is well in all quarters.

My love,

Nora

> VFX 94085 Capt N. Heysen
> Att. Group 824 Cairns, RAAF
> 24 June 1945

Dearest Mother and Daddy,

Firstly safe and welcome arrival of the parcels of goods. I'm settling down somewhat. The landscape here compensates for all the rest, and I've lost my heart to the mountains and cane fields, the only difficulty is trying to concentrate on WAAAF work when I want to go roaming the hills with my colours. Thank you Daddy for the extra colours and hope they'll produce something.

At the moment I'm painting a dispatch rider and a cook, both under difficulties—the former poses hanging over the low doorway into the signal office, a busy thoroughfare amidst telephones and milling women. The latter in the kitchen with me sitting on the table, almost on the stove.[32] What with the heat and the dust and flies and the sight of yards of bully beef and dehydrated mashed potato pie, well,

---

32   These paintings are *Despatch Rider (Leading Aircraftsman George Mayo), Cairns* (1945), oil on canvas, Australian War Memorial (ART24367) and *WAAAF Cook (Corporal Joan Whipp)* (1945), oil on canvas, Australian War Memorial (ART24394).

painting is the least of the problem. This painting is causing keen concentration, as I want the bully beef pie in the scheme, which means it is on the menu and hated by all.

Lovely sunny days, warm to hot, with cool nights. A huge full moon tonight, a farewell party to one of the men last night which continued till dawn, even a straw mattress looks inviting tonight. There's plenty of entertainment, concerts, movies, dances and dinners at nearby units. For the most part, I stay in, as I can't make the pace and do my work at the same time.

My love to all,
Nora

Att. No. 2 MAETU Group 291, RAAF
Pacific

Dearest Mother and Daddy,

Well, I'm here at the place I spoke of. Three days solid flying with wretched nights at transient staying camps has left me a little weary. It is steamy and hot, this camp is in a coconut plantation by the sea. It rains every day and the mud is deep all round. The first night I spent at Higginsfield way up on the tip of Cape York, then Madang, Wewak, Hollandia and Biak, all round New Guinea and up. Tomorrow there is a dance. I move still further up, I'm going with a couple of the flying sisters to bring back the battle casualties. I'll be away three or four days, then will return here, I hope, with my subject matter. It will be difficult working on the plane full of stretcher cases over the eight hour flight, I don't know how it will go and can't say I'm thrilled with the idea, but having undertaken this job I must go through with it and take the rough with the smooth.

The air is electric with rumours and every hour brings the peace nearer in talk. I only hope, and with all the others, dream of being home again … It will be bedlam here if news comes through. Everyone is hanging over the wireless waiting, the guns are ready to go off in the blast of victory. The island will tremble.

I share a room with three other sisters. The showers and toilet are communal. This lack of privacy I still find intensely embarrassing and will never accustom myself to it. I'm sitting outside the mess, an army hut that the sisters have brightened up with gay cushions and red tables, the palms wave gently in the breeze off the sea, a welcome breath indeed as it has been stifling all day. Washing and ironing are still the major problem. It just takes too much and I'm afraid I trade on being a little bohemian and therefore above starched cleanliness.

A four o'clock getaway, so I must to bed. My love to all at home,
Nora

Unknown Photographer
Nora Heysen in Uniform 1944

Manuscripts Collection, MS 10041
National Library of Australia

Nora Heysen (1911–2003)
*Colonel Sybil Irving, Controller,
AWAS* 1943

oil on canvas; 76.4 x 56.0 cm
Acquired under the official war art
scheme 1945
Australian War Memorial, ART 22220

above
George Harvey Nicholson
*Captain Nora Heysen behind the
Barbed-wire Perimeter at the Nurses'
Compound, 106th Casualty Clearing
Station, Finschhafen, New Guinea*
1944

photograph
Australian War Memorial, 073884

Nora Heysen (1911–2003)
*Matron Annie Sage, Matron in Chief,
AANS* 1944

oil on canvas; 76.6 x 56.4 cm
Acquired under the official war art
scheme 1945
Australian War Memorial, ART 22218

Nora Heysen (1911–2003)
Theatre Sister Margaret Sullivan
1944

oil on canvas; 91.8 x 66.0 cm
Acquired under the official war art
scheme 1945
Australian War Memorial, ART 22234

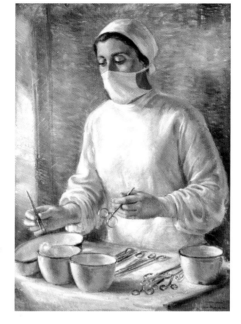

below
K.C. Rainsford
*Captain Nora Heysen, Official War
Artist, in her Studio at 138 Flinders
Street, Melbourne, Completing
Paintings which were Commenced
in New Guinea* 1945

photograph
Australian War Memorial, 085073

above
Nora Heysen (1911–2003)
*Transport Driver (Aircraftswoman
Florence Miles)* 1945

oil on canvas; 66.6 x 81.8 cm
Acquired under the official war art
scheme 1945
Australian War Memorial, ART 24393

Nora Heysen (1911–2003)
*Despatch Rider (Leading
Aircraftsman George Mayo),
Cairns* 1945

oil on canvas; 77.0 x 61.0 cm
Acquired under the official war art
scheme 1945
Australian War Memorial, ART 24367

Cairns, North Queensland
24 August 1945

Dearest Mother and Daddy,

I have received the telegram and Mother's letter. As you see I have changed my address yet once again, but am not very far from my last camp, only this time I'm army and back to hospitals. This camp is well established in a most beautiful spot—a valley of cane fields surrounded by mountains. From out my window I look upon a canvas all readymade, a strip of ploughed earth, the tender green of newly sprouting cane and a lovely line of hills. This time I have a cubicle to myself and actually a mirror and a chest of drawers and two chairs, luxury indeed, especially the privacy which I appreciate after being landed in with a dozen others.

I can't remember if I've written since coming down from Morotai, what with peace celebrations and all, the upheaval and change of plans and movement, my mind is confused. I'm waiting to hear from the Colonel as to what next, but until I do, I suppose I'll continue my itinerary. As a respite from flying, this is good and I'm glad to stay put. The very thought of moving again with all this luggage horrifies me ... I'm going to marry the biggest strongest man I can find, and sit back for the rest of my life.

It has come so suddenly I still cannot fully realise it. The thought that I'll soon be out of this job goes to my head, to be free to paint what one wants to, seems to me to be very Heaven.

My love to all and a hope that it won't be so long now,
Nora

Att. LGH Medical Research Unit
Cairns, North Queensland
4 October 1945

Dear Daddy,

A letter to wish you many happy returns of the day on the 8th and to say that my parcel has been delayed, and will follow later.

I wish you could see this landscape. You would be as fascinated as I am, but would be able to do something about it. It is not really Australian in the typical sense of being too lush, colourful and decorative, but it has a character and beauty all its own and is on a grand scale, the sun-filled skies, the blue of the mountains and the tender greens of the cane fields with splashes of red earth. At present it is the season for cane cutting, mostly being done by dark labour Afghans in white turbans and Italians, subject matter for a Van Gogh.

This is just a birthday message as I have only just yesterday posted
my news. I hear there is a new book out on Australian painting by one Bernard
Smith—have you seen it?

My love and birthday wishes,

Nora

Hahndorf, South Australia
2 November 1945

My Dear Nora,

This is just to tell you that the very much-delayed parcel has arrived at last!

Thank you so much dear Nora for sending me this decorative piece of '*your
country*', for it is quite obvious that you have fallen in love with your surroundings.[33]
Your description and your little picture excite my curiosity. It must be a delightful
countryside and quite *distinct* from these parts in form and character.

I would not be surprised if Cairns does not perform the miracle one day
of dragging Mother and I from this cosy nest at Ambleside. We are getting *older*.
Mother sends her love and many thanks for the little picture and much love,

With love from your Dad

Att. LGH Medical Research Unit
Cairns, Queensland

Dearest Mother and Daddy,

The Colonel has left it to me more or less when I return, so that now it
rests with the work I have to complete. At the moment I'm up to my ears in work
and have half a dozen portraits on the way, a landscape and some figure subjects.
I have yet to find a cooperative sitter. The CO of this research unit is a brilliant
young man, Bickerton Blackburn and has an amazing head on his shoulders
somewhere between Beethoven and Byron. Then there is the entomologist, the
only woman to hold that position and another Madam Curie in her own field,
an odd looking little person, ugly and interesting, bright intelligent eyes behind
glasses and a lined and pitted yellow face and grey wispy hair; a couple of full-faced
matronly matrons and a pathologist complete my itinerary for the portraits.[34]

---

33 Nora Heysen sent her father a small painting of the Cairns landscape, including the cane fields, for his
   birthday.

34 *Major Josephine Mackerras* (1945), oil on canvas, Australian War Memorial (ART24395). See also Tony
   Sweeney, *Malaria Frontline: Australian Army Research during World War II*, Melbourne, Melbourne University
   Press, 2003.

The work done here is interesting, six wards full of men or 'guinea pigs' as they are called used for experiments for malaria treatments. They are bitten with the mosquitoes which are bred here and are given the malaria by biting a patient with the fever. One sees a good bronzed Anzac go down to it and in a week he's lost 2 stone and looks at death's door, then when he's provided the pathologists with the right number of wogs and reactions, he's brought to again fed up to health and then down again to another attack.

It won't be long now before I can close my paint box on war work, a happy day. As Jim McGregor says in his last note 'come back and paint flowers as they should be painted'. At least I can try.

My love to the big three with thoughts turning homewards,
Nora

14 William Street
South Yarra, Melbourne
Friday 23 January 1946

Dearest Mother and Daddy,

A telegram has just come bringing a vision of white poppies—I would like to be home. Not knowing till the last minute that I was leaving Cairns, nor how long I'd be coming down, I did not write my decision. Now it seems I'll be held up here for a couple of weeks getting my discharge, and handing in the finished work to the Military History.[35]

The trip from Cairns took me nearly a week instead of a couple of days. I arrived yesterday feeling utterly exhausted and today am still in bed … Arriving at the Menzies more dead than alive, only to find they had no room, absolutely crowded out as was every other place I tried in Melbourne. At last I rang Sybil Irving and she has put me up, so here I am. I've had air travel once and for all. Of course I had 350 lbs of luggage, most of it in brown paper parcels, eleven separate ones to look after and lug on and out of trucks, and planes, and transient camps.

Written in haste and tiredness. I'll write again as soon as I straighten myself out. My love to all and hope it will be the Adelaide Express soon,
Nora

35 Nora Heysen was discharged from the AIF in early February 1946 and completed the work for her official war art commission in March and April of that year.

14 William Street
South Yarra, Melbourne
18 March 1946

Dearest Mother and Daddy,

Well here I am temporarily with a roof over my head ... Now that I am here with an opportunity of painting Brigadier Fairley I have nowhere to paint and will, I suppose, have to be content with a pencil portrait.

I hope you were able to locate the papers on top of the linen press. They were the preliminary notes for the cataloguing of my war work and I can't get on without them as I cannot remember the numbers or details.

The Morgue is more morguish than ever, the last flood came through the roof and flooded everything. It now smells like a morgue, real New Guinea atmosphere, and Mainwaring is the sole survivor still working there. Ivor Hele came through on the same train as myself, he's off to Canberra to do the Duke. He'll be made as a portrait painter henceforth.

My love to all at home,

Nora

These letters come from the National Library of Australia's 'Papers of Sir Hans Heysen, c.1880–1973', MS 5073, series 2, folders 157, 158, 159, 160, 163 and 164; and 'Papers of Nora Heysen, 1913–2003', MS 10041, series 1.3, folders 31 and 35.

To Liverpool, London
and back again
1946–1953

On completing her work for her official war art commission, Nora Heysen moved back to Sydney. Her letters recount meeting up with old friends after being away, the difficulties in finding accommodation and how some of her father's friends and other artists in her Society of Arts circle had fared during those years. The gap in correspondence from late 1946 and throughout 1947 suggests that Nora might have returned to 'The Cedars', where she may have painted *Anemones* (1947), or that some of the letters have not survived.

By early 1948 she is sailing from Adelaide to the United Kingdom to join Robert Black, an Army doctor with whom she fell in love while in New Guinea. After the war he travelled to England as a ship's surgeon in order to go to Liverpool to further his expertise in tropical medicine, which he developed while working in New Guinea, Sydney and Cairns. Between 1946 and 1948, he was a United Kingdom Medical Council Research Fellow at the Liverpool School of Tropical Medicine, until poor health forced him to return to Sydney. Nora stayed behind, moving to London. Ships were filled to capacity with British emigrants bound for Australia and so a ticket back to Australia was hard to come by. She finally arrived home in early 1949.

The Liverpool and London letters speak of postwar rations and difficulties in obtaining art supplies, set against her securing commissions, meeting up with other expatriate artists and the array of good, reasonably priced art on offer in various London galleries. The latter was of great interest to her father, who was a Board Member of the

National Gallery of South Australia and always on the lookout for opportune purchases for the gallery. She recounts what items were astutely purchased by their Adelaide collector friends, Ursula and Bill Hayward.

Back home in early 1949, Nora settles again in Sydney, this time with Robert, and re-establishes her art practice. Before long she is busy with numerous portrait commissions, painting flowers and entering her painting *Robert H. Black MD* in the 1950 Archibald Prize. By late 1951 she holds a solo exhibition at the Heysen Gallery. The letters between Hans and Nora are packed with art-world gossip, their respective and spirited views on exhibitions, Society of Artists exhibitions (in which each exhibit), gallery purchases and the winners of the Archibald and Wynne prizes. Hans's assessment of Nora's work is readily accepted—her respect for her father is such that any criticism is seen as just.

The year 1951 saw celebrations of 50 years of Federation and several letters talk about the Jubilee Art exhibitions, sponsored by the Menzies government, including the commission Hans received for what he called his 'big canvas'. Father and daughter continue to engage in a lively exchange about art. In one letter following an exhibition by Sidney Nolan of his Kimberley inspired work, Hans comments he was about to look in *The Bulletin* for a report, only to find that Nora had provided him with that very criticism. Nora is especially critical of Nolan's work because it is being talked about as presenting a new perspective on the landscape, whereas she finds the work to be 'phoney', since the subject matter was sourced from an aircraft window. This is the 1950s, when art styles were changing in response to international abstraction, and Nora points to simmering factions within the Society of Arts and to critics' proclivities for preferring one style or group of artists over another. She sums up the shift in style in the 1952 Society of Artists exhibition: 'Haefliger sits enthroned on the dais with three huge canvases of Jesus Christ and his apostles around him—Passmore, Kmit, Orban, Drysdale, Jean Bellette and his other friends of today'. Hans knows he will secure little praise for his 1952 David Jones retrospective in Sydney from *The Sydney Morning Herald* because the newspaper's critic, Paul Haefliger, prefers Dobell, Drysdale and Friend.

This group of letters concludes with the news that, as soon as Robert's divorce comes through, Nora and Robert marry in early 1953 in a simple registry office ceremony. Hans and Sallie are delighted and send their very good wishes, even though Hans comments dryly: 'yet it seems strange to congratulate you now when, in your own conscience, you had found your life's mate some years ago'.

Usher's Hotel, Sydney
Wednesday 22 May 1946

Dearest Mother and Daddy,

This afternoon we attended the opening of the Society of Arts exhibition of drawings at David Jones and everyone was there. It was interesting seeing the old crowd again after six years. Very few of them recognised me. It is a good show of very varied work, too much of a crowd to see anything and I must go again before commenting. I include one cutting that gives Daddy a mention—the bald hill did look well. After the show Stef and I had tea with the Haywards and Hera, Ure Smith was not there. I believe he has not been well.

Love to all at home,

Nora

Petty's Hotel
York Street, Sydney
3 June 1946

Dearest Mother and Daddy,

As you can see I've moved down and this place has none of the comfort of Usher's and nothing to recommend it. Hotels are only bearable if they are good.

I went down and paid my respects to Leo Buring with, of course, ulterior motives as I haven't been able to buy a bottle of sherry in the whole of Sydney. Actually he remembered me, the whole works with a glass or two of sherry to complete the atmosphere ... He has been very ill and still looks very shaky and pale. One realises how much the strain of these war years have told on everybody. I was quite shocked to see Will Ashton hobbling round on a stick, and Adrian quite grey and aged. Only Hera has survived the ravages and her hardness is such time couldn't get in edgeways, her only development seems to be in the adoption of a gushing manner that is most embarrassing.

Stef will have talked of the evening we enjoyed at Adrian's of Frank Clune and his rude remarks about the pretty, dolled-up food when what he wanted was a real bloody steak. He didn't give a damn for all that fancy period stuff glowering at Adrian's tastefully arranged table with candles in exquisite holders and fine glass and silver and every piece of china a rare piece.[1]

However the incongruity of Frank Clune sitting down to Adrian's table was in itself amusing and everyone's humour had been cultivated nicely on pink

---

1   Frank Clune (1893–1971) was a successful travel writer who portrayed the 'authentic' bush life.

champagne cocktails, so his every remark was howled down with laughter, and the party of oddly assorted people was a happy success. Mrs Clune is Dobell's latest subject.[2] I shouldn't have thought that she would land herself in this freakish interpretation but evidently they are quite taken with each other. Even Dobell on that evening was quite talkative—very unusual for him.

My love to all at home,

Nora

44 Macleay Street
Potts Point, Sydney
26 August 1946

Dearest Mother and Daddy,

You will be sorry to hear that Ure Smith had a very bad heart turn and nearly passed out—his condition is improving, but he has been ordered complete rest with no visitors at all, and will have to go very slowly from now on. I went along on private view day to have a preliminary look-see and to say 'hullo' to the old crowd.

Adrian, Murch, Wilson with Dundas, Dorothy Thornhill, Lloyd Rees, Appleton and Robertshaw hold the floor with six works apiece. Except for the Gallery purchases, the sales are very few. I'm glad that the Sydney Gallery bought the Carrington Smith portrait which appealed to me more than anything there— it is a quiet scheme in greys and browns and of whites, and has distinction and feeling and a quiet sincerity that is so lacking in the others work.[3] Daryl Lindsay made two purchases for Melbourne.

It isn't a good show. The few Gallery purchases stand out and one or two others, and that's all.

Today I had lunch with John Brackenreg and we did the show again—Howard Hinton was there looking very old and shaky. He's been very ill and he certainly looks as if he won't see another Summer. He wants to be remembered to you.

With my love to all,

Nora

---

2   Thelma Clune ran Clune Galleries. William Dobell's painting *Thelma Clune* was completed in 1945.

3   This is Jack Carrington Smith's portrait *Arrangement in Grey, Green and Brown*.

44 Macleay Street
Potts Point, Sydney
5 October 1946

Dearest Mother and Daddy,

I lunch with McGregor tomorrow. The Sunday luncheon parties are again on and the usual crowd there to enjoy them after my weekly scratch takings at the Cross, I'm more than ready for a good hearty meal with the nice accompaniment of wines. Ure Smith and the Will Ashtons were there last Sunday, and all send their warmest remembrances. Sydney Ure Smith is much thinner, has dropped a stone but looks better for it, though he says he feels very depressed and cannot throw off the heavy despondency.

Don't miss *The Overlanders* when it shows in Adelaide. I've seen it twice and want to go again, the scenery is grand and it's well photographed, really Australian. At last a film has caught the real atmosphere without any of the tricks and false glamour of Hollywood.[4] Parts so much like your pictures I'm sure you would appreciate it.

My love to all,
Nora

Hahndorf, South Australia
14 October 1946

My Dear Nora,

Another birthday has passed and with it the shortest 12 months of my experience, at least that is as it seems. Tuesday afternoon was spent in town attending a Board meeting. I was very reluctant about going, but as we were to meet Sir Keith Murdoch, Mother persuaded me to go, at the last moment, and so we went down together.

It was good to have your letter with its pleasant news and the Stanley Spencer to follow right on the birthday. Thank you ever so much Nora. His is certainly a most original art—with an extraordinary point of view. Not always pleasant, but always interesting with a combination not easy to understand. A wonderful sense of pattern with fine feeling of colour. I think he is a great artist and falls into place with John and Steer as the greatest trio in British art of the early 20th century.

Mother is fairly well, but some days feels very tired—she sends her love and so do I,
Daddy

---

4   *The Overlanders*, set in 1943 and featuring Chips Rafferty, portrays outback life in the time of the threat of Japanese invasion.

44 Macleay Street
Potts Point, Sydney
26 October 1946

Dearest Mother and Daddy,

I was glad to have Daddy's letter ... I'd love a glimpse of everyone but what with all these strikes it seems likely I'll be marooned here for some time yet. Even should the hold-up come to an abrupt end, the Melbourne Cup will make travelling difficult.

I still have my little room over the Harbour but the manageress is showing renewed signs of agitation and hints daily as to plans for leaving. All I can do is pretend I do not understand and continue with my painting. I have almost finished two more flower pieces.[5] On Sunday I spent the day at Turramurra with the Bronners and came back with a huge bunch of lovely flowers from their garden. I went to the Brahms concert last Saturday and called around after the performance to say hello to Bernard Heinze[6]. He sends his love and says he was conducting the concert for Daddy and that he hoped he'd enjoyed it.

My love to all,
Nora

Off Cape Guardafui, Somalia
Saturday 14 February 1948

Dearest Mother and Daddy,

My first sight of land after a very long two weeks and three days—Aden tomorrow with the possibility of posting, so I'll chance a short letter to tell you how things go. Already it seems a decade since I left home—time goes slowly when there is little to do.

We've just seen Cape Guardafui. A dim outline of hills and blinking lighthouse too dark to see any more. Aden will be arrived at and left all on a Sunday night ... Already it is getting cooler which is a relief after a very hot sticky spell. In another week we'll be shivering I suppose.

My love to all at home,
Nora

---

5   Nora may have painted *Flowers in a Delft Vase* (1946) during this time.
6   Bernard Heinze (1894–1982) was one of Australia's most influential conductors.

47 Croxteth Road
Liverpool, United Kingdom
Easter Sunday, 28 March 1948

Dear Mother and Daddy,

At last having found a room wherein to house myself and baggage and having more or less settled myself in, I can put pen to paper and give an account of my doings.

Although I have but a room it is fairly large, and the windows being big and high, the light will be good for painting. The lack of bathroom is the chief drawback, the kitchen-in-a-cupboard is amusing and I might add a bit cramping. I'm learning to adapt myself to cooking in a frying pan, washing and laundering in a fire bucket, living out of a suitcase and to restricting myself to the limitations of one room. Food, and the shopping for it, is the biggest problem and time waster, also washing and the continual battle against dirt. One queues up for everything and even to buy one's handful of rations takes hours.

I miss flowers, they are too expensive to buy. How I'm going to ever get enough to paint God only knows, I'll have to resort to pinching them out of the Gardens.

I must put the kettle on and smell coffee, what memories of home it always recalls. My love to all at home,
Nora

Hahndorf, South Australia
12 April 1948

My Dear Nora,

And now comes your letter from Liverpool—that you are 'settled in' with a lovely Chestnut tree outside your window already decorating itself in Spring green and beyond that the Gardens. At least this is some compensation for what you have left behind, and I think you are lucky in this when I think back on my impressions of Liverpool. You do not mention Robert and in what spirits and health you found him. I do sincerely hope all is well, and please convey my good wishes to him.

It makes us sad and apprehensive when you describe the children of your surroundings, it sounds unbelievable in this land of plenty. Here there is endless talk of growing and sending food to Britain, but with this everlasting string of strikes going on, I can't see how we can produce more than we actually consume.

I have never known the Gums to be more beautiful than this summer—so I have been out amongst them each morning and afternoon with some result, I think, when I compare them with older studies.

And now dear Nora, the pen has run dry and so has my time—Mother sends her love and so with it goes mine. Let me know when there is anything you want. And don't forget to tell me how you get along.

Always from your Dad

47 Croxteth Road
Liverpool, United Kingdom
Sunday 9 May 1948

Dearest Mother and Daddy,

Since last I wrote I have received Daddy's letter a very happy occasion and deeply appreciated even to the fine quality rice paper on which it is written. How one has come to really value the things of quality left to us—I am constantly reminded here that 'things are not what they used to be' and it is sad to see and feel the damage, and sadder to realise that there is little hope of any quick recuperations.

Trying to buy artists' materials I came away dumbfounded and empty-handed—no brushes, no turps, no paper, no canvas, no stretcher, a few restricted colours in stupidly small tubes. Evidently paint is considered a non-essential luxury, not to be encouraged or indulged in under any circumstances. I regret not bringing more canvas and paints and am busy trying to procure odd pieces of canvas, but then again one is curtailed as linen is couponed, and the ingredients for priming are nearly all unprocurable.

Since last writing I've been very busy painting flowers and have completed two schemes—One of the first Spring flowers in window light with light infused colours and the other a vivid exciting riot of June colour—the tulips here are rather lovely—their forms and colours new material for me, as I haven't had them to use before—the horrible expense of flowers here is a deterrent.

I'll be interested to hear the repercussions of the Henry Moore show.[7]

My love to all at home,

Nora

---

7   Courtesy of the British Council, Henry Moore's *Exhibition of Sculpture and Drawing* toured to Sydney, Hobart, Melbourne, Adelaide and Perth in 1947 and 1948. The catalogue for the exhibition stated that Moore is 'regarded as one of the most creative figures in British art today'.

Hahndorf, South Australia
1 June 1948

My Dear Nora,

It was exceptionally welcome to have your last letter, and to hear all your happenings, but I felt disturbed over the news of Robert. Let us hope your supervision of his diet or an improvement makes itself felt very soon.

You will have heard of Howard Hinton's death, no doubt. The last letter from him was written in a very quivering hand. *The Bulletin* paid him a just tribute and published a whole page dealing with his many generous acts and gifts to the Armidale College.[8] And so another friend has gone into the unknown, but to linger in our memory.

I hear Syd Smith is again in hospital—he is very ill and has resigned from the Presidency of the Society of Artists. I am much afraid he is not much longer for this world.

The Henry Moore sculptures and drawings have come and gone—it left me with a feeling of hopelessness. There was no joy in his life. He seemed obsessed with one type of form or shape which he repeats in nearly everything he touches, just as if his mind had been 'twisted' out of the normal by what he had seen, felt and experienced during the war years. With it all, however much you dislike his outlook on life, he seems utterly sincere and honest with his art and definitely has 'something to say'.

In every way what a contrast to the outlook on life of Tom Roberts who loves the sun, the trees and morning clouds in the sky … There are several pictures which are remarkably fine and included is our *A Break Away!* Altogether it is a delightful exhibition, full of good taste, charm and honesty of purpose, and also always searching.[9]

We are all well at home, all our good wishes go to you,

From your Dad

---

8   Howard Hinton donated approximately 1000 works of art illustrating the development of Australian art to the Armidale Teachers' College, along with an extensive art library. Today, the art collection is held by the New England Regional Art Gallery, New South Wales. See 'Mr Howard Hinton Dies', *The Sydney Morning Herald*, 24 January 1948; 'The Hinton Pictures', *The Bulletin*, 14 April 1948; E.S. Elphick, 'Hinton, Howard (1867–1948)', *Australian Dictionary of Biography*, vol.9, Melbourne University Press, 1983: 307–308.

9   Hans Heysen is referring to the National Gallery of Victoria's large Tom Roberts' touring exhibition, on show in Adelaide then, which consisted of an impressive exhibition of 82 oil paintings from state and private collections, and an additional six drawings and prints. Lionel Lindsay wrote the catalogue essay. The exhibition included Roberts' *A Break Away!*, held by the National Gallery of South Australia.

47 Croxteth Road
Liverpool, United Kingdom
26 July 1948

Dearest Mother and Daddy,

Since coming back from my second visit to Scotland, I've been busy painting flowers and have lost myself in a small burst of work.

I've managed to get here and in Edinburgh enough paints and canvas to keep me going. I did a little painting while staying with Shirley ... It was odd amid all that opulence and wealth to sit in the evenings before a fireless grate, because there was no wood to burn and at meal times to be ushered in in evening dress to a polished table and all the do-dahs, butler and servants to wait on one, to be served a slice of bacon on a piece of toast, or a piece of lettuce and a carrot, and then get up with an empty tummy.

It's probable that you will be seeing Robert if his ship calls in at Adelaide. He leaves here some time in August. His health has at last determined his return. I can only hope that Australian food and sunshine will mend the havoc Liverpool has caused to his health.

There are a few commissions floating around here, and also I'd like to spend some time in London before returning.

The crisis in Berlin has caused an uneasy alarm here. One dare not try and realise the conditions over there. I've inquired about sending food parcels to Germany from here but am told that it is no longer possible. A new law has come in against any food parcels going to Germany from here.

I'm enjoying the contents of your food parcel—the eggs are excellent for salads and for currying, and the bacon is a wonderful acquisition. The rations don't improve here. There's been another cut in butter which leaves 2 oz a week and meat is almost negligible.

My love to all at home,

Nora

47 Croxteth Road
Liverpool, United Kingdom
26 August 1948

Dearest Mother and Daddy,

I've received notice that it may be 3–4 years before a passage is available, which is cheering news. However, being an Australian returning home I have a priority, but what that will avail me awaits to be seen ... I'm going down to

London next week to look round for a room and to see the shipping office and what can be done.

I've been busy painting a couple of flower pieces—right in the middle of them who should walk in but Jeff Smart. I was staggered by surprise. His ship had docked at Liverpool, and having my address, along he bounced. There was I sitting painting a little bunch of flowers. Poor Jeff just couldn't believe his eyes—'what to come all the way to England, to sit in Liverpool, to paint flowers when the place was teaming with cracker slums'. For him the place was an artist's or rather a Smart paradise with subjects big, black and beautifully worded in all directions.

Well we talked non-stop for ten hours or more, went to the opera, dined out at the Adelphi, did the Cathedral and went in ecstasies over the slums. That latter item I didn't participate in. He can have all the slums in Liverpool for one white rose.

Robert arrives in Adelaide or is scheduled to arrive on the 15th of September and has 3 days there.

My love to all at home,
Nora

47 Croxteth Road
Liverpool, United Kingdom
17 October 1948

Dearest Mother and Daddy,

Still in Liverpool, but I'm just about to pack up and go down to London where I shall remain until my ship sails in either December or January.

While in London I stayed with the Haywards and had a very gay and entertaining time with them. Never a dull moment, people all the time, plays, concerts, nightclubs, parties and a delightful boat trip up the Richmond river. Nights were turned into days, and no one went to bed until 4 or 5 in the morning. I slept on the sofa, every bed, couch and table had someone sleeping on it. The hospitality of those people knows no limits. All the Australians in England congregate there to eat and drink and be merry. A great number of people are going to find life very flat now that they have gone.

Did the round of the Galleries with Bill Hayward, who has spent most of his time over here adding pictures to his collection. There are still good pictures at reasonable prices to be bought. I couldn't help wishing the Adelaide Gallery had a few thousand to spend to get some of these things before they are sold or the prices soar beyond reach … Dick Smart is mad on Matthew Smith. I don't see what he sees in him, but I must admit I've come round to thinking he definitely has his place amongst contemporary artists. Dick Smart also has an amazing collection of Stanley Spencers, some of his early figure work which is extraordinary to say the least of it.

The Haywards have added quite a number of names to their collection. The best thing Bill bought was a Stanley Spencer figure, I'm going to bring it out for them. It's a nude of his wife getting out of a voluminous pair of combinations with a caricature of himself to set off the picture.

Ursula bought a Vuillard, a lovely little thing and also has a Gauguin fan, a John landscape and a figure subject, a Derwent Lees and Epstein head of Churchill, a Victor Passmore and some others which I can't recollect.[10] You'll no doubt be seeing them before long, as they were very keen for you to see what they've got.

I've been working on the Blue Coat Commission and have almost completed a fair sized canvas of 9 or 11 girls entering the chapel in their Sunday uniforms. It's quite an interesting subject in a way, as the uniform is quaint—they wear poker bonnets and large white tippets which give a decorative effect. I'm working in the chapel which makes rather an ill-lit and very cold studio—my models are also a bit trying as the youngest of the girls are only 5 years—little monkeys who only giggle and scratch. Shirley Jones is one of the Trustees of this school which is for orphans and run entirely on charity (hence the Commission).[11]

My love to all at home,

Nora

Hahndorf, South Australia
20 October 1948

My Dear Nora,

Many thanks for the cable with the birthday message, it came on the very morning and was indeed welcome.

Our trip to Yankalilla, Normanville and Rapid Bay was all too short, but a real success, the weather proving perfect the whole of the 5 days!

The Gallery is now showing my Lucas–Constable mezzotints collection and to my surprise McCubbin has printed a nice catalogue for the exhibition.[12] I am not

---

10   These works are now in the Carrick Hill collection (www.carrickhill.adelaide.sa.gov.au). See J. Schoff (ed.), *The French Collection at Carrick Hill*, Adelaide, Carrick Hill Trust, 1989.

11   The paintings are *Coming out of Chapel* (1948) and *Dorothy James, Barbara Murray and Marion Lloyd, Young Ladies of the Liverpool Blue Coat School* (1948). Jeffrey Smart writes that Nora Heysen 'had a large portrait commission, a whole choir to paint. What a job! She had fifteen likenesses, and she brought them all off'. See Jeffrey Smart, *Not Quite Straight: A Memoir*, Vintage Books, 2008: 197.

12   In the catalogue Louis McCubbin quoted Constable, who said the prints produced by Lucas of the English landscape mark 'the influence of light and shadow on the landscape'. The 30 prints of c.1830s were drawn from Hans Heysen's collection.

entertaining much hope for a success, people as a whole are not interested in black and white work—especially so at the present.

I sold one of your flower pieces to a Melbourne man for 50gs.

Time and space is up my dear Nora so for the present I must say 'Farwell' and cheerio!

Your Dad

7 Hartley Crescent
Notting Hill Gate, London W11
22 November 1948

Dearest Mother and Daddy,

With moving and settling in and all the things of interest that London has to offer, I haven't had time to catch up with myself yet. Jeff Smart helped me find my present room ... It's a typical London bed-sitting room with nothing to recommend it save windows that open out onto a little park and lawn.

You'll be interested to have news of the Batemans ... I was shocked to see how much they had both aged. Bateman is a grey haired old man and not only has he aged physically, but mentally. His memory is so poor that he repeats himself over and over again, and at times gives the impression that he's losing his reason. He spends all his time at his studio now and only goes home to sleep.

He's working on a large intricate figure composition of the horse sale at Elephant and Castle (the only horse sale left in London)—he's been painting on it on and off for three years. It's a large undertaking crowded with figures and activity and character studies and for what it is, an admirable achievement ... He hasn't sold a picture for three years, and is feeling disappointed and bitter over this neglect shown to his work. He complains that the only people who are recognised and sell here are Sutherland, Moore, Piper and Picasso. He thinks that the art market is dead here, and that good work is no longer recognised. He blames Sir Kenneth Clark for extolling these few men at the expense of everyone else.

There's more than a certain amount of truth in what he says just as in Australia the only artists that receive favour from the critics are Dobell, Drysdale, Friend and Bellette.

Mrs Bateman has aged tremendously too and is finding life very dreary and monotonous. All day alone with the meals to cook and no companionship ... It is not until one meets people whom one has known before that one realises fully what the war here did to people. I was able to take a few tins of Australian food with me when I dined with them and Mrs Bateman was thrilled.

Cooking facilities in this place are almost non-existent. I'm only a few doors away from Jeff and Jac Hick so we do some exchange in cooking meals. They boast a kitchen, but for that privilege pay £5-5/- a week.

It's rather nice being back in the same district as it is not so strange to me ... Covent Garden is doing a season of Wagner Operas and I've been to three or four. I've discovered that standing room is sold for 7/6 when the house is full, so that is the way I've managed to see *Tristan and Isolde* and the four operas of *The Ring*—all of which last four hours apiece. So you can imagine how weary one's feet get.

I was very glad to have Daddy's letter to greet me when I arrived down in London. It had just arrived when I called in at the Bank, so the news was only a week old ... Glad to hear of the success of the Rapid Bay trip.

My love to all at home,

Nora

Hahndorf, South Australia
1 December 1948

My Dear Nora,

I met Bill Hayward when last in town, he was waiting for McCubbin to go down to Customs together. He told me you were looking extremely well and filled with enthusiasm for all the good things you had seen in London. It certainly does compensate for a very great deal. It's wonderful what influence good art can bring to many. Your description of his 'Spencer' makes me most eager to see it and the other good things he bought over there. It is a great pity that our Gallery can find no really reliable body to buy for us. Let us hope we may find such a person soon. It wants someone right on the spot, and whose judgement one could really trust. It is just possible we will try for the Boudin you spoke about at Barbizon House, it seems Hayward spoke to McCubbin about it.[13]

Perhaps Jock has told you about a large 'still life' of mine Steve bought at Bruce's Sale, and for which they ran him up to £190. It belongs to the same period as the one in the dining room and the same size. I told him to bring it up here, and after looking at it for a week I decided to have a *go*! And after another week transformed it into quite a decent thing—more sumptuous and richer. I entirely repainted the background, apples instead of quinces on the table, and so on. Now it's gone away to John Martin's Gallery, and I am not quite sure what Steve intends to do with it—but he should make a profit.

---

13   On Sir Edward Hayward's advice, the National Art Gallery of South Australia purchased Eugène Boudin's
      St Vaast-la-Hougue (1892), oil on canvas, from Colnaghi.

Did I tell you before that John Brackenreg is bringing out a book on my work—probably sometime next year.

While Brackenreg was in Melbourne he went up to Ballarat and wrote in high praise of your painting *Motherhood*. It is hanging in the centre of a wall and looks extremely well. In John you evidently have a great admirer. Time is up dear Nora so '*auf wiedersehen*'.

Mother and Jill send their love and with every good wish,

From your Dad

7 Stanley Crescent
Notting Hill Gate, London W11
12 December 1948

Dearest Mother and Daddy,

Daddy's letter written on 1st of December came yesterday and I was extremely glad to hear home news, yet anxious to know of Daddy being laid up with a poisoned foot. Such things can be dangerous. I hope all's well again now, and that the enforced rest has been a good tonic.

By now you will have had my letter confirming my date of departure and likely day of arrival in Adelaide, 25th January, just a month too late.

I've booked right through to Sydney to save unloading and reloading the stuff again—I just can't face it all over again. As my ship only spends a short day in Adelaide, I'll disembark there and continue the journey by train. That will give me a few days at home before getting to Sydney to get my luggage off at that end. News from Robert is disquieting. The temporary good effects of the trip out have evidently gone. He has too much worry and strain on his shoulders, and as the cause of it is also my concern, I feel I must be with him to stand by. So my anxieties are not only luggage troubles.

Yesterday evening I went to a party at the Becks—Melbourne people—he was the leading Cello player with the Orchestra there. Now he is playing here with the BBC Orchestra, anyway I was asked with Jeff Smart and Jacquie Hick, and we went along and who should be there but Colin Colahan. Do you remember him? His memories of his visit to Hahndorf are still very fresh. When introduced to me he said, Oh yes, of course I remember, your Mother is the best cake maker in the world! And he went on to tell me in detail what he'd eaten on his last visit to the Cedars.

He is quite grey haired now and much more self-assertive and confident, a nice house in Chelsea, Whistler's house he built for himself, and he has made his reputation here and sells well. I must go out to his studio and see just what he is doing. I'm to airmail him some gum leaves as soon as I get back. It is interesting to hear of the reincarnation of the flower piece.

Dick Smart of Tooths' leaves for Australia per Lancastrian tomorrow ... I believe he'll be angling to get the position of buyer over here for the Adelaide Gallery. In no time you'll have Matthew Smiths and Stanley Spencers and Tristam Hilliers etc. all over the place.[14] He's going to stay with the Haywards and they'll probably take him up.

My love and Christmas wishes to everyone until that day six weeks ahead,

Nora

Tuesday 11 January 1949

Dearest Mother and Daddy,

Colombo tomorrow where I hope to post this with Adelaide only a fortnight away, I'm already feeling excited and thinking it will soon be time to start packing again. Already we've been given yards of forms to sign.

The ship is overcrowded; four are squeezed into two-berth cabins and six into four-berth. At night most of the people, to get out of their stuffy cabins, sleep on the deck. If one wants to take a walk, one steps over bodies in the daytime.

Just remembered it is the 11th today. What a birthday and without one greeting.

My love to everyone,

Nora

44 Macleay Street
Potts Point, Sydney
Sunday 9 February 1949

Dearest Mother and Daddy,

Back at this place where at least I can count on a bed for few days. So far I've had all I can do to keep a roof over my head whilst looking for something more permanent. I've already had three changes within the week. When one does eventually find a place to take, there is a stipulation that it is only for 2 or 3 days and then it's starting all over again.

---

14   Richard Smart became a London buyer for the National Art Gallery of South Australia in 1956 and indeed purchased British modern work. See Edward Morgan, 'Gallery Buyers', *Art Gallery of South Australia Bulletin*, vol.33, no.3, 1972.

I dined with McGregor last night and he welcomed me back with opening a couple of bottles of the world's finest champagne, it was lovely. Only once before have I tasted champagne like it.

Love to all at home,

Nora

Onslow Avenue, Sydney
18 March 1949

Dearest Mother and Daddy,

I rang Ure Smith but haven't been along to see him yet. He says he's feeling a lot better, and everyone agrees that he's made a remarkable recovery from what he was a little while back. See quite a bit of Adrian now that he is my neighbour, have you seen his book yet?[15] The prints seem very good and he's very pleased with the publication's success.

I saw the Archibald exhibits, of course Dobell's portrait eclipsed everything else.[16] It is painted in a high key with a lot of cadmium making the canvases around it look like mud pies. That Bill should have carried off the Wynne Prize also I'm not so sure of. I thought Lloyd Rees' landscape much worthier, it had a really Australian feeling.

I'll be in my studio flat in another fortnight and can hardly wait to get out my brushes.

My love to all at home,

Nora

36 College Street, Sydney
10 May 1949

Dearest Mother and Daddy,

Well at last I'm temporarily settled and have an address which I can call my own. I only wish to God this studio was permanent.[17] I shudder at the prospects of starting to flat hunt again in a couple of months.

This is a nice big room with a good light (on bright days) for working—a pleasant liveable room with divans round the fire and bookshelves piled with books,

---

15   In 1948, Sydney Ure Smith published and edited *Adrian Feint: Flower Paintings*.

16   William Dobell won the Archibald Prize in 1948 for his portrait *Margaret Olley*. He won the Wynne Prize the same year for *Storm Approaching Wangi*.

17   This is Elaine Haxton's studio apartment. Haxton (1909–1999) was a painter, printmaker, designer and commercial artist. See Andrew Sayers, 'Elaine Alys Haxton', Dictionary of Australian Artists Online, accessed 11 May 2009.

simple nice furniture, and a little balcony leading off it which catches all the sun that's going and overlooks the park. There's a kitchenette too, small, but adequate enough with also a lovely view over trees and lawns.

I've seen Ure Smith a couple of times—he's looking painfully thin just a shadow of his former self.

I haven't been in to see the exhibition of drawings at David Jones but enclose the *Sydney Morning Herald*'s criticism, if criticism it can be called, since it is so dogmatic and destructive.[18]

Daddy's watercolour has pride of place over the mantel piece, unfortunately I had to leave the frame at home. Most sadly I do need my frames. None of the framers will do any framing here, they will provide standard sizes and that is all.

My love to all at home,

Nora

Hahndorf, South Australia

16 May 1949

My Dear Nora,

I don't know how long I shall be allowed writing this letter, but each previous attempt has been frustrated with one kind of interruption or another. We certainly have been inundated with visitors: more than is good for us! Still we did have some refreshing individuals like Sir Kenneth Clark and Professor Burke— both of whom I found most agreeably catholic in ideas about art, and both are 'livewires' and most enthusiastic[19].

Your letter was indeed welcome and it seems you are now happily installed, even if it is only for the time being. Something else will turn up in the meanwhile. Both Mother and I are greatly relieved.

The Melrose Prize was adjudicated on Thursday last, and the prize of £100 went to Drysdale. McCubbin, Professor Burke and myself were the jury and we were unanimous. *Woman in a Landscape* is good, a splendid interpretation of an 'isolated' individual of the outback but in no way typical. The picture does convey a

---

18   Hans Heysen had a work on show in this Society of Artists exhibition.

19   Kenneth Clark (1903–1983) was a former Director of the National Gallery, in London. When he visited Adelaide in 1949, he was Slade Professor of Fine Art at the University of Oxford. The National Art Gallery of South Australia was looking for a London buyer and, during this visit, he offered his services, making many good purchases over the next six years. See Edward Morgan, 'Gallery Buyers', *Art Gallery of South Australia Bulletin*, vol.33, no.3, 1972. Clark delivered a public lecture at the University of Melbourne on 'The Idea of a Great Gallery' on 27 January 1949. See Carrick Hill Archives. Joseph Burke, British born and educated, was the first Herald Professor of Fine Art at the University of Melbourne. He established the first art history courses at an Australian university and commenced teaching in 1948.

feeling of the hopeless life some of these women endure at drought conditions. The Drysdale's causing some excitement—3000 people visited the Gallery on Sunday.

There is always something depressing and sinister about Drysdale's work, and this applies to so much of the modern outlook. Rarely does one meet with a happy note as we find in the French impressionists with their feeling of light and space; in fact they deny sunshine, blue skies, life and movement. It's all cast in a mould to fit the modern pattern, and they seem afraid to paint what they see.

Our Northern trip was a great success after the first 4 depressing days. David came back a new man and I will say I have never felt better or more fit. Also I feel I struck a new note in some of the half-finished sketches which I hope I can develop. For 4 weeks we had continual sunshine, very little wind, it was warm but not hot. The only drawback was the *flies*, they assumed enormous proportions, and they remained in millions with us throughout the trip.

We had no mishaps despite our misgivings regarding the trailer, which of course is growing old, but it stood the journey and proved almost a welcome home. It was somewhat green the first week, but the landscape soon after assumed the warm and brown tones that I always associate with the North.

I must end with every warmest of good wishes to you my dear Nora—and good luck,

Your Dad

PS Steve came along with one of your English flower pieces for me to sign, I did, and after varnishing all the colours came up splendidly and rich.

36 College Street, Sydney
17 August 1949

Dearest Mother and Daddy,

It seems rather a long time since I had any news of home ... Robert is off to the Northern Territory for 2 or 3 months on a malarial survey scheme for the Government. He'll no doubt be passing through Adelaide on Monday ... I'll give him the Van Gogh letters for Daddy to read. They are so well worthwhile reading and thinking over that I cannot resist the opportunity for you to read them.

I've been pretty busy trying to finish and frame some work for the Society of Artists show. Stef sent me over a frame which helped me out at the last minute, the framing situation here is pretty hopeless.

I sent in three flower pieces and a portrait study of Robert. One a study of red camellias against intense blue is a slightly new note, but the others were typical bunches, rather richer and more intense in colour than usual perhaps. Anyway the hanging committee evidently didn't think much of them, for all, excepting one, have been put in corners in bays. I was in yesterday—varnishing day—for a first look, but I can't say that I came away feeling stimulated.

The three big D's are not exhibiting—Dobell, Drysdale, 'Donald'! Everyone will be disappointed not to see some of Dobell's New Guinea work, the one small Drysdale isn't convincing—a white naked figure dancing in the desert. It will be interesting to see how the sales go this year.

My love to all,

Nora

Hahndorf, South Australia
2 September 1949

My Dear Nora,

It seems very long while since I last wrote to you. There never seems time to sit down in a writing mood ... Your last letter was welcome and we always enjoy your 'picture making' in describing things, you certainly have the art of letter writing! It was good to hear all goes well despite the 'turmoil' the strike caused you.[20]

Robert paid a flying visit ... It was but a glimpse in the half-light that I got of him. He looked better than when we saw him last, but not *better* enough. He was cold and he seemed very nervous, and the darkness under the eyes showed strain which made me wish that I could give him some of my energy. The warmer weather of the Far North will help to bring him better health. Robert gave me the Vincent van Gogh book, which I know I am going to enjoy.

Steve has opened his gallery with success. Already a great number of people have called in, not only out of curiosity but had come to buy also.[21]

Ivor Hele has just painted a portrait of Don Bradman. The reproduction was not exciting, he placed his sitter in the usual chair with usual curtain with Orpen folds, and there was *no* bat. There was no imagination or invention shown anywhere.

Mother and I send our love to you,

Dad

---

20   This is the Australian coal strike which ran from June to August 1949.
21   Stefan Heysen left John Martin's Art Gallery, Adelaide, and opened Heysen Gallery, Hahndorf, which he ran from 1949 to 1953.

36 College Street, Sydney
8 February 1950

Dearest Mother and Daddy,

You will gather from the cuttings that the exhibits for the Archibald and Wynne prizes were rather dull. For once I agree with Haefliger's criticism. I felt glad when I heard that Murch had carried off the honours, his winning portrait isn't particularly good.[22] I thought it lacked form and solidity, the thing looked artificial.

At the moment we have an exhibition of Modern Art from New York on, but I haven't been in to see it yet. I sold both the flower pieces I had in at a show at David Jones Gallery, and Wal Taylor seems to be sitting up and asking for flower pieces so that I feel that I'm beginning to re-establish myself here.

Ursula is due over here shortly, also Vi Johns of John Martin's Gallery has warned me that she is coming and wants flower pieces, so that I'll be getting some Adelaide news.[23]

Love to all at home,
Nora

36 College Street, Sydney
7 March 1950

Dearest Mother and Daddy,

Wal Taylor invited me to an evening party at his flat, a gathering of artists, but it was a dull affair and the supper of barley water and cakes didn't help stimulate the conversation. I believe that old Wal Taylor is trying to brighten up his business contacts again to re-establish his Gallery.

I've been working on a couple of portraits, one of a doctor whom I met in Cairns and is now a pathologist to the Children's Hospital here, a man with a fine sensitive head but as he only has time at night to sit, it has meant working by night light. My other subject is Robert—I'm getting myself into working trim for the next Archibald! When I saw the entries for this year's competition I thought that if I couldn't do better I'd give up painting.

---

22   Arthur Murch won the 1949 Archibald Prize for his portrait *Bonar Dunlop*.
23   Vi Johns took over running John Martin's Art Gallery from Stefan Heysen.

Hannah Lloyd Jones wants me to do a drawing of her as a present for her husband. If I do the drawing, I can have flowers out of her garden any time I wish them—blackmail!

I'm including a packet of zinnia seeds for Daddy to try.

My love to everyone,

Nora

36 College Street, Sydney
29 March 1950

Dearest Mother and Daddy,

Lunched at Jim McGregor's on Sunday last and he said he'd been up with Freda—they are off to America this week for six weeks. Haven't seen the new Monet that Jim was responsible for buying for the Sydney Gallery.[24] I'll include the paper reproduction. Having promised a flower painting for the Ure Smith Memorial Exhibition, I'll have to stir myself to get it done.[25] I suppose Daddy is contributing?

Love to all,

Nora

36 College Street, Sydney
1 May 1950

Dearest Mother and Daddy,

The run of art shows has started again commencing with Nolan's prodigious display—Haefliger, in the *Herald* going so far as to say that the beginning of the Australian school of painting dated from that collection. All other Australian artists were usurped, with Nolan dawned a new era etc.[26]

The work certainly made an impression. David Jones Gallery covered with 6 ft canvases all in the same colour of hot red ochre! The criticism spoke of the marvellous subtleties to be found in that one all-pervading saturating colour, but for my part, I couldn't see the subtleties. It left an impression of overwhelming monotony and repetition, doubtless true enough to the landscapes in the Far North, but it doesn't necessarily make art. His subject matter was all gathered in a month of travelling by air over the Kimberley and the ranges and desert of

---

24   This is Claude Monet's *Port Goulphar, Belle Île*, oil on canvas, which was purchased in 1949.

25   Sydney Ure Smith died on 11 October 1949. Hans felt the loss deeply; he had just written a letter to him when he heard the news of his death. See Colin Thiele, *Heysen of Hahndorf*, Adelaide, Hyde Park Press, 2001: 264.

26   *Sidney Nolan: Exhibition of Central Australian Landscapes* was exhibited at David Jones Gallery from 31 March to 14 April 1950; James Gleeson's review on 31 March 1950 in *The Sun* carried the headline 'Landscapes Triumph for Australian Artist'.

the Northern Territory. Daddy would have been interested, and I couldn't help wondering what his criticism of the show would have been. To me it just didn't ring true. There was something phoney about it, too slick, one felt that he'd arrived at a very clever formula for depicting the arid mountains and vast desert land, without really getting down to a knowledge of it first. He paints with duco and his skies are sprayed on! The result is a rather thin and cheap quality to his paint, and the skies are dead flat and as monotonous as a piece of new blue linoleum. I must admit though that on first appearance the work produced an effect, one thought here's someone with a new vision doing something on a grand scale, the scale is certainly grand, but the content falls far below.

If I can locate my catalogue I'll post it along so that you can see the country that he's 'flown over'. It was amusing to see the dates on the canvases—60 canvases in as many weeks all equally spaced 1 to 7 days. Done in the studio, I should imagine, from photographs and cursory notes. The Sydney Gallery bought one of the best, of anthills and banyan trees.[27]

I saw quite a bit of Ursula and Bill when they were over. Ursula seems to be quite at home in Sydney, and enjoys the accelerated pace with which life moves over here. She must have mental and physical movement surrounding her all the time. Poor Bill seems to find it bewildering and boring, and it is pretty obvious that the environment which suits one of them is unbearable to the other. They leave on Thursday for London.

I feel like getting down to painting again, or rather I should say I feel as if I can cope with the chores so as to get to my painting. There is always such paraphernalia of tiresome necessary jobs which stand between a woman and any work she wants to do, apart from the demands of the home.

Douglas Dundas is trying very hard to carry on Ure Smith's role, but he's finding it more than he can carry.

Bill Dobell has retired to New Guinea for three months to paint the Natives. He now has a business manager and is almost entirely organised by Frank Clune.

My love to all with a hope that all is well,

Nora

---

27   The day before the opening of the 1950 exhibition, *Sidney Nolan: Central Australian Landscapes*, the National Art Gallery of New South Wales purchased *Dry Jungle*, showing ant hills and banyan trees.

Hahndorf, South Australia
5 June 1950

My Dear Nora,

Many 'washing days' have passed since I last wrote. Mother and I enjoyed your last letter, full of news and 'good pictures' although you may not think so. You certainly have the art of writing, but as you say—'if only it didn't take so long'. I find letter writing takes too much of my scanty spare time ... This reminds me, would you give me your friend's address who loaned you 'Dear Theo'. I could then post it onto him and perhaps slip in a little pencil sketch.

When reading the *Bulletin* about Nolan's central Australian landscape I was wondering what they could really be like, but you have given me the answers.

How did the Syd Ure Smith memorial show go? I sincerely hope all is well with you.

Mother sends her love in which I heartily join,

From your Dad

36 College Street, Sydney
18 July 1950

Dearest Mother and Daddy,

I did so enjoy getting Daddy's long letter full of home atmosphere and news.

You ask about the Ure Smith Memorial show ... The most successful part about it was the opening and the huge and diverse crowd which packed the gallery to bursting point, and spilled right down to the foot of the stairs. It was a rather wonderful tribute to Ure Smith to see the mixed crowd, the mink coats of Society mingled with the shabby bests of the local greengrocer, postman, and bottle-oh of Potts Point. Just everyone rallied. Disappointing too was the collection of pictures sent in by the artists. A poor show, I thought, as it is the artists who owe him so much ... Daddy's watercolour looked well, despite its being very badly hung in a corner of the entrance bay.

Actually, for a memorial tribute to Ure Smith, the little show of his publications and his private correspondence and sketches held at the Mitchell Library was to me much better and more dignified than the David Jones display. There were two or three of Daddy's letters to Ure amongst the collection at the Mitchell Library— letters from and to all his many friends, most of them illustrated humorously.

I was glad to finish the Hannah Lloyd Jones commission—halfway through, of course, I wished that I had never undertaken it ... She was impossibly restless, so that hourly sittings which were dealt out to me were cut in halves by her rushes to the telephone, or to give her maids orders ... Of course the finished result was not flattering.

She offered me the choice of her 500 odd vases for a loan. I selected a beautiful white Bohemian glass jug but she hastily said, 'Oh do you mind very much if you don't have that one I was just going to put some flowers in it for the reception to Menzies I'm giving' ... On the night of the big party I looked round for the flower piece in the white jug, but of course it wasn't there. These so and so women! They don't really mean a word they say.

To go back to the party given by the Lloyd Jones for Menzies—it was some party! French champagne flowed, oysters by the dress basket full and every luxury ever concocted in the way of delicacies to eat. The women were out in their prewar glory of jewels, Paris model frocks, minks and ermines. I felt as if I'd strayed there by mistake and it took several glasses of champagne to make me feel anything but an 'amused spectator' on the cream of Sydney social life.

I was amazed to see Lionel Lindsay there, Jim McGregor the driving force of course, Lionel Lindsay was in high spirits and looked not a day older than when I painted him, still as loquacious and still as vitally alive.

Goossens was there with his glamorous wife and fledgling daughter. He wanted to be remembered to you, and sent all sorts of messages of goodwill. Menzies also sent his good wishes and remembrances. Rather funny, next day Menzies in Parliament was asked to explain his presence at such an extravagant banquet. He was asked was it a fact that French champagne flowed like water and that all the women wore mink coats! His reply was, as usual, apt—he said that *he* didn't have any *champagne*, 'probably concentrated on Scotch whisky which was equally plentiful and that the mink coats resembled very much those worn by the opposition members wives on similar occasions, and that it was very pleasant to enjoy a gathering without any communists present'.

We have been having a season of ballet over here with the premiere of *Corroboree* to set all Sydney talking ... If you have heard Anthil's music for the thing you'll have an idea of the whole ballet. All the noise and monotony and staccato excitement were repeated in the movement. It was certainly a marvellous spectacle and new and all that, but for my part, I felt an intense relief when the noise stopped and with it the waves of monotonous jerking restless movements. Still it was interesting to see that we are capable of producing a new and actively alive ballet from the roots of Australian life, though I think had there been any Aboriginals present, they might have failed to recognise what it was all about.

My love to all,

Nora

36 College Street, Sydney
10 September 1950

Dearest Mother and Daddy,

I was alarmed to hear of Mother's illness and am wondering how things are going.

The opening of the Society of Artists show has come and gone, the usual gathering there with a good sprinkling of red dots, mostly gallery purchases, to stimulate further buying. I sent four things into the show—a couple flower pieces, a street scene done from my kitchen window and a portrait. They complain that my prices are too high over here but I'm sticking to them.

There are shows galore at the moment, Drysdale has his London exhibition on preview before he sails with it. I wonder how his work will be received over there. The best of the canvases were the solitary hopeless figures in the treeless waste, not any Australian types but Greeks, Italians and Malaceos. The same strips of veranda in perspective, with the deserted town main street, the horizontal sky, then of course there were the deserted homesteads with twisted sheet iron, the bed and the horizontal sky, and some dramatic abstract landscapes with a kangaroo or emu *and* a horizontal sky ... Margaret Preston is up to the mark with something *new*. A crucifixion with no visible cross and a large thing with a scheme of kangaroos and emus and native flora all mixed to produce a pleasant colour harmony, the latter bought by the Art Gallery.[28]

My love to all,
Nora

Hahndorf, South Australia
23 November 1950

My Dear Nora,

Jeff Smart and the Hick girl are back from their travels. Jeff already opened his exhibition at John Martin's yesterday, so he has lost no time. I am somewhat curious as to what his work is like.

Cheerio with love from all three,
Dad

---

28 This is *Adam and Eve in the Garden of Eden* (1950), which the National Art Gallery of New South Wales acquired in 1950. See Geoffrey Smith, 'Adam and Eve in the Garden of Eden' in Deborah Edwards, *Margaret Preston*, Sydney, Art Gallery of New South Wales, 2005: 236.

36 College Street, Sydney
Wednesday 28 November 1950

Dearest Mother and Daddy,

Ursula and Bill Hayward were here for a few days—Ursula looking very fit and animated with the stimulus of travelling, and Bill rather thin and worried and I think looking forward to being back. Ursula is very excited over her recent purchases. A Renoir, a Degas, two Rouaults, some Epsteins amongst others.

I'll be interested too in hearing how Jeff Smart fares with his exhibition. Love to all at home,

Nora

36 College Street, Sydney
14 February 1951

Dearest Mother and Daddy,

I managed to get a very nice easel by pooling my Christmas birthday cheques. It's an extremely good easel being strong and utilitarian without being massive or heavy and, made of natural maple, it looks nice as well.

John Brackenreg said he'd posted you the booklet on the Archibald exhibits so that I didn't send mine[29] ... The Ivor Heles held their own and were, I think, the best paintings of heads in the show, but he seems to fall down on the background and clothes etc. I think the poor drawing in the arms of his self portrait went badly against him in the judging, or so Jim McGregor said.

My love to all at home,

Nora

Hahndorf, South Australia
21 February 1951

My Dear Nora,

First of all I must thank you for your interesting and entertaining letter.

It is interesting what you say regarding Ivor Hele's portraits—he had just sent in a batch of drawings to John Martins to sell (and they sold immediately). Our Chairman bought one for our Gallery, it *looks* most effective, at first sight, then you *questioned* the form and things? Because, superficial in a way, with a very apparent display of technical ability.

---

29   Nora entered her portrait *Robert H. Black, MD* in the 1950 Archibald Prize. The work was on display from 20 January to 4 March 1951.

And you are right about Ivor's disinterestedness—when it comes to backgrounds and the painting of his clothes—both lack form and expression and do not help build up a 'general pattern'. I think this essential and in this respect I liked your portrait of Robert very much—the canvas was *one piece* and the likeness excellent. And it is the best thing you have so far done, in the portrait line. If I may make a comment, the hills against the sky—nearest the head—seemed too positive and detracted and the folds in the right sleeve are not sufficiently considered *in pattern* in relation to the whole. Still you have done a jolly good job, Nora.

I am glad you managed to get a really good solid easel for they are not easy to pick up at any time, and I can't see how you could have done without one.

We are all well and send our love to you,

From your Dad

36 College Street, Sydney
14 March 1951

Dearest Mother and Daddy,

I was very glad of Daddy's letter and most particularly for the few kind words about my portrait, they bucked me up considerably. Have just lugged Robert's portrait back from the Gallery to find a telegram awaiting me asking permission to show it in the Brisbane Art Gallery so now I have to turn about and trek it back to the Gallery for forwarding. The background in the original is in a tone darker than in the photograph, actually it is Moreton Bay Fig trees in a row receding. I tried to make a convention of an unconventional background. I wasn't altogether happy about the result but as you told me once, and I've since often remembered it, 'It's not the doing that is difficult, it's knowing what to do.' However often one paints a background it doesn't seem to get any simpler. I don't blame Ivor for trying to slide over the problem.

I'm wondering when Daddy's exhibition with Sedon opens—what with that in the offing and all the work entailed and the 56 x 42 on your mind there would be no room for anything else let alone requests for pictures—I've passed on your answer to the two clients here and they are willing to wait.

I've bought a table after much searching, had to pay £22 for it and just a natural maple wood, gate legged one. I couldn't help thinking of the one in my studio I paid 12/6 for and a much better job, and my walnut one sitting in the Heysen Gallery. Robert has plunged on the strength of his war gratuity and bought a refrigerator, a Crosley, just like the one at home, and you can imagine the boon it is in this place.

My love to all at home and a wish that all's well,

Nora

Nora Heysen (1911–2003)
Anemones 1947

oil on canvas; 47.0 x 37.0 cm
Private collection
Photograph by Michael Kluvanek

Nora Heysen (1911–2003)
Flowers in a Delft Vase c.1946

oil on plywood; 39.5 x 30.0 cm
Nora Heysen Foundation Collection
The Cedars, Hahndorf
Photograph by Michael Kluvanek

Unknown photographer
Nora Heysen and Robert Black
c.1940s

photograph
Manuscripts Collection, MS 10041
National Library of Australia

Unknown photographer
Nora Heysen and Robert Black
Wearing Berets c.1948

photograph
Manuscripts Collection, MS 10041
National Library of Australia

Nora Heysen (1911–2003)
Self Portrait 1948

red chalk on paper; 43.0 x 31.8 cm
Pictures Collection, nla.pic-an7946238
National Library of Australia

above
Nora Heysen (1911–2003)
Dorothy James, Barbara Murray and Marion Lloyd, Young Ladies of the Liverpool Blue Coat School 1948

oil on canvas; 44.3 x 39.7 cm
Blue Coat School Collection, Liverpool, United Kingdom

Nora Heysen (1911–2003)
Robert H. Black MD 1950

oil on canvas laid on composition board; 78.0 x 59.0 cm
Gift of the artist 1999
National Portrait Gallery

Hans Heysen (1877–1968)
In the Flinders–Far North 1951

oil on canvas; 102.0 x 141.0 cm
National Gallery of Australia
© Hans Heysen, licensed by Viscopy

left
Nora Heysen (1911–2003)
Portrait of Dr Robert Black 1953

oil on canvas; 40.9 x 30.6 cm
Pictures Collection, nla.pic-vn4804449
National Library of Australia

far left
Nora Heysen (1911–2003)
Portrait of Hans Heysen 1952

conté crayon on paper; 39.8 x 29.9 cm
Pictures Collection, nla.pic-an5263452
National Library of Australia

Hahndorf, South Australia
6 June 1951

My Dear Nora,

There have been many days, dull and breathless, when the light has been too feeble to work in the studio. It was well that I tackled my big canvases in April for it's been the only dry and pleasant month. Anyway it's finished as far as I can carry it, and it's somewhat of a relief.[30] As with each picture, one becomes somewhat depressed and disappointed when the final stage is reached. For while the picture is growing, there is always the hope of reaching one's *mental* vision of what one is striving for. Now the difficulty arises, how it gets over to Sydney and also the packing problem, for so large a work this has become a very real problem!

It was jolly good to get your last letter, and both Mother and myself thoroughly enjoyed and appreciated it. It is good news that you are to do the Gratton portrait! Is it to be a full length in robes?[31]

Are you having an entry for the Commonwealth Jubilee Open Competition? I see the entries have to be in by June 29, that is, in Adelaide, and they will be judged by 3 of us. We are to select 3 from the state to go before the final judging.

We had our first meeting with our new Director, a very affable man of 50 years, who I think we will find very agreeable to work with. Perhaps you have already met him? Robert Campbell—he is a watercolourist of standing, following in the Daryl Lindsay school.[32] It appears we have purchased a large Solomon Ruisdael landscape for our gallery and also a small Corot, so let us hope for the best.

If I can make it, I want to show a couple of watercolours—about 25 x 18—at the coming Society of Artists show, both Northern. Would you let me know in good time when their sending-in day is, or if you meet the secretary tell him to advise me well beforehand, so as to give me time to pack.

I have been asked by young David Jones to have an exhibition, a kind of retrospective one in their galleries next year.

Mother and I send our love. We were both extremely glad to hear that Robert cooks so well.

And again my love to you dear Nora,

Dad

---

30   Hans Heysen is referring to his commissioned painting, *In the Flinders*, for the Commonwealth Jubilee.
31   Norman Gratton was the Principal of Scotch College, Adelaide. He retired in 1951 and the portrait might have been a retirement gift.
32   Robert Campbell (1902–1972) was Director of the National Gallery of South Australia from 1951 to 1967.

36 College Street, Sydney
Sunday 17 June 1951

Dearest Mother and Daddy,

I enjoyed every bit of Daddy's letter, especially the news that the big canvas is finished and that others are growing to take shape. Thank goodness the weather held until the end.

I don't think I'll be entering for the Open Competition. I have more than I can cope with now and the time is slipping past in a most alarming way. I'm still hoping to hold a small show with Stef later in the year ... My immediate problem is the portrait of this Mr Gheysens which I begin on tomorrow. Why on earth he has picked on me to do his portrait God alone knows. He wants to be the subject of the next Archibald win, and apart from actually painting the thing, he has the portrait all worked out to the very size and scheme and all. As you may gather, he is a colossal egoist with a very inflated opinion of himself. His idea is to be painted with notes coming out of his head and musical instruments floating round to show that he is a composer, 'something new and different to catch the eye of the judges'! But he doesn't want anything ostentatious looking for he wishes everyone to know that he's a very modest man! At first I thought he must be joking, but alas no—to further my difficulties he is short, fat, bald and paunchy and wears glasses. The typical middle-aged continental type, a mixture of German, Dutch and Belgian, I should think, and he wants to be refined down and elongated to look distinguished. He says all the best artists elongate; take Dobell for instance and El Greco, and that I must put hair on and suggest with a shadow that he has some and do away with the paunch etc. Lord what am I to do?[33]

It's good to hear of the Heysen exhibition over here next year. It should give Sydney a much needed jolt to see some really good draughtsmanship again.

I've made tentative plans to do the Gratton portrait late in August running into September.

My love to all,

Nora

---

33   Dobell also painted Gheysens. His portrait *Camille Gheysens* was entered in the 1957 Archibald Prize. The painting is now in the collection of the Art Gallery of New South Wales.

36 College Street, Sydney
Tuesday 14 August 1951

Dearest Mother and Daddy,

I'm thinking of coming home for a couple of days before going down to
Ursula's and starting on the portrait ... This Gheysens bird has worn me down, in
fact, if I hadn't committed myself to this Gratton commission it would be a very
long time before I contemplated another portrait to order. I hope to have a more
sympathetic subject in Mr Gratton.

Jeff Smart has arrived here and is still looking for a flat, but having come
well furnished with letters of introduction to Ursula's friends, he doesn't lack for
free meals, drinks, entertainment—'he'll get on, not a bit stuck up or anything'.
I only wish that he wasn't staying so near, it is too convenient for him to pop in
whenever he feels inclined, or hasn't an invitation to dinner.

I'm waiting to hear that the Jubilee Prize entries are on view, I'm longing
to see Daddy's big picture.[34]

My love to all until Tuesday,
Nora

Hahndorf, South Australia
24 October 1951

My Dear Nora,

This should have been written exactly 16 days ago! Please forgive for
there have been endless jobs that simply had to be seen to and I dare not, from
experience, try my eyes at night.

Today my show opens at Sedon Galleries, Lady Latham is opening it, and
I do hope the Melbourne weather is better than ours. Sedon rang yesterday, 7
pictures had been sold and he said 'the show looked very well'. There are two large
watercolours, 24 smaller ones and half dozen drawings. I sold one watercolour out
of the Sydney Society of Artists, a 24 x 18 inch, price 170gs, but I do not know who
purchased it. I must write to Miss Swanton and find out.

The Jubilee show which finishes this week has proved a great success, and
personally I feel it's a good show, generally speaking, but with many gaps. The Tom
Roberts' seem to carry the day, I was simply charmed with his *Bourke Street*. Of
its kind it is a masterpiece. I was not so enthusiastic about Lloyd Rees (it won the

Wynne last year).[35] Splendidly composed but with no 'joy' in the actual handling of paint. There is no movement and little atmosphere, still it is a good picture ... perfectly composed but it lacks *something*, and despite a certain richness of colour there is a sadness. It must lie in Lloyd Rees' make-up and a reflection of his nature.

Mother sends her love and so do I. I hope Robert is well, and enjoying life, give him my best wishes,

Dad

36 College Street, Sydney
29 October 1951

Dearest Mother and Daddy,

Just to confirm my telegram to say that I've booked on Thursday's 1st November plane TAA which arrives about 1.30 pm so that makes the Adelaide office ten minutes to 2 o'clock, if she arrives on time!

I meant to write on Friday when I decided to go over for my opening, but got caught up in painting a small flower piece for Vi Johns' show.[36] I realised that I'd promised to do something and that it would have to be done before I left. I have committed myself for two so that I'm busy, and can foresee the usual last minute rush and the inevitable wet canvas for travelling.

It was good to have Daddy's letter and I appreciated it. Extra good to hear of the first-day sales and the success of the show. I'd like to be breaking my trip to see it in Melbourne—have booked my return for the 8th which gives me just a week at home.

Hoping all's well,

Love Nora

36 College Street, Sydney
New Year's Day, Sunday 1952

Dearest Mother and Daddy,

Mr Wieneke was in yesterday. I understand that Daddy is in writing contact with him, he's a picture dealer and runs a Gallery in Brisbane. He seems a quite decent sort of man with an honest wish to establish a market with good work

---

35   Lloyd Rees won the Jubilee Art Prize for *The Harbour from McMahon's Point* (1950), held by the Art Gallery of New South Wales.

36   This is Nora Heysen's exhibition, *Flower Paintings*, at the Heysen Gallery, in Hahndorf, which showed 25 works and ran from 2–18 November 1951.

and to encourage appreciation as far as he's able[37] ... I have half committed myself to a small show with him next year.

With again my thanks for the good things in the Christmas box, Robert sends New Year Greetings and wishes.

Hoping all's well, with love to all at home,
Nora

36 College Street, Sydney
Tuesday 12 February 1952

Dearest Mother and Daddy,

I suppose the Archibald has been the only event and that wasn't a very exciting show this year.

I was very glad that Ivor won this year[38] ... The head in the winning portrait was a good vigorous bit of straight painting and it carried well, but the head was all there was to it, though the colour, background and coat was pleasant and harmonious and much better than his usual colour.

Mr Gratton was given a good place among the upper four or five and he held his own in a quiet way, but the only mention I've heard about it at all was from Jim McGregor who liked it. Poor old Gheysens was completely overlooked and all the publicity he was angling for came to less than nothing, so that is the end of that beautiful friendship and I don't think I'll ever hear from him again.

The King's death has cast a gloom over the city's activities and all the animation in preparing for the Royal visit has ceased in mid-air.[39] Was just looking forward to that Garden Party too!

Robert sends his remembrances. With love to all at home,
Nora

Hahndorf, South Australia
13 March 1952

My Dear Nora,

It's been a hectic time ever since an urgent wire came from David Jones to remind me of my promise to hold a show with them covering the period of the Sydney show—the agricultural one. It completely took the wind out of my sails as I

---

37   James Wieneke (1908–1981) ran Moreton Galleries, Brisbane, from 1951 to 1967 and showed leading artists, including Margaret Olley, Sidney Nolan and Charles Blackman. Brisbane's Johnstone Gallery, however, was considered more avant-garde.

38   Ivor Hele (1912–1993) won the 1951 Archibald Prize for his portrait *Laurie Thomas*.

39   King George VI died on 6 February 1952.

had always connected this annual event with Easter which falls due a month later. This now gave me exactly a month to get everything together.

I thoroughly appreciated your description of the Archibald—the booklet made a poor showing, taken all in all. Ivor deserved the prize ... Your summing up was well considered and summed up the position with excellent judgement. Brackenreg could well have given your painting of Gratton more prominence. It was reproduced too small. Jim McGregor wrote very appreciatively of it and rightly mentioned its many excellent qualities. Under the circumstances, I feel you did jolly well.

A wire came today telling all arrived in good order at David Jones. So they have to hang the show decently opening on the 19th. I hope they send you an invitation. Tell me of your impression as a whole and how it is hung, and I can guess already Haefliger's reaction to the 'old fashioned painter'!

Cheerio and do keep well. Mother sends her love and I send lots more of it, Your Dad

36 College Street, Sydney
19 March 1952

Dearest Mother and Daddy,

I've been waiting to see the show before answering Daddy's letter. You will have heard the first fine burst of enthusiasm the exhibition received here[40] ... You would have felt as pleased and proud as I did when you walked in. The impression was excellent, the pictures well chosen and placed and hung, neither overcrowded nor too meagre. They filled the big rooms comfortably and it is a big room, enough to dwarf most artists.

The sketch for the Jubilee competition took the centre of one long wall and the turkeys held the other, the charcoal drawings were alone on terracotta coloured hessian screens on the short wall directly opposite when you walk into the large room, and they looked fine.

Adrian remarked on the beautiful framing and the dignified presentation of the work altogether, so did Will Ashton whom I met there and who was still there when I left over an hour later, hobbling round on his stick enjoying every picture.

I've been gathering up news items and criticisms. Haefliger, of course, gives vent to his usual splenetic reaction to good draughtsmanship and realism. He must

---

40   On 20 March 1952, *The Daily Telegraph* reported that 'buyers who queued outside the gallery doors from nine o'clock in the morning, bought 11 pictures in half an hour'.

have felt a bit bitter when the work was received with such enthusiasm from artists and public alike.

Have been enjoying Gieseking here. He impresses me as being one of the truly great, and to hear the piano played as he plays it is a rare and lasting pleasure and experience. There haven't been any demonstrations against him here and thousands have been turned away from his concerts.[41]

My love to all and a hope that all is well,

Nora

Hahndorf, South Australia
Monday 7 April 1952

My Dear Nora,

How time flies and the exhibition is over and done with. It was jolly good of you to telephone with the 'good news' on the opening day, the very first inkling I got of the excitement … It was quite a thrill to hear that the exhibition had such a good and excellent 'send off'.

Adrian Feint was the first to follow with an appreciative letter: 'The show came like a breath of fresh air,' he said. And that sounds jolly good. Then followed a letter from Mr Jewell in which he expressed himself in almost the same words, and on the same day your airmail came and gave us the *full news*. Many thanks. A telegram from Sir Charles Lloyd Jones followed on its heels—a telegram of congratulations … But I had no letter from Lloyd Rees or anyone else. The exhibition has meant a lot to me, but I really think it has been well worthwhile.

Cheerio much love from all,

Your Dad

---

41   Walter Gieseking (1895–1956) was a French–German pianist who was in the German army in the First World War and, on occasion, played to audiences in German-occupied France during the Second World War. This was the subject of controversy and demonstrations during a 1949 tour to the United States of America, with a concert cancelled in New York. He was later cleared in an Allied court hearing and resumed his concert career. See Theodore Baker, *Baker's Biographical Dictionary of Twentieth Century Musicians*, New York, Schirmer Books, 1997,

36 College Street, Sydney
11 May 1952

Dearest Mother and Daddy,

Just to say thank you for giving me a very timely break at home with all the comforts and considerations to make it a happy stay. The morning cup of tea was a great luxury, though I felt guilty accepting it.

My love and thanks for four weeks holiday.[42]

Nora

Hahndorf, South Australia
Sunday 1952

My Dear Nora,

This is just a hasty note to tell you the news. There was a Board meeting on Friday to receive the report and decision of the Melrose Prize result, as you know the adjudicators were Campbell, McCubbin and Millward Gray. And I did think that things were in your favour, but to my astonishment the name of Charles Bush was read out as the winner, and you a very close runner-up. I understand the decision was a toss-up, with the casting vote against you.[43] You will know the Bush well, a self portrait shown in the last Archibald competition. In it there are some good painting qualities and sense of form in the head. But in comparison yours was fresher and looked good.

Mother was terribly disappointed and took some time getting over the decision, but there you are and it is no use kicking. The only answer is to do better and I know you will.

There were about 50 entries for the Melrose, but I felt with 3 or 4 exceptions they were a sad lot.

Mother sends her love and wants me to thank you for your last letter, we both enjoyed it.

My love,

Your Dad

---

42 Nora would have completed *Portrait of Hans Heysen* (1952) during this time.

43 Nora's entry for the Melrose Prize was *Portrait of a Young Man*, depicting Robert Black (the same portrait she entered for the 1950 Archibald Prize but renamed). It was highly commended. See 'Melrose Prize Competition, 1952', *National Gallery of South Australia Bulletin*, vol.14, no.1, July 1952.

36 College Street, Sydney
Thursday 29 May 1952

Dearest Mother and Daddy,

Many thanks for news and cuttings regarding the Melrose. I must admit that I was disappointed to have just missed it but I was glad to know that my flesh tones were 'just right', some consolation, and glad to hear that the portrait stood up to the other entries.

I had a letter from Robert Campbell expressing his thanks for the contribution. I have the feeling that it was his vote that went against me.

Robert will be down on the 25th June so there's only a month to go—his return will coincide with the finalisation of his divorce, so it will be a happy homecoming and the end of eight years' wait.[44]

The Society of Artists show was a complete flop and the Wakelin show sold next to nothing, a sign of the times.

Love to all,

Nora

36 College Street, Sydney
7 August 1952

Dearest Mother and Daddy,

To see the Heysen book complete is a wonderful event, and to look through it and contemplate the production from all points of view, and to find it completely satisfying and more than meeting all expectations, is a still rarer event.[45] Then to be presented with one of the first copies hot off the press was an added thrill, then too coming as it did on a gloomy day in the midst of an all-time *low* here, the event was heightened.

Metaphysically the sun is shining here after a very dreary period—the coming of the book seems to have heralded better times. The lights are on again after being without electricity for over a fortnight, also the gas supply which has been practically nil for the last four months has at last been attended to. Trying to cook on a primus stove groping round by candlelight, no refrigeration, music, radio or warmth, a wet bleak spell of weather combined with a last minute hitch in the finalisation of Robert's affairs. Tuesday was a red letter day: the Heysen book, a cheque from Stef, electricity and gas restored, news that Vi Johns had sold two pictures I'd sent over some weeks ago, and a cheerful visit from John who was full

---

44   Robert had married Dr Dorothy Tandy in 1941.
45   This is Lionel Lindsay and James MacDonald, *Hans Heysen Watercolours and Drawings*, Sydney, Legend Press, 1952.

of his visit up home and glowing with the account of all he'd done and seen and talked of and eaten.

With the sending-in date for the Society of Artists almost upon us again I'm busy framing and finishing some work to go in.

With my love and thanks for the proud day of the Heysen book,

Nora

36 College Street, Sydney
1 September 1952

Dearest Mother and Daddy,

It was quite a surprise to see Stef over here and the offerings he brought fresh from home were lovely to receive ... Stef brought along Campbell and Lloyd Rees with him, so the biscuit tin was opened there and then to accompany the cup of coffee, and thankful I was to have something to offer. My first meeting with Campbell—he seemed friendly and enthusiastic, and I was very pleased to hear his opening speech for the Society of Artists show which wasn't unmixed with criticism. It ended on the note that it was a pity that the artists were not directing their talents towards seeing and feeling their own country, rather than becoming slaves to European trends and cults.

You'd get quite a shock to see the Society of Artists show this year. I've never seen so much derivative work in one show before—the movement which has been infiltrating Australian art and angling for supremacy is now in complete command, and like the dictatorship powers have announced their victory with a ruthless purge of all their enemies. Haefliger sits enthroned on the dais with three huge canvases of Jesus Christ and his apostles around him—Passmore, Kmit, Orban, Drysdale, Jean Bellette and his other friends of today ... Only a few canvases, which owing to the laws of the Society that one picture from each member's entries must be hung, are tucked away in corners where they don't interfere and ruin the grand advancement of the new and exciting modern group.

As you can imagine no gum trees or blue skies were to be seen in this show. I liked the Lloyd Rees canvases more than anything. At least I find depth and sincerity there that are not borrowed.

A lot of the members are feeling pretty sore about the ruthless rejection of their works ... Unfortunately, I won't be here for the next meeting. Hal Missingham has asked me to accompany an exhibition of landscape paintings from the Gallery to the country centre of Young, and to lecture on the works and open the show—15 guineas for 12 lectures, and fares and accommodation paid. At first I said 'No', appalled at the idea of public speaking, but I've been persuaded into thinking 'Why not!'

Hope all's well at home, that the sun is shining there too. Many thanks for all the good things,

Love Nora

36 College Street, Sydney
Monday 20 October 1952

Dearest Mother and Daddy,

I hope the birthday went off happily. It was a lovely day and I celebrated it by painting the scene from my kitchen window—the magic of tender Spring foliage in Spring sunshine.

I was at Jim McGregor's for Sunday lunch yesterday. He's just back and looking better than I've seen him for some time. He's terribly enthusiastic over the Heysen book and said the copies he took with him were received with great pleasure and amazement at the perfection of the reproduction. He says he's sent a dozen or more to friends all over the world and in his opinion each print in the book is a winner.

Yes, I suppose you did wonder at my launching out into public speaking. I wonder still how I came to do it, and vow that it will be the first and last time.

During the five days I was there, I had about 600 school children to lecture to and was kept talking solidly for 3 to 4 hours each morning. Quite hard work and more especially as it was all new to me and I was extremely nervous. The children from the Christian Brothers College and Convent were well behaved and interested, but the public school 'opportunists', so rightly named, were real little hooligans.

I talked to the children in groups of 40 at a time, but God knows how much of what I said went in and what was the use of it all. The show was quite an interesting collection, one Heysen, the oil of a haystack with a cart and horse against light. It had more sun in it than any other picture there and I was always glad when I came round to telling the kids that this picture was painted by my Father etc. It and Sali Herman's street scene in Woolloomooloo and the Drysdale and Streeton were the most popular pictures. I was surprised that the children liked the Drysdale and Sali Herman.

This must go before I start on another flower piece!

My love to all and I hope the good effects of the holiday still linger,

Nora

Hahndorf, South Australia
4 November 1952

My Dear Nora,

The mount cutter is proving a real success and most useful. As it makes such a clean cut and far more easily handled than the old mount cutters I have been using, thank you again for thinking of it.

What an entertaining experience you must have had at Young. I still can't get over the idea of you lecturing. I simply couldn't imagine myself surmounting the ordeal, and yet by the paper report, it appears you did jolly well, my hearty congratulations. Sometimes I doubt whether all this talk does much good, and yet one never knows when and where a seed will germinate ... I feel you were jolly brave to tackle the job.

You have my love always and Mother sends hers too,
Dad

Hahndorf, South Australia
6 January 1953

My Dear Nora,

You will be glad to hear, things are going along well—the wound has stopped draining yesterday and I have managed the studio several times—and my interest in painting is returning rapidly, so with each day I am getting stronger and stronger and it will not be long before I can get onto some concentration.[46]

I am really beginning to enjoy the *Spanish Painting* and like the writing as well when dealing with the earlier period. So far I have not got to the moderns, but there is a very fine Picasso, a beautifully set up figure finely constructed and carrying weight, also the two of his blue period. These are fine, but when it comes to the other stuff—well enough!

I am enclosing something for your birthday from both Mother and myself and whatever you get for it will, I sincerely hope, give you pleasure and of course we both send our hearty congratulations with the best of wishes for our New Year and may it bring you happiness and cheerio.

With love,
From your Dad

---

46   Hans Heysen, then aged 75, had gall-bladder surgery in December 1952. See Colin Thiele, *Heysen of Hahndorf*, Adelaide, Hyde Park Press: 269.

36 College Street, Sydney
21 January 1953

Dearest Mother and Daddy

I was very pleased to have my birthday greetings ... Very pleased too to have the cheque and many thanks. You'll be happy to hear what the cheque brought me to play a part in my big day. Robert and I were married yesterday, a very quiet wedding at the Registry Office with two witnesses, Elsie Buckle and a Tom O'Day, an air pilot and artist whom we met during the war. So now the lawful seal has been put upon our union, and I am officially Mrs Robert Black with a ring and all and very happy about it.

After all these years, I can scarce believe that our wish of ten years standing is now fulfilled. If anyone had told me that this is how I'd eventually do it, I wouldn't have believed them. After endless delays, Robert eventually received his clearance papers on Saturday then had to wait till Monday to fix a time and someone to marry us. So it was all rather hurried in the end. Robert took half a day off, we lunched on a couple of pies and walked down to the Registry Office which is just down at the end of the street. It was the hottest day imaginable. We arrived too early and sweating to await our turn in the queue were married at three o'clock, the whole ceremony only taking 15 minutes or less and as we were ushered out the next couple were escorted in. I had a few quiet chuckles at the disparity of my youthful visions and the actual matter of fact event and yet it is a miracle how the real thing can transform such factually unromantic surroundings into something significant and moving. We celebrated afterwards with champagne and then went on with the normal routine. So that's that and they lived happily ever after. I bought myself a new hat with the tenner, an armful of roses and the Skira book on Spanish Painting (the same). All for *the* day so that I felt that you were represented even though you couldn't be personally there.

I've been pretty busy painting, almost finishing a largish portrait of Robert and between sittings a little basket of crab apples just by way of relaxation from the exacting demands of portraiture.[47] On my birthday Jim McGregor invited us to lunch so I had a holiday from the kitchen and enjoyed some of the most lovely German wine I've ever tasted. Jim wanted to know exactly how you were and all your symptoms before and after—he knows all about it and is full of sympathy and concern for a quick recovery. He had just been judging the entries for the Archibald and says the standard is the lowest he's seen. It looks as though Dargie will have

---

47   This is *Portrait of Dr Robert Black* (1953), oil on canvas, 40.9 x 30.6 cm, National Library of Australia, Pictures Collection, nla.pic-vn4808449.

it again though Dobell has a portrait of Professor Marston in, which should be a winner. Also Ivor has sent in his portrait of Kenneth Wills.[48] Friday is judging day so will have to wait till then to know who's done what with whom and who's carried off the honours. I wish I had an entry in, perhaps this year will be a more settled painting year. I hope to do some work in the islands. It's not so long now before we're off to the Trobriands, late February or early March.

I was very pleased to have family news in Daddy's letter and to feel in the writing a return to strength and enthusiasm.

Love to all,

Nora

Hahndorf, South Australia
29 January 1953

My Dear Nora,

At last your letter has brought the long-awaited good news! Hearty congratulations—yet it seems strange to congratulate you now when in your own conscience you had found your life's mate some years ago. And congratulations can only come on the legal binding and so I am glad this has been accomplished (to everyone's satisfaction).

I see from your letter, so full of interesting news, that Robert and you will be off to the Islands within the early year. Let it be a kind of second honeymoon and a well deserved and enjoyable adventure, as well as a holiday away from city life.

I would like your ideas on the Dobell Archibald portrait of Marston. I always thought this would have been an ideal subject for Dobell. What has he done with him—is it a fine painting? I had the idea it might be suitable for our Gallery, as Marston has so long been associated with Adelaide.

You will be glad to hear we bought a fine Wilson Steer for the Gallery.[49]

My love goes with this,

Your Dad

48   Kenneth Wills (1896–1977) was controller of the Allied Intelligence Bureau in the south-west Pacific area in the Second World War. He was a prominent Adelaide businessman and Chairman of G. & R. Wills & Co. and Advertiser Newspapers, and Chancellor of the University of Adelaide. Ivor Hele's portrait *Sir Kenneth Wills* (1952) is part of the University of Adelaide's Art and Heritage Collection. See David Palmer, 'Wills, Sir Kenneth Agnew (1896–1977), *Australian Dictionary of Biography*, vol.16, Melbourne University Press, 1983: 559–561.

49   This is Philip Wilson Steer's *Bridgnorth* (1917), oil on canvas, purchased in 1953.

36 College Street, Sydney
2 February1953

Dearest Mother and Daddy,

Daddy's letter this morning and very happy we both are to have your recognition and blessing on our partnership and a very warm thank you too for the material part of it which will go a long way towards making (our second honeymoon) free from care and a happy holiday. I was just wondering how I was going to manage to get the necessary materials together and meet the fare with what I had saved up. It will just make all the difference and I can't express my thanks for such a timely and generous gesture. We leave per Qantas plane on the 28th February, with an overnight break at Cairns to Pt Moresby for a few days and then on to the Trobriand Islands via Samaria by boat. My painting materials with Robert's medical equipment have already left by ship.

I'm looking forward too to doing some drawings of the natives and getting different subject matter. The Trobriand Islands have an average rainfall of 4 inches a day, so the main enemy is going to be mildew and the difficulty of keeping paper dry enough to work on.

I don't quite know what conclusions to come to about the Marston portrait. It is certainly the tour de force of the show and is outstanding because of its luminosity, design and imagination—qualities so pathetically lacking in the other exhibits—but it's far short of Dobell's best. It's very sketchy and he's just 'flashed' over subtleties and difficulties in a fashion that is effective, but far from satisfying. As a portrait I don't think it is good—it gives the appearance of being painted entirely from memory and he's lost the real character of the man I feel. At least it doesn't give me the impression of the man as I remember him, and still it's interesting as a picture, but how much more he could have done. Jim McGregor, when he rang the other evening, spoke of the Marston portrait, expressed a wish that he'd like to buy it for the Adelaide Gallery, and when I told him who Marston was and of his long association with Adelaide, he was still more interested, but I haven't heard since if he's actually bought it.[50] If he hasn't I think he'd need very little persuasion to clinch it. I believe his vote went to the Dobell.

With love and thanks from Robert and myself and a hope that all continues well, Nora

---

50   Hedley Ralph Marston (1900–1965) was a prominent and colourful Adelaide scientist who also mixed in art circles. See Eric Underwood, 'Hedley Ralph Marston, 1900–1965', *Records of the Australian Academy of Science*, vol.1, no.2, Canberra, 1967.

36 College Street, Sydney
15 February 1953

Dearest Mother and Daddy,

Mother's letter with its 'nest egg' has come to enhance our state of well being and our hopes of building a home in the near future …

I heard indirectly that a wealthy wool buyer had bought the Marston portrait, so I assume it was Jim McGregor and that the portrait will be presented to the Adelaide Art Gallery. Even though it is not successful as a portrait it will stimulate a lot of interest.

My banking account is still in my name and I'll let it remain so, also my painting name will be Nora Heysen, only 'Mrs Black in private life' as the papers put it.

My love and thanks for so much,
Nora

These letters come from the National Library of Australia's 'Papers of Sir Hans Heysen, c.1880–1973', MS 5073, series 2, folders 158, 159, 162, 165, 166, 167, 168 and 173; and 'Papers of Nora Heysen, 1913–2003', MS 10041, series 1.3, folders 30, 31, 32 and 34. Some of the letters are also from 'The Cedars' collection.

Touring the Pacific
and settling in Sydney
1953–1959

The 1950s marked a busy time in Nora Heysen's career. Following her marriage to Robert Black in early 1953, the two set out for the Trobriand Islands, Robert to continue his work on tropical diseases and Nora to paint and draw. She was doing what several other modern artists were doing around these years, looking to the Pacific for subject matter. Her friend William Dobell had spent several periods in New Guinea from 1949 to 1953, and Margaret Olley too worked in the Pacific. Nora Heysen was back in the Trobriand Islands and again in New Guinea in 1954. Her letters home from these trips prompted her mother Sallie to comment that if ever her daughter decided to write about her travels, the letters said it all!

This decade was one of exhibiting. In 1953 Nora held a successful solo exhibition at Moreton Galleries, in Brisbane, and two solo exhibitions in Adelaide: one in 1956 at the Heysen Gallery, in Hahndorf, run by her brother Stefan Heysen, and a second in 1957 at John Martin's Gallery, in Adelaide. She continued to enter the Melrose Prize for portraiture, which she previously won twice. Her entry in 1959 was unsuccessful. This loss to the more modern artist Jacqueline Hick prompted Nora to comment: 'I've long since given up hope of winning prizes—my work is far too unexciting and conventional'. However, schooled by her father in the business of art, she saw value in entering competitions because it was 'a means of keeping one's name before the public and getting the odd commission'. She entered her portrait of *Professor*

C.G. Lambie in the 1957 Archibald Prize, but it went to William Dargie for his very topical portrayal of Albert Namatjira. She also twice entered *The Australian Women's Weekly* Portrait Prize; first, in 1955 with two entries, *Mrs David Jamieson and her Daughter* and *Sibella Anne Mannix*, and again in 1958 with *Self Portrait: Scheme in Grey*. Although she was no longer winning the prizes, she was getting a steady stream of commissions for portraits and flowers, was constantly sending off work to exhibitions and having work purchased, including her beautiful drawing of an islander, *Moulasi*, by the National Art Gallery of New South Wales in 1956.

Balancing the professional side of her career with her private life, and thus finding time to paint, is a subject she broaches on several occasions. In 1954 Nora and Robert purchase a charming historic house, 'The Chalet', at Hunters Hill, in Sydney. This resolves one major difficulty, having a home of their own and space for her studio, but its large garden causes her mother to ask what will happen to her daughter's painting if 'the gardening disease' gets hold of her. Nora, however, delights in having her own flowers to paint, especially her favourite but elusive rose, the Souvenir de Mal Maison, which her father grew especially for her from cuttings. Robert, meanwhile, is frequently away on field trips, often for lengthy periods of time. Nora comments she is sad to see him go: 'I sometimes think that we've had more than our share of enforced goodbyes'.

The 1950s were an important transitional period in Australian art and the rise in abstraction. This became an issue in the Hunters Hill Art Show, for which Nora served on the selection committee with Hal Missingham. They had to defend their selection of abstract art to a conservative local council. New galleries were opening, including Clune Galleries and Rudy Komon Art Gallery, the latter initially as an antique shop selling paintings. The Society of Artists continued to hold its exhibitions. Nora is networking at openings and conveying messages home to her father from numerous Sydney artists and collectors. This is not the quiet, reclusive life so often attributed to her.

Nora's parents have periods of ill health, especially Sallie, and numerous letters are full of enquiries about their wellbeing. Hans continues to be busy producing art, and enquiries come constantly to Nora from various galleries in Sydney wanting her father's work in their upcoming exhibitions. Some of these enquiries she sends on, other she fends off. In 1959, Hans is knighted and his portrait is painted by Ivor Hele and presented to the National Gallery of South Australia. Hans is a celebrity and he and Sallie are featured in *The Australian Women's Weekly*.

Papua Hotel
Port Moresby
3 March 1953

Dearest Mother and Daddy,

Just a brief note to say we have arrived so far ... here we are sweating 'till the launch takes us on to the Trobriands. It's as hot as Hades, and not a breath of air to fan the damp body. From out the hotel window I can see the groups of natives sitting in the shade of the trees—a decorative picture—the dark silky skinned bodies and the notes of primitive bright colours in their sarongs. Some of the young girls wearing grass skirts, some nursing fat black babies, while other babes are being hung in string bags from branches of the trees, and every now and again are given a slight push to set them swinging. Great bunches of green bananas and golden papaws add colour, and I can see a long stick strung along with fish.

It is interesting to see the changes that have taken place up here—one wouldn't recognise the place from when I saw it nine years ago. The couple of tin roofs have spread into a sizeable town with a couple of stores, picture theatre, hotel and quite presentable houses. It never was or will be, though, much of a place.

With love to all,

Nora

Losuia, Trobriand Islands[1]
23 March 1953

Dearest Mother and Daddy,

And so we have arrived in Losuia and this is our house—a whole house to ourselves standing on stilts by the edge of the sea surrounded by coconut trees, banana palms and pawpaw trees. We even have a couple of fowls! The whole front of the house is a large veranda-like room which I use for a studio, and is quite ideal as such ... I'm free to paint all day. A complete change in a new and fascinating world so teeming with interesting subject matter that I feel quite drugged and bewildered, and don't know how or where to begin.

Arrived just a fortnight ago today after a five and a half days' sea trip ... we threaded our way round tropic isles, stopping here and there to see a native village, and see what was doing. On one of the islands of the Amphlett group, we watched them making cooking pots. Quite fascinating to see with what simple means they were made and how perfectly symmetrical and efficient the finished product. Just some of the natural putty-coloured clay moistened with water, moulded

---

1   This is one of the few letters in which Nora Heysen included a drawing. See Plate 1.

with the hands and decorated with a shell, then burned in a fire. No pottery wheel, no kiln or tools and lo the pots come out all sizes and shapes and patterning. It is an object lesson up here to see how much can be done with so little. Their beautiful slender canoes are fashioned from a log with an adze and nothing else, except for the finishing polish which is achieved with the dried skin of a fish. There is a village near here which we visited yesterday, noted for its master wood carvers and there all their tables and bowls and figures, from the largest article to the most delicate intricate work, was done with an adze, a penknife and the old fish skin. I tried to make some drawings of them at work squatting in their huts, and quietly chipping away.

Quite a feature of Losuia are the native women who carry everything on their heads—to watch them going by is a real pleasure, such poise and grace of movement, like ballerinas in their grass skirts which are worn about eight inches below the waist. They are short and stand straight out, made from layers and layers of dried banana leaves stripped to resemble grass. Their Sunday best skirts are very decorative, made of different tiers of different colours, with a pattern of pandanus leaves around the top. Worn on that part of the lower hip they get the ultimate movement as they walk, and go bobbing up and down in a most attractive and seductive way. The young girls have beautiful bodies and are very good to look at.

The native men simply wear the briefest of G-strings made of a piece of pandanus leaf, and perhaps a hibiscus or butterfly in their hair, or a piece of fern in their woven arm bands. Their sense of just how to decorate themselves seems infallible.

I've had a long stream of sitters today beginning with the big chief Mitakata who is king of the black world. We visited the village where he lives surrounded by his yam houses and his thirteen wives, and with the help of an interpreter, asked if he'd be willing to sit for his portrait one day. Lo and behold, in he walked yesterday in full regalia, necklaces of pig tusks, beads, bangles and strings of shells dangling in festoons round ankles, wrists and calves and forehead. So loaded with decoration he could hardly walk—two attendants with him carrying his royal carpet, lime, gourd, betel nut and other appendages. Really an amazing performance, but as no one could speak a word of the other's language, it was frightfully awkward. In the end I gathered he'd come to sit for the portrait.

This morning he appeared again with all his royal jewellery carried in a bag. He's a wonderful subject really, but quite beyond me. One would have to be a Goya or a Jacovleff to cope.[2] He's an old man for a native, 65 years or 70, thin and

---

2   Alexandre Jacovleff (1887–1938) was a fashionable Russian émigré based in Paris, whose work shows the influence of the Ballets Russes. Hans Heysen held Jacovleff's *Fara Ali Afden, an Abyssinian* (1928). Jacovleff trained in St Petersburg, worked in Italy and Spain in 1913, and then Mongolia, China and Japan. He was awarded the Legion of Honour by the French Government in 1926 for his North African work.

wizened up but with a noble bearing and a highly intelligent face. The last of his blood, he brought three of his wives with him this morning and three piccaninnies, and they all sat round and giggled. Very trying for the artist ... Wherever you start to draw, hoards of natives crowd round to look. Even here in my studio, they stand round the door peer in the windows and if one isn't looking, they're in squatting round the floor.

You'd be amused at the 'trades people' here and the manner of shopping. The trading is conducted with sticks of tobacco, 2 sticks for a fowl, 1 stick for an enormous bunch of bananas, ½ stick for an egg and so on, and all day the natives come and squat by the back door selling their offerings. As there's no fresh meat up here, or butter and little bread, one's daily diet becomes a matter of what the natives bring in. Fish, sometimes wild pig, jams, pawpaw, bananas, odd looking beans and tiny tomatoes. But I can't hope to describe the life up here.

Meanwhile how is everything? I am so remote up here and mails are few and far between. Once a fortnight the seaplane lands with mail. I must prepare for the next sitter—a wood carver this time.

I hope Daddy is getting quickly stronger and that all's well.[3]

My love and thoughts,

Nora

Hahndorf, South Australia
2 April 1953

My Dear Nora,

You have given us a great pleasure with your last letter from the Trobriand Islands, it is full of interesting and fascinating pictures of natural life surrounding you. It is going to do you a world of good in more ways than one—quite apart from the complete break from Sydney life. It's quite a delightful sketch of the house you now live in and it's just the very thing to give us a picture of your surroundings, but all those mosquitoes, how they would make me curse.

Mother has at last some help ... also you will be glad to hear that your Dad is back to normal or almost so.

I have already got onto several things in the studio, the large oil of Gums and sheep I painted as a commission for the Bank of Australasia seems to have given full satisfaction, and they also bought the large watercolour study for the oil. This is to hang in their Board Room in Melbourne. The oil has already gone to London and is now in the framer's hands before being presented to Lord Inverforth.

---

3   Hans Heysen was still recovering from gall-bladder surgery.

Now I have just completed the oil I started about 20 years ago of *Bronzewings and Saplings*—somehow I have a feeling it's turned out trumps. Looks quite good. Full of sun and movement. Something to have ready for an exhibition.[4] This makes me ready to begin another biggish oil of open northern landscape of Arkaba for which I have already completed the watercolour study.

I had a fine opportunity of making a comparison between Dobell's portrait and the man himself some two weeks back. There was Marston standing in front of his picture! I at once felt where Dobell had failed and failed badly which no bravura of brushwork could override. The drawing and observation was very faulty and there was no real penetration into the character of the sitter. I was not surprised when Marston told me he did not actually sit for the big painting, and that it was done mainly from memory (a great mistake).

Mother sends her love and best of good wishes in which I join most heartily, Your Dad

Losuia, Trobriand Islands
20 April 1953

My Dearest Mother and Daddy,

The Catalina flying boat has just brought in Daddy's letter. I watched her landing in a flurry of white foam from out of my studio window … When I saw the handwriting my heart leapt for pleasure.

The latest *Turkey and Sapling* picture sounds fine. I have a vision of its sunshine and movement. Realising up here exactly how much energy, effort and sustained enthusiasm it takes to conceive and bring to conclusion a large picture, I feel that Daddy must be feeling quite himself again with the long convalescence behind. Our time up here is nearing an end all too soon. Only another week or so to go, and we leave for Pt Moresby on the 30th.

In some ways I won't be sorry to leave the tropics with the heat and mosquitoes, and I'm looking forward to a hot bath, some fresh butter and meat again and coffee! And most particularly do I look forward to hearing music again. The only music up here is the monotonous sound of the native drums, and the natives singing hymns at the Mission.

On the other hand, the time has been all too short for the work I've attempted up here. Not only are the natives a problem in flesh painting, but trying to pin them

---

4   *The Promenade* (1953) is held by the National Gallery of Australia. It was acquired in 1959 by the Commonwealth Art Advisory Board.

down to sittings, once the novelty has worn off, is my biggest headache … For a short time they make excellent sitters, but they can't sustain the effort and don't know what is expected of them.

I've done quite a bit of work, drawings and paintings, only one flower piece of red hibiscus. A largish oil of a native mother and child, a couple of paintings of young girls in grass skirts, some portrait heads and now I'm all out on the big canvas of Mitakata, the big chief. I am working against time, and hosts of other difficulties. Working on a tabletop in a conflicting light and with spasmodic sittings isn't making my task an easy one. The old boy lives out at a village some four miles out on jungle roads, and has to be brought in each time by a truck which is rarely available. He should make an unusual and striking portrait if I can carry it off.

Robert, of course, sees these people from a different angle, disease ridden with malaria, tuberculosis, yaws and everything else, living in congested unhygienic conditions, and for him, it is depressing. However, he's keeping remarkably fit and enjoying the freedom of life up here, and having our own house. I must say I'm enjoying absolute freedom from household chores.

I was amazed the other day when a native girl brought along a reproduction of a Woodside pastoral of Daddy's telling me that my Father had painted it, and how it was her treasured possession.

I was very interested to hear your criticism on the Archibald and Wynne prize exhibits lent to the Adelaide Gallery and particularly of the Dobell portrait of Marston which, I presume, didn't go to the Adelaide Gallery after all.[5]

And now to bed as I have a big day of sittings tomorrow from Mitakata and have to make the most of them. I'm just about snowed under with insects of all descriptions, ants, moths, beetles of every variety, twenty odd lizards chasing after moths on the ceiling and a couple of bats flying in and out round my head. Wonderful place for an entomologist! I forgot the mosquitoes.

My love and hope that all continues well and the help remains,

Nora

---

5   William Dobell's Archibald entry of Marston is held by Queensland Art Gallery. An earlier version, oil on board, was bequeathed in 1998 to the Art Gallery of South Australia by the subject's wife, Kathleen Nellie Marston.

36 College Street, Sydney
Wednesday 3 June 1953

Dearest Mother and Daddy,

It's difficult to realise that I've been back three weeks today and impossible to account for the time—it's just vanished.

Now I've got on top of things again, and am ready for the next chapter, preparing for my show in Brisbane.

Talking of shows, just then the postman blew his whistle and there was an invitation to the Heysen show at the Heysen Gallery, so you'll be in the throes of it yourself.[6]

Apart from unrolling and stretching my canvas, I haven't been able to get to work. It was quite a shock to see the work in these surroundings. The exotic colour and brown bare bodies seem strange in this grey atmosphere.

Dr Keogh was over from Melbourne the other day and was interested in the new work and bought two of the drawings—a red chalk drawing of a baby's back and one of a young native boy holding a golden cock. I didn't get the big portrait of the chief finished. In the end, time defeated me … the old chief went on strike.

I wonder that any work survived the boat trip back to Port Moresby and I was beyond caring if it did. The cabin was awash most of the time and everything tossed about unmercifully, and then the cockroaches and rats were so bad that they ate the very clothes on our bodies while we slept, and there was nowhere safe from them. As most of my paintings had had to be rolled up only half dry and had no protection from sea water or cockroaches, I gave away any thought of getting anything back whole. It's amazing what oil paintings will survive even when they are painted on paper! The drawings didn't fare so well as the portfolio got wet.

Sydney is aflutter with Coronation celebrations and everyone is frantic trying to enjoy the occasion.[7]

Robert sends his good wishes.

My love to all at home,

Nora

---

6   This was a Hans Heysen solo exhibition.
7   The Coronation of Elizabeth II occurred on 2 June 1953.

73 Arabella Street
Longueville, Sydney
25 September 1953

Dearest Mother and Daddy,

At last some news of my Brisbane venture to report … only today have I heard that the pictures have arrived safely, and that six were sold on the opening day. I enclose cuttings and catalogue.

The fight over the College Street evictions is still going on and it is frontline news in all the papers. Some of the tenants are still refusing to be evicted and one old dame threatens to hang herself to the tree outside if she is moved. It's a losing battle against such a powerful body as the RSL, but we may yet get some compensation? The last few weeks there were so nerve wracking with continual meetings and demonstrations that for our part we'd had enough and were glad to go quietly.

It's a pleasant spot out here—quite detached from the turmoil and noise of the city, in fact so quiet that I find myself staring curiously at the odd car that passes. It was the old Kingsford Smith home, with a bit of a rambling uncared-for garden and a little wooden house. Smithy's room is detached from the rest of the house so that when he came in at all hours after flying he wouldn't disturb the household. As the men folk are away all day, I can see myself taking advantage of the quiet and the garden and getting out the old palette and brushes. I have put up Daddy's two pictures and the pastel which has been enormously admired and the watercolour, so I have something about me.

Tom O'Dea is an artist so there is a studio ready set up with easel etc. Also he played round with ham radio, so there's a shack for Robert. Couldn't be better. Must run this up to the post.

With love to all at home with a big prayer that all goes well and that Mother is getting stronger every day.

Love and thoughts,
Nora

The Canberra Hotel, Brisbane
4 October 1953

My Dearest Mother and Daddy,

Firstly to wish Daddy Many Happy Returns on the 8th.

This Brisbane trip was in the end an eventuality, leaving Thursday we arrived here Friday evening, and were lucky enough to find a hotel to put us up.

Were just in time to see my show before it was unhung. I must say I was agreeably surprised to find two more red dots making the total sold 8, which isn't so bad for an introduction, and promises a future market here. The Moreton Gallery is really a good little gallery, a nice size and well lit for artificial lighting and right in the centre of the city.[8]

I had another agreeable surprise to see the Art Gallery here which has changed out of all recognition probably due to Robert Campbell's efforts.[9] The few pictures that were on view, being an exhibition of recent acquisitions, were well framed and beautifully presented. Some very 'nice' Tom Roberts and early Streetons and Conders amongst the collection. They evidently haven't bought a Heysen in the last few years. Mr Wieneke is still excited over his last visit to Hahndorf ... I'll include this last review of my show, as it's slightly more effusive than the two I sent before.[10]

The trip here was very enjoyable in lovely weather with the country looking its best. It brings home to one the vastness and variety of this country when you travel these distances. We went through a belt of Lloyd Rees canvases. I'd always thought he saw Australia with dark coloured glasses on, as it were, and the dark sombre tones were the product of his own melancholy outlook, but there it was so reminiscent of his paintings and I felt he hadn't exaggerated at all. Once through that belt, the light and colour scheme seemed to change completely to silver greys, blues and pale ochres, and from that to the grand mountain scenery with tropical gullies and foliage, and with all nothing resembling the Hahndorf and Woodside scenery.

Hope to see the Armidale collection on the home trip, when we won't have to run to a time schedule.[11] It's really a bit far to do the trip in two days. The car went very well and besides I'll be able to put all the leftover paintings in the back and save the air freight.

Love to all,

Nora

---

8   Moreton Galleries was located in the AMP Basement, Edward Street, Brisbane.

9   Robert Campbell (1902–1972) was the first Director of Queensland Art Gallery, from 1949 to 1951, before becoming Director of the National Art Gallery of South Australia. See Christine Finnimore, 'Campbell, Robert Richmond (1902–1972)', *Australian Dictionary of Biography*, vol.13, Melbourne University Press, 1993: 360–361.

10 Nora is referring to Gertrude Langer, 'Nora Heysen's Work on Show', *Courier Mail*, September 1953.

11 This is the Howard Hinton Collection at Armidale Teachers' College, in New South Wales.

Hahndorf, South Australia
29 October 1953

My Dear Nora,

I have felt very conscious for not writing to you long before this, but I know you will understand the upside down situation we have been in, which has absorbed all my thoughts, energies and time. An anxious period has passed or nearly so, for mother has made a remarkable recovery and getting back to normal, the stove already occupying her attention. Mother had not been herself for quite a long while and definitely losing ground, when the climax came with unbearable pains—I immediately called the doctor, who was here within ten minutes and injected. He diagnosed the trouble at once and you may imagine our feelings when an operation was suggested—and arranged for ... It amazed both the surgeon and Dr Roberts how quickly mother recovered from the ordeal, for within 3 weeks Mother was back home and much of my anxiety was passing.[12]

You certainly have given me a great and most pleasant surprise with the Berenson book on the Renaissance. Thank you ever so much, but how did you know that I had never read his, not ever seen it? I feel sure it will make excellent reading. There seems an abundance of things I have not seen in illustration before.

We have just bought a new Drysdale—a large canvas for the Gallery— a Nolan scene of death and desolation, and a Norton which I don't like at all ...

The Drysdale I like in its big design—but he still adheres to his elongation.[13] You will see this, as his centrepiece for his exhibition in Sydney very soon. In the Nolan picture I definitely feel he has caught something uncanny with desolation and decay. But both these pictures make me long for some clear, fresh and healthy paint. Surely we have had enough of these sombre and unhealthy skies with not a hope or a happy note anywhere—surely this is but (a very small note) in the Australian landscape. And yet it is acclaimed as the forerunner of an Australian school! Perhaps it is only a passing phase. I hope so.

Mother and I send our love and hope sincerely that you will soon, very soon, find a suitable place to live in and make a home.

Cheerio,

Your Dad

PS Remember me to Robert.

---

12   Sallie Heysen had gall-bladder surgery.
13   The Art Gallery of South Australia purchased Russell Drysdale's *Mullalonah Tank* (1953) and Sidney Nolan's *Near Birdsville*.

73 Arabella Street
Longueville, Sydney
17 November 1953

Dearest Mother and Daddy,

I was very glad to have Daddy's long letter reporting Mother's steady progress.

We are still marking time and, as the weeks go by, with more and more impatience. We have looked at innumerable houses but with no results. The lowest figure quoted so far was £4,700 for an old house that would need half as much again spent on it to make it habitable. The so-called modern new places we've had offered give me the cold shudders—with their gimcrack foundations, box rooms, suburban gardens and lack of space or privacy. My idea is to find an old place solidly built that we could add to and make to our requirements, but so far nothing approaching it has come along.

I don't find much time for painting and even if I did make the time, somehow I feel too unsettled and disorientated to find the state of mind to concentrate. I've begun on a couple of flower pieces, but they've remained unfinished.

We had a night off last week and went to the Artists' Ball—it was quite amusing seeing the varied ideas in fancy dress. As our chance of going only arrived a couple hours before the show began, our fancy dress was a very impromptu affair. I donned the sari I bought in Ceylon and, with a few curtain rings and dark paint, went as an Indian woman, while Robert wore his Batik sarong. I'll send some snaps when they come along.

Robert wishes to be remembered.

My love to all,

Nora

Hahndorf, South Australia
27 November 1953

My Dear Nora,

Just a hurried note to ask if you are willing to part with the Ronda portrait study? Mother has always intimated a great fondness for this painting and it has just occurred to me that it would be lovely if I could give it to her for Christmas. I have enclosed a cheque for 60gs—but if you feel you should have more, don't hesitate to tell me and I shall supplement the difference.

My love and Mother's love goes with this,

Dad

73 Arabella Street
Longueville, Sydney
2 December 1953

My Dear Daddy,

Many thanks for your letter and the cheque anticipating my 'yes' to your proposal to buy the Ronda portrait study for Mother. I willingly accept the 60 guineas and am glad to think that the portrait will remain in the home. Also it seems appropriate that Mother should own that first painting of 'Ruth', as she was instrumental in my getting her as a model. When I look back upon the quiet days in the studio with Ronda patiently and serenely posing and with refreshments brought to us, the more I appreciate the 'atmosphere' (for want of a better word) that made painting like that possible, and I realise that I have never since found a like set of circumstances—a studio with freedom from financial and domestic worries. Painting requiring contemplation demands some stability in one's way of life. I find I can't really settle down to doing what I want to do until I find some permanent home. That said home still seems as remote as ever.

We are both looking forward to being with you for Christmas Eve.

Love to all,

Nora

Windsor Road
Baulkham Hills, Sydney
Tuesday 24 January 1954

Dearest Mother and Daddy,

At last a chance to put pen to paper—these last few weeks have been one mad rush to pack and move and get Robert away ... This continual moving makes letter writing almost an impossibility.

Now I'm staying with the Blacks at Baulkham Hills trying to sort out our possessions into a reasonable space.

I've had a brief look at the Archibald entries—a very disappointing show this year with nothing outstanding. Ivor had an easy win, a win which no one disputes—not even Haefliger![14] His two portraits are the best that I've seen of his—the heads admirably painted with vitality and force, but as usual conception in both lacks design and distinction.[15] The backgrounds are merely filled in spaces.

---

14   Ivor Hele won the 1953 Archibald Prize with his portrait, *Sir Henry Simpson Newland, CBE, DSO, MS, FRCS*. Newland was an Adelaide surgeon who pioneered plastic surgery and transformed the mutilated faces of soldiers during the First World War. See Neville Hicks and Elisabeth Leopold, 'Newland, Sir Henry Simpson (1873–1969)', *Australian Dictionary of Biography*, vol.11, Melbourne University Press, 1988: 8–9.

15   Hele's second entry was *John Horner Esq.*

Amongst the Wynne entries I couldn't find one landscape to hold my attention or interest me in any way. I've never seen a poorer lot.

Vi Johns is over, as you know. I'm lunching with her tomorrow and then we are going on to see the Dobell show at David Jones.[16]

My love to all,

Nora

Baulkham Hills, Sydney
24 February 1954

Dearest Mother and Daddy,

It was good to have home news and I enjoyed and I appreciated Mother's letter ... Here things are gaining momentum as the day for my departure grows near ... I take off on the evening of Saturday and arrive in Moresby 7 o'clock next morning. From there we'll no doubt move straight on per trawler to the Trobriands.

I've been rather busy packing and getting away pictures for all these special Royal visit exhibitions that are cropping up.[17] The Fellowship of Australian Artists, the Adelaide Society of Artists and Vi Johns are also making a Royal effort.

Sydney caught the Royal fever badly ... my one effort was to go over to Mosman ... so that I could see the Royal arrival and the fireworks display. Watching the *Gothic* come in from a grandstand seat on one of the most lovely sparkling mornings was really an impressive sight, with every imaginable craft that could float out on the harbour bedecked with flags and bunting.[18] Then later we went up to Macquarie Street where Wal Taylor had offered us a seat on his balcony, and from there we had an excellent view of the procession. The Royal couple looked very youthful and gracious and slightly bored, but the enthusiasm of the crowds was infectious.

You've no doubt heard the second instalment of Vi Johns' news and all about the Dobell show and the Archibald and Wynne exhibits. There were some good things in the Dobell show, but not for sale. The best of them to my mind belong to his London period and that just following his return here. In his later work, he appears to be desperately trying to be modern and the result is crude with none of the drawing and technique of his earlier work, nor the beauty of colour. His prices were fantastic. The slightest thumbnail sketch was 45 guineas.

---

16   *William Dobell: Exhibition of Paintings* was held at David Jones Gallery from 2 January to 17 February 1954.

17   Queen Elizabeth II and the Duke of Edinburgh visited Sydney from 3–18 February 1954, as part of a two-month royal tour (3 February to 1 April), the first in 20 years.

18   The *Gothic* was the royal yacht used to transport the royal party during the Australian tour.

I can quite understand that Daddy hasn't any letter writing time, far more important that he's painting. I'm looking forward to finding freedom for some work in the islands, and only hope a house can be found for us there.

My next letter will be from the islands.

My love to all and Birthday Greetings,

Nora

Port Moresby
13 March 1954

Dearest Mother and Daddy,

Well, here we are once again sweating in the tropics … I was pleased to see Robert waiting looking extremely fit and well.

We are staying with Dr Gunther, who is Director of Public Health here, until the old *Hekeha* is made seaworthy to take us on to the Trobriands, that will be in about two or three days from now.[19]

I have no liking for the tropics and wonder how I'm going to get rallied into working again. I have brought sufficient paper and sepia to keep me occupied for 3 or 4 months, only the energy to begin is needed.

I don't know yet how long we will be in the Trobriands, probably about 5 or 6 weeks, then back here and up the Sepik River. The address in the Trobriands will be the same, Losuia, but I'm afraid the mails will be few and far between as the flying boat service has been discontinued.

By the time this reaches you Royalty will have hit Adelaide—you'll be lucky to escape being drawn into some social function.

My love,

Nora

Hahndorf, South Australia
1 April 1954

My Dear Nora,

The last word from you came from Port Moresby March 13—when you were awaiting the next leap with some anxiety. I do hope it was not as bad as anticipated, and that the energy begins to flourish.

Much love from,

Daddy and Mother

---

19   The Art Gallery of New South Wales holds Nora Heysen's drawing *Study of a Boat, the* Hekeha.

Esa'ala, on the way to Samaria[20]
Easter Sunday 1954

Dearest Mother and Daddy,

This time the visit to the Trobriands was a great disappointment, in most part due to having no house of our own, and no freedom or retreat from the confused unhappy state of affairs existing amongst the 'whites' there. We were the forced guests of the Assistant District Officer there, a position that didn't work out to anyone's satisfaction. Robert perhaps fared better than I, as he was away visiting islands and doing field work. I found it practically impossible to settle to doing any work, as I had no retreat where I could work or get peace in which to collect my thoughts and impressions ... In the end, I shut myself in the small stifling hot bedroom we shared and painted a flower piece.

The administrative problems in Losuia seem to break every officer out there. Not one has survived his term. The one who was in command on our last visit finished up in the madhouse, and the present man we stayed with was well on the way, speeded on by constant recourse to liquor.

Later

Evening and we are anchored in a small bay on the tail end of Papua. A great full moon rising over the water, hot and still, and a native on board strumming a guitar with an emerald green parrot sitting on his shoulder, and around natives squatting. The moonlight shining on a dark face here and there silhouetting it against an ink blue sky, and the dim shapes of coconut palms and native huts on the shore. We are loaded with 20 passengers travelling to Samaria and Moresby, so the boat seethes with dark bodies. No privacy whatsoever.

One mail arrived in Losuia while we were there. It was a great joy to find one letter for me (Mother's) amongst it. Lucky it was, as it arrived the day before we left. Home news is especially welcome and every morsel was devoured hungrily. The paper cuttings too with all the Royal shows made interesting reading. I'd have liked to have seen the exhibition of works from private collections. I felt quite pleased to have got a mention in such august company. And again I'd dearly liked to have seen the big 'unfinished' Northern one of Daddy's dominating the John Martin's rally.

---

20   See Plate 2 for the drawing that Nora Heysen included at the top of this letter.

Easter Monday, Milne Bay

We are tied up in a small inlet of the bay in the heat of a tropical midday sun while Robert goes off to catch mosquitoes in some native huts. One bay is like another with coconut trees along the foreshore backed by high jungle-clad hills. The only sign of life in this settlement seems to be a goat and a rooster. It is difficult to realise that this bay was the scene of so much activity during the war. No signs to tell the tale except that the native houses in these parts are made of galvanised iron, a relic of the American occupation and very ugly they are. The native huts may be unhygienic and all that, but they do fit into the scheme so very well.

We'll be in Samaria by this evening where I hope to get this long overdue letter posted.

Love to all at home,
Nora

Minj[21]
Sunday 1 May 1954

Dearest Mother and Daddy,

And here we are dropped from the blue into another world so completely different in every way that it all seems rather unreal—like a plan for a model village set on a plateau surrounded by blue mountains. After the foetid heat and lavish sprawling exotic Trobriands, this cool circumspect orderly place is wonderfully restful. Due to bad weather, the plane from Moresby was delayed and we only just made Wau before the clouds closed in and had to stay there the night ... The aircraft used up here seem so ridiculously small and frail when flying over these enormous sinister mountains with ravines and snake-like rivers creeping like corkscrews round their gullies. Next stop was Goroka and from there we chartered a small dragon plane, that just held the three of us (the third being Robert's assistant Laurie Gray) and the pilot and all our gear (800 pounds we weigh as a party), and were dropped down out of the mountains into this cool oasis.

Roses grow here and violets, and at nights one sits round a fire and goes to sleep with four blankets.

These Highland chiefs are very splendid and impressive, some of their head dresses are magnificent, made of birds of paradise. They paint their faces in vivid colours, reds, yellows and blues, discs of pearl shell through their noses, and

---

21   See Plate 3 for the drawing that Nora Heysen included at the top of this letter. Minj is in the Western Highlands of Papua New Guinea.

possum skins round their necks and tufts of fur in their ears. They look like exotic birds themselves. I don't know how one could paint them. All modelling of features is lost in the pattern of colour, but as a colour pattern they are superb ... They look pretty fierce, but are really very friendly. The women folk get so overcome with emotion when they see you, they clasp you to their bosoms and hug you in a bear's grip—somewhat an alarming experience, as they are covered with ash and ochre and grease. One comes out of the ordeal bearing the imprint. Except that the women have breasts, they look and are dressed exactly like the men—the only other distinguishing feature is that the men wear a big bustle of foliage on their behinds. They consider it highly immodest to show the crease.

Love to you all,

Nora

Hahndorf, South Australia
16 May 1954

My Dear Nora,

The many movements in your letter does not augur much leisure for work but no doubt you will have managed the wherewithal for later development. Anyway we've enjoyed the letters tremendously, and if ever the writing 'my travels' grips you, they are all here to refer to.

Daddy's time in the studio is a good deal taken up with letter writing unfortunately, but he manages to turn out quite a number of sketches that he had laid aside years ago half finished. I wish he could have a trip away to see something to excite him.

Another batch of English watercolours are being shown at the National Gallery, very interesting though the majority are definitely in modernistic manner. Frances Hodgkins' work gave Daddy much pleasure. He admires her unerring colour sense—also the work of Barbara Hepworth, her *Trio: Surgeons and Theatre Sister* is most intriguing and made me think how you would enjoy it—she is a sculptress in the Henry Moore tradition Campbell said, this delicate study was a sheer joy—but you don't want to hear me talk art.

Goodnight and goodbye.

Daddy sends much love,

Mother

Windsor Road
Baulkham Hills, Sydney
24 May 1954

Dearest Mother and Daddy,

Back again but still living out of suitcases and trying to find some semblance of law and order in which to collect my thoughts for writing. You'll see by the address that we've come back to the Blacks' home in Baulkham Hills.

I hope you eventually received my last letter from Minj. There being no Post Office there, letters had to be handed over to the pockets of the pilot of any plane that happened to be going in the right direction. Once I see a letter going into a pocket, I think 'Well that's the last of it!'

After flying back to Moresby from Minj, we only had a couple of days there before taking off for Sydney ... Meanwhile how are things at home? It seems a long time since Mother's last letter found me at Samaria on our way back from the Trobriands ... Also received a large paper cutting about Daddy from the *Herald* I think and various criticisms of an exhibition of drawings from the National Gallery of Daddy's.[22] Very glad to hear of both.

This is just to report that I'm safely back and well except for large sprinkling of grey hairs, I don't seem to have suffered any ill effects from the tropics. Robert is also fit and wishes to be kindly remembered.

Love,
Nora

Baulkham Hills, Sydney
1 July 1954

Dearest Mother and Daddy,

With all the business and excitement of finding a home, my intention of following up my last letter and filling in the gaps has been put aside ... Just when I was beginning to despair of ever finding a suitable place, I chanced to see an advertisement in *The Herald* that looked promising, so Robert took the day off and we went to have a look and with the first look decided that that was it, and we'd come to the end of our search. *It* is in Hunters Hill, an old Colonial type house overlooking the water in a peaceful spot.

---

22   Hans Heysen's work was exhibited in *A Royal Visit Loan Exhibition of Paintings* at the National Gallery of South Australia.

Ours is 'The Chalet' … it's an interesting place and has plenty of possibilities.[23] The large veranda and courtyard effect at the back of the house is quite charming and very liveable. The kitchen and bathroom have been modernised just recently, and are all new and spick and span. The rest needs attention and paint, but is liveable in its present state of disrepair, and can be done by degrees.

There are so many things about the old place that remind me of home. The heavy cedar curtain rods with the big rings, the big rooms with the French windows, the stable doors opening onto the back courtyard, the old black iron, the jam making pan lined with white, the hand painted porcelain pieces on the doors, and many odd things that bring a smile of remembrance. It has a quaint staircase too leading up into a huge attic, and a lovely little lemon tree loaded with fruit outside the kitchen. There's a beautiful big room with the right light for a studio—about 10 rooms in all, and after the congested living I've had for 10 years or more, it's going to be heaven to be able to move round in space. You can imagine how thrilled I am.

The present owner is a collector of antique furniture, and at the moment the place resembles a museum. I'm trying to retain a few bits towards furnishing, but how the old will shake down with our few modern pieces I don't know.

I'll post too some bits and pieces about the Marcus Clark collection.[24] I was in at the sale on Tuesday to see the Turner and Guardi sold and the English collection … There wasn't half the interest shown as in the Australian collection. The general feeling seemed to be that the pictures offered couldn't be genuine. Also a few art criticisms to compare with those of Elizabeth Young's. Jimmy Cook has taken over from Jeff Smart on the *Telegraph*—a big improvement and a more balanced outlook.

Hoping all is well in all quarters.

Love to all,

Nora

---

23   'The Chalet', built in 1855, is a rare example of early prefabricated housing. It was imported from Germany by Swiss builder Leonardo Bordier and erected as one of four in a French settlement in Hunters Hill. The prototype was exhibited in 1854 at the Paris Industrial Exhibition in Hamburg, Germany, where Bordier purchased it. Prefabricated housing was built in Australia in the 1850s to solve the housing shortage experienced during the gold rush era. See 'The Chalet', www.about.nsw.gov.au/collections/doc/the-chalet, accessed 20 June 2010.

24   Sir Reginald Marcus Clark (1883–1953) was a retailer, Director and later Vice-President of the Royal Prince Alfred Hospital and Trustee of the National Art Gallery of New South Wales. See Peter Spearritt, 'Clark, Sir Reginald Marcus (1883–1953)', *Australian Dictionary of Biography*, vol.8, Melbourne University Press, 1981: 11–12. The two-day sale was handled by James Lawson, fine art auctioneers, Castlereagh Street, Sydney.

Hahndorf, South Australia
3 July 1954

My Dear Nora,

This is just a hasty note. What a thrill it was to get your airmail yesterday telling us of your great 'find'. A just recompense for all your troubles over the last 12 months in trying to find a home for yourselves. Mother got a tremendous 'kick' out of it and could hardly control her excitement.

It was good of you to send the (priced) catalogue—and most interesting to me. I wonder what became of the bigger still life of mine? Perhaps it went to his brother.[25] What an extensive collection he must have built up—I wish we had been there to buy the Turner or supposed Turner, and certainly Tom Roberts' *Coogee*.

The work in the studio is going slowly, all *too* slowly, for there is a steady demand for watercolours, big and small. I had hoped to make a start on another large Northern subject for this year's Society of Artists, but it is not to be—better luck next year. So let it be. It is almost 3 years since I have been out sketching now—it is time that I refreshed my mind with new material. Perhaps next year a chance to get away will offer itself.

I am sure there are some things you would like to retain in your new home to come, something you feel should remain, so I am enclosing a cheque for £100—from Mother and myself to help you get it.

Mother sends her love and will write very soon.

Our good wishes go with this for your dear self and Robert,
Dad

Windsor Road
Baulkham Hills, Sydney
Wednesday 8 July 1954

Dearest Mother and Daddy,

It was wonderful to get Daddy's letter and when I found the cheque I gave three heartfelt cheers ... Never had a cheque been so timely ... Amongst the things I wanted to retain was an old oak dresser, a cedar wardrobe, an old leather chair for Robert's study, a very charming little walnut sewing table for still life studies, a couple of Windsor chairs, a cedar day lounge, a few copper saucepans and the jam saucepan, and the biggest item, which I thought too good an opportunity to miss,

---

25 The bigger Hans Heysen in the Marcus Clark collection was *Autumn Flowers and Fruit* (1927), which Nora Heysen noted in the catalogue as 'withdrawn' from sale.

a washing machine almost new for £50. Now I can have all the things and still £20 over for the odd items that crop up with a move.

We have been over to Hunters Hill to see our home a couple of times since last I wrote, and each time it seems even nicer. Last visit we met a few of our neighbours. Dr Reid, from next door, who said he's met me on a visit to you some 23 years ago when he lived at Mt Lofty, and the Amerys who have, like us, just bought an old home and are planning what they are going to make of it. Mr Amery was Director of David Jones Art Gallery. Hal Missingham lives a few minutes' walk away, and I hear that Norman Lindsay has just bought an old home and is coming down from Springwood to live at Hunters Hill, so there will be some folk around with my interests.[26]

We'll be moving in sometime next week.

I posted off ... a *Women's Weekly* in which I appear at the Marcus Clarke sale.

Many thanks for the cuttings. Also I'm interested that Stewart Cockburn is a freelance journalist now and is making a name for himself.[27]

This must go with warmest thanks for your wonderful contribution towards our home. Robert joins me in thanks and love to all,

Nora

Hahndorf, South Australia
26 July 1954

My Dear Nora,

We were wondering what will happen to your painting should you get the gardening disease badly.

Goodbye now my dear and lots of luck with your new home,

Mother

'The Chalet'
Hunters Hill, Sydney
Friday 1954

Dearest Mother and Daddy,

Mother's letter was indeed welcome today ... I'm glad the little posy carried its message. Yes, I have since found palms, violets and wallflowers and there are lilies of the valley and ferns of all varieties. When the Spring comes many things

---

26   Hal Missingham (1906–1994) followed Will Ashton (1881–1963) as Director of the National Art Gallery of New South Wales from 1945 to 1971.

27   See John Scales, 'Farewell to a Man who Sought Truth', *The Advertiser*, 11 July 2009: 32.

will come to light, as the garden is packed tight with all sorts of shrubs and bulbs—
forget-me-nots everywhere. Not a rose though, the Souvenir de Mal Maison must
be first in. This house is just the right setting for its simplicity, graciousness and its
quiet tones of white and greys. Will Daddy try and get a cutting started for me?

Yes I can too see the danger of becoming garden conscious—what with the
big house and its garden interest, where's my painting time going to be? At the
moment there's just so much to do both inside and out, I could wish the days twice
as long to be able to cope with it.

Since we have hung some pictures, the home looks a little less bare.
Daddy's pastel and watercolour have found their right positions at last in pride of
place and look fine. The pastel is everyone's favourite picture. The place continues
to charm me. It is full of delightful interiors. I'm going to find many new settings for
my still lifes. I cannot yet fully grasp that it is my home—I'm afraid it will vanish
like a dream and I keep wandering round and round it to substantiate reality.

I'm looking forward to the day when you'll come over to see it.

Hoping all's well in all quarters,

Nora

'The Chalet'
Hunters Hill, Sydney
25 August 1954

Dearest Mother and Daddy,

Many thanks for the reporting on advancement of furniture ... As you
rightly guess, my studio more than any other room, is greatly in need of the odd
table; and I'm quite determined when I do get the frames over that I will paint
pictures that will fit them.

I've been planting hollyhocks, foxgloves and mignonette and phlox.

The Society of Artists Show opened last week with a sherry flourish and
a gathering of some nine hundred people crowded into the Education Department
rooms.[28] The sales have been excellent with eight to nine Gallery purchases to
start the ball rolling. It's a good show this year. A more balanced selection and
hanging committee gave far better results than in the previous years, also the
older artists put forward a better effort. No doubt the intrusion of the new modern
experimentalists has put them on their mettle.

---

28   Nora Heysen had one painting in the show, *The Blue Vase*.

Adrian was inquiring after you and wishing you had sent over this year. Also Lloyd Rees said he was looking forward to seeing you very soon. He's driving over to South Australia with his son, and this time he promises himself a visit to you.

To further add to demands on my time, an Art Committee has been set up in Hunters Hill to arrange a loan show from the homes round here. I've been put on the selection and hanging side with Missingham and Amery and it's our job to go round to all the homes and select or reject pictures offered for loan, which is going to take as much tact and time ... Being on the Selection Committee will give me an entrée into these old homes, and it should be very interesting.

Much love to all,
Nora

Hahndorf, South Australia
3 September 1954

My Dear Nora,
The Lloyd Rees show was a great success. Daddy had to see the pictures with some of the Trustees and had selected one for the Gallery. Mr Rees seemed quite satisfied with results so far. £500 on the opening day is not bad for Adelaide. It has acted as a tonic for Daddy—they talked shop to their hearts content.

Mother

'The Chalet'
Hunters Hill, Sydney
26 October 1954

Dearest Mother and Daddy,
Now that I've started painting again it seems more than ever difficult to find letter writing time ... When I'd nearly finished the large flower piece, I got inveigled into starting another—the second led to a third. So I became properly ensnared in paint. I'm beginning to realise why Daddy was always pottering around late at night doing the odd jobs.

My potato patch is flourishing and blooming already—after being dependent on florists and the odd bunch from people's gardens, it is wonderful being able to pick a bunch from my own garden when and how I want it.

The Selection Committee has begun on its job of going round to the old homes of Hunters Hill and selecting pictures for the loan exhibition. Missingham,

John Amery, a cartoonist by the name of Lahm and myself make the foursome.[29] Up to date we've 'done' three homes, and it's been interesting seeing both the homes and the collections of pictures. The big Catholic school for boys, St Josephs, produced unexpected treasures, real old masters amongst a collection of two or three hundred pictures gathered from all over the world, and varying from curios of still life done in feathers, modern watercolours, historic Australian pieces to a Botticelli and Caravaggio. The next home proudly offered a Heysen. One of the Yankalilla Rapid Bay hills near the sea, a subject which was unanimously voted in—also a Lambert nude, a small Tom Roberts and a lovely little Fred McCubbin, a Blamire Young and a very Norman Lindsay bunch of nudes. The last home came good with a Dutch figure group and a little gem of a painting done by the grandmother, a double portrait of her parents. If the quality of work keeps up to this standard, it should be a surprisingly good and interesting show.

I was in at the National Gallery the other day delivering a portrait of Adrian Feint for the exhibition they are having of *Artists by Artists* in November— Missingham showed me Daddy's *Self Portrait*. You'd be amused too to see it next to mine, they are going to be hung together. The likeness, especially as the heads are painted in the same position, is absurd. Missingham is delighted.[30]

Much love to all,

Nora

'The Chalet'
Hunters Hill, Sydney
Sunday November 1954

Dearest Mother and Daddy,

I enjoyed Mother's letter ... David's suggestion that he could drive you over sometime during the Christmas holidays sounds wonderful, and I hope it will come off.

Robert left last Friday for the Philippines ... The opening day for the *Artists by Artists* show was unfortunately the wettest day I've known in Sydney— very few people turned up which was a great disappointment to Missingham and all those who'd worked so hard to get the show together. It's an interesting exhibition. The commissioned portrait is absent, there's a friendly contact between

---

29   Hardtmuth 'Hottie' Lahm (1912–1981) was a cartoonist for *Man* magazine, *Smith's Weekly* and *Sunday Sun*. Nora Heysen's portrait *Hardtmuth 'Hottie' Lahm* (1973) was included in the 2001 retrospective of her work at the National Library of Australia. See Joan Kerr, 'Hardtmuth Lahm', *Dictionary of Australian Artists Online*, accessed 14 July 2010.

30   Hans Heysen painted his *Self Portrait* in 1902 as a student in Paris. Nora Heysen's *Self Portrait* (1932) is held by the Art Gallery of New South Wales. See *Artists by Artists: Portraits of Australian Artists*, Sydney, National Art Gallery of New South Wales, 1954.

sitter and subject, and a feeling of artistic integrity in the portraits so lacking in the Archibald exhibits. You'll see me there looking very portly. Pity the photographer didn't have the imagination to get Daddy in as well, his portrait was hanging next to mine and looked well, I suggested it, but he had his own ideas.[31]

We've done some 25 odd homes of Hunters Hill on our quest for pictures, and it's been most interesting. Riverside is on our list for next Saturday, so I may meet Father Scott whom you mention was up to visit you.[32]

A Mr Komon rang me the other day saying he was just off to Adelaide and was hoping to go up to see you, and wanting to know if I had a message to take. He really wanted an introduction. I only met him once at an opening ... he seemed a man very interested in art and knowledgeable on the subject.[33]

My love to you and a hope that all's well,

Nora

'The Chalet'
Hunters Hill, Sydney
18 December 1954

Dearest Mother and Daddy,

I've been trying to finish a couple of paintings to get them into the Christmas market.

You ask about the Pewsey Vale watercolour that came up at the Marcus Clark sale. I remember it well and was surprised at the time that the bids didn't go higher. I can't find my catalogue at the moment, but I seem to remember that it went to 60 guineas and was withdrawn—more than that I can't remember. I've been asking and no one can add any information. It all seems very odd that it should be offered to the SA Gallery at £40. I hope it finds its way into the Gallery.[34]

Love to all from us both,

Nora

31   'Artists' Self Portraits', *The Sydney Morning Herald*, 5 November 1954. The photograph of Nora Heysen standing in front of her self portrait appeared in *The Sun Herald* on 7 November 1954.

32   Father Scott was well known to Adelaide artists, a friend of dancer Robert Helpmann and painted by Adelaide artist Jo Caddy.

33   Rudy Komon (1908–1982) ran an antique shop that sold paintings. The shop was originally located in Waverley, Sydney. Between 1959 and 1984, the Rudy Komon Gallery was located at 124 Jersey Road, Woollahra, Sydney.

34   Hans Heysen's watercolour, *Pewsey Vale*, was acquired by the Art Gallery of South Australia in November 1954.

'The Chalet'
Hunters Hill, Sydney
14 January 1955

Dearest Mother and Daddy,

It was lovely to have both your letters on *the* day, and to honour the occasion the postman blew two long blasts on his whistle. I scrambled out of bed and came back with the bounty. Warmest thanks for the cheques. As money has to go only to necessities these days, it's a real pleasure to have the extra for the little extras that make so much difference. I've had my eye on a new publication of Renoir's paintings and I'm going to treat myself to that.

What an anxious day that terrible Sunday must have been for you. I was appalled to read the cuttings you sent and to see the house at Marble Hill.[35] My heart goes out to the Grattons. A tragedy at their age to lose all their possessions and a lifetime's collection of books and souvenirs of the past. I've often wondered if Mr Gratton would like to have the preliminary oil sketch I did of him.

Jeff Smart was here yesterday, and he said Ursula was over, but I haven't seen her. I hadn't seen Jeff for over 6 months. He's been too busy making money. He says he's not going to paint until he has £7,000 and then he's off to Italy to do it. At the moment he's playing with the stock exchange and buying and selling houses.[36]

My love to all and my thanks for the Birthday,

Nora

'The Chalet'
Hunters Hill, Sydney
15 February 1955

Dearest Mother and Daddy,

You will have received 'Mr Gratton' by now ... I'm sorry too it isn't more like him. I hope he understands that it is just a preliminary note for composition and colour.

I've received my first Hunters Hill commission—to design and paint a large decoration of flowers, five times life size, to fill the space of a doorway. I must go and see the position to know if it is possible.

---

35   The Black Sunday bushfire burnt the Adelaide Hills district of Marble Hill and destroyed many houses, including the Governor of South Australia's summer residence.

36   Jeffrey Smart recounted: 'as soon as I had saved some money, I put it down on a deposit on a house in Paddington. My father said that ten workers cottages were enough to keep you, but I was modestly aiming for only four ... For a painter, even a small income spells independence and makes a great difference. Perhaps it is odd that I didn't look to painting to make a living'. See Jeffrey Smart, *Not Quite Straight: A Memoir*, Melbourne, William Heinemann Australia, 1996: 325–326.

The loan show comes off here next week and I can foresee myself being very busy. There are only four of us to arrange and hang the show in a day and a half, and then we have to take it in turns to mind the show and sell catalogues during the week it's open.

From my collection, Daddy's pastel and Dobell's washing steps have been selected.

Love to all at home and I hope the rains have come to ease fire anxiety,
Nora

Hahndorf, South Australia
21 February 1955

My Dear Nora,

The Gratton has arrived and Daddy is charmed with the colour scheme and is framing it with some concern, for it needs all of it kept within the mount, and he has found an oldish frame to suit. Stewart ... is taking it to Mr Gratton. He says the old man will be overcome with deep appreciation and you will hear more about it later.

We are sad to think of your problems—the house, the garden and the painting are more than enough ... You badly need one of those part-time housekeepers for the chores.

Much love,
Mother

Hahndorf, South Australia
2 March 1955

Dearest Nora,

This afternoon there was a party of another kind—Vi Johns brought up Anton Riebe (or vice versa) *and* Joshua Smith who is really too good to be true—it's hats off to Dobell for a most amazing portrait which everyone takes to be a caricature! He said and did things which kept one on the brink of hysterical laughter—have you ever met him? He even played the piano, and well too, and vowed he had the time of his life! Daddy was suffering from suppressed laughter, and ever since has been exploding at intervals—what an amazing person.

Vi Johns told us quite a bit about your house—she was enchanted with the rightness of the setting for you, but doesn't know how you are going to make time for painting! How did the Hunters Hill show go? *The Bulletin* only mentioned it happening.

Much love from us both,
Mother

'The Chalet'
Hunters Hill, Sydney
Friday 1955

Dearest Mother and Daddy,

I managed to get two small flower pieces painted somehow and fortunately Wal Taylor sold both without any trouble—he bought one for himself. What I do resent is paying out the 25% commission, but on the other hand I also resent giving up a lot of time to entertaining likely buyers, and putting up with their inane remarks about art and it's one thing or the other.[37]

Your mentioning of the lovely incomparable Souvenirs stirs my painting senses and I long to have a bush in. I can just see them in this setting. I plan to have the one Daddy has struck for me by the entrance door. 'Souvenir de Mal Maison', not so appropriate by name I suppose, but I chose it as my emblem and would like one planted on my grave when I die.

Much love,
Nora

'The Chalet'
Hunters Hill, Sydney
12 July 1955

Dearest Mother and Daddy,

It is with deep pleasure that I see the Souvenir in her place by the entrance to our home. She carried perfectly thanks to the beautiful packing—the roots still quite damp and no damage anywhere. And what a magnificent bush.

You will have probably guessed that my silence meant that I'd at last got going on The Women's Weekly prize … After a lot of searching around to find a mother who was both paintable and free to sit, I settled on a neighbour. She unfortunately is very pregnant and likely to be run into hospital at any minute, so I've been frantically working against time. The child is just two, so you can imagine I haven't chosen altogether an easy subject.[38] In fact the many problems have left me feeling half demented. As well as this, as a second string to my bow, I've begun

---

37   Commission was a hot topic in the Heysen household. Hans Heysen negotiated a low 15 per cent commission with Macquarie Galleries. See Jean Campbell, *Early Sydney Moderns: John Young and Macquarie Galleries*, Roseville, New South Wales, Craftsman House, 1988: 79–80.

38   *Mrs David Jamieson and her Daughter* was exhibited in the Sydney showing of the 1955 *The Australian Women's Weekly* Portrait Prize. The conditions for entry for this prize stated that the portrait should be of 'a woman, or a woman with baby or child up to 10 years, or a child under 14 years'.

on another painting of a red-headed four year old who is a perfect Renoir type.[39] I'm doing her in the garden but so far she's proved a perfect little devil, and to get anything out of her is almost impossible.

Much love,

Nora

Hahndorf, South Australia
26 September 1955

My Dear Nora,

This is just a hasty note—but first let me thank you again for the very happy week we spent with you and Robert. It was a wonderful *break* for Mother and me, but I am afraid it meant so much extra work for you. It was good to see your home and to feel the charm of your surroundings. I do really think you were extremely fortunate in getting it, and well worth all the trouble and inconvenience it caused in the process.

We had an uneventful trip home but I found the landscape around Bacchus Marsh most paintable and interesting. An afternoon and night was spent at Robe, as delightful as ever, very little changed in 70 years.

With love from,

Your Dad

Hahndorf, South Australia
Sunday 20 November 1955

Dearest Nora,

This has been a hectic week—the accompanying cuttings will tell you of Adrian Feint's wonderful success—the Haywards were the good Samaritans who made it possible. They also asked Daddy and me to have dinner with them as we wouldn't go the cocktail opening, and Daddy revelled in all the new acquisitions and much art talk. Adrian said he would see you soon and no doubt tell you of his good fortune, he seemed happy and looked well.[40] Adelaide will probably appeal to other Sydney artists as a best buyer, but they will have to stay at Carrick Hill!

Much love,

Mother

---

39   *Sibella Anne Mannix* was also exhibited in the same Sydney exhibition. The judges were the Directors (all men) of all the state art galleries. Jack Carrington Smith won the £1500 prize with *Arrangement in Green*. See 'Tasmanian Wins Richest Portrait Prize', *The Daily Telegraph*, 19 August 1958.

40   Adrian Feint's Adelaide exhibition was opened by Ursula Haywood at John Martin's Art Gallery, Adelaide, on 17 November 1955. He sold all but one painting before the show opened, including two works to the National Gallery of South Australia, *Embarkation* and *The Apple Tree*. See 'Artist has Quick Sale', *The Advertiser*, 18 November 1955.

'The Chalet'
Hunters Hill, Sydney
12 January 1956

Dearest Mother and Daddy,

First to arrive was Daddy's birthday cheque followed by Mother's letter and then your telegram … Part of my birthday cheque has gone into a pair of tubs to go either side of the front steps. They arrive this afternoon, a pink camellia in one and a white in the other, so my birthday present will be a permanent growing one to enjoy and remember.

The Persian carpet has made a wonderful difference to the entrance way, in fact gives the whole place a lift. It has settled in most happily. A couple of pictures have helped take the quality up to the walls.

The neighbour for whom I painted the child commission has just called down to say her husband doesn't like it, and will I do something to alter it so that he'll be pleased! As I haven't been paid I suppose I'll have to do something or take it back, and I know which I'd prefer.

All those weeks of exasperating work! I'd best stop before I vent my spleen on the givers of portrait commissions.

My love and thanks for a Happy Birthday.

Robert sends his love with mine,

Nora

'The Chalet'
Hunters Hill, Sydney
Tuesday 22 May 1956

Dearest Mother and Daddy,

You can blame the Souvenirs for the delay in writing—once again their subtle beauty has ensnared me to the neglect of all else. Three attempts to capture them and I still wonder if I'm any nearer to getting that certain illusive something I'm after … If only I could just admire those roses and not torture myself with trying to paint them.

The best of news items is that the Sydney Gallery bought the *Native* drawing I had in the Society of Artists show at David Jones.[41] A pleasant surprise indeed … It wasn't a good show, bits and pieces of no consequence and, except for the three Gallery purchases (Carl Plate and Desiderius Orban), not another thing was sold. Very disappointing.

---

41   This is *Moulasi, New Guinea* (1954) held by the Art Gallery of New South Wales.

However despite the slump in picture sales here, the Glad Gallery seems to be flourishing and Mrs Glad is always asking for more pictures.[42] I've retrieved a few Wal Taylor has had for years and given her those, and she's already found buyers.

Robert has gone up to Brisbane to give a paper at a Congress … My date for the Adelaide show is fixed for the first two weeks of October.

I thoroughly enjoyed Mother's letter … which reminds me of Treania Smith's amazement to find that Daddy wasn't intolerant of the Moderns and actually enjoyed looking at the Gleesons. She evidently had a long chat with Daddy when she was over with a show in August.

Must away to rob the neighbour's garden for my next flower piece.

Love to you all at home,

Nora

> *'The Chalet'*
> *Hunters Hill, Sydney*
> *20 September 1956*

Dearest Mother and Daddy,

A short letter to say that I've booked on 'The Cannon Ball' service TAA Tuesday 2nd October.

The last picture finished today[43] … I've been working overtime to finish a basket of wildflowers with framing at night, and at this point I vow I'll never be persuaded to have another show. I haven't lowered my prices and I'm dubious about results, for except for the pink roses and a few mixed bunches, the work isn't what people expect from me.

I just had another request for Daddy's pictures from Wieneke—he tells a sad tale of his clients waiting patiently and never giving up hope.

Love to you from us both,

Nora

---

42   The Glad Gallery in 10 Mount Street, Hunters Hill, was run by Jane Glad, Norman Lindsay's daughter.

43   This was for Nora Heysen's 1956 *Exhibition of Oil Paintings and Sepia Drawings by Nora Heysen* at John Martin's Art Gallery, Adelaide. It opened on 4 October and ran for two weeks. Twenty-six works were exhibited and 20 purchased. The National Gallery of South Australia purchased *Spring Flowers*. See 'Gallery Buys Women Artists' Works', *The Advertiser*, 5 October 1956.

Nora Heysen (1911–2003)
A Chieftain's Daughter 1953

oil on board; 78.0 x 57.0 cm
Private collection
Photograph by Sue Blackburn

right
Nora Heysen (1911–2003)
King Mitakata, New Guinea 1953

sanguine, pastel laid on paper;
63.5 x 48.5 cm
Gift of the artist 2003
Art Gallery of New South Wales
© Lou Klepac

far right
Unknown photographer
*Nora Heysen and Robert Black at
the Artists' Ball* 1953

photograph
Manuscripts Collection, MS 10041
National Library of Australia

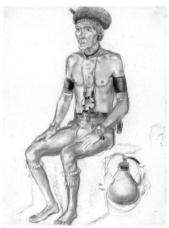

plate 1

plate 2

plate 3

above
Hans Heysen (1877–1968)
The Promenade 1953

oil on canvas; 106.7 x 76.2 cm
Purchased 1959
National Gallery of Australia
© Hans Heysen, licensed by Viscopy

right
Nora Heysen (1911–2003)
Self Portrait 1932

oil on canvas;
76.2 x 61.2 cm
Gift of Howard Hinton 1932
Art Gallery of New South Wales
© Lou Klepac

far right
Hans Heysen (1877–1968)
Self Portrait 1902

oil on canvas; 53.0 x 45.0 cm
The Cedars, Hahndorf
Photograph by Michael Kluvanek

right
Unknown photographer
The Chalet, Hunters Hill, Sydney

photograph
Manuscripts Collection, MS 10041
National Library of Australia

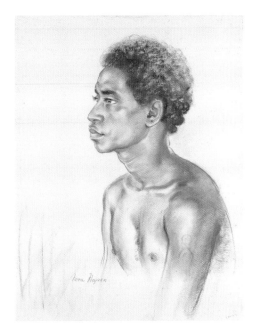

Nora Heysen (1911–2003)
Moulasi, New Guinea 1954

pastel on paper; 57.4 x 44.7 cm
Purchased 1956
Art Gallery of New South Wales

Ivor Hele (1912–1993)
Sir Hans Heysen, OBE 1959

oil on masonite; 106.6 x 81.3 cm
Gift of Mr and Mrs E.W. Hayward and
Ivor Hele 1959
Art Gallery of South Australia

below
Nora Heysen (1911–2003)
Self Portrait 1954

oil on canvas; 89.0 x 66.5 cm
South Australian Government Grant 1994
Art Gallery of South Australia

'The Chalet'
Hunters Hill, Sydney
Friday 1956

Dearest Mother and Daddy,

Just to say thank you for those two precious weeks. It seems I need to
return to the place and atmosphere of my youth for that renewal of the spirit.
Nothing else will work the cure, it's my 'magic adrenalin'. After going thoroughly
tired physically and mentally, I've come back with a fresh zest ready to begin again.

My love and thanks for a piece of home that remains with me,

Nora

'The Chalet'
Hunters Hill, Sydney
Christmas 25 December 1956

Dearest Mother and Daddy,

I've been trying to finish the portrait of David Sheumack which I'd
promised framed and complete for their Christmas.[44]

I went to the lunch party and was wryly amused—a real publicity stunt
in the American fashion. I don't know how I came to be asked amongst the 60 odd
celebrities. Frank Clune organised it—Ampol, who were presenting Namatjira with
a truck, paid the bill and everyone asked turned up to get a free lunch at Princes.[45]
Poor old Namatjira looked bewildered and unhappy sitting between Dame Mary
Gilmore and Doc Evatt with a battery of cameras fixed on him and Frank Clune
telling him what to do and when.[46] Dargie is doing Namatjira, no doubt for the
Archibald. He was given the sittings before old Albert took off back to the country
in his new truck.

The cuttings from Daddy's pink geranium are doing nicely, and one has
lovely large flowers.

The wireless is playing *Still Night Holy Night* and my thoughts are homing.
Love from us both,

Nora

44   David was 19 months old. The oil painting *David* (1956) was exhibited at S.H. Ervin Gallery in *D.R. Sheumack*
      Collection of Australian Painting from 17 May to 12 June 1983, along with Hans Heysen's *Winter Sunshine*
      (1953), *Sunlit Quarry* (1954), *In the Maralana Gorge* (1956), *Cottage Bunch* (1957) and *Rapid Bay* (1957).

45   See Unknown photographer, *Albert and his New Truck*, National Library of Australia, Pictures Collection,
      nla.pic-an24130689.

46   See Unknown photographer, *Mrs Frank Clune, Dr H.V. Evatt, Albert Namatjira, Dame Mary Gilmore and V.M.*
      Leonard at a Table having a Meal, National Library of Australia, Pictures Collection, nla.pic-an24039750.

Hahndorf, South Australia
7 January 1957

My Dear Nora,

My hearty congratulations for the birthday and with it the best of good wishes we drink to you on the day. Secondly my thank you for the Christmas book, and on skimming it over, it looks interesting and I have always been somewhat curious about this so called Arnhem Land and the people who lived there.[47]

Mother sends her love and much more,

Cheerio from your Dad

'The Chalet'
Hunters Hill, Sydney
15 January 1957

Dearest Mother and Daddy,

It was indeed good to have your birthday letter with wishes and handsome cheque.

My birthday was a warm Summer's day but, with Robert leaving on Saturday, there was little heart for celebration and I spent it ironing and packing. Still it was kind of the powers that be to make the day of departure the 12th and not the 10th. Robert should have arrived at Kuala Lumpur by now. He has a long strenuous journey ahead. He gets back to Sydney on the 2nd of May and he hates flying. So you can imagine he set out with very mixed feelings, and I was equally upset and reluctant to see him go.

I must begin to think of the job I've undertaken to do, the painting of Professor Lambie ... As the finished picture is to hang in the Great Hall of the University, I'll have to put my best foot forward.

Love to you both and Jill,

Nora

---

47   By 1957, the National Gallery of South Australia held the largest number of barks from the Australian–American Scientific Expedition to Arnhem Land, gifts from C.P. Mountford, and works by Namatjira, with Robert Campbell supporting further acquisitions. A selection of Aboriginal barks, watercolours and carved objects were also on permanent display in the gallery, including loans from C.P. Mountford and Dr Charles Duguid. See Elizabeth Young, 'A Heritage of the Aborigine [sic]', *The Sunday Advertiser*, 3 December 1955: 67; 'Special Shows at the Gallery', *The Advertiser*, 22 November 1955; National Gallery of South Australia Board Minutes, 16 May 1955, item 9. Hans Heysen also owned a bark painting, *Wambidbyer Anteater*, thought to have been given by his friend Baldwin Spencer in exchange for a painting.

'The Chalet'
Hunters Hill, Sydney
17 January 1957

Dearest Mother and Daddy,

I went to the preview of the Archibald and was depressed by the mediocre standard ... The Dargie of Namatjira was most uninspired and weak in design and construction. He'd got nothing of the rugged bigness of the man and his quiet dignity just a slick of empty painting, but there wasn't much else.

Adrian Feint was there, evidently back from Adelaide. He was asking after you—regretted not being able to get up to see you, but Ursula being so ill all the time he was over upset his plans.

I've been going ahead with painting the front of the house, but getting rid of the old cracked stuff is a tiresome business and I see precious little for my labours.

Robert is now in Calcutta.

I'm hoping that Mother is on the improve and the eyes mending quietly.

Love to you,

Nora

Hahndorf, South Australia
18 January 1957

My Dear Nora,

Hearty congratulations on the complete success of young David Sheumack's portrait; it's a beauty and it captivated both Mother and I completely. You have not only captured a splendid likeness but also the age and an *alive* little body—a very complete design and an interesting painting. We are both enthusiastic over its subtlety and the beautiful ways the eyes are set in the head, so full of childish wonder. Again my congratulations.

Mother sends her love and thoroughly enjoyed your last letter—so glad that Robert is finding so much success,

With love from Dad

'The Chalet'
Hunters Hill, Sydney
Wednesday 13 February 1957

Dearest Mother and Daddy,

It was indeed good to have Mother's letter this morning and to see the handwriting back to normal. And very nice too to hear 'my' *David* praised ... The parents' criticism is the only one I've had and theirs I judged a *little* biased, so I'm happy to have your approval, as it really means something.

Sydney is all agog with the design for the new Opera House to be built on Bennelong Point. I suppose the design figured in your papers. I went to the Gallery to see all the entries displayed, 5 galleries full of them, and I agreed that the one chosen was outstanding and had an imaginative conception the others lacked.[48] Most of them were Gropius inspired, more like factories or air terminals and tanks than a home for theatre and music.

I saw Ted Ford the other day, and he was asking after you and is most concerned to hear of Mother's collapse.

Tomorrow is sending-in day for the Society of Artists drawing exhibition.

My love and thanks for writing. I realise what an effort it must be but am so glad of news,

Nora

'The Chalet'
Hunters Hill, Sydney
Sunday 17 March 1957

Dearest Mother and Daddy,

Visiting time at the hospital and I'm wondering what the latest report is and how Mother is feeling. I only hope the operation followed up with the drugs have eased headaches and nervous tension. It was good to be able to talk to Daddy last Monday and gave me some comfort. It is reassuring to feel that the doctors are on the right track and that the operation was successful. I was talking to Ted Ford about Cerebral Fibrositis and he admitted that it was such a rare disease that he didn't know much about it.[49]

---

48   Danish architect Jørn Utzon (1918–2008) won the design competition. Eugene Goossens, the Director of the Sydney Conservatorium, successfully lobbied for an opera house at Bennelong Point. The competition for designs for the opera house was launched in September 1955. There were 233 submissions. The winning one, which received a prize of £5000, was announced in 1957.

49   Colin Thiele describes the condition as 'periarteritis nodosa'. See Colin Thiele, *Heysen of Hahndorf*, Adelaide, Hyde Park Press, 2001: 273.

A large part of my time has been gobbled up by this local exhibition. We finished the hanging late last night after an all-day effort. This year's show is the best up to date and looks well despite the intrusion of the abstractionists. After a furious outcry from the Council at the number of the rejects and the inclusion of the outrageous moderns, the selection committee consented to reconsider the rejects and accepted another five paintings.

I start on Professor Lambie tomorrow and am nervous at the prospect of launching a big portrait ... He's a little man, very Scotch and reserved and hard to know. A man with few friends, and no one regrets his retirement from the post of Professor of Medicine.

So I quail in the face of the problems ahead.

With a prayer that all is progressing well at home.

My love and hopes for a steady recovery back to health and home,

Nora

'The Chalet'
Hunters Hill, Sydney
Sunday 24 March 1957

Dearest Mother and Daddy,

It was reassuring to have Mother's letter to know that you were feeling well enough to write, but I was alarmed at the terrific drop in weight 7st 8lbs and the night sweats still continuing. Sounds a drastic sort of treatment. The worst part about having one of the rare diseases is the fact that as the doctors have so little experience with it, you become something of an experiment.

Professor Lambie is proving a very cooperative sitter and came every morning last week for a couple of hours. He has to be done in his robes, blood red and as he's only a small bald-headed man, the colour and bulk is inclined to swamp him.

Jane Glad came in with a big Norman Lindsay covered nude for me to touch up in places where it doesn't meet the frame.

With a hope that every day brings a little weight and strength back.

With all my love,

Nora

'The Chalet'
Hunters Hill, Sydney
8 April 1957

Dearest Mother and Daddy,

I'm at last free from the tension of the Lambie portrait—another couple of sittings will complete it … The more I saw of the little man the more I liked and respected him, and wanted the portrait to be good. Also I think that he's enjoyed himself and is actually sorry the end is in view … After the first week he stopped quoting French at me, and went off onto Plato, Shakespeare and Socrates, and eventually after loading him down with art books, he discusses art and critics. I've discovered that he writes poetry, plays the piano and loves coffee. I lent him the Heysen book of drawings and he was most enthusiastic and asked to be allowed to take it home for a few days.

I don't know yet when I have to begin on my next subject, the Headmaster of Sydney Grammar, but I was amused when I heard, after quoting my price, that he wanted to be done full length with his hands behind his back. This was the answer to my explanation as to why I charged so much for a head and shoulders, as against a three quarter length portrait. I said the painting of the hands entailed so much more work, and hence the extra price, and as he wished to be done large, and as the trustees didn't feel as if they could raise the extra £50, that seemed the solution! One certainly gets a few laughs out of this portrait commission business.

It was good to talk to Daddy the other evening and to know that Mother was home again.

All my love and I hope things progress well with every day helping a bit,

Nora

'The Chalet'
Hunters Hill, Sydney
30 April 1957

Dearest Mother and Daddy,

It was so good to get Mother's letter and to see the firmness coming back into the writing and feel health returning ... I was very interested to hear about what had actually taken place with the operations, and now will be able to satisfy Ted Ford's interest in the disease.

All my love to you three at home,

Nora

PS Interested to hear of the return of *Sowing New Seed* and would like to see it again.[50]

'The Chalet'
Hunters Hill, Sydney
Wednesday 22 May 1957

Dearest Mother and Daddy,

With Robert safely home and things back to normal again, I can settle to write.

Did I tell you we now have a sketch club at Hunters Hill with one evening a week a nude model? It's been going now some 4 months and I've welcomed the chance of drawing from the nude again. Only half a dozen of us, but all enthusiastic.

The presentation of my portrait of Prof Lambie has been postponed until June, owing to one of the sponsors being away overseas.

Part of the charm of the commission was that I exhibit it in the next Archibald! My love to you all, in which Robert joins,

Nora

'The Chalet'
Hunters Hill, Sydney
2 August 1957

Dearest Mother and Daddy,

I've delayed writing until after dining with the Sheumacks so that I could at last report on seeing *the* watercolour ... A beauty and without doubt one of the

---

50   William Orpen's *Sowing New Seed* (1913), which the National Gallery of South Australia returned to the artist, was later purchased in London by Melbourne collector Senator R.D. Elliot, who bequeathed it to the Mildura Arts Centre in 1956.

very top best. It should I feel be in the Adelaide Gallery ... I think that if I had to make a choice, between the watercolour and the large Northern oil they have, my vote would have to go with the watercolour with its lovely subtle light colour scheme yet, with such feeling of weight and form and the way the sheep are put in echoing the colour form of the hills is magic.

Mrs Sheumack turned on an elaborate meal with oysters mornay, chicken maryland with all the trimmings and a bomb alaska to top the bill of fare—and, as that wasn't sufficient, it was followed by a big supper of cakes and biscuits she'd made herself. Not of course up to my Mother's standard.

At the moment I'm trying to get a couple of flower pieces ready for the Society of Artists show sending-in day on Thursday, and as usual I've left the framing and finishing till the last moment. Is Daddy sending this year I wonder? I must admit I've no interest in sending in now, and would just as soon pull out of it altogether. That Society died with Ure Smith. There are no meetings at all now, and no unity or cooperation between the members, and it's so divided in interests and aims that it ceases to function.

Love from us both,

Nora

Hahndorf, South Australia
Sunday 11 August 1957

Dearest Nora,

Daddy's eyes shone to hear of the watercolour ... Daddy won the Wholohan prize for his watercolour in the last show.[51]

Everyone is asking did you perhaps go to the opening of Frank and Terry Clune's new gallery—it sounded quite a splash.[52] Goodbye to the poor old Academics—why don't they give a farewell exhibition? I'm sure it would pay.

Daddy and Mother

---

51   Hans Heysen won the first Maude Vizard-Wholohan Prize. See Colin Thiele, *Heysen of Hahndorf*, Adelaide, Hyde Park Press, 2001: 271.

52   Frank McDonald and Terry Clune opened Clune Galleries in Macquarie Street, Potts Point, Sydney.

'The Chalet'
Hunters Hill, Sydney
17 December 1957

Dearest Mother and Daddy,

At last a breathing space in which to write. The first item of news is that I've seen the flower piece. The Sheumacks dined with us on Friday and true to their word brought their latest Hans Heysen ... It's a beauty, different from any I've seen with all the detail submerged into a harmonious whole, with richness and yet a pervading silvery tone over all.[53] I told Mrs that you would send her the recipe for apple cake?

Wal Taylor died last week on the eve of his release from hospital and of the opening of his Christmas show. In a way it was best for him to go out then, as he himself didn't wish to live as a semi-invalid with nowhere to go, and no one to look after him.

The show went on and Elsie Buckle and I went to the opening which was more of a memorial to Wal than a social affair. I had a study of white roses in and sold it. The fate of the Grosvenor Galleries remains in the balance. The Maritime Board who own the building want to reclaim it, but there is pressure to keep it as a gallery.

So it was Ivor's Archibald, but it should have been Dobell's in my opinion.[54] The Ivor self portrait was an excellent piece of straight painting and a good likeness, Dobell's Mary Gilmour had neither of these qualities, but was imaginative, distinguished and the work of an artist. Dobell also had in a portrait of Camille Gheysens—remember I was commissioned to paint that man some years ago.[55] He's still trying to win the Archibald. Lambie was in, but was hung with the also-rans.

We lunched with Sir Jim last Sunday and he spoke of his hopes of getting a Heysen for German friends of his.[56] He looks well and glad to be back, but poor old Freda is frail and shaking.

Our love and wishes,

Nora

---

53   This is Hans Heysen's *Cottage Bunch* (1957).
54   Ivor Hele won the 1957 Archibald Prize with his *Self Portrait*.
55   Nora Heysen entered her portrait of Camille Gheysens in the 1951 Archibald Prize.
56   James McGregor had received a knighthood in 1956.

Hahndorf, South Australia
3 March 1958

Dearest Nora,

Ivor Hele is much in the news personal gossip. He brought home a dame from Canberra and installed her in his house, relegating no 1 to the house next door in which his mother lives![57] It is a queer set up, but he was frank about his impending divorce ... success has gone to his head.

Daddy has finished the Quarry – it's a beauty full of dignity and restraint and that rare quality, distinction.

Much love to both of you,

Mother

Hahndorf, South Australia
Monday June 1958

Dearest Nora,

The Hiroshima panels are causing a riot in Adelaide. Women faint and weep and Campbell is calling for extra police to control the crowd! I enclosed Eliz Young's comments.[58]

Mother

'The Chalet'
Hunters Hill, Sydney
19 August 1958

Dearest Mother and Daddy,

It seems quite a while since I last received home news.

My portrait of the doctor's daughter is at a standstill, as every time she's due to sit she rings and puts it off. To calm my irritation, I've started on a self portrait and now at least I have my sitter when I want and for how long I want, and with any luck I might get it through in time for the *The Women's Weekly* competition.

---

57   This is June Weatherly, who Ivor Hele met while working on the commission to paint the opening of Parliament. See Jane Hylton, *Ivor Hele: The Productive Artist*, Kent Town, South Australia, Wakefield Press, 2002: 26.

58   The Hiroshima panels, painted on rice paper scrolls by Japanese artists Iri Maruki and Toshika Akamatsu, were exhibited at the Art Gallery of South Australia from 7–25 June 1958. See Elizabeth Young, 'Atom Bomb Panels Hung: Epic Panels of Tragedy', *The Advertiser*, 6 June 1958; '5000 Queue to See Panels', *The Advertiser*, 9 June 1958.

Friday

I was pleased to hear that Daddy is to be painted and by Ivor and hope he makes a good job of it. I was only saying the other day that I wished Ivor could do it. He's not altogether the right artist, but the best for the job in Australia I think, and I agree it must be done. I had the chance and failed, so now it's up to Ivor.[59]

Must get back to self sitting, as the light is good.

Robert is well and extremely busy putting his tribe of students through exams. He sends his love with mine,

Nora

Hahndorf, South Australia
24 August 1958

My Dear Nora,

Your drawing gave him (Daddy) quite a thrill (he is unwell).

Mother

'The Chalet'
Hunters Hill, Sydney
Monday 15 September 1958

Dearest Mother and Daddy,

Mother's letter this morning to bring confirmation that Daddy was up and about again and I'm relieved and glad.

I painted my self portrait in a week in a scheme of greys using the opening looking out on to the back veranda as a background. It was still wet when we rushed it in to the Gallery an hour before closing date. The photographers were all there to catch the late entrants so we were taken offloading the thing from the back of the wagon. So you may see us in *The Women's Weekly*.[60]

Many thanks for getting my flower piece into Vi Johns—the news that I've sold both is good indeed and a pleasant surprise.

Love from us both,

Nora

---

59   Nora Heysen entered in the 1948 Archibald Prize a portrait of her father. The portrait was on display from 23 January to 5 March 1948.

60   Nora Heysen entered *Scheme in Grey: Self Portrait* in *The Australian Women's Weekly* Art Prize. See *The Australian Women's Weekly* file, Art Gallery of New South Wales Library.

'The Chalet'
Hunters Hill, Sydney
6 October 1958

Dearest Mother and Daddy,

It was good to hear in Mother's last letter that Daddy was feeling up to a Board meeting again, and I was also pleased to hear that the armchairs in the living room are at last being used to relax in.

I did get my self portrait in amongst the 96 pictures accepted for *The Women's Weekly* competition but only just I think. I didn't agree with the judging but there was very little good painting in the show—everyone trying so desperately hard to be 'Modern' resulting in a lot of crude experimental works, but you'll be seeing a selection of it for yourselves.[61] I went to the opening.

Love and greetings,

Nora

'The Chalet'
Hunters Hill, Sydney
Monday 10 November 1958

Dearest Mother and Daddy,

I was glad to have Mother's letter last week to know that ... art is on the upgrade in Adelaide. Many thanks for the cuttings.

Norman Lindsay's show opens at David Jones today.[62]

Wal Taylor's collection of pictures furniture etc. came up for auction last week.[63] I went along to see the pictures sold. A very hot day and the gallery was crowded, but whether due to the sticky heat or a general apathy towards the work available I don't know, but the pictures only fetched about a third of their current prices. Admittedly there were not any outstanding things, but there were names—

---

61   John Rigby won the 'best portrait' prize with *Margaret* and Albert Tucker the 'best subject picture' with *Australian Gothic*. Each prize was £1000. See 'Our 1958 Art Awards: Two Prize-winning Entries', *The Australian Women's Weekly*, 24 September 1958.

62   Rose Lindsay organised the exhibition of 200 etchings, *The Complete Collection of Etchings by Norman Lindsay*, which was held at David Jones Gallery, Sydney, from 12–25 November 1958.

63   Grosvenor Galleries operated from 1923 to 1958.

Lambert, Dobell, Gruner, Tom Roberts and none of them went over 75gs—
A Dufy watercolour fetched the highest price at £175 ... I could have had a good
Margaret Preston for 17gs, a Lawrence for 12gs, or a Michael Kmit for £10. I was
only thankful that there was nothing of mine there—nothing of Daddy's either.

Love to you both from us both with a hope that all's well,

Nora

> *'The Chalet'*
> *Hunters Hill, Sydney*
> *Sunday 23 November 1958*

Dearest Mother and Daddy,

I went in to see the Norman Lindsay show—a remarkable exhibition of
his complete works of etchings. The techniques and craftsmanship miraculous
but something illustrative and commonplace prevents me from accepting them
as works of art. However the show has roused a great deal of interest, and Bruce
Glad tells me over £500 worth of prints have sold, which seems to contradict the
generally accepted idea that there's no interest in black and white work.[64]

In the meantime heartfelt thanks for the parcel of home goodness and love
from us both,

Nora

> *Hahndorf, South Australia*
> *February 1959*

Dear Nora,

My portrait is not quite complete yet. Ivor wants more sittings—in the
meantime he is having a new studio built at Aldinga—so he is thinking of other
things. The painting is coming along well and I feel he has made a good job. He is
very keen and anxious to do one of his best,

Your Dad

---

64   The Norman Lindsay exhibition was popular with the general public but critical reception was mixed. *The
Sydney Morning Herald* described it as 'plain, unashamed and ribald sex', whereas Laurie Thomas in *The Sun*
commented that it was a 'display of fantastic craftsmanship'. See Lin Bloomfield, *The Complete Etching of
Norman Lindsay*, Sydney, Joseph Lebovic Gallery, 1998: 448.

'The Chalet'
Hunters Hill, Sydney
Friday 13 February 1959

Dearest Mother and Daddy,

Daddy's letter brought the disturbing news of Mother's ordeal.[65] What an anxious week, and there I was immersed in my large portrait with thoughts for little else than trying to complete it within the time limit. And now the worst seems over, I can only hope that now the haemorrhaging has been stopped and that recovery will be quick.

Glad to hear that *the* portrait is near completion. I guess you won't be sorry to see the end of sittings. It was very nice to have had the trip down that day and to have seen the portrait coming along so well. I hope Ivor has found that little something that was holding it back. I was amused when the wife of my last subject, on seeing my portrait, said she liked it very much but there was something a little strange somewhere. Exactly what I'd thought about Ivor's portrait of Daddy. I'm still convinced it was the modelling of the eyes.

Our love with a big hope that things are better again and Mother well on the way to recovery,

Nora

'The Chalet'
Hunters Hill, Sydney
25 February 1959

Dearest Mother and Daddy,

I didn't win the Queensland portrait prize but came near it—too much local interest in favour of the winner with her subject a Queensland identity and patron of the Arts[66] ... I see that Campbell was one of the judges! My subject was very disappointed and I'm now painting him a flower piece to compensate him.

Robert is going to a conference in Delhi leaving about the 19th of March, but will only be away about a fortnight this time. I'll be busy with the Hunters Hill show.

Much love from us both,

Nora

---

65   Sallie Heysen's health continued to deteriorate.

66   The winner was Betty Cameron (later Churcher) for her painting of Brisbane philanthropist J.V. Duhig. See Glenn Cooke, 'Betty Churcher', http://www.daao.org.au/main/read/7270, accessed 23 July 2010. Nora Heysen's entry was *R.K. Macpherson, MSc., MD, BS.*

Hahndorf, South Australia
26 March 1959

My Dear Nora,

Your Hunters Hill show will be in full progress by now. I've been hoping for a criticism in *The Bulletin*. Shows in Adelaide have been numerous but really one, that of Clifton Pugh, reaping some success. I saw it and shudder at the macabre and unhappy mind that could conceive the subjects ... Daddy has had a final sitting for his portrait, so surely it will soon appear in the Gallery.

Mother

'The Chalet'
Hunters Hill, Sydney
12 May 1959

Dearest Mother and Daddy,

It was good to have Mother's letter—with the cream of the news—both well again and Daddy able to get to his studio.

It's good too to hear that *the* portrait is at last complete and hanging in the Gallery. I'd very much have liked being in at the presentation ceremony[67] ... How does it look in the Gallery?

The watercolour of Daddy's fetching £187 at the auction will bring a fresh avalanche of demands for work.

Robert is down in Melbourne or rather Healesville some 38 miles out at an Army Medical School. He's been made a Lieut. Colonel, Consultant in Tropical Diseases to the Army ... I've been busy sewing on colour patches and marking things and digging things out from the attic.

Also the Society of Artists drawing exhibition came along in the middle of things. I sent three drawings amongst them one of Peter which was bought by the Newcastle Art Gallery ... It was a good show highlighted with a panel of Lambert drawings and some early Lloyd Rees. The Lamberts still look mighty good amongst all the modern experimental ventures, but apart from Gallery purchases, not much was sold.

---

67   Ivor Hele and Ursula and Bill Hayward presented Hele's portrait of Hans Heysen to the National Gallery of South Australia.

I sent a couple of portraits over for the Melrose Prize thing—my own *Self Portrait* and the one of Dr Macpherson. I've just begun on a commission to paint a young Commando, jungle greens and beret ... and also I've started on a nude painting Friday nights so I'm busy.

My love and wishes,

Nora

'The Chalet'
Hunters Hill, Sydney
2 July 1959

Dearest Mother and Daddy,

Yes, I can imagine the chaos at home and just how inundated you are with letters telegrams and visitations, even I have come in for some reflected glory.[68] Many have written telephoned or personally called to express their congratulations and pleasure over Father's knighthood ... I must not forget to pass on the warm congratulations of all the girls working at Parkers.

Three portrait commissions are keeping me more than occupied. The two new ones, children of 8 and 6 years, can only be brought to me on the weekends—both together! They live at Newcastle and their Father, a doctor, practises there and can only manage that time, also the young Commando I'm painting can only sit the weekends, so that I'm at my wits ends trying to cope.

Ivor has sent photographs of the portrait as promised ... Also a nice letter from which I quote: 'we had a grand time, I was the lucky one, as I had a greater opportunity to realise what a great man he is, and an even greater artist. Never was a knighthood more deserved, and I don't think he could care less. We feel that we should congratulate the Queen'.

And so say all of us.

Our love and the hope that you have the strength to bear up to this avalanche of publicity,

Nora

---

68   Hans Heysen's elevation to Knight Bachelor was announced in the Queen's Birthday Honours List of 12 June 1959.

Hahndorf, South Australia
Monday July 1959

My Dear Nora,

What do you think of Jacqueline Hick's achievement! I can imagine yours looking antiseptic beside it. All you have to do is to rub yours up and down the chimney or over a greasy stove, and you might win a prize! Daddy stood down when they notified him you were competing.

Mother

'The Chalet'
Hunters Hill, Sydney
Thursday 21 July 1959

Dearest Mother and Daddy,

I was glad to have Mother's letter with the news of Jackie Hick's win and the paper cutting of her *Self Portrait*.[69] Yes, I quite agree that mine must have looked antiseptic in contrast! Maybe the paper reproduction doesn't do it justice and the colour redeems it. I've long since given up hope of winning prizes, my work is far too unexciting and conventional. All the plaudits these days go to something *new* in the fashionable idiom even if the new only amounts to surface tricks of paint or unrealistic colour. However to enter for these things is a means of keeping ones name before the public and getting the odd commission.

I'm glad Jackie won the £100—though little enough, it will help for how she keeps going with four children to care for I just can't imagine. I find it difficult enough with none.

Love to you from us both,

Nora

'The Chalet'
Hunters Hill, Sydney
Tuesday October 1959

Dearest Mother and Daddy,

It was good indeed to have been able to be there for Daddy's investiture—an occasion to remember, smile about and feel proud.[70] The birthday, the trip

---

69   Jackie Hick won the 1959 Melrose Prize for *Self Portrait*. By the late 1950s, the Art Gallery of South Australia offered the Melrose Prize every fourth year. See *Bulletin of the National Art Gallery of South Australia*, vol.21, no.1, July 1959.

70   The investiture was on 14 October 1959 at Government House, Adelaide. Hans Heysen was too elderly to travel to Canberra, so the Governor-General, Sir William Slim, came to Adelaide for the ceremony. All members of the Heysen family attended.

down to Ivor's, waking up amongst the Birch tops to the song of birds and all the recollections of one's childhood.

With love and thanks and a big hope that all's well and you are not overtired, Nora

'The Chalet'
Hunters Hill, Sydney
30 December 1959

Dearest Mother and Daddy,

It was wonderful to hear you on the 'Eve'.

Sir Lionel was at Jim's on Sunday looking very fit and was talkative as ever. I relayed your message and he sends his love and fondest greetings, says he's writing. Peter was also there and I hardly recognised him, quite grey and middle aged. He says he's prodding his Father into writing his memoirs.

Lord Jim looks a little worn and tired and admits at last that he is heartily sick of travelling ... I think it must be something like 15 years since I last saw Sir Lionel and saw very little change in him. His mind and memory are still alert, but he says his eyesight is failing badly and he can no longer work.

I'm going to enjoy spending my Christmas cheques and have in mind the new Goya book just out, a down pillow and a Beethoven Symphony. Robert gave me a gramophone for my Christmas box. A thing I've always wanted and now all I want are the records to complete it.

Love from us both,

Nora

PS Robert is awaiting the exam results any day now!

These letters come from the National Library of Australia's 'Papers of Sir Hans Heysen, c.1880–1973', MS 5073, series 2, folders 167, 168, 169, 170, 171, 172 and 173; and 'Papers of Nora Heysen, 1913–2003', MS 10041, series 1.3, folders 29, 30, 31, 32, 34 and 35.

Success, anxiety and change
1960–1968

The 1960s was a stressful decade for Nora Heysen, and even though one of decline for Hans, it was still a productive one for both. A major anxiety overshadowing the early years was Sallie's prolonged ill health. She died in May 1962. Hans' feeling of loss was profound and he wrote to Nora that it seems like 'some horrible nightmare from which I hope to be suddenly released'. His long-time friend Lionel Lindsay had also passed away a year earlier. After Sallie's death Jill, then David Heysen and Lyly looked after the ageing Hans, and Nora's letters are addressed to them as well.

Nora and Robert Black made their third trip to the Pacific and were in the Solomon Islands from September 1961 to February 1962. Nora continued to exhibit in the Archibald Prize; her portrait of poet *James McAuley* was shown in 1961 and her painting of the very elderly and colourful *Miss Paul* was in the 1967 exhibition. However, Nora faces the ignominy of having her portrait of *Charles Rowley* rejected in the 1965 and writes home: 'for the first time I was turned out'. The issue of how modern artists are approaching portraiture threads its way through the letters with Nora commenting of the 1963 Archibald:

> Looking round I couldn't help but agree with Gleeson that portrait
> painting is in the doldrums. All the attempts to treat portrait painting
> in the abstract manner seem to fail dismally, and the old tired

academic representation is equally unsatisfactory. Only Dobell
seemed to be able to lift portrait painting out of the mediocre rut.

Both father and daughter exhibited in numerous solo exhibitions, and in a
joint exhibition at Hamilton Gallery in April 1963 organised by David Heysen. Hans'
work was honoured in a retrospective exhibition in the 1966 Adelaide Festival of Arts
when he was 89 years of age. A significant publication, *The Art of Hans Heysen*, by
David Dridan, was released at the same time. In 1960, an exhibition of Hans' work had
attracted record crowds to the Hahndorf Gallery and David Heysen, by then producing
prints of his father's most well-known work, showed them in a lucrative exhibition in
October 1967. Nora, for her part, was equally busy with a solo exhibition in Millicent,
in South Australia, in March 1963 and another in August 1967 at North Adelaide
Galleries. She was constantly sending in work to group exhibitions of the Society of
Artists and to other galleries. However, hovering over her work and its reception was
the changing fashions of the era. At one stage she enters paintings in the August 1962
Society of Artists exhibition and writes home: 'Now that I have my brown Mothers
and babies ready to meet the world, I'm sure they won't be accepted. A very 'modern'
selection committee this year and probably realism will be outed'. The work was
accepted but this sense of being out-of-step with fashion infuses her letters and
critical reception.

In his senior years Hans continued to receive commissions and requests for
work, at times more than he could manage. His commissioned watercolour, *White
Gums, Summer Afternoon*, was presented to Queen Elizabeth II on her royal tour
of 1963. He also appeared in two ABC television shows, was interviewed by John
Hetherington for his *Age* newspaper series on artists, as was Nora, and was the subject
of a biography by Colin Thiele. Nora, too, as a mid-career artist was busy, serving
on the selection and hanging committee for the Spring 1960 and Autumn 1961
exhibitions of the Society of Artists, and on their Executive Committee in 1964. She
was also on the selection committee for the Hunters Hill Art Show, then a judge and,
in 1962, a judge of the Robert Le Gay Brereton Memorial Prize for drawing.

The Society of Artists was struggling, and some letters touch on the issue of
the rise of the commercial gallery sector and the different patterns of buying by the
state galleries. Both father and daughter exhibit in the new galleries—Hans at Clune
Galleries and at the Dominion Gallery, and Nora writing home in 1966: 'when I was
last in at The Hungry Horse Gallery I was asked for work which surprised me'.

International abstraction hit Australia with a fanfare in 1967 in *Two Decades of American Art*, a touring exhibition about which Nora reports rather coolly. What constituted Australian art in the early 1960s was also the subject of the 1963 Tate exhibition, which is alluded to in an exchange between Nora and her father.

Nora is increasingly living alone. Her husband Robert, an expert in tropical medicine is frequently away on fieldwork or at conferences for extended periods. The stresses of managing a large home, maintaining a career and having an elderly father in Adelaide consume her energy. Finally in 1968 she goes on an overseas trip to visit galleries in New York, London and Spain with her sister and brother-in-law, but receives word in Madrid in mid-June that her father is unwell. Hans Heysen died in early July, aged 90 years.

Hahndorf, South Australia
7 January 1960

My Dear Nora,

My hearty congratulations dear Nora and may your birthday be a happy one. I am up to my neck in commissions, but little time left to do my studio work. My interests in the work never fails and I itch to do more.

All the very best of good wishes to you and Robert,

From your Dad

Hahndorf, South Australia
25 January 1960

Dearest Nora,

Daddy has just finished a flower picture! The first for many a long year and it's a beauty, also an oil of the Arkaba range, a splendid thing which goes to Sedon for his yearly show. Isn't it wonderful he can stand up to do oils, but he does get badly tired and has cramps at night.

Much love to you both,

Mother

'The Chalet'
Hunters Hill, Sydney
Thursday 18 February 1960

Dearest Mother and Daddy,

Mr Mason rang a couple of days ago to tell me of his wonderful visit to you—said you'd treated him like royalty and he was enchanted with you both, the home and everything and now wants to make the film just on Father with my Mother featuring too.[1] I think he appreciated it immensely.

I have been thinking of coming over during Festival time for a brief visit if I can manage it.[2] I haven't fixed on any definite plan as I've just started on a scheme to paint the neighbour's cleaning woman with her child, I had her sitting for me yesterday. An interesting woman who I'd had my eye on for some time. Jill met her and will remember her. Dark olive skinned of Greek Egyptian Belgian extraction, fine eyes and a great dignity of bearing, but I don't know if I'll be able to cope with

---

1   Richard (Dick) Mason, who worked with Robert on a film about malaria, earlier made *An Introduction to Australian Art*, featuring William Dobell, Russell Drysdale and Roy Dalgarno, for the Department of Information Film Unit (later Film Australia).

2   Adelaide was the first Australian city to hold an arts festival. It commenced in 1960 and is held biennially.

the kid whom she will not come without and who's just at that grizzling destructive age, so disrupting to the concentration.[3]

Love from us both,

Nora

'The Chalet'
Hunters Hill, Sydney
Thursday 7 April 1960

Dearest Mother and Daddy,

Sir Richard Boyer opened the Hunters Hill show and devoted his entire address to how he opened Sir Hans Heysen's exhibition in Hahndorf and what he'd said.[4] I met him afterwards (of course he didn't remember meeting me at Daddy's show) and he sends his love to Daddy and to tell you how honoured he was to meet you and what an occasion the whole thing was. He was most eulogistic over his Festival visit and had the highest praise for Adelaide and how the Festival was managed.

Lloyd Rees is back and wishes to be remembered to you both.[5] Asks did you receive his congratulations on the knighthood? He has aged a lot I thought and looks tired and ill. All he could say on his impressions of art abroad was confusion, confusion and more confusion! I met him at a meeting of the Society of Artists last week. Everyone there had heard of Daddy's successful show and were amazed at the rally of 16 000 to view it.

I've heard about Daddy's broadcast to schools and everyone is thrilled with it.

Love from us both,

Nora

---

3   They are the subjects of *Mother and Child* (1960), held by Bathurst Regional Art Gallery.

4   *An Exhibition of Oil Paintings, Watercolours and Drawings by Sir Hans Heysen* was held at the Hahndorf Gallery. Sir Richard Boyer opened the exhibition on 13 March 1960 and 17 000 people visited it within a fortnight. See Colin Thiele, *Heysen of Hahndorf*, Adelaide, Hyde Park Press, 2001: 276; 'Exhibition is First in 30 Years', *The News*, 5 March 1960.

5   In 1959, Lloyd Rees (1895–1988) was in Britain and Europe. See Jancis and Alan Rees, *Lloyd Rees: A Source Book*, Sydney, Beagle Press, 1995: 27.

'The Chalet'
Hunters Hill, Sydney
Monday 6 June 1960

Dearest Mother and Daddy,

It was good to have Mother's letter telling of John Dowie's commission to do Daddy and of the sittings in my old studio. Is the finished result to be in bronze? All very exciting and I long to see how it progresses. I like John Dowie and have faith that he will do a good job.

Here too the weather has been bleak and cold. One lift was to see an exhibition of Carl Plate's work at the Macquarie Galleries.[6] Another lift was to visit Adrian in his new flat. A happy Adrian painting in reds and golds at last, thanks to Jim McGregor, in a place where he's always wanted to be, and with security of ownership. He's a different person; was inquiring after you both, and sends his very best wishes.

My thoughts are at home wondering how things are,

Nora

'The Chalet'
Hunters Hill, Sydney
10 June 1960

Dearest Mother and Daddy,

Before I forget, I've promised to put forward a request to Daddy for two watercolours for a show at Anthony Horderns in October. Tony Marinato is organising the exhibition, commission goes to charity. He's the bloke who has established the Watson's Bay Gallery and also holds yearly shows at Anthony Horderns.[7] The October one is a special with Menzies to open it and all the best artists asked to contribute. Tony is a pleasant fat Italian who doesn't seem to ask for any profit for himself—the couple of times he's called here to collect work he's brought a big fresh fish as caught by himself. He rang to ask if I'd ask if you'd be good enough to contribute, 20% commission I think he works on.

Love to you both from us both,

Nora

6   Carl Plate (1909–1977), who spent time in America, Europe and Britain, worked as an international modernist. He ran Notanda Gallery, in Rowe Street, Sydney, which his sister Margo Lewers established.

7   Tony Marinato ran the Watson Bay Wharf Art Exhibitions at Tony's Café and Art Gallery from 1947 to 1963.

'The Chalet'
Hunters Hill, Sydney
Thursday 22 1960

Dearest Mother and Daddy,

Interesting too to hear of Harley Griffiths' success, as I've been hearing from all sides that there's a slump in the picture market.[8] Certainly here it seems true enough, for show after show comes and goes with one or two sales, and even a glowing criticism hasn't brought forth sales of abstract work.

I'm going to be tied up with a couple portrait commissions, one of a girl of 21 years and the other of a young man a couple years older. Also the subject I have in mind for an Archibald entry, the poet and critic Jim McAuley (remember the Angry Penguins and the hoax put across some years back, he's the poet who figured), he has consented to sit. Unfortunately he's only Saturdays free. I don't know how I'm going to manage, as all have to be finished before Christmas. To paint a portrait with one sitting a week is maddening, to paint three at the same time under those conditions will be three times as maddening.

Love from us both and I hope the sun has come to cheer you,

Nora

PS The walnuts and raspberry jam have been a real treat and the eggs a good standby.

'The Chalet'
Hunters Hill, Sydney
27 August 1960

Dearest Mother and Daddy,

This year my magnolia, the Japanese variety which blooms so elegantly on bare stems as in the Orovida tempera, flowered and is a real joy, an aristocrat in the garden.

This year I was on the hanging and selection committee for the Society of Artists. I've been a member for 29 years and this was the first time I've been actually voted in, a mixed blessing I soon found, as it meant a couple of days of really hard work. Some 450 entries, which first had to be unpacked, then selected and arranged. I was the only woman, but I was also some 20 years younger than the 5 other men so couldn't take advantage of my sex and let the men do all the carting of heavy pictures. A big and very mixed show this year and difficult to hang

---

8   Harley Griffiths (1878–1951) exhibited with the New South Wales Society of Artists and was manager with
      Hardy Wilson and Julian Ashton of the Fine Arts Society, Sydney, from 1911 to 1914.

even with the advantage of Farmers new gallery.[9] A better show than last year, but the Galleries didn't buy and the sales very poor up to date.

The *Exhibition of Women's Achievements in the Arts* opens tomorrow.[10] I was in last week to take my three contributions and was amazed at the variety and quality of the paintings gathered. I felt like packing mine up again and retiring, they looked so prosaic and, yes, pedestrian.[11]

Love from us both,

Nora

'The Chalet'
Hunters Hill, Sydney
Wednesday 26 October 1960

Dearest Mother and Daddy,

Mother's letter relating the strenuous and happy birthday celebrations made good reading.

I finished the portrait of the girl to everyone's satisfaction and commence on the young man on Saturday. Unfortunately the portrait of James McAuley has temporarily been suspended, as he was invited to go India as a guest to represent Australia in the literary field for a six-week tour, and won't be back till just before Christmas, which rules him out as an entry for the Archibald. So now I'll have to think again.

We saw the *Shirley Abicair Program* on TV with Daddy amongst the gums. Has it come to you yet? Not as good as I'd hoped. Far too much Shirley Abicair and not enough care taken with lighting.

Love to you from us both,

Nora

---

9   This is Blaxland Gallery.

10   This Exhibition of Women's Achievements in the Arts, hosted by the National Council of Women of New South Wales, Arts and Letters Committee, was held at David Jones Gallery from 31 August to 6 September 1960.

11   Nora wrote home that she was offended when Adelaide critic Elizabeth Young called her work 'pedestrian', which Nora now uses to describe her own painting.

'The Chalet'
Hunters Hill, Sydney
Tuesday 15 November 1960

Dearest Mother and Daddy,

Mother's letter dated 31st October is still unanswered and I can't think how the time has gone. A large flower piece has consumed most of it.

Drysdale has received terrific publicity over his big retrospective show at the Gallery.[12] I went to see it two or three times as it was a great opportunity to assess his work. A very fine show and he has certainly made a contribution, if a limited one, but somehow I can't be moved by the work as I should. I feel he paints with the head and not the heart, and is concerned more with making a striking impact rather than extracting true values. His middle period seemed to me most satisfying. In a lot of the later work, there is a curious combination of abstraction and realism that I find difficult to reconcile, but at his best in a few landscapes and in the lone figure compositions he gets that utter loneliness and stillness of forgotten souls.

I did get the drawing done of Peter Tansy, nephew or rather grandson of old Lane Mullins. I drew him when he was 7 years, so it was very interesting to see him again and draw him at 30 years.

But I must get back to my painting. The infernal background problem is with me again. Small wonder artists find a satisfactory formula and stick to it.

Love from us both with a hope for better report on the neuritis,

Nora

'The Chalet'
Hunters Hill, Sydney
17 February 1961

Dearest Mother and Daddy,

I was glad to have Mother's letter to fill me in on scraps of home news.

I've had a couple of quick trips into the Gallery to see the Archibald, Wynne and Sulman entries. Judy Cassab didn't have much opposition. I didn't think her portrait of Rapotec was a happy compromise of abstract and realism. It is a realistic, if somewhat shallow statement of a vital and forceful personality jazzed up with meaningless squares and rectangles of colour to bring it up to date with contemporary fashion. But it is a large vigorous painting and a good likeness.

---

12   Russell Drysdale's retrospective exhibition, covering his work from 1937–1960, was shown at the Art Gallery of New South Wales, October–November 1960.

I came away feeling, especially with the portraiture, that trying to combine realism and abstraction was a failure, and yet the old academic portrayal looked tired and dead.

Love from us both with a hope that the fires are keeping their distance and the heat relaxing,

Nora

Hahndorf, South Australia
3 March 1961

My Dear Nora,

The River Art show again a colossal success, Daddy's contribution as usual snapped up by Campbell for Menzies (a standing order). Kym Bonython has opened a new art Gallery, abstract only.[13]

Art is flourishing in Adelaide. Daddy has two orders to fill, two thousand pound cheques!

Goodbye for now,

Mother

'The Chalet'
Hunters Hill, Sydney
Sunday 15 March 1961

Dearest Mother and Daddy,

Robert left early on Friday and will now be in New Delhi and back home again in a fortnight, I'm hoping.

I had a long chat with Drysdale yesterday ... I've always liked Drysdale and find him both easy and interesting to talk to. He's travelled widely, though much loves Australia and wants to paint it. He also has the deepest admiration for Daddy's work and spoke of a print of sheep in a yellow dusty landscape he'd always kept with him. The charcoal drawing of the pine appealed to him tremendously and the small Northern drawing that Daddy gave me a couple Christmases ago.

Since coming back from Europe he's been roaming round the far west coast of Australia and is fascinated with Broome and the outback places and natives.[14] And by the way, he asked could he possibly meet you one day. He's always wanted to, but has felt too shy to bother you ... I presumed to tell him that I was sure he'd be welcome.

---

13 Kym Bonython opened Bonython Gallery in Jerningham Street, North Adelaide, in March 1961.

14 Russell Drysdale, born in the United Kingdom in 1912, settled with his pastoralist family in Melbourne in 1923, returning to the United Kingdom and Europe in 1932–1933, 1938, 1950 and 1957.

Must off and bake a cake. My love and thoughts and may you both be feeling stronger every day,

Nora

PS Many thanks for the recipe for the Dutch tart.

'The Chalet'
Hunters Hill, Sydney
22 May 1961

Dearest Mother and Daddy,

Lloyd Rees is showing his last series of paintings done in Italy at the Macquarie Galleries.[15] I'll enclose Wallace Thornton's criticism. On the whole I had to agree with his opinion. I found it vaguely disappointing, and only in a couple of small things did I feel that he'd in any way resolved his problem of trying to compromise between romantic realism and the newer idioms in painting. He's trying desperately to lighten his palette, but his melancholy mood persists and the natural daylight never enters.

The division in the Society of Artists is becoming open warfare between the traditionalists and the so-called moderns. Dundas is resigning and a new President being elected. I'm wondering who on earth can fill the role and hold the Society together. There's not another Ure Smith.

Robert sends his love with mine to you both,

Nora

Hahndorf, South Australia
8 June 1961

Dearest Nora,

I did want to tell you of Daddy's visit to the Bonython Gallery to inspect Gleghorn's work! Daddy was quite interested and finished up by buying one for the Gallery, much to Bonython's delight, Ivor and the Trustees had refused.[16] They are all old diehards and won't even *look* at the abstracts.

---

15   Lloyd Rees toured Italy in 1959. The exhibition was *European Motifs by Lloyd Rees.*

16   The National Art Gallery of South Australia purchased Tom Gleghorn's *Landscape and Coast* (1960), oil on composition board, from Bonython Gallery in 1961.

Lionel's death has shaken Daddy, as you can imagine, and now the news of Will Ashton's unfortunate marriage already breaking up.[17] Daddy is well enough to withstand shocks.

Much love from us both, especially from Daddy who so enjoys your letters and me also,

Mother

'The Chalet'
Hunters Hill, Sydney
Thursday 15 June 1961

Dearest Mother and Daddy,

I am dismayed to hear of Daddy's fall with the painful consequences and only hope that at least the painful part is over.

Lever Brothers have offered Robert a job in the Solomon Islands to investigate their native labour from a medical and psychological point of view ... for my part, I feel I could do with a break from domesticity with a change of subject.

Very interested to hear of Daddy's visit to the Gleghorn show and of the purchase of one of his works for the Gallery ... He spent 7 years studying under Dobell, and although the Dobell influence is not apparent, I feel that he's gained painting qualities from him. I think you'd like Gleghorn if you met him.

It was sad to hear of Lionel Lindsay's death knowing how it would shake you. Last time I saw Lionel Lindsay he was still alert and interested and interesting.

Much going on in the art world over here, but I am out of time and space and it must wait.[18]

We are both well and send our love,

Nora

---

17   Lionel Lindsay died on 22 May 1961.

18   The major art world event was Bryan Robertson's exhibition, *Recent Australian Painting*, which opened in June at Whitechapel Gallery, London. Robertson, aware of the Commonwealth Art Advisory Board's selection of artists for the 1963 Tate exhibition of Australian art and dissatisfaction about the 'safe' version being assembled, worked closely with Hal Missingham, from the Art Gallery of New South Wales, and Eric Westbrook, from the National Gallery of Victoria, to ensure a contemporary selection. His artists included Godfrey Miller, Jeffrey Smart, Margo Lewers and Brett Whiteley, and their work was well received by London critics. See 'Australian Art at Flood Tide: The Post Nolan Era', *Times* (London), 27 March 1961; Sarah Scott, 'A Colonial Legacy: Australian Painting at the Tate Gallery, London, 1963' in Kate Darian-Smith, et. al., *Seize the Day: Exhibitions, Australia and the World*, Clayton, Victoria, Monash e-Press, 2008: 19.1–19.6; Simon Pierse, 'A Horse Designed by a Committee', *Art and Australia*, vol.47, no.1, 2009: 120–125.

'The Chalet'
Hunters Hill, Sydney
25 August 1961

Dearest Mother and Daddy,

I was alarmed to hear of Daddy's 'sick' turn and can imagine how worrying it was.

I've delayed writing hoping that any day would bring forth a decision on our Solomons trip. Provisionally we are due per ship on the 25 of September.

I made an effort to go along to the private view and opening of the Society of Artists exhibition to welcome Lloyd Rees as our new president. Back in the old Education building and everyone glad to be 'home' again after a three-year term at the Blaxland Gallery. Certainly the show looked much better and the sales seem better too, despite the usual condemning of the art critics.

The honours seem to go to Wakelin this year, with a large painting of the Conservatorium and landscape, and a still life, all fine paintings and all sold, the first to the New South Wales Gallery.[19] The only Gallery to buy this year.

Poor Lloyd Rees is worried about the social angle of being President. He and his wife, as he explained, have always retired from a social life and now they feel unable to cope. When I went along on the afternoon of the opening, I found Lloyd Rees in the back room trying to make all the savouries for the evening opening, shirtsleeves rolled up and fussing around with paper doillies, bits of cheese and biscuits, so Adrian Feint and I took over.

Love from us both,

Nora

Yandina, British Solomon Islands
Sunday 15 October 1961

Dearest Mother and Daddy,

Well arrived at last at our destination, but not settled. The accommodation scheme went sadly awry and when we landed there was no house for us, and no one could put us up. So back to the ship for another day and night until she'd finished loading copra and had to sail on and then we were off-loaded, and eventually collected with crates of frozen meat and our other supplies and taken to the Manager of Plantations, a very smart new home, and stored in our own air-conditioned bedroom until our situation could be resolved.

---

19   Roland Wakelin's *Down the Hill to Berry's Bay* was purchased by the Art Gallery of New South Wales in 1961.

My painting equipment has all been neatly stored away in a cupboard, and all Robert's stuff is still on the wharf.

Have just been told that mail will have to go in a few minutes if it is to catch this week's mail. A plane calls here only once a fortnight.

Must stop with a warm cheerio from this far-flung post.

Love with a hope all is well,

Nora

Yandina, British Solomon Islands
Sunday 27 October 1961

Dearest Mother and Daddy,

At last a little mail has found us, and in it Mother's letter which was a joy to have with all the news of the birthday. The unveiling ceremony and the paper cuttings to bring pictures of the big day, and what a hectic day it must have been.[20]

Still, I'm afraid no chance of getting more workable accommodation, so must I suppose make the most of it. Robert is finding plenty to interest and stimulate him, and is going ahead collecting volumes of data. His tireless enthusiasm and stamina amaze me.

There is very little here to excite me in the way of subject matter, nothing like the interest that I found in the Trobriands. For here, the natives are recruited from other islands to work on the plantations and in the copra mill etc., single men mostly who are housed in wretched galvanized iron huts. Only very recently have a few wives and children been permitted to come with them, so that there are no native villages and natural living to interest me.

As for the scenery, well, it's deadly monotonous, just rows upon rows of coconut palms on a well nigh flat surface, and as for the climate, words fail me ... I've been out with my sketchbook down to the copra mill, or anywhere that a few natives are working to get some studies.

With absolutely no domestic chores and all the time in the world to paint, it's ironic, and appears one can never gain anything without losing. However the shed being put up in the 'garden' as a studio for me is now almost complete. A square 12' x 14' box with a galvanized iron roof, but just what I'm going to paint there remains a question, as the homestead here is too remote to get natives to come and sit for me. In the meantime, I've been trying to get the natives a bit used to me and to understand what I'm doing. No artists have been here, but a few

---

20   See '84th Birthday: Bronze Head by John Dowie Unveiled', *The Advertiser*, 9 October 1961.

cameras have led them into thinking that they must pose all stiff and straight on for a minute, and it's all over ...

I was alarmed to hear of Mother's heart attack and hope all is well again. Love from us both,

Nora

Yandina, British Solomon Islands
Sunday 12 November 1961

Dearest Mother and Daddy,

It was a joy to receive the photograph with your letter ... I took it down to show my native subjects who had been asking if I had any pictures of my Father and Mother, and you just should have seen the interest in everyone to have a look. When I told them that you were 84 they shook their black heads in disbelief. It is exceptional for these people to reach the age of 70, and 50 is considered a fair span. Now when I appear I'm besieged with 'Can we see the photo of your Father?' A few of the bright ones have worked it out that I must be very old.

Robert is having a lot of fun finding out how the place is managed, or mismanaged, and the European and native points of view. It's difficult for him carrying on an enquiry as a guest of the Managing Director, a real exercise in tact, as well as other difficulties involved.

With love from us,

Nora

Yandina, British Solomon Islands
25 November 1961

Dearest Mother and Daddy,

I'm hoping that the mail plane will bring me a home letter tomorrow. For three hours I've been battling with my Mother and baby subject ... I've found myself a very patient 'Mother' and an exceptionally good baby, but even so the subject is a difficult one to cope with under the best conditions. But this theme never ceases to interest me, and I find myself everlastingly trying again to express the fundamental timeless feeling it holds, forgetting previous failures and all the many difficulties. Anyway, up here lack of time is not one of them. Having a fine weather studio isn't very practicable, as it rains every other day. Also having the light coming in all round makes the flesh painting of the dark bodies so complicated that I just tear my hair out.

We enjoyed an unexpected break last week. Our hosts went off to Honiara for a week, and we were left in charge with five native servants to look after us. It was pleasant to be free from being guests and we also had the use of the car to run round in. I guess the other Europeans were somewhat startled to see the manager's car with natives sitting up in front with the driver. Here natives do not ride with Europeans, and do not walk with them, and only of necessity talk with them—very much the master–servant relationship. Great raising of the eyebrows when we do all the 'not dones' and enjoy it. Robert has now won the confidence of the natives. They realise that he is not a member of Levers organisation and are willing to open up and talk, making his work a lot easier. In the course of events, when his report goes through, there will be considerable changes for the better for labour here.

Everyone is now counting the days till the arrival of the *Tulagi* to replenish food supplies. She's a week and a half overdue—no butter or meat or flour left. Almost everything has to come up from Australia. In this land of the tropical fruits, we eat tinned fruit salad from Australia, and yes, desiccated coconut imported from Ceylon.

I wonder how all goes at home … We heard that Drysdale had a most successful show with the New South Wales Gallery buying one for £2000.[21] Also that Jeff Smart did well with people queuing up to buy his work and a glowing critique to boost it further.[22]

Love from us both and another thank you for the photograph,
Nora

Hahndorf, South Australia
1 December 1961

Dearest Nora,
Your letter dated 25 November has just come, many, many thanks. We were hoping for better news as far as the weather and ability to work is concerned. As you say, 'all the in the time in the world' and so much else could be added, but that's the way it goes alas, and we here imagining you with all the tropical fruits you could wish for and all the natives to draw … When the 'not dones' come back, you'll probably enjoy the sternly raised eyebrows.

---

21 The Drysdale retrospective exhibition was held at Queensland Art Gallery from April to June 1961.
22 Jeffrey Smart's October 1961 exhibition at Macquarie Galleries resulted in the Art Gallery of New South Wales acquiring *The Stilt Race*, which had also been in *Recent Australian Painting*. See Wallace Thornton, 'Neo-realist Sets his own Pace', *The Sydney Morning Herald*, 18 October 1961.

We also heard of Drysdale's and Nolan's success and saw TV pictures of them, not too inspiring. Indeed we hear little of the Sydney art world.

Lots of love and good wishes to you both,

From Daddy and Mother

Yandina, British Solomon Islands
13 December 1961

Dearest Mother and Daddy,

Much news good and not so good in Mother's letter of the 1st of December which arrived last mail. Interested to hear that John Hetherington is to have the next interview with Daddy. I met him some years ago and liked him. He seemed different from the usual reporter journalist type, ideals and some sensitivity and integrity.

JoJo in her last letter spoke of seeing Daddy on television and how good it was and how thrilled she was to see you working in your own studio and walking amongst the gums. I hope they'll show it again when we get back.

Our plane bookings are for the 13th of February, we return via Rabaul and Pt Moresby, spending two days in each for Robert to see people.

I did hear that Judy Cassab has an entry, a portrait of Robert Helpmann, in for this year's Archibald, but I should think that Jacqueline Hick could out-paint her any time, but Dobell will probably be well in the running this year, and Ivor is bound to show so that I don't think that the women painters will be in the running. I'm showing James McAuley, that is, if it is accepted, but have no hopes at all.[23] I suppose the show will be off before we return. In the meantime I'm plodding away with my damp mothers and babies and my drawing. We found some families of Polynesian people from Sikiana at another labour camp on this island amongst whom I found some good studies also. One day we took a launch to a neighbouring island and enjoyed ourselves amongst a new set of faces. Russell Islanders true—who gave us a very warm reception and showered us with pineapples, eggs and tomatoes.[24]

This will be the last letter to reach you before Christmas, so with it go my thoughts and blessings for a happy Eve ... Here we'll be suffering it English fashion, the turkey is already in the deep freeze and the pudding also.

Love from us both,

Nora

---

23   Nora Heysen's portrait of James McAuley was in the 1961 Archibald Prize.
24   The Russell Islands are in the Central Province of the Solomon Islands.

Hahndorf, South Australia
26 December 1961

Dearest Nora,

Your letter dated November 25th was enjoyed by several of the family though it doesn't sound too good to me. You have too much to put up with, good reading but not so good for you who must feel much waste of good time. Even if you could achieve one Mother and Child up to your standard, you will forget the unpleasant rest.

Mr Hetherington came and 'did' Daddy for about 3 hours, was obviously pleased with the session, and afterwards over coffee we had a great pow-wow over present and bygone art of which he was glad to have a few details.[25] He had never met Lionel or Norman Lindsay, Blamire Young, Gruner or Tom Roberts, before his day of course. We like him as you thought, he is anxious to add you to his list of subjects.

Daddy sends his love, lots of love to you both,
Mother

Yandina, British Solomon Islands
9 January 1962

Dearest Mother and Daddy,

We leave tomorrow for our island retreat.

Robert wants to make a study of the Tikopians living on Somata for a thesis to complete his Anthropology course, and I'll be glad to have Polynesian types for models instead of Melanesian which predominate here. I've been trying to complete a few of the subjects I've started on, a fishing scene, another mother and child, and another child asleep on a mat in a native hut. These, with a couple of portrait studies, are the only oils I've done. I seem to find chalk drawings more manageable in this climate and under these conditions.[26]

My big *Mother and Child* was the only canvas I was able to get sittings for, and even then it was hard work getting the car to collect and deliver, and hardening one's heart to the wailing of the four other children left behind when I took their Mother.

Love from us both,
Nora

---

25   See John Hetherington, 'Sir Hans Heysen: Artist of the Tree', *The Advertiser*, 10 February 1962.
26   It is likely that the drawing *Mary* (c.1962) was completed then.

Butete[27]

18 January 1962

Dearest Mother and Daddy,

You will see that we have at last reached our island retreat and it so happens it is more isolated than we thought. The launch we were promised broke down on our first trip to Somata leaving us helplessly rocking between two islands. We were eventually rescued by some natives passing in a canoe who paddled us to shore, and from there we had a four mile walk to the home of the European manager, and ultimately a Chinese trading launch took us back to Butete. That was my first and last chance of getting off this island. Robert has found himself a crew of Tikopians with a canoe and has been able to get to nearby islands and do some work, but I've been marooned. Not that I've cared about that ... I've been contenting myself with painting a few flowers in a jam tin.

I certainly had a unique birthday. We did actually get away on that day. Mr and Mrs Ungless accompanying us with our two house boys, all our furniture and household requirements on board, and only too literally everything on but the kitchen stove.[28] All went smoothly till we were just about to land at the Butete wharf, and then a sudden hail squall hit us and we were drenched in a matter of minutes, and the wharf was washed away, and then just as suddenly the rain stopped but the water remained rough. You can imagine the fun and games off-loading everything into a small dinghy, and getting it to the beach and off ...

The refrigerator wouldn't work—the wrong parts having been sent—and full of frozen meat, bread, butter etc. That was the unkindest cut of all. It was as well the Manager was there to witness his arrangements but he didn't stay long, he and his wife sailed off and left us to it. We at least had a primus on which to cook, and we borrowed a knife and fork apiece from a neighbouring islander and some plates and off-loaded the frozen meat and butter in lieu of. The fun really began when we tried to go to bed, and found the place infested with rats, literally thousands of them—so no sleep ... that was my birthday.

Since then things have improved a bit—we can now use the toilet, though there is no seat and no water. New parts have been sent for the refrigerator and it works a bit.

We have a kerosene stove and are gradually getting a little peace at night by poisoning off the rats, our two house boys have stayed with us, though

---

27   See Plate 4 for the drawing that Nora Heysen included at the top of this letter.
28   Ungless was the Plantation Manager at Yandina.

I wouldn't have blamed them had they shot through back to all the conveniences they are used to.

However the end is near, and the time of our departure from this 'island paradise' approaches. I can't say that I'll be sorry to return to Hunters Hill. There's a lot of interest here, but the conditions have been too difficult to enjoy it and the freedom from domestic chores has been somewhat annulled by complete loss of other freedoms, and any privacy in which to work.

Love from us both,

Nora

Hahndorf, South Australia
23 January 1962

Dearest Nora,

I do hope the new island venture has proved a success and will make up for some of the lapses so far. We were even hoping that you would make Adelaide some time during the Festival, but realise that you will be fairly fed up and longing to get into your own home at Hunters Hill and shut yourself up with your canvases and drawings.[29]

How Daddy would just long to be with you there. Bother this old age business, it is boring us badly, and I am not pulling my weight. Daddy has taken over the 6 o'clock chores as well as all his other bits and pieces. He can't spend all his time in the studio, of course not, but one wants him to go there whilst he is fresh and eager for work; enough grumbling today.

Daddy sends much love with mine to both of you,

Mother

Butete
31 January 1962

Dearest Mother and Daddy,

At last we've had a mail day at Butete bringing two home letters dated 7th and 23rd January. We were so pleased to get mail again that we overlooked the fact that the launch that brought it hadn't any of the provisions on it ordered more than a week ago. No meat for nearly two weeks, and no fish has been caught so that we are down to a strange diet of tinned strawberries and mushrooms and sweet

---

29 The 1962 Adelaide Festival of Arts was significant because it included the first showing of the highly contentious 1963 Tate exhibition of Australian art, *Antipodean Vision*. The Prime Minister of Australia, Robert Menzies, admitted in the opening speech to have pressured the Commonwealth Art Advisory Board to select Australian art that would present a positive image to future migrants. See Sarah Scott, 'A Colonial Legacy: Australian Painting at the Tate Gallery, London, 1963' in Kate Darian-Smith, et. al., *Seize the Day: Exhibitions, Australia and the World*, Clayton, Victoria, Monash e-Press, 2008: 19.9–19.10.

potatoes. Our cook boy has washed his hands of the whole business and comes in looking hopelessly dejected at meal times 'Everything Nothing Missus'.

Our whole stay here has been one long bungle of frustration and neglect. We have indeed been cut off on a desert island, but eventually we did get a launch after Robert, thoroughly fed up, threatened to cancel the rest of his work here and return. So that we had several trips to Somata where I enjoyed drawing the Tikopians, and Robert was able to get on a little with his work. Also did a few trips to nearby islands, saw the people living in their own made villages, which was a pleasant relief after the tin hut labour line conditions of Yandina. The Tikopian people have a great appeal, tall, handsome with a lovely golden brown skin, straight hair and fine features. Also their temperament is open and happy.

I wish that I could have had more time to work amongst them, but every launch trip meant three hours sailing, some of the way in open sea, so that attempting oils was impossible.

A letter from Adrian Feint says that Drysdale made £10,000 at his show at the Macquarie Galleries just recently.

Must try and pack up on the chance that we do get away from this God-damned island. More later.

Yandina, British Solomon Islands
1 February 1962

At that moment Robert came dripping in saying can we be ready to leave in 1½ hours. He'd found that a ship was up in the neighbourhood with one of the plantation managers, and they'd be willing to take us back with them. A mad rush to get all our goods and chattels onto the launch in heavy rain … Now it's a matter of tying up a few loose ends and finally packing to leave on the 13th—a journey that will be in three stages of air travel, a couple days at Rabaul, another couple at Pt Moresby, and again it's a headache to know what to do with wet canvases, for in this humidity the surface remains sticky even after a few months 'drying'. This will probably be the last letter from these parts.

Nora

Hahndorf, South Australia
3 February 1962

Dearest Nora,

Your letter of January 18 with the delightful little wash-in of Robert canoeing off to work reached us safely in spite of your fears ... is this a sample of the tropics to whites! I hope to heaven that you get back to Yandina safely.

From both of us,

Daddy and Mother

'The Chalet'
Hunters Hill, Sydney
Tuesday 24 April 1962

Dearest Mother and Daddy,

I wonder how Easter has passed and I only hope Mother's improvement has gone ahead again with no more setbacks ... I curse the distance which makes it so difficult to keep in touch ... It is too tempting to ring up and get a direct answer to the ever present question: 'How is Mother today?'

An exhibition of recent acquisitions was showing at the Gallery and I was pleased to see amongst them a *Portrait of Thea Proctor* by George Lambert, a very early work which holds its own and looks fine.[30] Also Daddy's *Delphiniums and Lilies* was on show today set between Tom Roberts' *Roses* and Gruner's *Daffodils*, first time I've seen it on view for years—a whole gallery of flower pieces, even my *Petunias* had come out for an Easter airing.

You will know that my thoughts are with you all. I hope that Mother is back to solids again and regaining from day to day.

Love from us both,

Nora

'The Chalet'
Hunters Hill, Sydney
18 May 1962

Dearest Mother and Daddy,

Lord Jim invited us to lunch at 'Neidpath'. Jim had just got back from America. I just don't know how he stands up to all this travelling. I noticed that his hands were shaking badly as he passed round the cocktails, so it must take its toll and poor old Freda looks the worse for wear.

---

30   This was George Lambert's first painting exhibited at the Royal Academy in 1904.

Adrian Feint was there worried about his forthcoming show in Brisbane, also Peter Lindsay was there, rather depressed because he says he's been working ever since his Father's death to get things cleared up, and has only got rid of the first layer.[31]

The Dobell sale has certainly stimulated art prices and sales. I saw a couple of films last week on Drysdale and Dobell showing at Qantas House here. Both excellent especially the one on Dobell.[32] Both films showed the artists painting, their palettes and techniques and most of their life's output of work. Qantas own the films but I couldn't find out who had taken them.

The Hunters Hill Art show opens on Monday. It is still going. Also Frank Bennett's life classes are on again, so that every Friday night the artists of Hunters Hill gather round to draw the nude.

My thoughts are with you all and I hope the days go more quickly for Mother with peaceful recuperating sleep.

Love to you all from us both,

Nora

Sallie Heysen dies 23 May 1962

'The Chalet'
Hunters Hill, Sydney
6 June 1962

Dearest Daddy,

My thoughts are with you and I'm hoping that the aches and pains left by the fall have gone by now. It was hard leaving you, and I only hope that soon the incentive to paint again will come and help sustain you.

Robert was truly delighted with your drawing of the home gum … needless to say what I feel about owning the charcoal of my old studio—it is a very special one for me.

Yesterday I found that I'd been appointed with Eric Lander and Kilgour to judge the Le Gay Brereton Memorial Prize, a prize awarded here annually worth £75 to an art student of promise, and to encourage the art of draughtsmanship.

---

31   Adrian Feint's forthcoming exhibition at Johnstone Gallery was from 18 September to 4 October 1962. Peter Lindsay was Lionel Lindsay's son.

32   Qantas commissioned both films and a third on Nolan. The films were produced by Collings Productions. See James Gleeson, *William Dobell*, London, Thames and Hudson, 1964: 208.

There were 18 entrants and it took us over three hours to go through thousands of drawings, and come to some agreement ... Hal Missingham was there and wished to be remembered to you.

My love to you all,

Nora

Hahndorf, South Australia
20 July 1962

My Dear Nora,

My thoughts are still wrapped up with Mother and it seems I cannot accept finality. It is all still like some horrible nightmare from which I hope yet to be suddenly released. There is so much to do, and so many clamouring for work, and yet I cannot get sufficiently excited to get to work in the studio. I feel happier outside doing physical occupation and there has been enough sunny weather to draw me out. Time I feel will be the only healer. And more sunshine.

I am afraid I must stop, my eyes can't write any more, so forgive me.

My love to you,

Dad

'The Chalet'
Hunters Hill, Sydney
24 July 1962

Dearest Daddy and Jill,

I had a long session with John Hetherington last week and found him easy to talk to, but what will come out of his article I don't know. Kahn came along too to do a drawing of me while Hetherington did the interview. I felt a bit drawn and quartered after 4 hours of being dissected. John says that he knows nothing about art and I'm inclined to believe him, but he's a nice fellow and we got along well.

I certainly didn't expect Daddy to write, and much appreciate the effort of eyesight and thought. I find too that I'm avoiding trying to paint and turn too to physical occupations.

Many thanks again for your letters,

Nora

'The Chalet'
Hunters Hill, Sydney
Wednesday 8 August 1962

Dearest Daddy and Jill,

Sending-in day for the Society of Artists exhibition and I've been frantically busy trying to get some of my island paintings finished and framed in time … Now that I have my brown mothers and babies ready to meet the world, I'm sure they won't be accepted. A very 'modern' selection committee this year and probably realism will be outed.[33]

David seems delighted with his success in selling Daddy's drawings in the South East.

I'm gradually feeling and bullying myself back into a painting frame of mind and will probably launch out into a different way of painting, having definitely made up my mind that I'm not satisfied with anything I've done. David is taking a risk in wanting to put on a show of mine in Millicent in March. I might suddenly produce a lot of abstracts!

Love to you all from us both,

Nora

'The Chalet'
Hunters Hill, Sydney
Monday 20 August 1962

Dearest Daddy and Jill,

So glad to have Jill's letter full of home news. I went to the opening of the Society of Artists' exhibition on Tuesday. Lloyd Rees had rung to ask if I'd help with the preparation of savouries for the sherry opening … I didn't see much of the show, however enough to see that my three native subjects had all been hung. The general impression of the show, despite it being as Wallace Thornton said in his criticism 'a melange of mediocrity', was that there was much more realism than in the few past years and that it was bright, varied and interesting. No Gallery purchases to give it a boost.

---

33 They were accepted and Nora Heysen exhibited *Miuri, Melanesian Mother* and *Tropical Siesta* in the 1962 Society of Artists Spring Exhibition, which ran from 14–30 August.

Later

At the moment the Sydney art world is madly excited over an exhibition of Ian Fairweather's work—the critics heralding him as Australia's greatest artist, a genius of worldwide standard. People queuing up all night for the privilege of buying a work of his for £400.[34]

I find his great big all-over designs in dull colours repetitive and rather dull, no life or lift or joy—a monsoon or a festival or a self portrait all treated in the same pattern of colours. But, you can't dismiss it as rubbish, for it is extremely well organised and executed, a blend of East and West cultures, and no doubt very intellectual in content if one had the knowledge to fathom the work. The gallery yesterday was jammed with people, even though the show has been on a week, the day was bad and it wasn't the lunch hour.

A very different story at the Society of Artists exhibition, where a handful of people wandered round with even fewer red spots. Fairweather had sold every painting at high prices—hard to work this art world out.

With love to you both,

Nora

> *'The Chalet'*
> *Hunters Hill, Sydney*
> *Tuesday 3 September 1962*

Dearest Daddy and Jill,

I'm making plans towards coming over, probably it will be the 14th of September ... meanwhile, Robert's itinerary has become more and more full and complicated.[35] He is due to go to a conference in Manila in September, back to Australia to give a lecture to the Army in Melbourne and then overseas again to Jakata for another conference, all of which makes things rather strenuous for him. I'm hoping that he can be relieved of at least one trip, as his commitments here are heavier than ever.

We entertained a beautiful Indian woman doctor the other night. I'd rather had been painting her in her glorious rose silk sari than preparing a meal for her.

---

34   The *Ian Fairweather* exhibition at Macquarie Galleries, Sydney, ran from 15–27 August 1962. Reviews were ecstatic: on 15 August *The Sun* published 'The Work of a Master' and *The Sydney Morning Herald* proclaimed 'Fairweather Now Seen as our Greatest Painter'.

35   During this visit, Nora would have accompanied her father to judge children's art entries at the Royal Adelaide Show.

Spring has come in with a rush here and my Japanese magnolia is a lovely elegant picture with a hundred or more flowers in bloom. If only the Bulbuls would respect them.

Love to you both from us,

Nora

'The Chalet'
Hunters Hill, Sydney
Thursday 1 November 1962

Dearest Daddy and Jill,

Two responses so far from the Hetherington article on me, both directed to you, so I must pass them on.[36] A letter from an Oscar Challman saying that he and his wife were so taken with the drawing of me, that he'd like me to accept a poem he wrote in tribute to Daddy. I'll enclose it.

Also a telephone call from a Dame Mary Daly who rang to ask how you were. She wanted you to know that the proceeds from the book *Cyntie* had been remarkably high and had already built a swimming pool for the disabled children. To tell you also how much your illustration was appreciated and how it helped sell the book. [37]

Robert got back safely, well, but tired. In a couple of weeks he's off again to Fiji.

Love from us both,

Nora

Hahndorf, South Australia
3 November 1962

My Dear Nora,

At long last the collection of Australian art has left our shores for London after a great deal of criticism and condemnation.[38] Poor Robert Campbell was completely run down and really looked a wreck. However, we are giving him a holiday! And he's going with the collection, and a stay in London, a valuable experience for him. I wish him good luck. He deserves it.

---

36   John Hetherington, 'I don't Know if I Exist in my own Right', *The Age*, 6 October 1962.

37   Nora is referring to Dame Mary Daly's book, *Cinty and the Laughing Jackasses, and Other Children's Stories* (Melbourne: Herald Gravure Printers, 1961), to which Hans Heysen contributed illustrations. The publication was written to support the Yooralla Hospital School, Melbourne.

38   The 1963 Tate exhibition, *Australian Painting: Colonial, Impressionist, Contemporary*, did not have the contemporary focus the Tate wanted. Numerous artists, including Albert Tucker, objected. On 27 January 1963, London's *Observer* reported that the exhibition came 'trailing clouds of controversy'.

Ursula and Bill are back from England, Ursula looking quite recovered and particularly well.

My love to you dear Nora,

Your Dad

'The Chalet'

Hunters Hill, Sydney

Wednesday 23 November 1962

Dearest Daddy and Jill,

It was indeed good to receive Daddy's long letter ... Much appreciated the letter, as I know what an eye-strain and effort it is, as well as the difficulty in finding time and concentration for letter writing.

I was in at the new Dominion Gallery the other day and the two young men who manage it were asking if there was any possibility of getting some work of yours— they had had many requests for Heysens ... I told them that you were inundated with demands for work and there was little or no chance, but that I'd ask you.

Love to you both and thank you for writing. Robert joins me, he's off on Sunday,

Nora

'The Chalet'

Hunters Hill, Sydney

30 January 1963

Dearest Daddy and Jill,

I'll just scrape through to have all 24 pictures ready for David.[39] How he's going to load them all on is another matter. I expect David towards the end of next week.

I did get into the opening of the Archibald and Wynne, but there was such a crowd of society women there, I didn't take more than a quick look round. I didn't like the winning portrait by Kahn, too theatrical and gimmicky and all that corroded looking paint was repellent[40] ... Looking round I couldn't help but agree with Gleeson that portrait painting is in the doldrums. All the attempts to treat portrait painting in the abstract manner seem to fail dismally, and the old tired academic representation is equally unsatisfactory. Only Dobell seemed to be able to lift portrait painting out of the mediocre rut.

---

39   This is for Nora Heysen's solo exhibition at Millicent in March 1963 and her joint exhibition with Hans Heysen in April 1963.

40   This is Louis Kahn's painting *Patrick White*.

I hope that you've had some relief from the heat and have been able to get on with the Queen's watercolour. Is it a pastoral scene?

Bits about the Tate show of Australian paintings have appeared in our papers rather contradictory reports. Some say it was greeted with a lukewarm reception, others that it was applauded as launching Australian painting abroad. What is the truth? You, no doubt, have the inside story from Campbell.

Love to you both from Robert and me,

Nora

Hahndorf, South Australia
20 February 1963

My Dear Nora,

It was good to hear your clear voice full of vim over the phone and that all was well with David's arrival.

I have delayed sending you the paper cuttings because it had been misplaced and could not find it, but here it is. At the moment, it is being shown in the window of the Government Tourist Department in King William St with two policemen on guard.

Campbell wanted to show it in the Gallery (which has been repainted and re-floored) but our Premier ruled otherwise, for the Tourist Department is his pet. He is to present the picture at the end of the tour (45 minutes) of the Gallery. And I only hope they or the Premier calls me in, for it is to be presented privately![41]

Campbell is back from London but looking very tired and nervous, but I have not yet spoken to him. Jill is asking him and his wife up very soon for lunch so I will probably hear all the news.

By the by—much love from both of us,

especially your Dad

---

41   *White Gums, Summer Afternoon* (1963), for which Heysen was paid a fee of £210, was presented to the Queen during her 1963 Royal Tour. Her visit was part of the Jubilee of Canberra celebrations.

'The Chalet'
Hunters Hill, Sydney
Thursday 26 February 1963

Dearest Daddy and Jill,

Just a short letter to say that I'll be seeing you soon. I've booked on TAA on Monday the 4th March. That will give a couple of days with you before going on to David's, probably on the Thursday to give time to arrange and hang the show.[42]

Thrilled to have the Queen's picture, if only in reproduction. It looks a beauty to have all the feeling of the early work with the simple treatment of the later.

Love to you both and looking forward to Monday,

Nora

'The Chalet'
Hunters Hill, Sydney
24 March 1963

Dearest Daddy and Jill,

I went to see the big Olsen show that all the critics are raving about.[43] Still my opinion of his work is unchanged—an engaging doodler ... No form no draughtsmanship, no intellect, no quality of paint. Almost every painting sold and the prices ranging from £200 to near a £1,000. When Mrs Clune asked me what I thought of the work I told her. She looked at me pityingly and said, but everyone thinks they are marvellous, the finest show held in Australia. The critics are raving about it.

I'll look forward to hearing your opinion of *the* Drysdale we gave the Queen.[44]

Love to you both,

Nora

---

42   The show is *A Special Retrospective Exhibition of the Work by Nora Heysen*, which was held from 10–17 March 1963 in the Masonic Hall, Millicent. Fifty works were shown.

43   This is *Exhibition of Recent Paintings, Gouaches and Drawings by John Olsen* at Clune Galleries.

44   Russell Drysdale's *Man in a Landscape* (1963), portraying an Aboriginal stockman, is part of the royal collection and has never been exhibited in Australia. See Geoffrey Smith, *Russell Drysdale 1912–1981*, Melbourne: National Gallery of Victoria, 1997: 168.

Nora Heysen (1911–2003)
Mother and Child 1960

oil on board; 86.0 x 66.0 cm
Purchased with the assistance of the
Ministry of Arts and donations
Bathurst Regional Art Gallery

Peter Medlin
Sir Hans and Lady Heysen 1961

photograph
Pictorial Collection, B 14450/13
State Library of South Australia

Unknown photographer
*With Love and Good Wishes
from Dad* 1961

photograph
Manuscripts Collection, MS 10041
National Library of Australia

With love & good wishes from Dad. 1961.

Nora Heysen (1911–2003)
James McAuley 1961

oil on canvas; 115.5 x 95.5 cm
University of Tasmania
Fine Art Collection
Photograph by Peter Angus Robinson

Nora Heysen (1911–2003)
Melanesian Mother and Child 1962

oil on masonite; 96.0 x 65.0 cm
Private collection

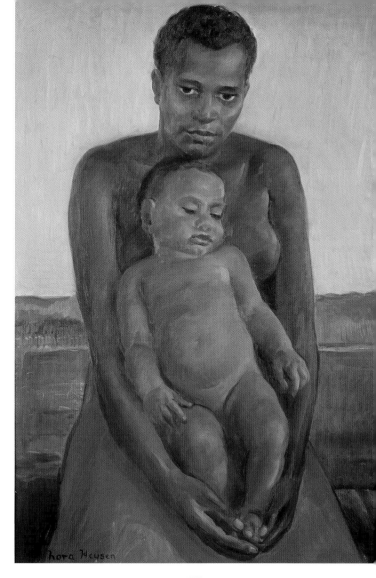

below
Nora Heysen (1911–2003)
Mary c.1961

charcoal on paper; 41.0 x 25.5 cm
Private collection
Photograph by Michael Kluvanek

below right
Nora Heysen (1911–2003)
Butete, 18 January 1962

watercolour and ink on paper
Manuscripts Collection, MS 10041
National Library of Australia

plate 4

Unknown photographer
Hans and Nora Heysen Judging Children's Art at the Royal Adelaide Show 1962

photograph
Manuscripts Collection, MS 10041
National Library of Australia

Unknown photographer
An Exhibition of Nora Heysen's Work, Millicent, South Australia 1963

photograph
Manuscripts Collection, MS 10041
National Library of Australia

Unknown photographer
Hans Heysen Presenting White Gums, Summer Afternoon *to HRH Queen Elizabeth II and HRH the Duke of Edinburgh* 1963

Manuscripts Collection, MS 5073
National Library of Australia

'The Chalet'
Hunters Hill, Sydney
Easter Sunday 1963

Dearest Daddy and Jill,

I hope that Daddy has been able to get some painting done. A batch of photographs has arrived from David including the extra nice one of the presentation of *the* picture with Daddy and the Queen and Duke. Excellent of the Queen who really looks animated and interested (for once) and of the Duke too.

With them came the views of my show ... I hear from David that your show at the Hamilton Gallery was a great success, and the few that were for sale all sold, and more wanted.[45]

I was glad to know that the Gallery there bought my *Dedication* so that eventually it found its right home in a country Gallery. An odd letter from old George saying that it is surprising that I can sell over a £1,000 at this exhibition while he has no demand at all for my work.[46] He concludes by asking, begging for two more rose pictures.

With love to you both and hoping all is well,

Nora

'The Chalet'
Hunters Hill, Sydney
5 May 1963

Dearest Daddy and Jill,

I've been re-reading Pissarro's letters to his son and marvel to read that he usually had four or five canvases going at once. I'm finding those letters more interesting now than when I first read them, perhaps it is because Pissarro and his contemporaries' attitudes towards painting is so refreshingly different from what it is today. Their delight in trying to capture the natural beauties of native fields and skies and simple peasants working. The petty jealousies among the artists, the blindness and greed of art dealers and the interminable battle for enough money to be able to paint without worrying where the next penny is coming from, these things are the same. Having met Lucien and his wife and daughter Orovida make those letters all the more interesting. What a grand old man he was. As an artist much superior to his son Lucien.

---

45   The joint *Exhibition of Paintings and Drawings by Sir Hans Heysen and Nora Heysen* was held at Hamilton Art
      Gallery in April 1963. Hans Heysen showed 18 works, Nora 12.

46   George Holman was antique dealer in Pirie Street, Adelaide,

I could wish I'd been there for the picnic to Maslin Beach with Marcel Marceau—that man intrigued me.

Love to you both from us two,

Nora

'The Chalet'
Hunters Hill, Sydney
Tuesday 4 June 1963

Dearest Daddy and Jill,

This last week end has been hectic. A party at John Brackenreg's Gallery in honour of Ray Crooke and his successful show in Brisbane. He sold £5,000 on the opening day.[47] John who has just returned from Brisbane and seen the show was very impressed, thought it the best one-man show he'd seen. Most of the artists were there quite a number of them just back from Margaret Preston's funeral.[48] Lloyd Rees, Dundas and Adrian Feint were asking of news and wished to be remembered.

This year there were some 350 entries for the Hunters Hill show, more than ever. Having resigned from the Art Council I was surprised to be asked to adjudicate.

I'm afraid this is a very disjointed letter but with it goes my love to you both,

Nora

'The Chalet'
Hunters Hill, Sydney
22 July 1963

Dearest Daddy and Jill,

This will be just a short letter to keep a promise I made to Mr Evatt of the Dominion Gallery. He just rang to ask me if I would ask my father to make a special concession, and let him have a couple of watercolours for a show he's putting on next month depicting the story of landscape painting in Australia. A very important show he says concentrating on Hans Heysen (he hopes), Conder, Tom Roberts, Streeton, McCubbin etc. He would, of course, like one or two for sale and then could borrow others from private collections. Anyway I said that I'd ask. I've told him that you were inundated with requests for work, and would most likely not

47   Ray Crooke portrayed islanders off the coast of Australia, including on Thursday Island. Paintings for this exhibition were drawn from Aboriginal subjects at Yorkeys Knob, near Cairns, Queensland. See Rosemary Dobson, Focus on Ray Crooke, St Lucia, Queensland, University of Queensland Press, 1971: 34.

48   Margaret Preston died on 28 May 1963.

want to be bothered. The Gallery he has is a very attractive one and pictures look well there. One of the new galleries in Castlereagh St.

Love to you both hoping all is well,

Nora

> 'The Chalet'
> Hunters Hill, Sydney
> 9 September 1963

Dearest Daddy and Jill,

It was nice to have your telephone call and actually hear your voices—good to hear that Daddy is feeling a little better.

I actually got into the city last Friday, and I saw the landscape exhibition at the Dominion Gallery where Daddy's *Quarry* is showing.[49] It's well hung, centre of a wall, with Roberts and Conder flanking it and it looks fine ... The show has been a great success and is to be extended for another week. Evatt hopes to sell *The Quarry* and he's had many enquiries.

Much love to you both,

Nora

> 'The Chalet'
> Hunters Hill, Sydney
> 8 October 1963

Dearest Daddy and Jill,

Everyone is talking about the picture of Daddy on his 86th birthday that appeared in this morning's *Herald*. Dr Reid has just sent over his copy thinking that I'd like an extra one, so I'll include it with this letter so you can have the Sydney version. Evidently the interviewer was out to provoke Daddy into making some bitter comment on the moderns, and didn't succeed.

Robert came back from Rio de Janeiro very tired and with one bung eye. Anyway it has at last cleared up and he's getting ready to take off again on the 20th for Pakistan, London and America—this time he'll be giving lectures as well as attending conferences, so he's busy writing papers. I've been trying to paint some Spring flowers.

The Society of Artists show has come and gone. A very small select show held at David Jones Gallery, it was supposed to be a very high standard to put the

---

49   Nora had been recovering from major surgery.

Society back into the limelight.[50] The critics blasted it, very few sales and rather poor attendances, definitely very disappointing from all points of view. I think, on the strength of this, Lloyd Rees will suggest the close of the Society. He hasn't been very happy about being President of a dying society. Only a man like Ure Smith could have held it together. Lloyd Rees hasn't the time nor the social contacts needed. Anyway there no longer seems the need for Societies these days. So many Galleries, so many one-man shows. The youngsters can arrive overnight with a successful show.

Love to you both,

Nora

'The Chalet'
Hunters Hill, Sydney
13 November 1963

Dearest Daddy and Jill,

Busy painting roses ... I've been painting all day and all night trying to get something of their illusive quality. This obsession to paint those roses. If I could just be content to look at them, what joy they'd bring.

Good news came through at last on Thursday. Robert was elected to the Chair of Tropical Medicine and is now Professor.[51] The title he should have had some six years ago, but to get it because of some politics between the University and the State, the position Robert held had to be reopened and applied for.

I include a cutting, Wallace Thornton's criticism of the exhibition of Australian painting going to London. You'll no doubt be seeing the show in the Adelaide Gallery soon. I saw it here last week and haven't recovered yet from the chaotic impression left by all those abstracts.

I'm determined to get this letter away tonight so must stop.

Love to you both,

Nora

---

50 The 'Foreword' to the 1963 Exhibition Catalogue reads: 'Because of a somewhat smaller wall area, the Society has deemed it advisable to make this exhibition a closed one except for a small group of invited artists'.

51 See Yvonne Cossart, 'Black, Robert Hughes (1917–1988)', *Australian Dictionary of Biography*, vol.17, Melbourne University Press: 107–108.

'The Chalet'
Hunters Hill, Sydney
Tuesday 19 November 1963

Dearest Daddy and Jill,

Good to have all the home news—Daddy in the studio again.

I don't blame you not being able to keep up with Robert's activities. I'm finding it difficult enough trying to work out mail to catch him in so many different places. He's on his way back through America now.

With love to you both,

Nora

'The Chalet'
Hunters Hill, Sydney
17 January 1964

Dearest Daddy and Jill,

Daddy's letter arrived right on the day making it feel like a real birthday … Thank you Daddy for the cheque. Something for the house and very timely as our thoughts have a fixation on the house at the moment. We are busy painting the halls and have been sweating at it solidly through the heat. The colour scheme for the walls is soft pale grey, the doors the dark grey with notes of black on the stairways and the wrought iron chandelier. It looks cool and austere and makes a very nice setting for my collection of Heysen drawings. Wish that you could see how well they look in their new fresh setting—much satisfaction for all the hard slogging.

Love to you both.

From Robert and me,

Nora

'The Chalet'
Hunters Hill, Sydney
5 May 1964

Dearest Daddy and Jill,

You must be feeling relieved that the television ordeal is all over. When is the screening date? I hope it is shown over here.

Most of the Adelaide Festival events have come on to Sydney. The exhibition of American paintings is on at the Gallery and on second viewing doesn't improve at all.[52] Despite the praise the critics gave it, I think there are only half a

---

52   The touring exhibition *Contemporary American Painting: A Selection from the James A. Michener Foundation Collection* from the Allentown Art Museum, Pennsylvania, was shown in all state galleries in 1964.

dozen pictures in the whole show worth anything at all. Most of it is utter nonsense and not worthy to be shown in any art gallery.

I find that I can only get the red and blue Pentel pens over here. Robert has an invitation to go to Geneva in October, also there is a trip to Pakistan in the offing.

Love to you both and thank you for a letter,

Nora

'The Chalet'
Hunters Hill, Sydney
Monday 24 May 1964

Dearest Daddy and Jill,

I was talking to John Brackenreg the other day and he said to tell you that he sold a flower piece of Daddy's for 800gs. Cash. Mixed flowers in a bowl with yellow gloves on the table. He said you'd painted it for Pavlova.

Glad to hear that your luncheon party for the Governor and his lady went off so well and that you found them genuine friendly folk and easy to entertain.

I'm hoping that Daddy's been able to start on the oil for the Commonwealth Bank. I know all too well the reluctance to start on a painting without the guarantee of free days ahead. In the end the only thing is take the plunge and ignore all interruptions. Must back and have another go at those persimmons.

Thanks again for thinking of sending over that box—the scent of those apples still lingers.

Love to you both from us two,

Nora

'The Chalet'
Hunters Hill, Sydney
8 July 1964

Dearest Daddy and Jill,

It has been cold too but the days are bright and sunny and I've been painting out on the veranda. The next occasion here is the opening of Bill Dobell's retrospective show. Two big receptions are to be given at the Gallery in his honour and Missingham is working day and night to make the show a really big thing. I'll have to make an effort and get into full evening regalia to drink champagne with the Governor at the formal reception. Darling of the ABC is opening the exhibition.

Love to you both,

Nora

'The Chalet'
Hunters Hill, Sydney
5 August 1964

Dearest Daddy and Jill,

A long letter from Jill bursting with activities past, present and to come …
I've just been bogged down with the painting and repairing business we've
undertaken, and except for the two receptions given at the Gallery in honour of
Dobell, I haven't been out.

The first, a preview exclusively for Dobell's friends, patrons and models,
was a really enjoyable affair, a real reunion of the old days in Sydney when Dobell
had his studio in Kings Cross. The second, a big glittering social affair with a
thousand or more filling the whole Art Gallery. Poor Dobell was suffering, as the
whole evening he had to stand and receive a long queue of people who wanted to
boast that they'd met and touched the great man.

I had a wild scramble getting myself there—first I had to borrow clothes
here there and everywhere—even made the local hairdresser and had my hair done
in a glamorous coiffure on top with the Spanish comb. This was to set off the old
fur coat I borrowed from Mrs Reid next door, a relic of her nursing days in Canada.
I felt Jill's wondering eyes on me as I took off for the ferry reeking of turpentine
instead of French perfume.

The Dobell show itself is magnificent and places him as a fine artist and a
very versatile one—a hundred portraits alone all hung together gives one an idea of
his range and depth. I had not realised that his output was so big or varied. I wish
that this show was going on to Adelaide so that you could see it. The expense as well
as the two years that have gone into assembling it would suggest it should be seen in
all states, but Missingham says no categorically. I'll post the catalogue to you.[53]

Someone to whom I was speaking at the reception said: 'Why hasn't an
exhibition of this sort been held of your Father's work?' Why indeed. Jill suggests
there could be something arranged for the next Adelaide Festival with a publication
of the works exhibited. I do hope it comes off. With David Dridan's enthusiasm
behind it I'm hopeful.

---

53   The Art Gallery of New South Wales' exhibition, *William Dobell: Paintings from 1926 to 1964*, ran from 15 July
to 30 August 1964. It prompted wider discussion, such as Elwyn Lynn's 'Portraiture in Australia, *The Bulletin*,
22 August 1964: 40–41.

I'm sorry to hear that Dr Schneider couldn't help remove the blurriness from Daddy's sight. It must be a deterrent to trying to start on the big oil.

Thanks for your long letter,

Love Nora

'The Chalet'
Hunters Hill, Sydney
25 August 1964

Dearest Daddy, David and Lyly,

Still very busy with the painting project—a never ending job and this takes in only the back and front verandas, the back is almost finished. I ultimately decided on a pinky tone for door and windows on the back veranda, it's a pleasant change from the all grey and white. Robert isn't very keen, says that he supposes he'll get used to it in time. The front is to remain all white, with dark grey shutters and a blue front door.

I'm now a member of the executive council for the Society of Artists, and there have been long meetings at Lloyd Rees' home trying to work out ways and means to revive the Society. John Brackenreg ... is keen to get the Society on its feet again. Lloyd Rees has agreed to continue as President for another year, so we'll see what happens.

I was very interested to read in David's letter about the proposed retrospective show of Daddy's for the next Adelaide Festival ... The Dobell show has been a tremendous success. I was in again today to see it and had to fight my way in and the Gallery was teeming with people and I had to queue up to see the pictures. For the whole six weeks, it's been the same. It is indeed a fine show and I think has done a lot to re-establish the worth of fine draughtsmanship and the realistic school of painting.

Love to you all from us both. Robert is well but overworked and tired. He leaves for New Guinea on 7th September.

Nora

'The Chalet'
Hunters Hill, Sydney
Sunday 11 October 1964

Dearest Daddy and Jill,

I have just returned from lunching with Sir James to an empty home. Even the cats seem subdued, and it's a very quiet Sunday afternoon.

Robert's plane left at noon a day earlier than he'd expected to take off so I had to go to the lunch party without him. Jim was in good form. He was very interested indeed to hear of the retrospective exhibition. Freda not so good, she has gone practically blind with cataracts. Adrian Feint was also there having just returned from a successful exhibition in Brisbane, at least successful on the face of it, for after paying off the 33 per cent commission, he made £1,000. Out of that, he still has his framing bill, transport and taxes etc, so for a year's work it's not so much.[54]

It was wonderful to have those two weeks at home,

Nora

> 'The Chalet'
> Hunters Hill, Sydney
> 29 October 1964

Dearest Daddy,

It was certainly a thrill to see your *Lively Arts* program … The charcoal drawings came out splendidly and there were some excellent portrait close-ups of you. The introduction was nice, I couldn't place all the shots amongst the gums— the trees looked so close together, like a mystic morn scene. I couldn't recognise my own voice at all and didn't feel exactly complimented when the neighbours instantly knew it was me talking, yet didn't recognise my self portrait. The drawing of David came out well and the still life. Your speaking voice registered well and very true I thought. The few hesitations and your searching for words were not obvious, and didn't detract.

Saturday

I shall add a few words about the opening of the Society of Artists before posting. A very successful opening—it was decided to dispense with opening speeches and instead we had Flamenco dancing and ballet with supper and sherry served.

Lots of the artists were talking about your *Lively Arts* program and saying what a treat it was and how much they enjoyed it. One and all were impressed with the charcoal drawings and several remarked on the beautiful close-ups of you. The general impression was that you seemed so relaxed and had no trouble in talking at all, so there you are.

---

54   Adrian Feint's exhibition was at Johnstone Gallery, Brisbane, from 15–30 September 1964.

Only one painting sold in the Society show up to date, and that was one of Adrian's. I put in two flower paintings and was surprised to see them hung.[55]

With love to you and Robyn and Lyly and David,

Nora

Hahndorf, South Australia
20 December 1964

My Dear Nora,

Your father is growing old, there's no doubt about it. It's becoming more and more difficult and an effort to reach the studio without a stick.

The picture market has never been as good as it is at present, and George is constantly asking for more and more. Unfortunately I cannot keep pace, as I do not go out sketching and have to rely on completing older work. Also there's a growing demand for the older sketches I did in Italy, Scotland and England and with David's framing they come up well.

Just got a letter from Ballarat asking for a typical Heysen oil for the new gallery at Shepparton—£500 by February. Can I do it, I doubt it.

Your Dad

'The Chalet'
Hunters Hill, Sydney
9 March 1965

Dearest Daddy and Jill,

Not much news from this quarter. Robert spent a few days down Jervis Bay way looking at Aboriginal settlements. He has now been selected to be one of a board of men who have been formed to make a study and assessment of the housing conditions etc. of the Aboriginals. He has also been made a full Colonel in the Army as their consultant in Tropical Medicine. He's off to Melbourne this week to lecture to the Army. In April over Easter he's off again to Wreck Bay and I hope to go also and get some new subject matter. I've never had a chance of drawing Aboriginals and look forward to the chance opportunity.

Freda Nesbitt died suddenly of a heart attack last week. Poor Jim, he'll miss her sadly.

John Brackenreg and Colsey have opened their new Gallery with a highly successful show of Godfrey Miller's work. We went to the pre-preview. A very nice

---

55   Nora Heysen's two exhibits in the Society of Arts annual exhibition (30 October to 13 November 1964) were *A Touch of Spring* and *A Gift of Red Roses.*

but small Gallery off William Street. I wonder how many more Galleries this city
can sustain?

     Love to you both from us,
     Nora

'The Chalet'
Hunters Hill, Sydney
25 March 1965

     Dearest Daddy and Jill,
     The AGA conversion to oil and a Wonder-heat in the dining room are
achievements which are going to save a lot of labour and dirt.[56] Daddy will be
relieved of that endless carting of wood and the stoking of the AGA. No longer can
it be held responsible for late meals and collapsed dishes!

     Well, the Hunters Hill exhibition is on again and the big fight is on
between the Town Council and the Art Council. The Town Council objected strongly
to our selection and judging and the Lord Mayor on the opening night made it very
clear that the residents of Hunters Hill were not going to stand for that sort of
thing—that sort of thing being abstract art. The rate payers were not going to see
their money fostering abortions and having them hung on the walls of their Town
Hall. The Art Council stands by the selections, and judges are all seething mad and
ready to resign … Thankless job, this judging business, two whole days we sweated
over it.

     Love to you both from us,
     Nora

'The Chalet'
Hunters Hill, Sydney
Tuesday 1 June 1965

     Dearest Daddy and Jill,
     Many thanks for your long letter and cuttings Jill. Wonderful light for
painting but I don't seem to be able to get to it. I've started a big portrait of a man,
Charles Rowley, who was principal of the School of Pacific Administration and is
now in charge of a big Aboriginal scheme—a willing subject but, as usual, with very
little time to sit, so progress is slow.

---

56   The AGA is the kitchen stove at 'The Cedars'.

This is leading to your query, when can I come over again and now I can see a possibility. That's the 4th of July. I'll bring my paints and might have a go at painting a portrait of Jill!

Love from us both to you both,

Nora

'The Chalet'
Hunters Hill, Sydney
5 September 1965

Dearest Daddy and Jill,

I seem to have been extremely busy with very little to show for it. Certainly no letters written. The highlight of this last week has been the Opera. I went to *The Elixir of Love* and was delighted with it. Harwood and Pavarotti were singing the leading roles and it would be difficult to imagine more suitable voices for the parts Then on Thursday I suddenly realised that Joan Sutherland was singing Lucia in a matinee performance and rushed in on the chance of getting a seat. My lucky day and an experience I'll never forget. She was magnificent.

I've been busy painting Spring flowers while I'm waiting for my sitters. I've got as far as deciding on clothes and colour scheme for the portrait of Persia Porter and now wait for her to find the time to give me.[57]

We have just come back from lunching with Jim McGregor. He has just returned from his trip abroad and looks well, though considerably older. The first Sunday luncheon party since Freda's death, so everyone was a bit subdued thinking of other occasions and missing the familiar figure. Jim was asking after you both and sends his love. Also Adrian was there looking rather frail.

Robert is off to New Guinea next week for a couple or more weeks and is busy preparing his papers for the various meetings he has to participate in. I'm hoping the trip will provide a break as well, as he's in real need of a tonic.

With love to you both and hoping all is well and the 'sap rising'. Robert sends his love too,

Nora

---

57   Persia Porter, later Lady Galleghan, was Chair of the Red Cross.

'The Chalet'
Hunters Hill, Sydney
13 October 1965

Dearest Daddy and Jill,

Thank you for both your letters Jill, the latest with the Madame Schuurman cuttings made record time in arriving in less than 24 hours. Since the Schuurmans have been in Sydney for the last couple of years this sudden desire to renew acquaintanceship with me, when on a brief trip to Adelaide, seems odd.[58] And as for the long friendship which culminated in her sitting for the Archibald portrait! Well, I hadn't met the woman until I painted her, and I haven't seen her since. There was never any ill feeling between us, just lack of any interest to continue relationships. However I was quite interested to see that she still looks like her portrait. Incredible to realise that 35 years have passed since then.

Robert returned from New Guinea on Sunday—he caught me in the middle of trying to clean up after an orgy of painting ... Now I'm frantically busy trying to restore order, and get back to some sort of routine before Robert takes off again next Monday for Ceylon. Before then, all the clothes have to be washed and ironed. Also I'm trying to finish the portrait of Charles Rowley and have a couple of sittings to cope with this week. Twenty-four hours in a day are not near enough.

I did manage to get my portrait of Persia Porter in for the competition.[59] With dozens of other women I arrived in a taxi with my wet canvas a few minutes before closing time ... I nearly killed my poor sitter and myself trying to get the portrait completed. What a difficult business this portrait painting is—no wonder that so few good portraits are painted.

Interested to hear that Daddy had bought an abstract and look forward to seeing it.

Robert sends his love with mine to you both,

Nora

---

58   See 'Keen to Renew Friendship', *The Advertiser*, 5 October 1965. Tom Schuurman was in Canberra as Ambassador of the Netherlands from 1964 to 1966.

59   The competition was the Portia Geach Memorial Award, open only to women artists, for the best portrait painted from life of a man or woman distinguished in arts, letters or science, or a self portrait.

'The Chalet'
Hunters Hill, Sydney
11 November 1965

Dearest Daddy and Jill,

Well the Portia Geach has been awarded. As you will have heard it went to Jean Appleton's *Self Portrait*. Personally I think that it should have gone to Jackie Hick who had a very strong and convincing *Self Portrait* competing and which to me was outstanding. The pose in the winner was unfortunate, and the figure had little relation to the background. A realistic figure with a few modern motifs strewn round to give it a contemporary look. I went to the cocktail party opening with Persia Porter, my subject, and was relieved to find my picture hanging. Only a third of the 189 exhibits were hung. But all told, it was a very good show and pretty high standard. I was surprised that there are so many women portrait painters. A more interesting show than the Archibald. I didn't get on the main wall, which was entirely given over the 'forward looking' artists, but was well placed amongst the conservatists.

Do you remember the woman who was up to do a tape recording of Daddy way back in 1960? She was doing a series of the artists for the Commonwealth Archives. Well she caught up with me six years and 200 artists later last week, and I submitted to the ordeal. It was a couple of hours before she got what she wanted. A shocking business trying to formulate sentences that made sense when faced with a microphone.[60] Anyway she remembered her visit to Hahndorf and was impressed, talked glowingly of Daddy. She thought how interesting to have Daddy at the head of the tapes, and me at the end!

Robert arrived back from Ceylon last Saturday, and left for Darwin the following Friday.

My love to you both and thank you for news,

Nora

---

60   Hazel de Berg's interviews of about 250 artists are held by the National Library of Australia. Daniel Thomas and Hal Missingham advised on the selection of artists. See Graeme Powell, 'De Berg, Hazel Estelle (1913–1984)', *Australian Dictionary of Biography*, vol.17, Melbourne University Press: 310–311.

'The Chalet'
Hunters Hill, Sydney
26 December 1965

Dearest Daddy, Lyly and David,

And so another Christmas has come and gone and now at last there is a little breathing space to collect one's thoughts.

Now I have my portrait to get into the Archibald, and Robert to get off to Vietnam and then perhaps there will be some peace … Robert is off again some place in February, but March looks clear and I definitely will be over.

Blessings and love,

From Robert and me to all at home

'The Chalet'
Hunters Hill, Sydney
13 January 1966

Dearest Daddy,

Your birthday 'Card' has just arrived—I'm sure no one has ever received such a superb 'Card'. It is indeed a beautiful drawing and I'm proud and happy to have it and to add one more treasure to my Heysen collection.

Madame Elink Schuurman and her husband called to see me on Sunday morning. It was quite interesting seeing them again after 30 years. Madame and I looked each other up and down both secretly thinking 'Heavens I hope I don't look as old as that'. She still has her vivaciousness and her charming insincerity, they seemed taken with the old home and took a lot of photographs.

I've heard from Robert as far as Bangkok. He should be in Saigon now and from there goes to a conference in Pakistan before returning on the 22nd—I've been hoping that peace would be declared before he had to go, but now it seems that any agreement is further off than ever.[61]

With a great warm thank you for that very fine drawing and hoping that all is well with you,

Nora

---

61   Robert's visit to Saigon was related to Australia's involvement in the Vietnam War. By late January 1966, Harold Holt became Prime Minister of Australia and, by March, he had increased troop numbers going to Vietnam, aided by the introduction of conscription.

'The Chalet'
Hunters Hill, Sydney
25 January 1966

Dearest Daddy and Lyly or Robin,

It's good to hear that the book is near its launching and that you are pleased with the reproductions.[62] I suppose David is busy now getting the pictures in order for the exhibition.

I'll include the Archibald and Wynne prize entries and criticisms with this. I went along to the private view and was very disappointed not to find my own portrait hanging. For the first time I was turned out. Poor Charles Rowley was very upset too. On the whole I thought that the work for landscape and portraiture was a higher standard this year, and I agreed with both selections for prizes. Far less experimental abstracts amongst the portraits which seemed to hint at a return to straight realism. This didn't hold for the landscapes.

More anon as I must be off to the kitchen.

Much love,

Nora

'The Chalet'
Hunters Hill, Sydney
Tuesday 28 March 1966

Dearest Daddy and David,

I have certainly come down with a bump, and it's now back to chores with a vengeance with three weeks accumulation to catch up on.

I look back on those three weeks with all their events and memories and that wonderful freedom from responsibility of meals and dishes and domestic chores to give me time and mind to enjoy it all. A wonderful holiday indeed with the highlights the opening of Daddy's exhibition and the visit of Brenton Langbein and his group of musicians.[63] Both unique occasions to enrich the years, and wonderful to look back on. Now when I take out my pictures of home there will be the memory of the house filled with music and the sight of those lovely violins lying on the dining room table. What an exciting afternoon it was and what luck to be there and not miss it.

---

62   See David Dridan, *The Art of Hans Heysen*, Adelaide, Rigby, 1966.

63   *Hans Heysen Retrospective Exhibition, 1901–1965* was held during the 1966 Adelaide Festival of Arts at John Martin's Art Gallery, 9–30 March 1966. Brenton Langbein (1928–1983) was an Adelaide-born violinist and conductor who became Concertmaster of Collegium Musicum Zurich and, in 1983, received the Canton of Zurich Award of Honour.

We enjoyed the mushrooms I brought back, also the few odd apples. And to close, my special love to you Daddy and a very big thank you for those three weeks

Love to all,

Nora

> *'The Chalet'*
> *Hunters Hill, Sydney*
> *Tuesday 10 May 1966*

Dearest Daddy, Lyly and David,

I went into the private view of the Lloyd Rees show at the Macquarie Galleries in their new quarters at the corner of Clarence and King St. A much more spacious Gallery than their old one in Bligh Street, but after 45 years it is strange to find them in a new place. Lloyd Rees was showing over 50 carbon and wash drawings —very pleasant and free and subtle landscape drawings with washes of delicate colour. A different approach for Rees, but basically the same reliance on old conventions.

We send our love to you all,

Nora

> *'The Chalet'*
> *Hunters Hill, Sydney*
> *Thursday 26 May 1966*

Dearest Daddy, Lyly and David,

Your last letter told me of Robert's visit and I was pleased to hear that he'd been able to get up to see you all. I've been plying him for every detail, especially about Daddy's health and the shingles.

Robert was so glad to see you all again said that nobody had changed at all and he said that Daddy knew who he was even after all those years. I know that Freya buttered his scone, that you all sat round a fire in the living room, that he met Dr Lawson and liked him and that Daddy was cheerful and bright.

Love to you all, a big hope that all is well.

Nora

'The Chalet'
Hunters Hill, Sydney
10 July 1966

Dearest Daddy, Lyly and David,

I've just been in to the opening of the Portia Geach Memorial prize exhibition. I did not know that this prize was to be a yearly event until I received an invitation to the opening. I felt sour about this as I should have liked to have had an entry, and also felt strongly that artists who contributed last year should have received notice or that the entry date should have been publicised. So I went along to drink the cocktails and to complain, both of which I did to the utmost of my capacity, but I don't think my complaints were really necessary, as it was all too obvious that I was only one of many who hadn't heard that the competition was going to be held. There was no portrait worthy of the $1000 prize. Poor show all round. One cannot help but feel that because this is a prize exclusively for women, it is not given importance. I had a few words to say to the Manager of the Trust and their publicity man. With a few whiskeys under my belt I let them have it. I'm not an aggressive feminist, but I can be roused!

With much love to you all three,
Nora

'The Chalet'
Hunters Hill, Sydney
8 August 1966

Dearest Daddy, Lyly and David,

So glad to have Lyly's letter from Derrymore. I only pray that the sun has come out to warm and cheer your stay and tempt Daddy out with his sketchbook!

I went along to see John Brackenreg's $100 show at *Art Lovers* and was pleased to see red stickers on my two little flower pieces. Saw John for a brief chat, he'd just come back from Thea Proctor's funeral and he was looking fairly well and complaining about putting on weight.

It was sad to hear of Thea Proctor's death, only a week previously I'd met her in at Parker's looking well and bright. She also wanted to be remembered to Daddy and was talking about her stay in Hahndorf.

Love from us both to you all,
Nora

'The Chalet'
Hunters Hill, Sydney
Tuesday 6 September 1966

Dearest Daddy, Lyly and David,

Did you hear that Terry Clune's Gallery had been burnt out? I missed the news here and when I took my guest along to see an exhibition there was staggered to find it in ruins.[64]

I only hope you got the cheque out of McDonnell or he'll be using this fire as an excuse to delay payment further.

I'm hoping all is well at home.

Much love to you all,

Nora

'The Chalet'
Hunters Hill, Sydney
Monday 28 November 1966

Dearest Daddy David and Lyly,

Lyly's telephone call was the last contact and what good news to make the wires sing. I can imagine David's excitement at being present at the sale and hearing the bidding going over the thousands. It's going to stimulate the Heysen market even further … Only wish that the law in France, where the artist gets a share in any sale, applied here.

Robert arrived home unexpectedly on Thursday last, a couple days earlier than I'd expected … Those couple of weeks in America he took as part of his leave, so that only leaves him ten days at Christmas time. I foresee a very quiet Christmas at 'The Chalet' this year as I too will be working flat out till then trying to get a portrait commission through. This is a job I've just been given to paint Professor Walsh, director of the Blood Bank here, and they want a three-quarter length portrait finished before Christmas. Also two pencil portrait commissions have come along, also to be done before then. Must get ready for a sitting. Hoping all's well at home.

Love from Robert and me to you all,

Nora

---

64   Under Martin Sharp's inspiration, the disused Clune Galleries became the Yellow House.

'The Chalet'
Hunters Hill, Sydney
10 May 1967

Dearest Daddy Lyly and David,

It's good to hear that Daddy is looking so well and I only hope that he is feeling as well as everyone is saying that he looks.

Very interested to hear that David has launched into 'printing' himself. Splendid idea and I should think that you couldn't go wrong financially—which one of Daddy's have you selected to print? ... I haven't seen John Brackenreg for some time but when I do I'll get his reaction. Anyway he hasn't the copyright on getting Heysens printed.

Robert got safely home from Geneva last Thursday ... I've been horribly busy painting this old lady. She lives in St Mark's Cottage at Darling Point and I've been lugging my paints and gear out there every fine day—three hours and more travelling time each day to get three hours painting, if I'm lucky. Very wearing, and how a car would help. The only thing that keeps me going is the challenge of a well nigh impossible subject. She's a wonderful old lady for 101 and can still walk a bit and feed herself, but that's about all. She just sits in an old wicker chair and dozes off to sleep, collapsed in a heap of pink woollies with an old straw hat with flowers round the brim perched on her head. Out on the veranda, as the inside is dark and dingy in the extreme. So I have sunlight to contend with ... By the time I get home in the evenings I've had it.

Love from us both to you all,
Nora

'The Chalet'
Hunters Hill, Sydney
Wednesday 24 May 1967

Dearest Daddy, Lyly and David,

It will be good to see a new Heysen print on the market. I remember *The Road* in the retrospective show. I think John Brackenreg would be the best agent you could have and you'll need a distributing agent here to extend sales and he has a big clientele.

Glad too to hear that the Old Academy building is at last having a face lift with plans for displaying prints and giving space for exhibitions. The idea to christen the new rooms with a show of Daddy's working drawings sounds fine and with Walter's enthusiastic help should go forward without too much work falling on you.[65] And while on the subject, tell Wally that it won't be possible for me to have a Festival show with him this time. I would rather wait until later when I could perhaps have a combined selling and retrospective show similar to the one you put on in Millicent. It's going to take all my time to get this show with Dridan over, and next year I hope to get in that trip abroad, and if I do get away it will have to be in March or April to fit in with Robert's plans.

Hoping you are all safely back and better for the break.

Love to you all,

Nora

'The Chalet'
Hunters Hill, Sydney
Wednesday 7 June 1967

Dearest Daddy Lyly and David,

I've been busy taking advantage of dull days and getting a bit of framing done. Back and forth to Parkers lugging frames and not over happy with what is offering and less happy about the rising prices. Yesterday when in at Parkers they were all very excited about the big prices at the auction of Dr Norman Paul's collection. I'll jot down a few that I remember, but no doubt you will have heard about the sale. Four of Daddy's came up—a Northern oil *Oratunga* $5,000; *Summer* W.C. $1,000; *Fruit and Flowers* $2,500; *Morning Light* W.C. $850.

Also one of my still lifes, the only work of mine, went for $500 which was far higher than anything my work has ever fetched.

I wonder has the new Director for your Adelaide Gallery been decided on and if John Baily got the position?[66] It appears that Brisbane too is gaining through the process of getting a new Gallery Director. I'll include a couple of

---

65   Walter Wotze, the Director of the Hahndorf Gallery, lobbied successfully for the restoration of the Hahndorf Academy. The opening in October 1967 was marked by an exhibition of Hans Heysen's work, *Historic Hahndorf.*

66   John Baily's appointment as Director was announced on 13 May 1967 and he remained in the position until 1975. An unsuccessful appeal against the appointment was lodged on the grounds that Baily, an artist and a school inspector of art, did not have a museum background. See 'What is Happening in Brisbane?', *The Australian,* 27 May 1967; 'Vigor of New Art Director ', *The Advertiser,* 20 May 1967.

cuttings. I haven't heard yet if Wieneke's appointment is final.[67] Trouble on trouble and now they've lost their Picasso![68]

We've been hearing a lot about your new premier—St Peters must feel proud of turning out such an accomplished young man.[69]

Love from us both to you all,

Nora

'The Chalet'
Hunters Hill, Sydney
June 1967

Dearest Daddy, Lyly and David,

I was very glad to have news of Daddy's progress and hope complete recovery comes quickly.

I did at last hear from David Dridan and it appears that my show opens on the 20th August, a month earlier than I'd thought, so it's going to take me all my time to get the work together and over by then.

It's a surprise to hear that Colin Thiele's book has gone so far and is in reading form already and good to hear that you think so highly of it. When is the book expected to be out? I hope that Daddy is enjoying looking back with another's eyes and sensibilities.

Over here the battle over the Power Bequest is raging and poor Bernard Smith, who as you know has been appointed Director of the new-found Faculty of Art at The Sydney University, is having a rough time.[70] You didn't say who had got the directorship of the Adelaide Gallery?

I must take advantage of a glimmer of light and finish a flower piece.

Love to you all and it won't be long before I'll be seeing you all I hope,

Nora

---

67   James Wieneke's appointment, finally announced on 21 June 1967, provoked controversy, including the resignation of two Trustees. Some thought him unqualified and he was appointed on the condition that he sell Moreton Galleries and his art collection. See 'Mr Wieneke Tells all about the Art of Patience', *The Australian*, 24 June 1967.

68   The missing Pablo Picasso, *La belle Hollandaise* (1905), was part of the larger unrest at Queensland Art Gallery, where significant paintings were being sold to pay for a new art gallery. The Picasso was found in the home of Mrs Rubin, the widow of the donor. It seems the 'thief' asked her to look after it for a month, then to return it to the gallery. See 'Rumours behind Theft', *Adelaide Chronicle*, 8 June 1967.

69   Don Dunstan was appointed Premier of South Australia in June 1967. He was a social reformer and supporter of the arts. Prior to studying law, he was educated at the elite St Peter's College, Adelaide.

70   Bernard Smith, former education officer at the National Art Gallery of New South Wales (1944–1952), senior lecturer in art history at the University of Melbourne (1955–1963) and art critic for *The Age*, took up the post of Director of the Power Institute in early 1967. The interpretation of terms of the Power Bequest 'to make available to the people of Australia the latest ideas and theories in the plastic arts' was debated in Letters to the Editor and a meeting of the Contemporary Art Society. Smith was criticised for setting up art history courses with little contemporary art focus and for overlooking studio-based courses. Artists also objected to the bequest's lack of support for public programs about contemporary art.

'The Chalet'
Hunters Hill, Sydney
27 July 1967

Dearest Daddy, David and Lyly,

I've been up to my ears in painting camellias and a fair-haired lass—not together, but at almost the same time. In the middle of it came the yearly inundation of the DTM's for afternoon tea.[71] That meant 14 doctors to bake cakes for and entertain— also another visitor from overseas had to be entertained for dinner, and as a little extra, the chimney threatened to catch on fire so had to have the chimney sweepers in and they, the clots, persuaded me that with modern methods no covering or protection of the room would be necessary. I'm still trying to clean up after the avalanche of black soot over everything. So if anyone came forth just now with the discussion of why women didn't achieve much in the painting field, I'd give them more than a piece of my mind. Which reminds me that I went to the cocktail opening of the Portia Geach Memorial exhibition and felt proud of what the women had achieved in the portrait painting field. The standard was good and Jo Caddy's winning portrait deserved the prize.[72] The head was very well handled, indeed the only criticism I had was that there was nothing else in the large canvas to support it. My portrait of Professor Walsh was well hung and I was relieved to see that it had been accepted, only half the entries were hung.

At last the Rodins are in Sydney on view, and the big American exhibition of two decades of painting. I'm waiting to get in to see both. The crowds to get in to the Gallery are huge and more than ever anticipated or gathered before.[73]

My plan at the present is to fly over on the 18th August if that will be OK with you. At the moment my chief concern is to get my work finished and off and then I can begin to think again.[74]

It's very good to hear that Daddy is on the improve and feeling more himself again, only hope the days keep cheerful to help recovery.

Love to you all,

Nora

---

71   Robert taught international doctors enrolled in the Diploma for Tropical Medicine (DTM).

72   Jo Caddy was a Canadian artist who taught painting and ceramics at the South Australian School of Art from 1957 to 1963. Her winning portrait was of fellow artist Lawrence Daws.

73   The Rodins were toured by the Peter Stuyvesant Trust. New York's Museum of Modern Art touring exhibition, *Two Decades of American Painting*, which came with a stylish catalogue, was held in Melbourne (6 June to 9 July) and Sydney (26 July to 20 August). It included work by Joseph Albers, Willem de Kooning, Jackson Pollock, Mark Rothko and Andy Warhol. Debate surrounding the show was fierce. See 'The Three Black Squares', *The Australian*, 18 August 1967. See also Daniel Thomas, 'Australia's Most Important Exhibition', *The Sydney Morning Herald*, 15 July 1967.

74   The exhibition, *Oils and Drawings by Nora Heysen*, opened at North Adelaide Galleries on 20 August 1967 and was noticed by critics. See 'Nora Heysen Back with Exhibition', *The Advertiser*, 21 August 1967.

'The Chalet'
Hunters Hill, Sydney
Sunday 7 November 1967

Dearest Daddy, Lyly and David,

John Brackenreg rang as soon as he returned from his stay over with you, full of appreciation for your hospitality and the wonderful time he'd had with you. He seemed very happy with everything and said that Daddy looked so well and was right on the ball.

It's good I hear that the Heysen show was such a tremendous success.[75] John told me last night over the phone that David had sold 160 prints, he was staggered finding it difficult to credit. Congratulations, what next for the Hahndorf Academy!

I see that Canberra is to build its own National Gallery at a cost of $4 million so maybe funds are short.[76] News from Robert is good as far as Afghanistan. He's due home on the 15th.

Much love to you all,
Nora

'The Chalet'
Hunters Hill, Sydney
19 December 1967

Dearest Daddy, Lyly and David,

I have several invitations for Christmas dinner and the neighbours the Reids have asked me over for the Eve.

Now the news of Mr Holt has obliterated all that.[77] Somehow one never connected Mr Holt with sudden tragic drama and the news came with a shock.

I've heard from Robert as far as India where he'll be spending his birthday tomorrow. Geneva for Christmas and not home until March seems like a long time ahead.

Love to you all and every wish for Christmas,
Nora

---

75   The exhibition was *Historic Hahndorf: Paintings by Sir Hans Heysen OBE*, Hahndorf Academy, 8–29 October 1967.

76   A Committee of Inquiry looked into setting up a national gallery. The gallery's establishment was announced by Harold Holt in November 1967. See 'A Great Gallery in Canberra', *The Australian*, 28 July 1967'; 'PM Promises Arts Council and Gallery', *The Australian*, 2 November 1967.

77   Harold Holt disappeared while swimming at Cheviot Beach, near Portsea, Victoria, on 17 December 1967.

Hahndorf
July 19th

My dear Nora,

The news contained in your last weeks letter, that you had signed on for another 12 months, came as a rather rude shock.. Ofcourse we had been wondering along what lines your plans were developing and I can quite imagine, that when a decision had to be made, what your feelings were, for it would be no easy matter to make up your mind on so important a period in a young painter's life. But now that you have made the decision you will feel very much happier — you will have a definite date to work to — which in itself will be an incentive. Eighteen months seem a long time to wait before you will be with us again but at the same time I do feel you are wise in having made this decision, so as to consolidate what you have learnt — & also to further your studies in the painting of the nude & composition. It will all help to discipline you in art. You have never again mentioned your intention to copy the "Nativity" by Pierro della Francesca — & I wonder if you ever began it. I shall be most interested to hear from you about it; for I do think you would derive great benefit from the work, besides taking home a 'record' which will bring joy & constant pleasure. Its a lovely thing which never fades from ones memory. The quality of its colour & its luminosity is an object lesson to the moderns. The word moderns reminds me; having read of another interesting Exhibition being held at the Lefevre galleries - from Corot to Cezanne; with a list of excellent names, Manet, Pissarro &c. If these are not again "remnants" it should prove worth seeing. & I shall look forward to your verdict on the show. The mention was made in the Illus London News - with a delightful Manet, illustrated - "Washing day.

PS. All is well at home. - Dimbar is beginning to recover. - Mills & David both work — being in the best of milk. David milks Bertha 12 lbs.

"Dimbar is beginning in her Treatment — "!

TO MY WIFE,
MARCH 1 1920

above
Unknown photographer
*Nora Heysen at the Hans Heysen
Auction, Leonard Joel* 1970

Manuscripts Collection, MS 10041
National Library of Australia

left
Hans Heysen (1877–1968)
Gums under Mist 1917

watercolour on paper; 46.8 x 61.5 cm
Bequest of the artist in memory of
his wife 1969
Art Gallery of South Australia

below
Hans Heysen's Paint Box

The Cedars, Hahndorf

36 College Street
19th March

Dearest Mother & Daddy.
I've been waiting
to see the show before answering Daddy's
letter. You will have heard the first
fine burst of enthusiasm the exhibition
received here. When I went in about an
hour before it officially opened Mr
Fox . . . was dancing about smiles
all over his face telling everyone what
a success he'd had - I wonder how often
in this age of queues pictures have
been the objective - the surprise & wonder
as people passed on the news was
really quite amusing. Fortunately
the gallery wasn't crowded when I
first went in so that my first
impression was uncluttered with people
& you would have felt as pleased
& proud as I did when you walked
in - the impression was excellent
the pictures well close & placed &

'The Chalet'
Hunters Hill, Sydney
28 January 1968

Dearest Daddy, Lyly and David,

I've been trying to get going on some painting but there's always some interruption—kind people think that as I'm alone I must also be lonely and need company, or to be taken out, and I'm forever battling to retain some free days. I did go into the opening of the Archibald and Wynne show, a very reduced exhibition this year as only 19 per cent were selected for hanging. I was lucky to get in with my portrait of the old lady, and to have her well hung.[78] It was a move in the right direction, as now the woman who commissioned the portrait is going to take it and pay me at long last. The prize was well won by Judy Cassab with the best portrait I've seen of hers.[79] I'll include a paper cutting in case it didn't appear in your papers. Quite an impressive tone and colour scheme and well painted, though I felt that the balance between realism and abstraction wasn't completely happy, and it lacked a human feeling. Clifton Pugh had a good portrait and Adelaide's Jo Caddy showed well.

In the landscape section Sali Herman's painting was my choice, also but it was by no means the best of his work.

I hope the heat is not too much for Daddy and that all is well,

Nora

'The Chalet'
Hunters Hill, Sydney
24 February 1968

Dearest Daddy, Lyly and David,

Sorry to hear about Daddy's fall while at Derrymore and hope his arm has healed now.

I'm tentatively feeling round June and July for my trip overseas but until Robert gets home and plans can be made, it is only a vague thought.

Pat just rang to say that in the last Australian *Vogue* there was a splendid picture of Daddy—had I seen it? I'll have to try and get a copy.[80]

Eventually I got round to seeing over the Opera House. Very interesting indeed and impressive. Now all I want is to see Utzon back to finish it. I went to a

---

78   Nora Heysen exhibited *Miss Paul*. The exhibition was held from 20 January to 18 February 1968.
79   This is Judy Cassab's portrait of artist Margo Lewers.
80   In March 1968, *Vogue* published an article about Hans Heysen, Max Harris, Don Dunstan and Stan Ostoja Kotkowski. See 'Adelaide Image Makers', *Vogue Australia*, March 1968.

big meeting organized to that end last week. It was held in the Sydney Town Hall and 2000 turned up and voted for Utzon's return. I'm hoping that the agitation will lead to something. Lloyd Rees made a strong plea at the meeting and I noticed quite a few artists in the crowd.

Very glad to hear that Jackie Hick is now on The Board.[81] I think she'll be an asset with her level head and open mind.

In regard to a choice of illustrations for the Heysen book I feel that you, Daddy, David and Colin are the best judges and that the choice will be determined by the text, availability and price of reproductions as well as making a selection for variety of subject matter and the best phases of Daddy's work ... I'd certainly like to help if I can in any way.

Painted a couple of flower pieces last week, but it was a battle against time to get anything.

I'll be glad when Robert gets home, as I've just about had trying to hold the place together. Hoping all is well on all sides.

With love to you all,

Nora

'The Chalet'
Hunters Hill, Sydney
6 March 1968

Dearest Daddy, Lyly and David,

Glad to hear that the new Northern print has come out so well and that you were so pleased with it. I noticed David's last print *Road to Hahndorf* in a Rowe St shop window when last in the city—$21.19. It was nicely framed and looked well.

Robert arrived home safe and well early Sunday morning and is already speaking of his next trip to Malaya in April, and a two- or three-day trip to Melbourne later this month. So any thought of resuming a normal routine seems very temporary, and I'd best make the most of having a man round the home again—I do hope to fit in a trip over to see you all before I set off on my overseas jaunt ... I have in mind to do that drawing of Daddy and to take him up on that promise to sit.

Love to you all in which Robert joins,

Nora

---

81   Jacqueline Hick was the second woman to join the Board of the Art Gallery of South Australia. Ursula Hayward was the first.

London
Sunday 16 June 1968

Dearest Daddy, Lyly and David,

Just packing up to leave for Paris ... it's been good to put down here for ten days ... Can you imagine what a feast I have been having.

I must have walked hundreds of miles seeing galleries and wandering around the parks. Have never thought of London as a beautiful city, but now that the buildings are all cleaned, it takes on a new look completely and is light and clean and more like the silvery tone of Paris. All coal has been banned, so smog and fogs are a thing of the past. The National Gallery looks fine, a beautiful creamy pale grey and even Lord Nelson has had a wash, though the pigeons are doing their utmost to whitewash him again.

Love to you all,

Nora (D'Arcy, Deirdre and Nora)

El Washington Hotel
Madrid
19 June 1968

Dearest Daddy, Lyly and David,

Your cable has just arrived with its disquieting news. How very worried you must have been trying to make contact with us ... We arrived here yesterday after a hectic but wonderful two days in Bores. So far find Madrid is disappointing, but haven't had time yet to look around. Spent a couple of hours in the Prado and of course was impressed with all the Velasquezs and El Grecos and Goyas, but the Gallery is so dark and dreary after The National in London and the Louvre in Paris. Everything seems to need cleaning and lightening and the noise is terrific.

Tell Daddy that *Les Meninas* of Velasquez looks superb in a room all to itself.

Forgive this scrawl I'm tired and worried too,

Nora

Hans Heysen dies 2 July 1968

These letters come from the National Library of Australia's 'Papers of Sir Hans Heysen, c.1880–1973', MS 5073, series 2, folders 157, 163, 164, 170, 171, 172, 173, 174, 175, 176, 177, 178 and 179; and 'Papers of Nora Heysen, 1913–2003', MS 10041, series 1.3, folders 28, 31, 34 and 35.

Epilogue

Nora did not make it back to Australia to see her father before he died in Mount Barker hospital on 2 July 1968, nor for his private funeral at Hahndorf Cemetery two days later. She was still overseas with her sister Deirdre and her brother-in-law D'Arcy. Tributes flowed in and newspaper coverage was that of losing a treasured citizen and artist. The Art Gallery of South Australia immediately mounted a special exhibition of 42 of Hans Heysen's paintings, watercolours, drawings, etchings and monotypes.[1] *The Advertiser*'s art critic Elizabeth Young commented on how many who never knew him would mourn his loss:

> He shared with everyone his own entrancement with nature, with the loveliness of light, the incidence of form, and particularly he taught us to see the subtleties, the individualities of the landscape of South Australia—the dramatic peaks of the Flinders Ranges, the intimate and often lyrical pastoral countryside of the South-East and the Adelaide Hills, and above all the eccentric beauty of the gum tree from the slim saplings to the grand old men. As with all great artists, this probing of the particular gave birth to something that is universal.[2]

---

1   'Special Show of Heysen Works', *The Advertiser*, 4 July 1968.
2   Elizabeth Young, 'He Shared Concepts of Beauty', *The Advertiser*, 6 July 1968.

The Australian's art critic Laurie Thomas described his passing as the death of a father figure who, striding around the Adelaide Hills in his knickerbockers, created his own personal tradition in landscape 'as distinctive as his own unbending self'.[3] In his tribute 'Death of Father Figure', published on the day of the funeral, Thomas dwelt on how Hans had given the landscape tradition 'a fresh twist' due to his fascination with light: 'I think it was Sir Kenneth Clark who said that the history of landscape painting is the history of the treatment of light. Heysen looked right into it'. Thomas also drew attention to the artist's own words describing his essentially international approach: 'everything in nature is much the same wherever you are, when once the eye has become more or less trained to seize upon the underlying rhythm of nature'.[4]

Once back from her overseas travels, Nora had the unenviable task of sorting through the work in her father's studio. Hans, with an eye for detail and believing that an artist's reputation beyond his lifetime rested on protecting the circulation of his completed works, had, in his will, entrusted Nora with this responsibility. For her, this included signing work her father had forgotten to sign, something each had done for the other over the years.[5] She was still sorting through her father's work in November 1968 when Colin Thiele's biography, *Heysen of Hahndorf*, was launched at 'The Cedars'.

To research his subject, Thiele had stayed with Hans and spent long periods talking to him. His intimate account and detailed knowledge of the family, events and the art was commented on by reviewer Pat Rappolt: 'Sir Hans was so familiar a part of the South Australian mystique that, so soon after his death, it is still difficult to evaluate a biography—especially one written as lovingly as this has been'. Despite this implied lack of objectivity between the biographer and his subject, she concluded that Thiele's work makes a 'vital and important contribution' to art and to the history of the region.[6]

Hans died in an era of death duties and one of the saddest tasks facing the family was to sell much of his precious art collection built up over the years to pay those duties. The collection included works by Rembrandt, Augustus John and Louis Buvelot and by Hans himself. Just before the two-day auction at Malvern Town Hall, in Melbourne, in June 1970, Nora said: 'it's a shame to sell father's paintings, these paintings have been like a family to me—I grew up with them all my life'.[7]

---

3   Laurie Thomas, 'Death of a Father Figure', *The Australian*, 4 July 1968.

4   Hans Heysen, quoted in Laurie Thomas, 'Death of a Father Figure', *The Australian*, 4 July 1968.

5   Robert Black to Nora Heysen, 4 November 1968. See 'Papers of Nora Heysen, 1913–2003', series 1.2, folder 2, National Library of Australia, Manuscripts Collection, MS10041.

6   See Pat Rappolt, 'An Artist's Life: *Heysen of Hahndorf*', *The Advertiser*, 9 November 1968.

7   See 'Her Family is on Sale', *The Age*, 18 June 1970.

Within a space of four years, Nora 's life changed dramatically. After losing her father, with whom she had conducted an extraordinary conversation about art in the letters each wrote to the other for more than 30 years, her marriage floundered. Robert's constant travel led to an inevitable growing apart, separation and divorce, with Nora staying on at 'The Chalet'. So began a new chapter for Nora.

Chronology

1839 Hahndorf, near Adelaide, is established by German migrants

1877 Hans Heysen is born in St Pauli, Hamburg,Germany, the sixth child of Louis and Elize Heysen

1884 Hans, his mother and siblings migrate to Adelaide; his father had arrived in 1883

1893–1894 Hans enrols at James Ashton's Norwood Art School, Adelaide

1895 Hans enrols at Ashton's Academy of Art, Grenfell Street, Adelaide, and joins the Easel Club

1895–1899 Hans exhibits with the Easel Club and the South Australian Society of Arts

1898 Hans studies part time at the South Australian School of Design under H.P. Gill

1899–1903 Funded by four Adelaide businessmen, Hans travels to Paris and studies at Académie Julian under Jean-Paul Laurens, at Académie Colarossi and at the École des Beaux Arts under Leon Bonnat

Hans also visits the United Kingdom, Holland and Italy

1904 Hans opens his own studio and art school in the Adelaide Steamship Building, Currie Street, Adelaide

Hans wins the Wynne Prize for *Mystic Morn*, which the National Gallery of South Australia purchases

Hans and Selma (Sallie) Bartels marry

1908 Hans holds a successful solo exhibition in Melbourne
The Heysen family moves to Hahndorf, South Australia

1911 Nora Heysen is born, the fourth of eight children

Lionel Lindsay writes in *The Bulletin* that Hans is a great watercolour painter

1912 Hans holds a second successful solo exhibition in Melbourne

Hans and Sallie purchase 'The Cedars', a 36-acre property in the Hahndorf district

1914 First World War is declared; Australia is at war with Germany

1915 Hans is caught up in a wider anti-German sentiment and refuses to declare his allegiance to Australia, stating that his paintings of Australian sunlight speak for him

Hans resigns from the Australian Art Association and the South Australian Society of Arts

1917   Hahndorf renamed Ambleside, one of 69 placenames anglicised under the 1917 Nomenclature Act

Hans' paintings are excluded from the National Art Gallery of New South Wales's *Loan Exhibition of Australian Art*, due to the artist's German background

1918   First World War ends

1920   *Art in Australia*, under Sydney Ure Smith, publishes *The Art of Hans Heysen* special issue

1920–1926   Hans holds four successful exhibitions

1926   Hans first travels to the Flinders Ranges, South Australia, where he travels annually until 1933

1928   Hans hold a successful Sydney solo exhibition of his Flinders Ranges work

Art in Australia publishes a second Hans Heysen special issue

Nora commences exhibiting with the South Australian Society of Arts

1929–1933   The Great Depression makes it difficult for Hans to sell his work

1930   Nora illustrates K. Langlow Parker's (Catherine Stow's) *Woggheeguy: Australian Aboriginal Legends*, published by F.W. Preece, Adelaide

1930–1933   Nora studies at the North Adelaide School of Art and establishes her own studio at 'The Cedars'

An Australian airmail service to England commences in the early 1930s

1932   Howard Hinton presents Nora's *Self Portrait* to the National Art Gallery of New South Wales

1933   Nora wins the Melrose Prize for *A Portrait Study*

Nora holds a successful solo exhibition in Adelaide at the Royal South Australian Society of Arts and uses proceeds to fund overseas study

1934   Good sales from Hans's exhibition in Perth fund a nine-month trip to Germany and the United Kingdom for Hans, Sallie and four daughters, including Nora

Nora stays in London, lives in Duke Street, Kensington, and studies at the Central School of Art

The England-to-Melbourne Great Air Race is held as part of Melbourne's Centenary Celebrations (October)

William Moore's *The Story of Australian Art: From the Earliest Known Art of the Continent to the Art of Today* is published

1935 Hans holds a successful exhibition of 98 works at the National Art Gallery of New South Wales and an exhibition of 36 Australian landscape watercolours at Colnaghi, London

Nora and Evie travel to Paris

Nora continues at the Central School of Art, London

Nora and Evie spend time at Rempstone Farm, Dorset

Nora meets Orovida Pissarro and Lucien Pissarro

Ambleside is renamed Hahndorf

Bernard Hall, Director of the National Gallery of Victoria, dies in London

Leslie Wilkie, Director of the National Gallery of South Australia, dies

1936 Nora and Evie travel again to Paris

Nora enrols at Byam Shaw School of Art, London

The Ballets Russes tours Australia for the first time

Louis McCubbin becomes Director of the National Gallery of South Australia (1936–1950)

James MacDonald becomes Director of the National Gallery of Victoria (1936–1941)

1937 Hans holds a successful solo exhibition in Adelaide

Hans is the South Australian representative and foundation member of the Australian Academy of Art

The Contemporary Art Society, Melbourne, is formed

Nora continues at Byam Shaw School of Art

Nora and Evie travel mid-year to Italy

Nora returns to Adelaide (October)

Will Ashton becomes Director of the National Art Gallery of New South Wales (1937–1945)

1938 Nora moves to Sydney, where she lives at Elizabeth Bay Road and then Onslow Avenue

Nora is elected to the Society of Arts

The Ballets Russes tours Australia for the second time

1939 Nora wins the 1938 Archibald Prize for *Madame Elink Schuurman*; her portrait *The Hon. John Lane Mullins* also shown

Robert Gordon Menzies becomes Prime Minister of Australia

Exhibition of French and British Contemporary Art is held at the National Gallery of South Australia (21 August to 17 September), the Lower Town Hall, Melbourne (16 October to 1 November), David Jones Art Gallery, Sydney (20 November to 16 December) and the National Art Gallery of New South Wales (January to June 1940)

Australia enters the Second World War

The Contemporary Art Society is formed in Sydney

1940   Australia sends troops to the Middle East

Hans appointed to the newly formed Board of the National Gallery of South Australia (1940–1968)

Nora moves to Montague Place, Sydney

1941   Nora wins the Melrose Prize for *Motherhood*

Nora commissioned by James McGregor to paint Lionel Lindsay

Hans and Sallie purchase two adjoining properties, taking the size of 'The Cedars' to 150 acres

The appointment of Australian official war artists commences

John Curtin becomes Prime Minister of Australia

Daryl Lindsay becomes Director of the National Gallery of Victoria (1941–1956)

1942   Nora's painting *Sir Lionel Lindsay* is hung in the 1941 Archibald Prize (January to February)

Darwin Harbour is bombed (February)

Sydney is attacked by Japanese midget submarines (May to June)

The Contemporary Art Society is formed in Adelaide

Art in Australia ceases publication

1943   Nora and Stella Bowen are appointed the first female official war artists; Nora commences her appointment in Melbourne (October)

1944   Nora shows three portraits in the 1943 Archibald Prize (January to March): *Colonel Sybil H. Irving, Controller, AWAS; Group Officer Clare Stevenson* and *First Officer Sheila McClemans, WRANS*

Nora posted to New Guinea, where she meets Dr Robert Black (April to October)

Nora returns to 'The Cedars' for four weeks to recover from dermatitis and is then sent to the Blood Bank, Sydney Hospital

William Dobell's Archibald Prize portrait of Joshua Smith is challenged in a controversial court case

The National Art Gallery of New South Wales holds an exhibition of Hans' drawings

1945 Nora returns to Melbourne, before being posted to North Queensland, Morotai and Wewak

Sybil Craig is appointed the third Australian female official war artist

Hans becomes an Officer of the British Empire (OBE)

Bernard Smith's *Place, Taste and Tradition: A Study of Australian Art since 1788* is published

Hal Missingham becomes Director of the National Art Gallery of New South Wales (1945–1971)

The Second World War ends in Europe (May) and in the Pacific (August), after nuclear attacks on Japan

1946 Nora discharged from the army (February) but stays on in Melbourne to complete her commission

Nora moves to Sydney (May)

1947 The British Council tours Henry Moore's *Exhibition of Sculpture and Drawing* to state galleries in Sydney, Hobart, Melbourne, Adelaide and Perth (1947–1948)

Hans spends five weeks working in the Flinders Ranges

1948 Nora's portrait of her father is hung in the 1947 Archibald Prize (January to March)

Nora travels to Britain to join Robert Black in Liverpool

Nora moves to London, where she meets up with other Australian artists (November)

The National Gallery of Victoria's exhibition, *Tom Roberts*, tours

Joseph Burke, the first Herald Professor of Fine Art at the University of Melbourne, commences teaching the first art history course in an Australian university

Sir Kenneth Clark, former Director of the National Gallery, London, and Slade Professor of Fine Art, University of Oxford, visits Adelaide, is appointed a London buyer for the National Gallery of South Australia and delivers a public lecture in Melbourne

Sydney Ure Smith retires as President of the Society of Arts; Douglas Dundas takes over (1948–1961)

1949 Nora returns to Australia, where she and Robert Black move into Elaine Haxton's vacant flat at 36 College Street

Russell Drysdale's *Woman in a Landscape* is controversially awarded the Melrose Prize, of which Hans is a judge, along with Louis McCubbin and Professor Joseph Burke

Hans visits the Flinders Ranges for the last time

The Heysen Gallery, Hahndorf, opens and is run by Stefan Heysen until 1953

Sydney Ure Smith dies

Robert Gordon Menzies becomes Prime Minister of Australia for the second time

Robert Campbell becomes Director of the Queensland Art Gallery (1949–1951)

1950   Sidney Nolan's exhibition of central Australian landscapes at David Jones Gallery, Sydney, presents a new direction in landscape painting

John Anthil's *Corroboree* is performed as a ballet in Sydney by Melbourne's National Theatre Ballet

1951   Nora's portrait of Robert Black is hung in the 1950 Archibald Prize (January to March)

Hans Heysen completes a commission, *In the Flinders*, for the *Commonwealth Jubilee Exhibition*

Robert Campbell becomes Director of the National Gallery of South Australia (1951–1967)

Robert Haines becomes Director of the Queensland Art Gallery (1951–1960)

1952   Nora's portraits *Camille C. Gheysens* and *Norman M.G. Gratton Esq.* are hung in the 1951 Archibald Prize (January to February)

King George VI dies

Buyers queue outside Hans' exhibition at David Jones Art Gallery, Sydney

Nora's portrait of Robert Black, renamed *Portrait of Young Man*, is highly commended in the Melrose Prize

Legend Press publishes Hans' *Watercolours and Drawings*, with text by Lionel Lindsay and James MacDonald

1953   Nora and Robert Black marry

Elizabeth II is crowned Queen

Nora accompanies Robert to the Trobriand Islands (March to May)

Nora holds an exhibition at Moreton Galleries, Brisbane

1954   Nora accompanies Robert on a second trip to the Trobriand Islands (March to May)

Nora and Robert purchase 'The Chalet' at Hunters Hill, Sydney

Nora's and Hans' self portraits are hung side-by-side in *Artist by Artists* at the National Art Gallery of New South Wales

1955   Nora enters two portraits in *The Australian Women's Weekly* Portrait Prize

Hans and Sallie visit Nora and Robert in their new home in Sydney

1956   The ABC national television service commences

The National Art Gallery of New South Wales acquires Nora's *Moulasi*

Exhibition of Oil Paintings and Sepia Drawings by Nora Heysen is held at John Martin Art Gallery, Adelaide

Eric Westbrook becomes Director of the National Gallery of Victoria (1956–1973)

1957   Jørn Utzon's design is selected for the Sydney Opera House

Clune Gallery, Sydney, opens

Wal Taylor of Grosvenor Gallery dies

Nora's portrait *Professor C.G. Lambie, MC, MD, FRACP, FRS is* hung in the 1957 Archibald Prize Exhibition (December to January 1958)

1958   Australia shows works by Arthur Streeton and Arthur Boyd at the Venice Biennale

Nora enters *Scheme in Grey, a Self Portrait* in *The Australian Women's Weekly* Portrait Prize

Frank Norton becomes Director of the Art Gallery of Western Australia (1958–1976)

1959   Nora enters her portrait *R.K. Macpherson MSc., MD, BS* in the Queensland Centenary Portrait Prize

Hans receives a Knighthood in the Queen's Birthday Honours

Nora enters the Melrose Prize with *Self Portrait* and *K.J. Macpherson MSc, MD, BSc*

Ivor Hele's portrait of Hans is presented to the National Gallery of South Australia

1960   Adelaide's biennial Festival of Arts begins

Bernard Smith's *European Vision and the South Pacific* is published

An Exhibition of Oil Paintings, Watercolours and Drawings by Sir Hans Heysen is held at Hahndorf Gallery

Hans is interviewed by Hazel de Berg for the National Library of Australia

1961   Douglas Dundas resigns as President of the Society of Arts; Lloyd Rees takes over (1961–1965)

Kym Bonython opens Bonython Gallery in Jerningham Street, North Adelaide (March)

Nora travels for the third time with Robert to the Pacific, to the Solomon Islands (September to February 1962)

Hans is interviewed by John Hetherington for *The Age*

Lionel Lindsay dies

Bryan Robertson's exhibition *Recent Australian Painting* opens at Whitechapel Gallery, London

Laurie Thomas becomes Director of the Queensland Art Gallery (1961–1967)

1962   Nora's portrait *James McAuley* is hung in the 1961 Archibald Prize Exhibition (January to March)

Lady Heysen (Sallie) dies

Bernard Smith's *Australian Painting Today 1788–1960* is published

Australia enters the Vietnam War

John Hetherington's interview with Nora, 'I don't Know if I Exist in my own Right', is published in *The Age* (6 October)

1963
Australian Painting: Colonial, Impressionist, Contemporary opens at the Tate Gallery, London; there is much objection to the poor showing of contemporary work

Hans presents *White Gums, Summer Afternoon to* Queen Elizabeth II during her tour of Australia

A Special Retrospective Exhibition of the Work by Nora Heysen is held at the Masonic Hall, Millicent, South Australia (March)

Exhibition of Paintings and Drawings by Sir Hans Heysen and Nora Heysen is held at the Hamilton Art Gallery, Hamilton, Victoria (April)

Margaret Preston dies

Art and Australia commences publication

1964
Contemporary American Painting: A Selection from the James A. Michener Foundation Collection from the Allentown Art Museum, Pennsylvania, tours Australian state galleries

William Dobell Retrospective Exhibition is held at the Art Gallery of New South Wales

Hans appears in an episode of *Lively Arts* on ABC television

1965
Nora is interviewed by Hazel de Berg for the National Library of Australia

Nora enters her portrait of Persia Porter in the Portia Geach Memorial Award; Jean Appleton wins with *Self Portrait*

Final exhibition and closure of the Society of Artists

1966
Menzies retires as Prime Minister of Australia and is succeeded by Harold Holt (26 January)

Decimal currency is introduced in Australia (14 February)

Australian troop numbers are increased in Vietnam and conscription is introduced

Hans Heysen retrospective exhibition is held at John Martin's Gallery and David Dridan's book *The Art of Hans Heysen* is launched during the Adelaide Festival of Arts

Thea Proctor dies (August)

1967
Referendum passed to count Indigenous people in the Australian national census

Oils and Drawings by Nora Heysen is held at North Adelaide Galleries

Bernard Smith becomes Director of the Power Institute, University of Sydney

The Musuem of Modern Art's *Two Decades of American Art* is held at the National Gallery of Victoria and the Art Gallery of New South Wales

It is announced that a national gallery will be built in Canberra

John Baily becomes Director of the Art Gallery of South Australia (1967–1975)

James Wieneke becomes Director of Queensland Art Gallery (1967–1974)

Prime Minister Harold Holt disappears while swimming at Cheviot Beach, Victoria (17 December)

1968
Nora's portrait *Miss Paul* is hung in the 1967 Archibald Prize Exhibition (January to February)

John Gorton becomes Prime Minister of Australia

Public meeting calls for Utzon to return to Australia to complete the Sydney Opera House

Nora travels with her sister Deirdre and brother-in-law D'Arcy to America, Britain, France and Spain

Hans dies (2 July) and is buried in Hahndorf Cemetery (4 July)

The Australian Council for the Arts is established

The newly designed National Gallery of Victoria opens

Colin Thiele's biography *Heysen of Hahndorf* is published

1972
Nora and Robert separate, then divorce

1974
Nora's portrait *Hardtmuth 'Hottie' Lahm* is hung in the 1973 Archibald Prize (January to February)

1976
Nora's portrait *Dorothy Hewitt* is hung in the 1975 Archibald Prize (January to February)

1978
The Art Gallery of South Australia holds an exhibition, *Heysen*, under Coordination Curator Ian North

1984
Nora's portrait *Merv Lilley* is hung in the 1983 Archibald Prize (December 1983 to January)

1988
Australian celebrates its bicentenary year

Nora's *Self Portrait* a finalist in the Doug Moran Portrait Prize

Creating Australia, an exhibition marking Australia's bicentenary, tours state galleries and includes Hans' *Red Gold*

1989
S.H. Ervin Gallery, Sydney, holds a retrospective exhibition of Nora's work, *Faces, Flowers and Friends*

Lou Klepac's monograph, *Nora Heysen*, is published

1993
Nora receives the Australia Council's Award for Achievement in the Arts

1995
Heritage: The National Women's Art Book, edited by Joan Kerr, is published and includes an entry on Nora as an official war artist

1998
Nora receives an Order of Australia

2000
The retrospective exhibition, *Nora Heysen*, with catalogue by Lou Klepac, is held at the National Library of Australia

2003
Nora dies

List of illustrations

Introduction
(between pages 8–9)

Nora Heysen, *Self Portrait* c.1932
Unknown photographer, *Hans and Sallie Heysen* c.1920s
Nora Heysen, *Phyllis Paech* 1933
Harold Cazneaux, *The Cedars* 1926
F.A. Joyner, *Heysen in the Flinders* 1927
Hans Heysen, *The Land of the Oratunga* 1932
Hans Heysen, *Aroona* 1939
Nora Heysen, *Spring Light* c.1938
Hans Heysen, *Flowers and Fruit (Zinnias)* 1921

Cosmopolitan London, 1934–1937
(between pages 72–73)

Unknown photographer, *Nora Heysen with her Parents in Wales* 1934
Hans Heysen, *Brachina Gorge* 1944
Unknown photographer, *Sallie Heysen in Front of Nora Heysen's Studio* c.1920s
Harold Cazneaux, *Hans Heysen in his Studio, Hahndorf, South Australia* 1935
Nora Heysen, *Self Portrait* 1934
Nora Heysen, *Student Bust, London* 1935
Nora Heysen, *Self Portrait* 1936
Nora Heysen, *Portrait of Everton (Evie)* 1936
Nora Heysen, *Ruth* 1933
Hans Heysen, *White Gums* 1936
Nora Heysen, *Down and Out in London* 1937

Sydney and the Archibald Prize, 1938–1943
(between pages 104–105)

Nora Heysen, *Poppies* 1938
Nora Heysen, *Madame Elink Schuurman* 1938
Nora Heysen, *Adrien Feint* 1940
Nora Heysen, *Motherhood* 1941
Nora Heysen, *White Cacti* 1941

Life as an Official War Artist, 1943–1946
(between pages 168–169)

Unknown photographer, *Nora Heysen in Uniform* 1944
Nora Heysen, *Colonel Sybil Irving, Controller, AWAS* 1943
George Harvey Nicholson, *Captain Nora Heysen behind the Barbed-wire Perimeter at the Nurses' Compound, 106th Casualty Clearing Station, Finschhafen, New Guinea* 1944
Nora Heysen, *Matron Annie Sage, Matron in Chief, AANS* 1944
Nora Heysen, *Theatre Sister Margaret Sullivan* 1944
K.C. Rainsford, *Captain Nora Heysen, Official War Artist, in her Studio at 138 Flinders Street, Melbourne, Completing Paintings which were Commenced in New Guinea* 1945
Nora Heysen, *Transport Driver (Aircraftswoman Florence Miles)* 1945
Nora Heysen, *Despatch Rider (Leading Aircraftsman George Mayo), Cairns* 1945

To Liverpool, London and back again, 1946–1953
(between pages 200–201)

Nora Heysen, *Anemones* 1947
Nora Heysen, *Flowers in a Delft Vase* c. 1946
Unknown photographer, *Nora Heysen and Robert Black* c.1948
Unknown photographer, *Nora Heysen and Robert Black Wearing Berets* c. 1940s
Nora Heysen, *Self Portrait* 1948
Nora Heysen, *Dorothy James, Barbara Murray and Marion Lloyd, Young Ladies of the Liverpool Blue Coat School* 1948
Nora Heysen, *Robert H. Black MD* 1950
Hans Heysen, *In the Flinders—Far North* 1951
Nora Heysen, *Portrait of Hans Heysen* 1952
Nora Heysen, *Portrait of Dr Robert Black* 1953

Touring the Pacific and settling in Sydney, 1953–1959
(between pages 248–249)

Nora Heysen, *A Chieftain's Daughter* 1953
Nora Heysen, *King Mitakata, New Guinea* 1953
Unknown photographer, *Nora Heysen and Robert Black at the Artists' Ball* 1953
Plate 1: Nora Heysen, *Minj, 1 May 1954*
Plate 2: Nora Heysen, *Our House—Losuia, 23 March 1953*
Plate 3: Nora Heysen, *Esa'ala, Easter Sunday 1954*
Hans Heysen, *The Promenade* 1953
Nora Heysen, *Self Portrait* 1932
Hans Heysen, *Self Portrait* 1902
Unknown photographer, *The Chalet, Hunters Hill, Sydney*
Nora Heysen, *Moulasi, New Guinea* 1954
Ivor Hele, *Sir Hans Heysen, OBE* 1959
Nora Heysen, *Self Portrait* 1954

Success, anxiety and change, 1960–1968
(between pages 296–297)

Nora Heysen, *Mother and Child* 1960
Peter Medlin, *Sir Hans and Lady Heysen* 1961
Unknown photographer, *With Love and Good Wishes from Dad* 1961
Nora Heysen, *James McAuley* 1961
Nora Heysen, *Melanesian Mother and Child* 1962
Plate 4: Nora Heysen, *Mary* c.1961
Nora Heysen, *Butete, 18 January 1962*
Unknown photographer, *Hans and Nora Heysen Judging Children's Art at the Royal Adelaide Show* 1962
Unknown photographer, *An Exhibition of Nora Heysen's Work, Millicent, South Australia* 1963
Unknown photographer, *Hans Heysen Presenting White Gums, Summer Afternoon to HRH Queen Elizabeth II and HRH the Duke of Edinburgh* 1963

Epilogue
(between pages 320–321)

Hans Heysen, *Page of Letter to Nora Heysen* 19 July 1936
Unknown photographer, *Nora Heysen at the Hans Heysen Auction, Leonard Joel* 1970
Hans Heysen, *Gums under Mist* 1917
Hans Heysen's Paint Box
Nora Heysen, *Page of Letter to Hans Heysen, 19 March 1952*

Index

HH refers to Hans Heysen.

NH refers to Nora Heysen.

A

ABC (Australian Broadcasting Commission), 6, 302
Abicair, Shirley, 6, 274
Aboriginal art, 83–84, 250, 250n47
Aboriginal people, 167, 197, 306
abstract art, 13, 125, 218, 253, 269, 307
Académie Colarossi, Paris, 8, 32n8
Académie de la Grand Chaumière, Paris, 38n16
Académie Julian, Paris, 8, 32n8
Adelaide Festival of Arts, 270, 270n2, 271, 286, 286n29, 301
Adelaide Steamship Company, 4, 10, 12, 59, 59n37
Adler, Larry & Mrs, 107, 107n22
The Advertiser (Adelaide), 5, 325
The Age (Melbourne), 18
Akamatsu, Toshika, 258n58
Albers, Joseph, 319n73
Albrecht, F.W., 84n58
Allentown Art Museum, Pennsylvania, 301n52
American art exhibitions, Sydney,
American war art, 163, 163n28
Amery, John, 238, 240, 241
Anderson, Stanley, 40, 40n20, 55
Andrews, Rebecca, 8
Anthony Horderns (department store), 272
Antill, John, 197
Appleton, Jean, 70, 176, 310
Archibald Prize, 26, 102, 199, 202n33, 312
   (1938), 100–105, 100n14, 104n17, 107
   (1944, 1948), 141, 259n59
   (1949), 189, 189n16
   (1950), 193, 193n22
   (1951, 1952), 205–206, 205n38, 213–215
   (1953, 1956), 229, 229n14–n15, 251
   (1957), 217–218, 257, 257n54–n55
   (1960, 1961), 275–276, 283, 283n24
   (1962, 1968), 294, 294n40, 321
   NH wins, 2, 100–105, 100n14, 104n17, 107
   NH's entries, 19, 134, 138, 138n9, 199n29,
      259n60, 267, 321, 321n78
Armidale Teachers' College (NSW), 2, 181, 181n8,
   226
Arnhem Land (NT), 250, 250n47
Art Gallery of New South Wales. *see also* National Art
   Gallery of New South Wales
   exhibitions, 275n12, 303n53

Art Gallery of South Australia. *see also* National
   Gallery of South Australia
   Heysen exhibitions (1968, 1977), 6, 325
Art in Australia (magazine), 6, 17, 46, 52, 109n25
art market, 11, 82, 134, 159, 164, 260–261
art supplies, 212
   easels, 199, 200
   oil paints, 32, 35, 164
   postwar Britain, 180, 182
   Second World War, 135, 141
Arthur Tooth & Sons, 9, 36, 36n13, 42
The Artist (magazine), 45
Artists' Ball, Sydney (1953), 228
Ashcroft, Peggy, 58
Ashton, Howard, 110, 123
Ashton, Julian, 273n8
Ashton, Will, 99–100, 114, 175, 177, 206, 278
   exhibition, 159
   gallery director, 102, 137, 137n8
Australia, National Journal, 109, 109n25, 113,
   120n37
The Australian (Sydney), 326
Australian Academy of Art, 6, 6n5, 58, 58n36, 66–67,
   67n45, 71
   exhibitions, 106, 106n21, 116, 118–119, 118n34
Australian Army Medical Women's Service (AAMWS),
   152
Australian Club, Sydney, 105, 107–108
Australian War Memorial, 136n3
   art collection, 138n9, 141n13, 149n17, 154n20,
      167n32, 170n34
   Art Committee, 5
The Australian Women's Weekly, 5, 218, 238
   Portrait and Art prizes, 16, 218, 245–246,
      245n38, 246n39, 259–260, 259n60, 260,
      260n61
avant-gardism, 7, 7n9

B

Bailey, John, 317, 317n66
Bakst, Léon (ballet costume designer), 81
ballet, 81, 99, 117, 197
   drawings, 117
Ballets Russes, 81n55, 100n13, 117n32–n33, 220n2
Bank of Australasia, 221
Baronova, Irina, 100, 100n13
Barr, Alfred, 7n9
Bateman, James, 35, 35n12, 40, 185
   HH on, 37, 39
   on NH, 57–58, 60–62, 75
   NH on, 36
   paintings by, 29, 29n5, 30, 30n6, 63n40, 64
Bateman, Mrs, 185

Bathurst Regional Art Gallery (NSW), 271n3
Battarbee, Rex, 83–84, 83n57, 84n58
Bell, Vanessa, 17, 36
Belle Époque Paris, 8
Bellette, Jean, 185
Bellini, Jacapo, 82
Bennett, Frank, 289
Best, Kathleen, 139–140, 139n10, 140n12
Binyon, Laurence, 50
Black, Robert (NH's husband), 173–174
    career, 173, 217, 223, 263, 300, 319n71
    domestic life, 200–201, 266, 304
    health, 181, 182, 187, 192
    marriages, 174, 209n44, 213–215, 327
    NH's portraits of, 191, 193, 199n29, 200,
        208n43, 213n47
    Solomon Islands work, 278, 280–282
    trips, 19, 191, 241, 250, 262, 269, 292, 299,
        308–311
    Trobriand Islands work, 223, 232
Black family, 229, 235
Black Sunday bushfire, Adelaide Hills (1955), 243,
    243n35
Blackburn, Bickerton, 170
Blackman, Charles, 205n37
Blamey, General, 162
Blaxland Gallery, Sydney, 104n16, 274n9
Blood Bank, AIF Unit, Sydney Hospital, 161, 161n26
'Bluey' (Queensland logger), 134, 149, 149n17
Blunden family, 122
Bone, Muirhead, 137
Bone, Nurse, 97, 97n9
Bonnat, Léon, 32n8
Bonython, Kym, 276, 276n13
Bonython Gallery, Adelaide, 277, 277n16
Bordier, Leonardo, 236n23
Botticelli, Sandro, 241
Boudin, Eugène, 186, 186n13
Bourdelle (sculptor), 38
Bowen, Stella, 2n3, 15
Boyer, Richard, 5, 271, 271n4
Brackenreg, John, 112n29, 115–116, 199
    art dealer, 108, 298, 302, 306–307, 314, 316,
        320
    and NH, 106, 111–113, 120, 123, 176, 187
Bradman, Don, 192
Braque, Georges, 83, 125
British art, 9, 10, 177
British Council, 117n32, 180n7
Buckle, Elsie, 116, 118, 213, 257
Buckle, William G., 116, 118, 119n35, 120
The Bulletin (magazine), 12, 164, 181, 196, 244
Burdett, Basil, 64
Buring, Leo, 175

Burke, Joseph, 190, 190n19
Burlington Gallery, London, 14, 67
Burn, Ian, 6–7
Burns, Mrs James, 109n25
Bush, Charles, 208
Butete (Solomon Islands), 285–287
Butler, Rex, 8n18
Buvelot, Louis, 326
Byam Shaw School of Art, London, 69–72, 69n46

C

Caddy, Jo, 242n32, 319, 319n72, 321
Café du Dôme, Paris, 41, 41n22
Cairns (Qld), 166–171
    NH's paintings of, 170, 170n33
Cameron (later Churcher), Betty, 262n66
Campbell, Robert
    art prize judge, 208–209, 262
    gallery director, 201, 201n32, 226, 226n5, 234,
        258, 293, 295
    Society of Artists, 210
Canberra (ACT), 130, 130n47
Carravaggio, 241
Carrick Hill, Springfield (SA), 5, 63n40, 109, 109n24,
    184n10, 246
Cassab, Judy, 16, 275, 283, 321, 321n79
Cazneaux, Harold, 2, 46, 46n26
Central Saint Martins College of Art and Design,
    London, 69n46
Central School of Art, London, 23, 40
Cezanne, Paul, 14, 76
Challman, Oscar, 293
Chekov, Anton, 58
Chinese art exhibition, London (1935), 45, 49–50,
    52–53
Christmas
    in London (1934), 27–28
    NH's plans for, 97–98, 129, 138, 229
    in the Solomon Islands (1961), 283
Clark, Kenneth, 185, 190, 190n19, 326
Clark, Reginald Marcus, 236, 236n24, 237n25, 242
Clausen, George, 29, 29n5
Clune, Frank, 175–176, 175n1, 195, 249
Clune, Terry, 256, 256n52, 315
Clune, Thelma, 176, 176n2, 249n46, 296
Clune Galleries, Sydney, 176n2, 256n52, 315,
    315n64
coal strike (1949), 192, 192n20
Cockburn, Stewart, 6, 135, 135n1, 238
Colahan, Colin, 12, 187–188
Cole, Rex Vicat, 69n46
Collings Productions, 289n32

Colnaghi (gallery), London, 37n14, 42, 44, 45, 186n13
colour in painting. *see* painting palettes
commercial art galleries, 268, 300, 307
Commonwealth Art Advisory Board, 278n18, 286n29
Commonwealth Bank, 302
Conder, Charles, 226
Connard, Philip, 29, 29n5
The Connoisseur (magazine), 159, 164
Constable, John, 6, 77, 184n12
Contemporary Art Society, 6n5, 124–125, 124n41, 318n70
Cook, Jimmy, 70, 152, 236
Corfe Castle, Dorset, 60, 62, 63n39
Cornish, Reverend and Mrs, 23
Coronation celebrations (1953), 224, 224n7
Corot, Camille, 56, 61
Craig, Sybil, 165, 165n31
Crooke, Ray, 298, 298n47
Curtin University, Perth, 19

D
Dadswell, Lyndon, 122
daffodils, 44, 63
The Daily Telegraph (Sydney), 206n40, 236
Dalgarno, Roy, 270n1
Daly, Mary, 293, 293n37
Darcy, Constance, 123
Dargie, William, 15, 161, 167, 213–214, 249, 251
David Jones Art Gallery, Sydney, 93n4, 137n8, 194, 206, 238, 260
Daws, Lawrence, 319n72
de Berg, Hazel, 310, 310n60
de Kooning, William, 319n73
de la Mere, Walter, 25
de Maistre, Roy, 76
Degas, Edgar, 117n32, 199
della Francesca, Piero, 82
Dobell, William, 117, 133, 185, 195, 261, 278
    exhibitions, 131, 131n49, 230, 230n16, 302–303, 303n53
    films about, 270n1, 289, 289n32
    HH on, 222
    Marston portrait, 214–215, 222, 223, 223n5
    in New Guinea, 195, 217
    and NH, 106, 106n20, 113, 115
    NH on, 108, 110, 123, 215, 257, 294
    paintings by, 108, 110, 118, 123, 123n39, 176, 176n2, 202n33, 244
    prizes won, 141, 189, 189n16
    Second World War, 152
Dominion Gallery, Sydney, 294, 298–299
Dorset (England), 58–60, 62–63, 66

Doug Moran Portrait Prize, 19
Dowie, John, 272, 280n20
drawings (HH's), 276, 289, 305, 311
drawings (NH's), 116, 117, 123, 126
    Mary (c.1962), 284n26
    of Michael Whitehead, 126
    Moulasi, New Guinea (1954), 247, 247n41
    Peter (Peter Tansy), 124, 125, 263, 275
    Study of a Boat, the Hekeha, 231n19
Dridan, David, 303, 312n62, 317, 318
Drysdale, Russell, 185, 270n1, 276n14
    exhibitions, 198, 275, 275n12, 282, 282n21, 287
    films about, 270n1, 289, 289n32
    and HH, 276
    HH on, 191, 227
    Melrose Prize, 190–191
    NH on, 192, 198
    paintings by, 190, 211, 227n13, 296, 296n44
    Second World War, 152, 163n28
du Boulay, Merle, 109, 109n24
Duguid, Charles, 250n47
Duhig, J.V., 262n66
Dundas, Douglas, 13, 116, 176, 195, 277
Dunstan, Don, 6, 318n69, 321n80
Dupain, Max, 116
Durand Ruel Galleries, Paris, 9, 75

E
École des Beaux-Arts, Paris, 9
Edinburgh, Duke of, 230n18, 297
Edwards, Mary, 105, 105n18
Edwards, Mrs, 123
Eggardun (Eggerdun), Dorset, 10, 59, 59n38
Elder Bequest (National Art Gallery of South Australia), 128n45
Elias, Ann, 8n16
Elizabeth II, Queen, 5, 224n7, 230, 230n17, 295n41, 297
Elliot, R.D., 255n50
England
    NH in (1934–1937), 14, 23–85
    NH in (1948–1949, 1968), 15, 179–188, 323
    postwar shortages, 179–180, 182
England-to-Melbourne Great Air Race (1934), 25
Epstein, Jacob, 17, 26, 63n40, 117n32, 128, 199
Evans, Edith, 25, 58
Evatt, H.V., 249, 249n46
Evatt, Mr, 298, 299
'Evie'. *see* Stokes, Everton
exhibitions (HH's), 268
    An Exhibition of Oil Paintings, Watercolours and Drawings by Sir Hans Heysen (1960), 271, 271n4

Art Gallery of South Australia (1968, 1977), 6, 325
Colnaghi exhibition, London (1935), 37, 37n14, 44, 45
David Jones exhibition (1938), 93, 93n4
David Jones exhibition (1952), 5, 205–207
Exhibition of Paintings and Drawings by Sir Hans Heysen and Nora Heysen (1963), 297, 297n45
Hahndorf Gallery exhibition (1953), 224, 224n6
Hans Heysen (2009), 8
Hans Heysen Centenary Retrospective (1977), 6
Hans Heysen Retrospective Exhibition 1901–1965 (1966), 312n63
Historic Hahndorf: Paintings by Sir Hans Heysen OBE (1967), 320, 320n75
National Art Gallery of New South Wales (1935), 5, 31, 38, 38n15, 39–40, 42
Royal South Australian Society of Arts (1937), 68, 78, 78n49
Sedons exhibition (1951), 203
Victorian Artists' Gallery (1936), 66, 66n44, 68
exhibitions (NH's), 16, 217, 268
Exhibition of Oil Paintings and Sepia Drawings by Nora Heysen (1956), 248, 248n43
Exhibition of Paintings and Drawings by Sir Hans Heysen and Nora Heysen (1963), 294, 294n39, 297, 297n45
first solo exhibition (1933), 2
Hahndorf Gallery exhibition (1951), 18, 204, 204n36
Oils and Drawings by Nora Heysen (1967), 319n74
S.H Ervin retrospective exhibition (1989), 18
A Special Retrospective Exhibition of the Work by Nora Heysen (1963), 16, 294, 294n39, 296, 296n42

F
Fairley, Brigadier, 172
Fairweather, Ian, 292, 292n34
Fantin-Latour, Henri, 17, 17n31, 33–34, 42, 47, 49
Farmers (department store), 104, 104n16, 274
Federation (Australia), 6, 7
Feint, Adrian, 13, 93, 111, 175–176, 272, 308
book on flower painting, 189, 189n15
exhibitions, 114, 246, 246n40, 289, 289n31, 305, 305n54
and HH, 206, 207, 240, 251
and NH, 122
NH's portrait of, 116–119, 121, 241
paintings by, 123, 123n39–n40, 159
Fellowship of Australian Artists, 230

Felton Bequest (National Gallery of Victoria), 31n7, 75n48
Fern, Mr, 66, 68, 78, 91, 159
Fields, Gracie, 25
Fine Arts Society, Sydney, 273n8
Finlayson, Mr, 78
Finschhafen (New Guinea), 144, 151
flannel flowers, 127–128
Fleischmann, Mr (Hungarian artist), 113, 124, 125, 128
Flett, James, 165
Flinders Ranges (SA), 7, 10–11
Florence (Italy), 80, 82
flower paintings. *see also* roses
in England, 180, 183, 191
exhibitions, 33–34, 36
Feint book, 189, 189n15
HH's, 17, 71, 77–78, 80, 257, 270, 288, 302
HH's views on, 47, 49, 65
in New Guinea, 150
NH's, 17, 24, 42–43, 45–46, 93, 109, 119, 127–128, 146, 191–192, 259
food
in New Guinea, 144, 149, 155–156
postwar England, 179, 182, 185
Sallie Heysen's, 12, 13, 133, 187
in Trobriand Islands, 282, 283, 286–287
Ford, Ted, 252, 255
Francis, Ivor, 17
French art, 9, 14, 56, 67
Friend, Donald, 165, 185

G
Gabain, Ethel, 137n6
Gauguin, Paul, 63, 63n40, 76, 115, 184
Geelong Gallery (Vic.), 146, 159
George V, King, 53, 53n32, 54
George VI, King, 205, 205n39
German placenames, 28n2, 54
Gheysens, Camille, 202, 202n33, 203, 205, 257, 257n55
Gielgud, John, 25, 58
Gieseking, Walter, 207, 207n41
Gill, Harry P., 17n31
Gilmore, Mary, 249, 249n46, 257
Glad, Bruce, 261
Glad, Jane, 248, 248n42, 253
Glad Gallery, Hunters Hill, Sydney, 248, 248n42
Gleeson, James, 248, 294
Gleghorn, Tom, 277, 277n16, 278
Goodchild, John, 165
Goossens, Eugene, 197, 252n48
Gothic (royal yacht), 230, 230n18

Grand Hotel de la Haute-Loire, Paris, 32n9, 41n22
Grant, Duncan, 117n32
Gratton, Norman, 201–202, 201n31, 203
Gratton family, 243, 244
Gray, Laurie, 233
Gray, Millward, 208
Great Paris Exhibition (1937), 83, 83n56
Green, Christopher, 7n9
Griffiths, Harley, 273, 273n8
Grosvenor Galleries, Sydney, 91n2, 114, 257, 260n63
Gruner, Elioth, 2, 6, 106, 261
    Memorial Exhibition, 119, 119n35
    paintings by, 94, 102, 164, 288
gum trees, 7, 8, 10, 179
Gunther, Dr, 231

H
Haefliger, Paul, 174, 193, 206–207, 229
Hahndorf (SA), 28n2, 54
Hahndorf Academy (SA), 317n65, 320, 320n75
Hahndorf Gallery (SA), 5, 16, 192n21
    HH's exhibitions, 224, 224n6, 271, 271n4
    NH's exhibitions, 18, 204, 204n36
Hall, Bernard, 11, 31, 31n7
Hamilton Art Gallery (Vic.), 16, 297, 297n45
Harris, Max, 6, 321n80
Haxton, Elaine, 189n17
Hayward, Edward (Bill), 165n30, 186, 186n13, 195, 263n67
    art collector, 5, 43n24, 183–184, 186, 246
    and NH, 164–165, 175, 198
Hayward, Ursula, 5, 109, 142, 164, 175, 195, 251, 263n67
    art collector, 5, 43, 43n24, 63, 63n40, 184, 199
    Feint exhibition, 246, 246n40
    in London, 183–184
Heinze, Bernard, 178, 178n6
Hekeha (boat), 231, 231n19
Hele, Ivor, 258
    HH on, 192, 199–200
    NH on, 136, 162, 199–200, 205
    official war artist, 136, 161–163, 165, 172
    paintings by, 192, 214, 214n48
    portrait of HH, 259, 261–264, 263n67
    prizes won, 64, 64n41, 205n38, 257, 257n54
Helpmann, Robert, 242n32, 283
Hepworth, Barbara, 13, 234
Herbert, Harold, 133, 135, 141
Herman, Sali (Solomon), 165, 211, 321
Hermannsburg (NT), 83–84
Hetherington, John, 17–18, 283–284, 284n25, 290, 292–293, 293n36

Hewitt, Dorothy, 19
Heysen, David (NH's brother), 28, 79n51, 191, 241, 267
    art dealer, 16, 268, 291, 297, 306
    HH's prints, 16, 268, 316, 320, 322
    NH's exhibitions, 16, 294
Heysen, Deirdre (NH's sister), 79n51, 325
Heysen, Freya (NH's sister), 110, 110n26
Heysen, Hans
    art prize judge, 64, 190, 201, 292n34
    Australian Academy of Art, 6, 6n5, 66–67, 67n45
    awards, 5, 162, 162n27, 163
    birthdays, 54n35, 280, 280n20, 299
    book illustrations by, 293, 293n37
    books about, 187, 209, 211, 268, 312n62, 318, 322, 326
    death and tributes, 269, 323, 325–327
    Dowie bronze head of, 272, 280n20
    in Europe (1899–1903 & 1934), 8–11, 23, 24–25
    exhibitions (see exhibitions (HH's))
    German heritage, 5, 8
    health, 136, 187, 212n46, 221n3, 278–279, 313
    knighthood, 5, 264–265, 264n68, 265n70
    marriage, 12
    motor car, 59, 66
    on nature, 32, 35, 75
    paintings (see paintings (HH's))
    portraits of, 259, 259n60, 261–264, 263n67
    television programs on, 6, 274, 305
Heysen, Jill (NH's sister), 267, 270, 303
Heysen, Josephine (Jill) (NH's niece), 87, 97, 97n9–n10
Heysen, Josephine (NH's sister), 87, 94
Heysen, Lyly (NH's sister in law), 267
Heysen, Mike (NH's brother), 111, 111n27, 126, 126n43
Heysen, Nora
    art prize judge, 289–290, 292n35, 307
    awards, 2
    birthdays, 51, 247, 285, 301, 311
    book illustrations by, 65n43
    divorce, 19, 327
    domestic life, 247, 251, 301, 304, 309, 319
    in England (1934–1937), 14, 23–85
    in England (1948–1949), 15, 179–188
    exhibitions (see exhibitions (NH's))
    famous-father syndrome, 17–19, 87, 104n17
    financial affairs, 67–68, 69, 77–79, 107
    marriage, 174, 213–215
    paintings (see paintings (NH's))
    photographs of, 140, 140n11, 242, 242n31
    school lectures by, 210–211
Heysen, Sallie, (nee Bartels) (NH's mother)
    on art, 12–13, 234, 263

and Cazneaux, 46
death, 267, 289, 290
food and cooking, 12, 13, 133
health, 198, 227, 227n12, 251–253, 262,
    262n66, 281, 288–289
marriage, 12
Heysen, Stefan (Steve) (NH's brother), 47, 97n8, 175,
    210
art dealer, 186, 191–192, 192n21
NH's exhibitions, 16
NH's portrait of, 97
Second World War, 111, 111n27, 126, 126n43
Heysen Gallery. *see* Hahndorf Gallery (SA)
Hick, Jacqueline
art career, 265, 265n69, 283, 310, 322, 322n81
and Jeffrey Smart, 186–187, 198
Hinton, Howard, 38, 60, 99, 114, 176, 181, 181n8
Hiroshima panels, 258, 258n58
Hodgkins, Frances, 13, 234
Hodgkinson, Roy, 143, 161
Hokusai (Japanese artist), 54
Holman, George, 159, 297
Holmes, Charles, 68, 69–70, 71, 74
Holt, Harold, 311n61, 320, 320n76–n77
Home (magazine), 109n25
Hooton, Joy, 18
Hordern family, 139
Hotel Australia, Sydney, 100, 100n12
Hunters Hill, Sydney, 238, 243
    Art Committee, 240–242
    Art Show, 218, 244, 271, 289, 298, 307
    life classes, 255, 264, 289
Hyde, Miriam, 50, 50n30
Hylton, Jane, 13–14

I

The Illustrated London News (magazine), 9, 58
impressionism
    exhibition (1939), 112, 115, 116
    and HH, 8, 9
    and NH, 14, 56
international abstraction, 174, 269
Inverforth, Lord, 221
Irving, Sybil, 137–139, 138n9, 160, 162, 171
Italian art, 10, 38
Italy
    HH in (1902), 9, 80, 81, 84
    NH in (1937), 14, 78, 82

J

Jackson, Mr, 69–70, 71, 72
Jacovleff, Alexandre, 29, 29n5, 81, 81n54, 220,
    220n2

Jewell, Mr, 207
John, Augustus
    art works, 105, 115, 117n32, 184, 326
    book about, 163–164
    HH on, 39, 177
    NH on, 36, 94
John Martin's Art Gallery, Adelaide, 16, 186, 192n21,
    193, 193n23, 199
    exhibitions, 198, 246n40, 248n43
Johns, Vi, 193, 193n23, 204, 230, 244, 259
Johnston, Mr and daughter, 105–108, 111
Johnstone Gallery, Brisbane, 205n37, 289n31
Jones, Brewster, 64, 64n41
Jones, Shirley, 99–100, 184
Jubilee Art Prize (1951), 201, 203–204, 204n35
Julian Ashton School, Sydney, 108

K

Kahn, Louis, 290, 294, 294n40
Kennington, Eric, 137
Keogh, Dr, 224
Kilgour, Jack, 289
Kingsford Smith, Charles, 225
Klepac, Lou, 13
Kmit, Michael, 261
Knight, Laura, 57, 117n32
Kokoda Trail (New Guinea), 143
Komon, Rudy, 242, 242n33
Kotkowski, Stan Ostoja, 321n80
Kurrajong (NSW), 122

L

Lae (New Guinea), 151
Lahm, Hardtmuth 'Hottie', 241, 241n29
Lambert, George, 241, 261
    drawings, 29, 29n5, 263
    NH on, 92, 102
    paintings, 92, 97–98, 97n7, 105, 288, 288n30
Lambie, Professor, 250, 253–255, 257
Lander, Eric, 289
Langbein, Brenton, 312, 312n63
Latham, Lady, 203
Laurencin, Marie, 94
Laurens, Jean Paul, 32n8
Lawson, Dr, 313
Lees, Derwent, 184
Lefèvre, Camille, 39n17
Legend Press, 112n29
Lehmann, Lottie, 77
Leonard, V.M., 249n46
letter writing, 1–5
Lever Brothers, 278, 282
Lewers, Margo, 272n6, 278n18, 321n79

light in paintings, 8, 9, 14, 326
Lilley, Merv, 19
Linderman, Grant, 160
Lindsay, Daryl, 64, 136, 137, 146, 176
Lindsay, Lionel, 197, 241, 266
    death, 267, 278
    exhibitions, 98
    and HH, 2, 98
    and NH, 96, 103
    NH's painting of, 129
    writings, 6, 17, 125, 181n9, 209n45
Lindsay, Norman, 2, 108, 117, 238
    exhibitions, 260–261, 261n64
    paintings by, 164, 253
Lindsay, Peter, 266, 289
Lindsay, Rose, 260n62
The Listener (magazine), 45
The Lively Arts (television program), 6, 305
Liverpool (England)
    NH in (1948), 15, 179–184
Lloyd Jones, Charles, 109n25, 117, 123, 197, 207
Lloyd Jones, Hannah, 117, 194, 196–197
London (England)
    NH in (1934–1937), 23–58, 67–85
    NH in (1948, 1968), 185–188, 323
    NH's comments on, 27–28, 41, 323
Long, Syd, 102
Losuia (Trobriand Islands), 219–223, 232
Louvre, Paris, 38–39, 39n17, 56
Luxembourg Galleries, Paris, 25, 56
Lyceum Club, Sydney, 108

M
MacDonald, James, 31, 64, 65, 209n45
Mackerras, Josephine, 134, 170, 170n34
Macquarie Galleries, Sydney, 245n37, 313
Madrid (Spain), 323
Mainwaring, Geoffrey, 137, 137n7, 141, 161, 172
malaria, 171
Manet, Édouard, 14, 25, 167
Manunda (ship), 10, 59, 59n37, 63, 155, 155n21
Marceau, Marcel, 298
Marinato, Tony, 272
Marston, Hedley Ralph, 214–216, 215n50, 222, 223
Marston, Kathleen Nellie, 223n5
Martin, John. see John Martin's Art Gallery, Adelaide
Maruki, Iri, 258n58
Mason, Richard (Dick), 270, 270n1
Mates, Capt., 148–149
Matisse, Henri, 115
Maude Vizard-Wholohan Prize, 256n51
McAuley, James (Jim), 273–274, 283, 283n23
McClemans, S., 136, 138n9

McCormack, Lady, 114
McCormack, Mr, 101
McCormack, Mrs, 106, 114
McCubbin, Frederick, 241
McCubbin, Louis, 5, 53, 53n33, 67n45
    exhibitions, 162, 184n12
    Melrose Prize judge, 190, 208
    and NH, 134
    SA gallery acquisitions, 78, 84, 84n58, 159
    SA gallery extensions, 64, 64n42, 82, 84–85, 85n59
McDonald, Frank, 256, 256n52
McEachern family, 127–128
McGregor, James (Jim), 4–5, 109n25, 141, 148, 197,
        199, 272
    art dealer, 42, 81, 194, 215–216
    health, 266, 288, 308
    and HH, 29, 158–159, 211
    knighthood, 257n56
    and NH, 42, 78, 92, 103, 105, 111–117, 126–127,
        135, 142, 160, 163, 189
    NH's paintings, 94–96, 100–101, 115–116, 118,
        123, 129, 171, 206
McInnes, W.B., 11
Melbourne (Vic.)
    NH in (1944), 135–142
    NH in (1945), 161–165, 171–172
Meldrum, Max, 11, 53, 101, 101n15, 102
Melrose, Alexander, 2n2, 44n25
Melrose Prize, 2n2, 64n41, 265, 265n69
    HH judges, 64, 190–191
    NH entry (1952), 208–209, 208n43
    NH entry (1959), 217, 264
    NH wins, 2, 16, 87, 127, 127n44
Meninsky, Bernard, 24, 27, 27n1, 29, 33
Menzies, Mrs Robert Gordon, 117, 141
Menzies, Robert Gordon, 126, 197
    art exhibitions, 272, 286n29
    Australian Academy of Art, 58n36, 67n45, 117–118
    Heysen family friend, 4–5, 6, 141, 197, 276
Menzies Hotel, Melbourne, 142, 143
Milan (Italy), 82
Mildura Arts Centre (Vic.), 255n50
Miller, Godfrey, 278n18, 306
Miller, Harry Tatlock, 117, 117n33
Millett, Jean F., 29, 29n5
Millicent Masonic Hall exhibition (1963) (SA), 16, 294,
        294n39, 296, 296n42
Minj (New Guinea), 233–234, 233n21
Missingham, Hal, 210, 218, 238, 240, 290
    gallery director, 238n26, 241, 278n18, 302
Mitakata (Trobriand chief), 220–221, 223
Mitchell Library, Sydney, 196
modern art
    exhibitions, 124–125, 193, 269, 300–302

and HH, 248, 309
  NH's views on, 26, 260
modernism, 6–7, 7n9, 26
Monet, Claude, 9, 10, 75, 194, 194n24
Moore, Henry, 13, 76, 180, 180n7, 181, 185
Moore, John, 124
Moreton Galleries, Brisbane, 16, 226, 226n8, 318n67
Mountford, C.P., 250n47
Mullins, John Lane, 95–96, 95n6, 98–101, 103
Mullins family, 117
Munro, Ronald, 140n11
Murch, Arthur, 70, 121, 176
  Archibald Prize, 193, 193n22
  art works, 108, 118, 159
Murdoch, Keith, 177
Museum of Modern Art, New York, 319n73
music, 43, 50, 197, 222, 312

N

Nadzab (Papua New Guinea), 152–153, 153n19, 154
Namatajira, Albert, 83n57, 84, 84n58, 249, 249n45–
    n46, 250n47, 251
Nan Kivell, Rex, 117n33
National Art Gallery of New South Wales. see also Art
    Gallery of New South Wales
  exhibitions, 119n35, 131, 131n49, 241–242,
    275n12
  HH's exhibition (1935), 5, 31, 38, 38n5, 39, 40, 42
  NH's paintings, 2, 3, 87, 93n5
  trustees, 4–5
National Council of Women of New South Wales,
    274n10
National Gallery, London, 25, 76
National Gallery of Australia, 320, 320n76
National Gallery of South Australia. see also Art
    Gallery of South Australia
  Aboriginal art, 250n47
  directorship, 11, 53, 53n33, 201, 201n32, 317,
    317n66
  European buyer, 186, 188, 188n14
  exhibitions, 112, 112n28, 159, 234, 235n22
  gallery extensions (1935–1937), 44, 44n25, 64,
    64n42, 82, 84–85, 85n59
  HH as Board Member, 1–2, 97, 97n7
  Melrose Prize, 2n2
  NH's paintings, 32n8, 128–129, 128n45
National Gallery of Victoria, 63n39, 75n48
  directorship, 11, 31n7, 64, 65
  exhibitions, 136, 136n2, 137, 158–159, 158n22,
    181n9
National Library of Australia, 50n30, 249n45–n46,
    310n60
  Heysen holdings, 19, 65n43, 213n47

Heysen retrospective (2001), 241n29
National Portrait Gallery, Canberra 33n10
Nazism, 25–26, 30
neo-impressionism
  and HH, 8, 9
  and NH, 14, 26
Nesbitt, Freda, 94, 117, 194, 257, 288, 305
  death, 306, 308
  NH's portrait of, 16, 111, 113–116, 118
New England Regional Art Gallery, Armidale, 181n8
New English Art Club, London, 27n1
New Guinea (1944), 143–158
  Casualty Clearing Station (CCS), 144n16, 147–
    148, 154
  criticism of NH's work, 134, 152
  food, 144, 149, 155–156
  mosquitoes, 145, 146
  NH's skin complaints, 152, 153, 155, 157–158,
    160
  nursing sisters, 142, 143, 144–145, 148, 151–
    152, 154–157
  operating theatres, 146, 147, 154, 155, 156
  paintings, 144–147, 149–156, 161–162, 165
  Papuans, 144, 147, 151, 154, 156
  rats, 153–154, 156
  trip to, 142–143
New Guinea (1954), 232–235. see also Trobriand
    Islands (New Guinea)
New South Wales Society of Artists. see Society of
    Artists, Sydney
Newcastle Art Gallery (NSW), 263
Nolan, Sidney, 205n37, 227n13, 289n32
  exhibitions, 194–195, 194n26, 195n27, 196
  HH on, 227
  NH on, 174, 194–195
Nora Heysen Foundation Collection, 40n21
North, Ian, 6, 7, 8
North Adelaide Galleries, Adelaide, 16, 319n74
Norton, Frank, 161, 227
Notanda Gallery, Sydney, 272n6
nude drawing and painting, 70, 255, 264, 289
nursing sisters (Second World War), 142, 143, 144–
    145, 148, 151–152, 154–157, 168

O

The Observer (London), 39, 293n38
O'Dea (O'Day), Tom, 213, 225
official war art scheme, 135, 152, 163, 163n28, 165.
    see also New Guinea (1944)
  exhibitions, 136, 136n2, 162
  NH joins, 135–136, 138–139
  NH leaves, 171–172, 171n35
  Treloar's criticism of NH's work, 134, 152

oil paints, 32, 35, 164
Olley, Margaret, 189n16, 205n37, 217
Olsen, John, 296, 296n43
opera, 186, 308
    Sydney Opera House, 252, 321–322
Orban, Desiderius, 247
Orovida. see Pissarro, Orovida
Orpen, William, 64, 97, 255n50
Our Country: Australian Federation Landscapes,
        1900–1914 (2001 exhibition), 7
The Overlanders (film), 177, 177n4

P

painting backgrounds, 99, 119, 199–200, 275
painting exhibitions. see exhibitions
painting palettes, 14, 24, 48, 50–51
painting prices. see art market
paintings (HH's). see also drawings (HH's)
    From the Apartment Window, Paris (1901), 41n22
    Aroona (1939), 7, 80
    Autumn Flowers and Fruit (1927), 237n25
    The Brachina Gorge, 39
    Cottage Bunch (1957), 249n44, 257, 257n53
    Delphiniums and Lilies, 288
    The Farmyard Frosty Morning, 39
    In the Flinders—Far North (1951), 5, 201, 201n30,
        203n34
    Flowers and Fruit (Zinnias) (1921), 17
    Fruit and Flowers, 317
    Hillside by the River, 40–41, 40n21
    The Land of the Oratunga (1932), 7
    In the Maralana Gorge (1956), 249n44
    Morning Light, 317
    Mystic Morn (1904), 7, 12
    Oratunga, 317
    Pewsey Vale, 242, 242n34
    The Promenade (1953), 222n4
    The Quarry, 42, 47, 298
    The Quarry Scenes, 39
    Rapid Bay (1957), 249n44
    Self Portrait (1902), 241, 241n30
    The Shadowed Hill, 40
    Summer, 317
    Sun-parched Hills, 40
    Sunlit Quarry (1954), 249n44
    At Sunrise, 80
    White Gums, 4, 59, 59n37, 63, 133
    White Gums, Summer Afternoon (1963), 5, 295,
        295n41, 296
    Winter Sunshine (1953), 249n44
    Zinnias, 77, 78, 80
paintings (NH's). see also drawings (NH's)
    Anemones (1947), 173

The Blue Hyacinth, 91
The Blue Vase, 239n28
Bluey (1944), 149n17
The Chestnut Tree, 94
Colonel Sybil Irving (1943), 137, 138, 138n9, 139
Coming out of Chapel (1948), 184n11
Corn Cobs (1938), 14
David (1956), 249n44, 251–252
Dedication (My Murray Madonna) (1941), 12, 126,
        127, 128–129, 297
Despatch Rider (Leading Aircraftsman George
        Mayo) (1945), 167, 167n32
Dorothy Hewitt (1975), 19
Dorothy James, Barbara Murray and Marion Lloyd,
        Young Ladies of the Liverpool Blue Coat
        School (1948), 184n11
Down and Out in London (1937), 80, 80n53
Dr Macpherson, 264
First Officer S. McClemans (1943), 136, 138n9
Flinders Street Station, 141, 141n14
Flowers in a Delft Vase (1946), 178n5
A Gift of Red Roses (1964), 306n55
Group Officer Clare Stevenson (1943), 138n9
Hardtmuth 'Hottie' Lahm (1973), 241n29
Interior (1935), 49, 49n28
Lieutenant Colonel Kathleen Best (1944), 139–
        140, 140n12
Madame Elink Schuurman, 93, 93n3, 95–96,
        98–101, 108, 117, 128
Major Josephine Mackerras, 170n34
Matron Annie Sage, 140–141, 141n13
Melanesian Mother, 291, 291n33
Merrie at Six Months (1941), 120n36
Merv Lilley (1977), 19
The Ming Bowl, 94
Miss Paul, 316, 321n78
Miuri, 291, 291n33
A Mixed Bunch, 2
Mother and Child (1960), 270–271, 271n3
Mother and Child (1961), 284
Motherhood, 126, 127, 186
Mrs David Jamieson and her Daughter (1955),
        245, 245n38
Petunias, 2, 3, 288
Phyllis Paech, 2
Portrait of a Young Man, 208n43
Portrait of Hans Heysen (1952), 208n42
Portrait of Robert Black (1953), 213n47
A Portrait Study, 2
R.K. Macpherson MSc., MD, BS, 262n66, 264
Robert H. Black MD, 199n29, 200
Ruth (Ronda) (1933), 32, 32n8, 121, 228–229
Scabious, 2, 127, 159

Scheme in Grey: Self Portrait (1958), 258–260, 259n60
Self Portrait (1932), 241, 241n30
Self Portrait (1934), 33, 33n10
Self Portrait (1936), 14, 51–52, 52n31, 54
Self Portrait (1938), 14
Sibella Anne Mannix (1955), 245–246, 246n39
Spring Flowers, 70, 93, 93n5, 248n43
Spring Light (c. 1938), 14, 24
Theatre Sister Margaret Sullivan (1944), 154, 154n20
A Touch of Spring (1964), 306n55
Tropical Siesta, 291, 291n33
WAAAF Cook (Corporal Joan Whipp) (1945), 167–168, 167n32
White Cacti, 128–129, 128n45
White Roses, 105–108
Papua New Guinea. see New Guinea
Paris (France)
    HH in (1899–1903), 8–9, 10, 32, 32n9, 41n22
    NH in (1935, 1936, 1937), 38–39, 41, 55–56, 82–83
Parker, K. Langloh. see Stow, Catherine 'Katie'
Parliament of South Australia, 64n41
Passmore, Mr, 70
Passmore, Victor, 184
Paul, Norman, 317
Pergamon, Berlin, 39
Peter Stuyvesant Trust, 319n73
Phaidon Press, 164
Philipoff, Alexander, 81, 81n55
Philipoff, Madame, 81
Picasso, Pablo, 76, 83, 94, 125, 185, 212, 318, 318n68
Piper, John, 137, 185
Pissarro, Camille, 9, 48, 52, 164
    letters to his son, 164, 297
    paintings by, 48n27, 72–75, 75n48
Pissarro, Lucien, 18, 48, 52, 72–74, 79
    paintings by, 25, 52, 74, 75, 78, 78n50
    SA Gallery purchase, 78, 78n50
Pissarro, Orovida, 18, 50–51, 79
    and NH, 14, 24, 36, 47–48, 52, 73
    on NH, 14, 24, 48, 72
    paintings by, 36, 44, 46–47, 48, 52, 74
Pissarro family, 14, 19, 74
Plant, Margaret, 6
Plate, Carl, 247, 272
Pollock, Jackson, 319n73
Port Moresby (New Guinea), 143, 219
Porter, Persia, 16, 308–309, 308n57, 310
Portia Geach Memorial Award, 16, 309–310, 309n59, 314, 319
portrait commissions (NH's), 16, 87, 202, 254

portraiture, 16, 88, 97, 134, 267–268, 294
Power Bequest, 318, 318n70
Preece (Adelaide bookshop), 164, 164n29
Preston, Margaret, 116, 118, 131, 131n49, 261
    death, 298, 298n48
    paintings by, 198, 198n28
    prints (HH's), 16, 113, 268, 316, 320, 322
Proctor, Ernest, 10, 25, 35, 35n11, 52, 59, 59n38
Proctor, Thea, 16, 116, 288, 314
    portrait of, 288
Pugh, Clifton, 263, 321

Q
Qantas, 289, 289n32
Queenscliff (Vic.), 136
Queensland Art Gallery, 2, 223n5, 226, 282n21
    directorship, 317–318, 318n67
    missing Picasso, 318, 318n68
Queensland Centenary Prize, 16

R
Radford, Ron, 7
Rafferty, Chips, 177n4
Ragless, Max, 165
Rappolt, Pat, 326
rats, 153–154, 156, 224, 285
realism, 13, 291, 312
Red Cross Blood Bank, Sydney, 161, 161n26
Redfern Galley, London, 117n33
Rees, Lloyd, 6, 116, 271, 271n5, 322
    exhibitions, 240, 277, 277n15, 313
    and HH, 2, 240
    HH on, 203–204
    NH on, 189, 210, 277
    prizes won, 203–204, 204n35
    Society of Artists, 176, 263, 277, 279, 291, 300
Reid, Mrs Malcolm, 110
Reid family, 238, 299, 303, 320
Rembrandt van Rijn, 326
Renoir, Auguste, 71, 106, 199
Reynolds, Joshua, 30, 30n6, 52
Reynolds, Mrs, 76
Riebe, Anton, 244
Rigby, John, 260n61
Robert Le Gay Brereton Memorial Prize, 289–290
Roberts, Hera, 89, 92, 94, 111, 175
Roberts, Tom, 226, 241, 261
    exhibition, 181, 181n9
    paintings by, 130, 203, 237, 261
Robertshaw, Freda, 176
Robertson, Bryan, 278n18
Robertson and Marks Architects, 100n12
Rodin, Auguste, 319, 319n73

roses
    growing, 28, 53, 115, 239, 245
    NH's paintings of, 17, 105–108, 110, 247, 257,
        300
Rothko, Mark, 319n73
Roualt, Georges, 199
Rowell, John, 159
Rowley, Charles, 19, 307, 309, 312
Royal Academy of Arts, London, 35, 35n12, 36, 37, 57,
    75–76, 77
Royal Adelaide Show (1962), 292n35
Royal Australian Air Force, 126n43
Royal College of Music, London, 50
Royal Jubilee (1935), 39, 39n19
Royal South Australian Society of Arts, 2n2, 78n49,
    84n58, 159
Royal Tour (1954), 230, 232
    Adelaide exhibition, 235, 235n22
Royal Tour (1963), 295, 295n41, 297
A Royal Visit Loan Exhibition of Paintings (1954), 235,
    235n22
RSL, 225
Rubin, Mrs, 318n68
Rudy Komon Art Gallery, Sydney, 242n33
Ruisdael, Solomon, 201
Russell Islanders (New Guinea), 283, 283n24
Rutherford, Mrs, 92

S
Sage, Annie, 140–141, 141n13
Sainthill, Loudon, 117, 117n33
Satelberg (New Guinea), 145, 148–149
sausages, 122, 123
Schoukhaeff, Basil, 29, 29n5
Schumann, Elisabeth, 25, 43
Schuurman, Elink, 93, 93n3, 95–96, 98–101, 117,
    128, 309, 311
Schuurman, Tom, 93n3, 128, 309, 309n58, 311
Scott, Father, 242, 242n32
Second World War, 41, 110–111, 120, 126. *see also*
    New Guinea; War Artists Scheme
    art exhibitions, 136–137, 136n2, 137n6
    in Sydney, 88, 111, 129–131, 130n48
Sedon, R. and Galleries, 81, 159, 203, 270
Segantini, Giovanni, 125
self-portraits
    HH's, 241, 241n30
    NH's, 14, 19, 24, 33, 33n10, 51–52, 52n31, 54,
        241, 241n30, 258–260, 259n60, 264
S.H. Ervin Gallery, Sydney, 18, 249n44
Sharp, Martin, 315n64
Shaw, George Bernard, 25
Shaw, John Byam, 68n46

Sheumack, David, 249, 249n44, 251–252
Sheumack, Mr & Mrs, 255–257
Shirley Abicair in Australia (television program), 6,
    274
'Shorty' (Scot), 149
Sickert, Walter, 36
Simon, Lucien, 30, 38
Sisley, Alfred, 9, 75
Sketch, 39
Slim, William, 265n70
Smart, Jeffrey, 159, 159n23, 236, 243, 243n36
    exhibitions, 198, 278n18, 282, 282n22
    and NH, 183, 185–186, 203
    on NH, 184n11
Smart, Richard (Dick), 183–184, 188
Smith, Bernard, 170, 318
Smith, Jack Carrington, 176, 176n3, 246n39
Smith, Joshua, 118, 123, 141, 244
Smith, Matthew, 63n40, 183–184
Smith, Sydney Ure, 91n1, 111, 114–115, 124
    health, 175–177, 181, 189–190
    and HH, 4, 194n25, 196
    Memorial Exhibition, 194, 196
    and NH, 89, 91–94, 106–107, 128, 163
    publications, 6, 91n1, 109n25, 120, 120n37,
        189n15
    Society of Artists, 4, 122–123, 181, 256
Smith, Treania, 248
Society of Artists, Sydney, 14–15, 159, 268
    decline of, 256, 277, 300
    drawing exhibition (1959), 263
    exhibition (1939, 1940), 108–111, 121–123,
        123n38
    exhibition (1946), 175–176
    exhibition (1949), 190, 190n18, 191–192
    exhibition (1950, 1952), 198, 210
    exhibition (1954, 1956, 1957), 239, 247, 256
    exhibition (1961, 1962), 279, 291–292
    exhibition (1963, 1964), 299–300, 300n50,
        305–306
    hanging and selection committee, 273–274
    and Lloyd Rees, 277, 279, 291, 300
    and NH, 93, 273–274
    NH's exhibition entries, 16, 122, 191–192,
        239n28, 291, 306
    and Ure Smith, 4, 122–123, 181, 256
Sodersteen, Emil, 100n12
Solomon Islanders, 280–282
Solomon Islands visit (1961–1962), 278–297
Somata (Solomon Islands), 285, 287
South Australian Centenary Prize, 64n41
South Australian Society of Arts. *see* Royal South
    Australian Society of Arts
South Australian Women's Association, 104

Spencer, Baldwin, 250n47
Spencer, Stanley, 164, 177
　art work, 42n23, 63n40, 184
　HH on, 45
　NH on, 36, 42, 94
St Josephs School, Hunters Hill, Sydney, 241
Steer, (Philip) Wilson, 62, 116, 177, 214, 214n49
　book about, 163–164
Stevenson, Clare, 138n9
Stokes, Everton (Evie)
　in Australia, 87–88
　Evie's baby, 120, 120n36
　in London, 24, 28–29, 37, 46, 55, 78
　marriage, 46, 51, 87
　NH's paintings of, 40, 42, 49, 53
　NH's parents views on, 31, 33, 34
Stokes, Henry, 87, 88, 130n47
Stow, Catherine 'Katie', 65, 65n43
Streeton, Arthur, 62–63, 63n39, 130, 226
　exhibitions, 79, 79n52
　Memorial Exhibition (1944), 158–159, 158n22
Stubbs, George, 159
Sullivan, Margaret, 154, 154n20
The Sun (Sydney), 194n26, 261n64
Sutherland, Graham, 185
Sutherland, Joan, 308
Sydney (NSW)
　College Street (NH's flat 1949–1953), 189–216,
　　224–225
　Montague Place (NH's flat 1940), 120–131
　NH in Sydney (1946), 175–178
　NH in Sydney (1949), 188–189
　NH in Sydney (1953–1954), 225–237
　Second World War, 88, 111, 129–131, 130n48
　'St Ravenna' (NH's flat 1938), 89–96
　'The Chalet', Hunters Hill, Sydney (1954–1968),
　　236–322
　'Westchester' (NH's flat 1938–1939), 96–120
Sydney Morning Herald, 102, 123, 190, 194, 261n64,
　299
Sydney Opera House, 252, 321–322

T

Tandy, Dorothy, 209n44
Tansy, Mrs, 122
Tansy, Peter, 122, 124, 125, 263, 275
Tate Britain, London, 27n1
Tate Gallery, London, 52, 64, 77
　Australian art exhibition (1963), 278n18,
　　286n29, 293, 293n38, 295
Taylor, Wal, 114, 116, 230
　art dealer, 79, 91, 91n2, 193, 245, 248
　death, 257, 260–261

'The Cedars', Ambleside (Hahndorf) (SA), 12,
　128n46, 307, 307n56
　garden, 44, 53
　and NH, 88, 126, 249
'The Chalet', Hunters Hill, Sydney, 236n23, 246
　garden, 238–240, 247, 273, 293
　home improvements, 247, 251, 301, 304
　purchase, 218, 235–239
Thermopylae (ship), 85
Thiele, Colin, 252n49, 318, 326
Thomas, Laurie, 261n64, 326
Thornhill, Dorothy, 176
Thornton, Wallace, 277, 291, 300
Tikopians, 284–285, 287
The Times (London), 39
Tintoretto, Jacapo, 82
Tonk, Henry, 116
Tony's Café and Art Gallery, Sydney, 272n7
Treloar, John, 134, 135, 142, 152, 160, 162–163
Trobriand Islanders, 219–223
Trobriand Islands (New Guinea)
　1953 visit, 215, 219–224
　1954 visit, 230, 232
Tucker, Albert, 260n61, 293n38
Turner, J.M.W., 9, 236, 237

U

UNESCO Exposition Internationale d'Art Moderne,
　Paris (1948), 16
Ungless, Mr & Mrs, 285, 285n28
University of Adelaide, 214n48
University of Sydney, 318
Utrillo, Maurice, 115, 116
Utzon, Jørn, 252n48, 321–322

V

Van Gogh, Theo, 19
Van Gogh, Vincent, 19, 71, 191–192
　NH on, 14, 56, 67, 83, 115
Velasquez, Diego, 323
Verne, Henri, 39n17
Victorian Artists' Gallery, Melbourne, 66n44
Vietnam War, 311n61
Vogue Australia (magazine), 6, 321, 321n80
Vuillard, Edouard, 184

W

Wakelin, Roland, 13, 279, 279n19
Wallace, Lillie, 104
Walsh, Professor, 315, 319
Warhol, Andy, 319n73
Watt, Ernest, 105–106

Watt, Mrs Ernest, 103, 106
Weatherly, June, 258n57
Webster, Mrs, 45, 77, 78, 80
Wentworth Hotel, Sydney, 160
Westbrook, Eric, 278n18
Whitechapel Gallery, London, 278n18
Whitehead, Michael, 126
Whitehead, Peter, 92
Whiteley, Brett, 278n18
Wieneke, James, 204–205, 205n37, 226, 248, 318,
        318n67
Wilkinson (journalist), 102
Wills, Kenneth, 214, 214n48
Wilson, Eric, 79, 118, 125, 125n42, 176
Wilson, Hardy, 64, 65, 273n8
women artists, 57, 101, 101n15, 309n59, 310
    exhibitions, 274, 274n10, 310, 314, 319
Women's Auxiliary Australian Air Force (WAAAF),
        137, 137n5
Women's International Society of Artists, 73–74
Women's Royal Australian Naval Service (WRANS),
        136, 136n4
Wood, Christopher, 115, 116
Woodside (SA), 47, 75
Wotze, Walter, 316–317, 317n65
Wynne Prize, 102, 189, 230, 312, 321
    HH wins, 1
    winners, 102, 189, 189n16, 203–204

Y
Yandina (Solomon Islands), 279–287
The Yellow House, Sydney, 315n64
Young, Blamire, 2, 241
Young, Elizabeth, 236, 258, 274n11, 325
Young, Lady, 76
Young (NSW), 210–212

Wakefield Press is an independent publishing and
distribution company based in Adelaide, South Australia.
We love good stories and publish beautiful books.
To see our full range of books, please visit our website at
www.wakefieldpress.com.au
where all titles are available for purchase.
To keep up with our latest releases, news and events,
subscribe to our monthly newsletter.

Find us!

Facebook: www.facebook.com/wakefield.press
Twitter: www.twitter.com/wakefieldpress
Instagram: www.instagram.com/wakefieldpress